A HISTORY OF SECONDARY EDUCATION IN ENGLAND, 1800–1870

*To the pious memory of Sir William Harpur
and Dame Alice, his wife*

A History of
Secondary
Education in
England,
1800–1870

John Roach

Longman
London and New York

Longman Group UK Limited
Longman House, Burnt Mill, Harlow
Essex CM20 2JE, England

Associated companies throughout the world

*Published in the United States of America
by Longman Inc., New York*

First published 1986

British Library Cataloguing in Publication Data

Roach, John
    A history of secondary education in England,
    1800–1870.
    1. Education, Secondary—England—History—
    19th century
    I. Title
    373.42   LA634
    ISBN 0-582-49703-5

Library of Congress Cataloging in Publication Data

Roach, John, 1920–
    A history of secondary education in England,
    1800–1870.

    Bibliography: p.
    Includes index.
    1. Education, Secondary—England—History—
19th century. 2. Public schools, Endowed (Great
Britain)—History—19th century. 3. Private schools—
England—History—19th century. I. Title.
LA631.7.R6 1986   373.42   85-19850
ISBN 0-582-49703-5

Set in 10/12 pt Baskerville
Produced by Longman Singapore Publishers (Pte) Ltd.
Printed in Singapore.

Contents

Contents

Preface and acknowledgements

This book has been planned as the first half of a two-part study of secondary education in nineteenth-century England. The second volume will continue the story from about 1870 to the report of the Bryce Commission of 1895 and the welter of argument and counter-argument out of which the Education Act of 1902 finally emerged. Since, during the first two-thirds of the century, a staged organization of the educational system into primary, secondary and higher had not fully developed, the word 'secondary' is really an anachronism. It has been useful to retain it as a convenient adjective to describe education during the period of adolescence – from 11 or 12 up to 18 or 19. It is with this sector that the book is primarily concerned, though both grammar and private schools took in much younger children as soon as they could read.

The research on which this book is based was directed by certain specific intentions. I wanted to look at schools of many different kinds and to examine as closely as possible the ways in which they actually worked – what was taught in them, what the masters and mistresses thought and felt, how effectively they carried out their plans and what were the major obstacles they met with. I wanted to find out all I could about the parents who patronized the schools – what their social and financial background was and what they sought from their children's education. At the other end of the educational process I was anxious to discover all I could about the careers followed by the boys whom the schools trained, especially those who went outside the well-documented professions like the Church and the law. There was a lot to investigate too about individual personalities. Some of the public-school heads like Thomas Arnold and Edward Thring have always been well known, but there were many heads of grammar and private schools – and among the latter group many women – whose careers are well worthy to be commemorated, though they have been largely forgotten by later generations.

In an area as vast as the whole field of secondary education between 1800 and 1870 no one scholar could discover everything, but anyone working in the 1980s has resources at his command which were less available 30 or 40 years ago. The counties and cities of England now possess well-organized record offices which contain a mass of information on education and on many other subjects of interest to the social historian. I have made considerable use of these resources, more particularly of school governors' minute books, of the private papers of heads of schools and of family correspondence. Detailed acknowledgements are made elsewhere, but I should like to express here a general word of thanks to all those archivists and librarians who have helped me. The valuable material available from these local sources makes it possible to put much more flesh on to the skeleton of generalities than was formerly the case. There is, of course, much more to be done in exploiting these resources than I have been able to achieve.

The book which has emerged from the study of this archival material and of printed sources which have not been much used, like the voluminous reports of the 'Brougham' Charity Commissioners, reaches certain conclusions which modify traditional interpretations. It is claimed that the grammar schools were less tightly bound within the strait-jacket of the classics and that they made greater attempts at innovation than has usually been thought. The private schools played a major role in the education of the middle class and were in many cases useful institutions standing in the forefront of innovation and often unfairly tarnished by the image of Dotheboys Hall and of Matthew Arnold's 'educational homes'. Finally the public schools had to struggle to achieve the supremacy which they enjoyed in the latter part of the nineteenth century and the reasons why their fortunes changed in the 1850s and 1860s need careful study.

Any author makes his case, the truth of which must stand or fall by the judgment of his readers. The arguments put forward here are backed by a substantial corpus of documentary and anecdotal evidence which is close-packed and which may sometimes appear over-detailed. It is to be hoped that the main lines stand out clearly enough for the reader to be able to interpret the generalizations in relation to the detailed evidence on which they are based. The method of exposition, based on the careful examination of examples taken from all parts of the country, has been deliberately adopted. What I have done has been to work from the periphery to the centre. It seemed logical to start from the diverse pattern of the towns and counties of England because, in the absence of any national planning, that is where the work was done and the future decided. Early-nineteenth-century England was still a very localized society, and that was particularly true of its schools. So much depended, in secondary schools of all types, on the initiatives of individuals and on their success in attracting pupils. Only a 'localized' interpretation of the story could do justice to their efforts, and this must depend on the accumulation of many examples. Moreover it would have been less than fair to the reader for the author to offer him such a picture without the detailed evidence to support it.

In conclusion I should like to thank the Leverhulme Trust, who awarded me an emeritus fellowship for 1984–85, and the British Academy who gave me a grant from the Small Grants Research Fund in The Humanities. Two of my friends, Mr J C Barry and Professor W H G Armytage, have read the typescript and made many useful suggestions about it. I am under particular obligation to Professor Armytage, whose probing comments have made me think hard about both the form and content of what I was trying to say. I owe him a great debt of gratitude – not least because he took the trouble to conduct the dialogue from the other side of the Atlantic. Lastly, I am grateful to Dr and Mrs J P T Bury for reading the proofs, and to the following for their permission to quote from archive material in their possession: Buckinghamshire County Council; The King's School, Chester; Council of the City of Chester; Cheshire County Council; Cumbria County Council; Durham County Council; Essex County Council; Gloucestershire County Council; Hampshire County Council; Lancashire County Council; City of Liverpool; Lincolnshire County Council; City of Manchester; The John Rylands University Library of Manchester; Norfolk County Council; Nottinghamshire County Council; City of Sheffield; Staffordshire County Council; Suffolk County Council; Wigan Metropolitan Borough Council; Wiltshire County Council; North Yorkshire County Council; West Yorkshire County Council.

List of tables

List of abbreviations

CathC *Report of Her Majesty's Commissioners appointed to inquire into the state and condition of the Cathedral and Collegiate Churches in England and Wales*, 3 vols 1854–55

CCR *Reports* of Commissioners to inquire concerning Charities. 1st, 1819; 2nd, 1819; 3rd, 1820; 4th, 1820; 5th, 1821; 6th, 1822; 7th, 1822; 8th, 1823; 9th, 1823; 10th, 1824; 11th, 1824; 12th, 1825; 13th, 1826; 14th, 1826; 15th, 1826; 16th, 1826–27; 17th, 1826–27; 18th, 1828; 19th, 1828; 20th, 1829; 21st, 1829; 22nd, 1830; 23rd, 1830; 24th, 1831; 25th, 1833; 26th, 1833; 27th, 1834; 28th, 1834; 29th, 1835; 30th, 1837; 31st, 1837–38; 32nd: Pt I, 1837–38; Pt II, 1837–38; Pt III, 1837–38; Pt IV, 1839; Pt V, 1839; Pt VI, 1840.

CSE *Central Society of Education*

DNB *Dictionary of National Biography*

ER *Edinburgh Review*

NC *Report* of the Commissioners appointed to inquire into the state of popular education in England ... (Newcastle Commission), 6 vols 1861

PP *Parliamentary Papers*

PSC *Report* of Her Majesty's Commissioners appointed to inquire into the revenues and management of certain colleges and schools ... (Clarendon Commission), 4 vols 1864

QJE *Quarterly Journal of Education*

RO Record Office

SIC *Report* of the Commissioners appointed by Her Majesty to inquire into the education given in schools in England, not comprised within Her Majesty's two recent commissions on popular education and on public schools (Taunton Commission), 21 vols 1867–68

TSSA   *Transactions of the National Association for the Promotion of Social Science*

VCH   *Victoria History of the Counties of England*

Map of selected schools

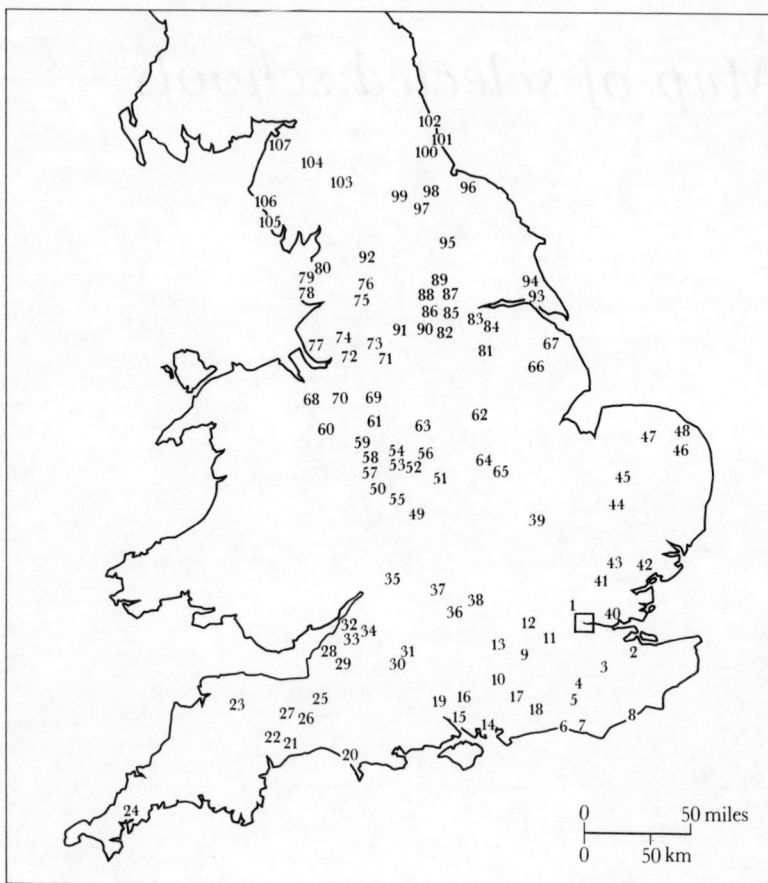

Map of selected schools

0   50 miles

0   50 km

1. London and environs:
   Charterhouse
   Christ's Hospital
   Dulwich
   Harrow
   Merchant Taylors'
   St Olave's, Southwark
   St Paul's
   Westminster
   Bedford Coll.
   Birkbeck Schs
   Blackheath Proprietary Sch.
   Cheam: Dr Mayo's Sch.
   Clapham Proprietary Sch.
   Finsbury: Cowper Str. Middle-Class
   Sch.
   'Laleham', Clapham Park

   Lewisham/Caterham
   Mill Hill
   North London Collegiate Sch.
   for Ladies
   Queen's Coll., Harley Str.
   Tottenham: Bruce Castle
   Univ. Coll. Sch.
2. Rochester: Cathedral GS
3. Tonbridge
4. Ardingly
5. Hurstpierpoint
6. Lancing
7. Brighton: St Mary's Hall
8. St Leonard's: Society of the Holy Child
   Jesus
9. Wellington Coll.
10. Basingstoke

Map of selected schools

11. Eton
12. High Wycombe
13. Bradfield
14. Southsea: St Paul's Sch.
15. Southampton Coll.
16. Winchester
17. Alton
18. Midhurst
19. East Tytherley (Hants): Queenwood Coll.
20. Dorchester: William Barnes's Sch.
21. Honiton
22. Uffculme
23. West Buckland
24. Truro
25. Somerton
26. Ilminster
27. Taunton: GS
 Wesleyan Proprietary Sch.
28. Bristol: GS
 Trade Sch.
 Clifton Coll.
29. Bath
30. Marlborough Coll.
31. Ramsbury: C.E. Meyrick's Sch.
32. Dursley: Agricultural and Commercial Sch.
33. Wotton-under-Edge
34. Tetbury
35. Cheltenham: Coll.
 Ladies' Coll.
36. Radley
37. Bloxham
38. Brill: Joseph Randell's Sch.
39. Bedford: GS
 English Sch.
40. Brentwood
41. Felsted
42. Colchester
43. Sudbury
44. Bury St Edmunds
45. Thetford
46. Norwich
47. East Dereham: William Buck's Sch.
48. North Walsham: Paston GS
49. Stratford upon Avon: 'Avonbank
50. Kidderminster
51. Rugby
52. Coventry
53. Birmingham: King Edward's GS
 Hazelwood
 Oratory Sch.
54. Oscott
55. Bromsgrove
56. Atherstone
57. Kinver
58. Wolverhampton: GS
 Cotton Coll. (at Sedgley Park until 1873)
59. Brewood
60. Shrewsbury
61. Stafford
62. Nottingham: Standard Hill Acad.
63. Repton

64. Leicester: Leicester and Leicestershire Collegiate Sch.
 Proprietary Sch. for Leicester and Leicestershire
65. Uppingham
66. Lincoln: Middle Sch.
67. Louth
68. Chester: King's Sch.
 Science Sch.
69. Macclesfield
70. Witton/Northwich
71. Manchester: GS
 J. R. Beard's Sch.
 Commercial Sch., Stretford Road
72. Warrington
73. Bury
74. Rivington
75. Blackburn
76. Stonyhurst
77. Liverpool: Collegiate Institution
 Institute Schs
 St Domingo House, Everton
78. Bispham
79. Rossall
80. Lancaster
81. Worksop: Dr Heldenmaier's Sch.
82. Sheffield: GS
 Collegiate Sch.
 Wesley Coll.
 Milk Street Acad.
83. Ackworth
84. Doncaster: private schs at
85. Wakefield: GS
 West Riding Proprietary Sch.
 Crofton Old Hall
86. Silcoates
87. Leeds: GS
 Mechanics' Institution Sch.
88. Bradford
89. Woodhouse Grove
90. Huddersfield: Coll.
 Collegiate Sch.
91. Rishworth
92. Giggleswick
93. Hull: Kingston Coll.
 Hull Coll.
94. Beverley
95. York: St Peter's
 Bootham
 The Mount
 Yeoman Sch.
96. Kirkleatham
97. Richmond
98. Darlington: Polam Hall
 H. F. Smith's Sch.
99. Bowes: William Shaw's Acad.
100. Houghton le Spring
101. Sunderland: Dr Cowan's Sch.
102. Newcastle upon Tyne: The Bruces' Sch.
103. Penrith
104. Uldale
105. Bootle: Hycemoor GS
106. St Bee's
107. Silloth: Green Row Acad.

PART ONE
The endowed schools

CHAPTER ONE
The basic structures of schooling

No synoptic history of English secondary education in the nineteenth century has been published since R L Archer's book of 1921.[1] Scholars have given much attention to the education of the mass of the people – in particular, during recent years, to the thesis that elementary education offered a means of 'social control'. The universities and the public schools have also been much studied. Between the national school and Eton or Rugby lies the broad field which the Victorians named 'middle-class education'. This is difficult for the historian to handle because it is not represented by any single institution. Historically the grammar school fulfilled that role, but the grammar schools, as we shall see, developed many different functions. It is conventional wisdom to say that the grammar schools had declined, and there is indeed much truth in the statement. It would be truer, however, to say that they had become more differentiated. Some of them had risen into the group of boarding schools from which the nineteenth-century public schools were to emerge. Others had become parish schools teaching elementary subjects, the three Rs of reading, writing and arithmetic. Many grammar schools straddled uneasily the two worlds of secondary and elementary education. They taught the classics to a few boys, some of whom proceeded to university, and they gave a more limited education – part classical, part modern – to a more numerous group of boys who left early for business or trade. The harmony between the two objectives was poorly attained, and diversity of function meant that no single function was performed successfully.

By 1800 the grammar schools had lost their educational monopoly. During the eighteenth century private schools, both for boys and girls, had grown up in increasing numbers to serve the divergent needs of many divergent clienteles. Some of them offered a more

3

modern curriculum than the classical fare provided by the grammar schools. They taught modern languages, surveying, and sometimes the natural sciences. But it is an error to think of them as offering a modern curriculum while the grammar schools offered a classical curriculum. Things were more complex than that. Many private schools were classical schools, just as many grammar schools offered modern subjects. In both sectors, and particularly in the private, the soundest rule to remember is that the parent got what he paid for. Many private schools were simply elementary schools teaching the basic subjects, going down to the dame schools which were child-minding institutions more than anything else. At the other end of the scale good private schools taught a wide range of subjects at a good level. Naturally, since they were the private ventures of the individuals who owned them, they lacked permanence, but their very nature also made it easier for them to adapt to new demands.

An attempt will be made later to provide some statistics of the number of grammar school pupils in the 1820s and 1830s (see Table 1, pp. 56–7). In the case of the private schools this is impossible. Two statements can, however, be made with reasonable confidence. First of all, most private schools were small, and secondly they provided a large part of the education available to the children of the middle classes. J G Fitch, when he reported on the schools of the West Riding for the Taunton Commission of 1864–68, estimated that more than three-quarters of middle-class boys were educated in private schools in that area.[2] It is not possible to make generalizations covering the whole country, but something like the same proportions may have applied elsewhere. It is possible that between the beginning of the century and the 1860s the private schools had grown in total importance as many grammar schools had declined. However, throughout the whole period, the private school was a very important institution. Its national importance is difficult to estimate since the grammar schools are so much better documented, but the tendency, both of contemporaries and of later historians, has been to undervalue the contribution made by the private schools to the education of the Victorian middle class.

The provision of schools of all types must be related to the steady rise in the population and in the numbers of those who were likely to want a secondary education for their children. The numbers of the child population can be given from the censuses, though it is impossible to relate them precisely to numbers in secondary schools, particularly in private schools where there are no statistics at all. The numbers of persons of both sexes, aged 10–14 and 15–19, were as follows (in thousands)[3]:

	1841	1851	1861	1871
10–14	1,732.1	1,913.4	2,105.2	2,424.3
15–19	1,586.8	1,727.2	1,932.6	2,180.4

Since much attention is given in Ch. 13 to private and proprietary schools in towns the increase in the populations of large towns should be especially noted (in thousands)[4]:

	1841	1851	1861	1871
Birmingham	183	233	296	344
Leeds	152	172	207	259
Liverpool	286	376	444	493
Manchester	235	303	339	351
Salford	53	64	102	125
Sheffield	111	135	185	240

Within these overall figures the numbers of boys and girls belonging to the upper and middle classes who were likely to require secondary education can only be estimated. Dr William Farr made a calculation for the Taunton Commission of 1864–68 of the number of children within the scope of their inquiry, and his estimates of the numbers of children in the middle and higher classes in 1864 were as follows[5]:

Ages	Boys	Girls	Total
10–15	161,194	158,763	319,957
15–20	150,262	148,044	298,306

Certainly rising numbers meant an increasing demand, and up to the 1860s at least much of that demand was met by the private schools. However, the pressure for more school places must not be exaggerated. There is plenty of evidence that children were sent to school for only short periods, and that boys went into trade and business very early. Few boys remained at school over the age of 16. Yet within those rather narrow limits the market for schooling was expanding, and there were plenty of masters and mistresses anxious to provide what middle-class parents wanted.

5

The private school has suffered because it has always had a bad press. Dickens created in Mr Squeers of Dotheboys Hall an archetype, part cruel part comic, which has been remembered when the efforts of many honest and conscientious masters have been forgotten. Matthew Arnold with more elegant satire completed a picture in which dishonesty and pretentiousness mingled in approximately equal parts. In modern times there has been little attempt at a serious evaluation of the work of the Victorian private school.[6] Much of what has been written relates to the Hill family of Hazelwood and Bruce Castle, largely, one would suppose, because an account of their work has survived.[7] An attempt will be made in Part Two to redress the balance, but a few general comments may be made here. First of all, the private schools provided for the education of girls as the grammar schools did not. Much of what they provided was indeed of little value, but some girls' schools did give a more solid education, and the better private schools formed one of the roots of the great development of girls' education in the last third of the century.

Another type of private school which made a distinctive contribution to English education was the school with denominational affiliations, particularly those with Nonconformist affiliations, providing for the education of a community which still laboured under social and legal handicaps. Some of these were simply the private ventures of individual ministers. Others were congregational schools, like the Quaker schools of Ackworth and Bootham and The Mount in York. The Quakers, in their anxiety to provide what they called a 'guarded' education for their own children, made a contribution considerably greater in proportion to that which might have been expected from such a small body.

The congregational schools like Ackworth might be called semi-public. So too were the proprietary schools of the 1830s and 1840s which attempted to base a sound secondary education on the joint stock principle as a means of collecting funds from a large number of subscribers. Many such schools were funded, and more will be said about them in Ch. 13. Most of them achieved only a limited success, partly because of difficulties in raising money, and partly through denominational rivalries.

Yet the same corporate idea could be applied to the education of the lower middle class – clerks, small tradesmen, artisans. It was for people of this kind that 'middle schools' were established in the 1840s in connection with the newly created training colleges for teachers, though this was a particularly difficult area in which to work, and none of these 'middle schools' survived very long – at least in their original form. The grading of schools adopted by Nathaniel Woodard, though it was not exclusive to him – first class up to about 18 years, second class up to 16, third class up to 14–15 – was another form of the same idea.[8] Woodard was a successful pioneer, but he found few imitators. Members of the lower middle class had been closely involved with the Mechanics' Institute movement which aimed at improving the education of adult workers: at the more ambitious level through teaching them science and at the humbler level of teaching them to read and write. In some cases the larger and richer institutes set up schools to give elementary and sometimes secondary education.

These congregational schools, proprietary schools, middle schools and Mechanics' Institute schools were all in their different ways semi-private and semi-public. They were public in the sense that they were sponsored by groups of people sharing a common interest which endured over a long period. They were private in the sense that they lacked the charters or Acts of Parliament which regulated the grammar schools, and even more in the sense that, like schools run by individuals, they lacked endowments and they survived only as long as they could pay their way. 'Private foundation school' is a convenient term to define their status. A grammar school, with a formal legal personality and an endowment, could survive much more serious blows of fortune than schools of this kind. Yet the conventional dichotomy between the grammar school and the private school is false in that very few of the grammar schools, apart from a few of the richest foundations, survived on the strength of the endowment alone.

All the schools which were successful – with very few exceptions – had become so because the master had succeeded in attracting boarders and sometimes paying day pupils in addition to the local boys who were entitled to claim either a free education or an education at very low charges. A F Leach pointed out long ago that historically there was no difference between a 'public' and a 'grammar' school and that the cleavage had grown up in the nineteenth century as easier communications made it easier to concentrate the boys of the upper classes in a few schools.[9] Apart from the collegiate foundations of Eton, Winchester and Westminster, the public schools like Harrow and Rugby were those which at an early date had been able to attain a more than local celebrity and to maintain this for a considerable period of time. In several cases – for example at Harrow – this led to long continued complaints that the interests of local boys had suffered from the perversion of the school to serve the interests of the boarders. In 1809–10 this led to a Chancery case in which the Master of the Rolls, Sir William Grant, found in favour of the school governors against the parishioners. In his judgment the Master of the Rolls asked whether the parish would gain if Harrow became merely a parochial school.

> It cannot be supposed, that for the present Salary a man of talents would be found to fill the place of Master; and to give him a large Salary is the last method that prudence would devise for securing diligence and exertion in the obscure sphere, to which he would be confined.[10]

Over and over again the reports of the first Charity Commission (1818–37) make it clear that a successful school was one in which the master had succeeded in attracting boarders and paying day pupils as well as boys on the foundations. At Norwich in 1833 there were twenty-four free boys on the foundation, twenty boys boarding in the headmaster's house, and twenty-seven paying day scholars, a fairly typical mixture for such a school.[11] The essential point is this: in very few places were there sufficient foundation boys to maintain an effective grammar school. That could be done only by attracting private pupils who bought their education from a grammar school in the same way as they might have bought it from a private school. In other words all grammar schools were private schools as well, and those which flourished did so because they had been able to develop the private side.

The balance between private and foundation purposes was not easy to maintain, as we shall see, and it frequently came down too much against the foundation scholars. At Bath, for example, there were no boys on the foundation. The master had seventy–eighty boarders and paying day scholars, and he spent more than his statutable salary in keeping the premises in repair.[12] The school was, in fact, a private school within the shell of a public corporation. At Taunton in the same county Mr Norris, a townsman and old boy of the school, 'did not believe that the people of the town had any idea that it was a free grammar school, and that they had any right to send their children there'.[13] Both of these were clearly felt to be extreme cases which could not be defended, but they reinforce the point that the public and private elements of the early-nineteenth-century grammar school are very difficult to disconnect. Sir William Grant in his Harrow judgment already quoted made two very important points. The first is that a man of education could not, in most cases, live on his basic salary as master of a grammar school. Therefore he needed to take private pupils. The second is that, if the master was able to live on his salary, he would have no stimulus to exert himself. There was a strong belief at the time that dependence on endowments was enervating. Men and institutions needed the stimulus of private profit to attain both public and private ends. Unfortunately the two could not always be reconciled, and local boys sometimes suffered in the interest of the boarders who brought the master profit.

The development of both grammar schools and private schools in the eighteenth century has been studied by Nicholas Hans and R S Tompson.[14] There was considerable criticism of the traditional classical curriculum, and pressure to teach subjects like mathematics, French, geography and history. Tompson argued that the grammar schools changed considerably during the century. The introduction of modern subjects meant that fewer pupils learned classics. More schools charged fees and more schools were attracting boarders. By the end of the century there was growing public concern about the administration of charities. In 1782 Gilbert's Act required the collection of information on charities from all parishes, and although no immediate use was made of the returns, they prefigure the much more active concern for charitable reforms of the early nineteenth century.

The major problem, from the point of view of the late twentieth century, in discussing both grammar and private schools of this period is that no clear dividing line existed between elementary and secondary education. The twentieth century is accustomed to public educational systems which are clearly structured. They begin with elementary or primary schools taking children up to the ages of 11 or 12. These are followed by secondary schools covering the period of adolescence up to 18 or 19, when higher education begins. Such clear divisions were beginning to emerge only towards the end of this study. The average grammar school took boys as soon as they could read. Such a school might teach only a few boys Latin. It might have a small classical upper school with some boys working for university entrance alongside a much larger lower school in which boys would leave quite early in adolescence in order to go into trade or industry. Almost every combination of ages and of levels of study can be found, with the result that the term 'secondary education' as we use it today is an anachronism, though it is extremely difficult to avoid its use.

Two writers of the 1830s who examined the problem were Thomas Arnold of Rugby and the Irish educational reformer, Sir Thomas Wyse. Arnold was chiefly concerned with what he called 'English, or commercial schools'.[15] There was, he wrote, no regular system of secondary education, no standard which measured the effectiveness of the schoolmaster and the value of the education he provided. Such a standard could be created only through the intervention of government which could provide something analogous to the standards set for the upper classes by the public schools and universities. Wyse's analysis of the problem was remarkably far-reaching. He was critical of the dominance of the classics, and he stressed the importance of the physical sciences. What was needed was 'a *real* or reality Education, as the Germans term it ... the Education best fitted for the practical, the reality-men – for the active classes of the community'.[16] Wyse was concerned with the education of the whole community, which should, he argued, be divided into three sections: primary, secondary and superior. The secondary schools should be divided into lower and higher. In both divisions the curriculum should include the mother tongue, modern languages, geography and history, mathematics, the natural sciences and Latin, with Greek only in the higher schools. What Wyse has to say about the curriculum is commonplace enough, and represents the standard pattern put forward by educational reformers. What is interesting about his ideas is that he was one of the first – if not the very first – in this country to put forward the idea of an educational structure divided into three clear stages with a specific programme of what the secondary stage should contain. Modern writing on education takes all this so much for granted that it is difficult now to appreciate how original all this was in the 1830s.

Since we cannot look at early-nineteenth-century education in terms which relate attainment to age, are there any other principles or measures by which we may categorize it? Thomas Arnold, in the essay already quoted, says that a man's education has two aspects. The first, the professional, fits him for his daily work. The second, the liberal, fits him for citizenship, and if that aspect is neglected, he is not educated.[17] The use of the word 'liberal' in this context should be noted. It links on to the idea of a liberal education, based on the study of the classics, and valuable, not because of the actual amount of Greek and Latin learned, but because it was argued that these subjects had a unique value in training the mind.[18] The tradition had ancient and medieval roots. It had been reinterpreted at the Renaissance in terms of the much more rigid literary standards rediscovered by the humanists. It survived as the basic equipment of the educated man who could, it was argued, readily adapt himself to new situations and was better equipped to do this than a man who had been more intensively trained on narrower lines. Classics – and in this respect mathematics were put alongside them – were uniquely educative because they forced the learner to work out his own solutions and to avoid drilling by rote. If the grammar school had an inner coherence, this is where it was to be found.

Nor was this argument thought to apply only to the education of boys who were being prepared for university. The Trustees' Minute Book at Warrington Grammar School contains a very similar view in the report of the external examiner for Christmas 1853, and in this case applied to a very different group of boys. He argued that classics and mathematics were of great value even for boys who were designed for business, since they instilled principles which made it easy to acquire any branch of knowledge, and taught 'mental habits of analysis and discrimination'.[19] By the middle of the nineteenth century views such as these were coming under growing attack, but they were remarkably influential and very long-lived. Of course their proponents were in a sense expressing their own personal interest. Since they were people who had themselves learned the old classical and mathematical curriculum and often very little else, they naturally wished to pass on their own knowledge. The conservatism of the established curriculum is in all generations an enormously powerful pedagogical force. Even so these men believed what they said, not least because they tended to give moral as well as intellectual value to the traditional studies. The classical languages had a strong link with religious education and traditional morals, while the sciences, even before Darwin, already suggested a danger to the established intellectual order. The persistence of Latin in the humblest school formed a link with long-standing traditions of education and religion which many teachers were unwilling to jettison.

By 1800 the 'liberal' tradition had run very thin in many places, and in many cases it is very difficult to decide whether a school is or is not a 'grammar school'. The standard used here is inclusion in, or exclusion from, the *Digest of Schools and Charities for Education as reported on by the Commissioners of Inquiry into Charities . . . Grammar Schools*, published in 1842. There seem to have been included in this all schools where the foundation deeds or later practice contain any mention of Latin or of 'grammar', even if studied by only a few pupils. It is fairly clear that the line was very difficult to draw between grammar schools, so interpreted, and endowed charity schools. For example, in the West Riding parish of Guiseley, Rawdon Free School is included, Guiseley Free School is not, though the entries describe schools which seem to have been very similar.[20]

It is an over-simplification to talk of the 'decay' of the eighteenth- and early-nineteenth-century grammar schools, since most of them had adapted themselves to changing circumstances as best they could. Certainly there were some schools which had in a real sense 'decayed', had closed, or were educating only a tiny number of boys. There were many schools like Chesterfield in Derbyshire of which the Charity Commissioners wrote: 'We are informed that this was formerly a grammar school of some reputation but of late years it seems to have been of little public benefit.'[21] However, there was much more flexibility in the grammar schools than has usually been allowed, and throughout the first half of the nineteenth century initiatives were being taken in many places to adapt to new situations. After having said that, it must be added that new initiatives often produced very disappointing results. Yet the reforms of the Taunton and Endowed Schools Commissions did not come out of the blue. Local communities had been trying to make changes for many years, and it is reasonable to regard the major changes of the 1860s and 1870s as merely an important stage in a long process.

When the Charity Commission was set up in 1818, it was excluded from 'the two universities and their colleges, six public schools (Eton, Winchester, Westminster, Harrow, Rugby and Charterhouse), institutions having special visitors or overseers, cathedral or collegiate churches, and Jewish or Quaker schools'.[22] The small group of major public schools already stood apart, although, according to the rules under which the Charity Commissioners operated, this did not include Shrewsbury, which had as good a claim to inclusion as the others.[23] The same group, with the addition this time of Shrewsbury and of the two London schools, St Paul's and Merchant Taylors', was investigated by the Public Schools Commission of 1861-64. The public schools will be discussed in Chs 15-18; for the moment it is sufficient to note the exclusion of the six schools from the Charity Commission inquiry. The schools attached to cathedrals were not investigated until the appointment of the Cathedrals Commission (1852).

One group which stands on its own is the London schools. St Paul's had a large endowment, the value of which was likely to increase, and the high master enjoyed a large salary. One hundred and fifty-three boys were admitted on the foundation and there were no others. A more extensive benefit might be provided, the Charity Commissioners thought, 'than the mere instruction in classical learning of 153 scholars'.[24] Merchant Taylors' was considered to be exempt from inquiry since it was supported out of the general funds of the company, but Carlisle in 1818 recorded that there were 250 foundation boys and that the masters also took boarders.[25] The most remarkable of the London foundations was Christ's Hospital, though its character was unique and it is difficult to relate it to other schools. The commissioners gave a very lengthy account of it.[26] With an income in 1835 of £50,000 it educated 1,150 children including 70 girls. Of these about 700 boys were in London and the younger boys and all the girls at Hertford. Most of the boys left at 15 and only a very small number stayed at school in order to be candidates for the university exhibitions. The commissioners commented that, since most of the boys left so young, their classical attainments were moderate only. They were anxious to introduce teaching in modern languages since this would be very useful for boys who were likely to go into commerce. The girls received only a basic elementary education, and were very few in number. There were too many schools in London and its suburbs to note them all, but one worth mentioning, because of its mid-Victorian metamorphosis into a major school, is Dulwich College. When the commissioners went there, there were twelve poor scholars, learning reading, writing, arithmetic and the elements of history and geography. Two of them were learning Latin, and the master did not think it his duty to give the boys a 'good Latin education'. The school did not grow in numbers because better-off families were not willing to associate with the charity boys and the poor preferred to send their children to another school nearby.[27]

Schools like St Paul's or, in a very different field, Christ's Hospital, maintained a position of permanent importance, but this was true for very few. In the eighteenth and early nineteenth centuries the fortunes of schools varied very markedly. Success was linked very much with the personalities of individual masters and even within a short period of time large variations in numbers were common. It was not until the late Victorian period that a stable group of public schools appeared, and until that happened, many schools had a more or less brief period of glory before they faded into obscurity. A number of schools, however, maintained a prominent position for a long time and among these I have selected two for closer examination. Repton School in Derbyshire, like many others, formed part of a joint school and almshouse charity. The total rental of the properties in 1837 was £2,268. There were sixteen almsmen in the hospital at Etwall. The school had a headmaster, two ushers and a writing master. There were eight foundation boys who were admitted as boarders, and the sons of parishioners of Repton and Etwall were admitted free. In August 1836 there were twenty-two free scholars including the eight foundationers, between forty and fifty boarders and from four to five paying day scholars. The instruction was classical 'with the addition of writing, accounts, mathematics, history and geography', and there were two university exhibitions.[28] At Tonbridge in 1819 the total receipts of the school properties were £4,578 per annum, but only a small part of this was used to maintain the school and the bulk of the money went into the general funds of the Skinners' Company, a practice which the commissioners questioned. There were ten boys on the foundation, all day scholars and the 'sons of gentlemen or respectable tradesmen in the parish and neighbourhood'. They were taught classics free but they paid one guinea a quarter for reading, writing, arithmetic and mathematics. The master had thirty-two boarders who, like the day boys, received their classical instruction free. The small number of foundation boys was due, it was thought, to the limited demand for a classical education in the town, and this demand might be increased if more money could be spent on university exhibitions.[29] At Tonbridge the headmaster received only a small statutory salary. At Repton he received £400 a year, but individual salary figures are very difficult to compare because bases of computation differed and there were wide variations about how much was received in kind.

The two schools just described had developed as boarding schools. At the other end of the scale, particularly in rural districts, many so-called grammar schools were really elementary schools, and indeed it is difficult to believe that many of them had ever filled any other role. These grammar/elementary schools were common in some remote rural areas, like Cumberland, the remoter parts of Lancashire and the North Riding of Yorkshire. One which forms a useful example because the Trustees' Minute Book has survived is Uldale in Cumberland.[30] The Charity Commissioners in 1821 reported the income as £46 19s. 0d., all of which was paid to the master. There were fifty/sixty children, none of whom were learning Latin, though classics had formerly been taught.[31] In 1839 a new Chancery scheme was made for the management of the school. The schoolmaster was required to teach 'the rudiments of grammar Latin English Writing Arithmetic and the elementary parts of practical Mathematics such as mensuration surveying book-keeping &c and other useful learning and in the principles of the Christian religion according to the doctrine of the Church of England'. He was also required to teach the Sunday school children and to take them to church. 'Quarterages', that is fees paid quarterly, were laid down for learning the various subjects, the residents of those properties which had originally contributed to the school funds paying less than other parishioners, and the poor being admitted at an especially low rate. Like all Chancery schemes the cost of this was substantial. The trustees had to pay £160 5s. 6d., which was about 3½ years' income at the 1821 values.[32] It is possible that Uldale School became more purely elementary as the years went on. At least that would be a possible interpretation of the fact that in the 1840s and early 1850s the number of free scholars grew steadily.[33] In 1855 the first step was taken towards asking for a government grant, and in 1856 a government grant of £54 was successfully obtained.[34] To accept government grant under the supervision of the Committee of Council for Education meant definite acceptance of elementary status, though this was probably rather a formal recognition of a situation which had long existed than in itself an important change in objectives or curricula.

Many similar examples could be given of rural schools very like Uldale.[35] Many of them, like Uldale, took girls, and some of them had a mistress as well as a master. For example, the trustees of Bispham Grammar School in Lancashire decided in 1845 to appoint both a master who would be able to teach classics and a schoolmistress 'to superintend the Female Department in Reading, Knitting, Sewing &c in addition to the Writing and Arithmetic to be taught by the Master'.[36] They duly appointed a master and a mistress (as the names are the same, she may have been his wife or his sister). The master went on until 1874. When he retired the chairman was asked to have the school placed under government inspection, the same outcome as at Uldale some twenty years earlier.[37]

These were country schools in remote places where there can have been little demand for classical learning. But similar developments had taken place in town schools as the Charity Commissioners' reports make clear. At Horsham in Sussex, for example, a gross endowment of £461 educated sixty poor boys free of expense. They learned reading, writing and arithmetic. Only four of them learned Latin, and the master had no private pupils.[38] At Thetford in Norfolk the corporation adopted new regulations in 1825 which limited the number of foundation boys to thirty, only eight of whom were to learn classics, and none of whom were to remain on the foundation over the age of 14. At the time of the inquiry in 1834 there was one boy on the foundation as a grammar scholar and twenty-one foundationers under the usher, learning English subjects. Though the master had paying scholars as well, the foundationers clearly had little opportunity to gain a grammar school education, not least because they could not remain over the age of 14. 'As a grammar school', the commissioners concluded, 'this appears to have been of very little use to the town of Thetford for many years.'[39]

Many such schools were not flourishing anyway, but some of these changes represent a process of readjustment which may have been valuable because it was accommodating the school to the needs of its district. The Charity Commissioners did not normally welcome such adjustments because they related all the schools to a model which gave absolute pre-eminence to classical learning. But sometimes a school which had diverged from that model may have been doing a good job under its own particular circumstances. For example, in London, Alderman Hickson's Grammar School, Allhallows Barking, had a fairly small endowment and a total expenditure in 1816–17 of just under £100 a year. The school for twenty foundationers was always full. The boys learned reading, writing, arithmetic and the catechism. Latin grammar could be taught but there was no demand for it. The master was allowed to take paying scholars and had about twenty of them. The school was, we are told, 'well conducted on its present plan', and was perhaps doing the most useful job possible in an area on the border of the City and the East End, where there was not likely to be a demand for more literary studies.[40] A rather different example is that of the grammar school at Stafford where in 1824 the master had about fifteen classical scholars and about the same number of English scholars. The usher did not normally teach Latin, but he had about seventy boys who learned reading writing and accounts. Boys were admitted when they could read and the school was free to inhabitants of the borough of Stafford. The commissioners commented rather adversely on 'the present mixed mode of instruction pursued in it', but perhaps that was what the townspeople of Stafford wanted. In terms of the school populations of that day a school with 100 pupils could be counted as successful and likely to be meeting local demand.[41]

NOTES AND REFERENCES

1. Archer R L 1921
2. *SIC* IX, p 255
3. Mitchell B R, Deane P 1962, p 12. The 1841 figures are approximate only
4. *Ibid.* pp 24–6. The large Salford increase 1851–61 seems to represent a boundary change
5. *SIC* I, Report of the Commissioners Appendix II 'On the number of boys within scope of the inquiry'
6. An exception is the thesis by Leinster-Mackay D P 1972

7. Hill M D 1825
8. See Heeney, Brian 1969
9. Leach A F 1903 vol II pp lxxxv–lxxxvi
10. Quoted in Carlisle, Nicholas 1818 (reprinted 1972) vol II p 142
11. *CCR* 27, p 526
12. *CCR* 4, p 282
13. *CCR* 5, p 488
14. Hans N 1951; see also Simon, Joan 1979: 179–91. Tompson, Richard S 1971
15. Arnold, Thomas 1845 Education of the middle classes, p 227
16. Wyse, Thomas 1836 vol I p 164. For Wyse's career see Auchmuty J J 1939
17. Arnold T 1845 p 232–3
18. For a fuller treatment see Roach, John 1981: 57–66
19. Warrington GS, Trustees' Minute Book 1840–89: 23 Jan 1854 (Ches RO)
20. *CCR* 15, p 653 (Guiseley, Township of Guiseley); p 658 (Guiseley, Chapelry of Rawden).
21. *CCR* 18, p 149
22. Owen, David 1965 p 188
23. For Shrewsbury, see *CCR* 24, p 213
24. *CCR* 3, p 241
25. Carlisle, Nicholas 1818 vol II p 61
26. *CCR* 32, Pt VI pp 74–384, and particularly pp 269–84, 'The education of the children'. For a modern account of the school in the later nineteenth century, see Seaman C M E 1977
27. *CCR* 29, Pt II pp 904–6, 922 (Camberwell, Dulwich College). For a recent account of the mid-Victorian reforms, see Hodges, Sheila 1981
28. *CCR* 32, Pt II pp 605–8
29. *CCR* 1, pp 154–6
30. Uldale GS, Trustees' Minute Book 1726–1886 (Cumbria RO, Carlisle)
31. *CCR* 5, p 94
32. Uldale, Trustees' Minute Book, 21 June 1839
33. Six were admitted, 16 Jan 1840. Twenty-three were admitted, 7 Aug 1854
34. Minute Book, 2 March 1855, 23 May 1856
35. See Hycemoor GS, Bootle, Trustees' Minute Book 1811–1910 (Cumbria RO)
36. Bispham GS, Trustees' Minute and Account Book 1830–78, 7 Feb 1845 (Lancs RO)
37. *Ibid.* 4 April, 9 June 1845; 1874 accounts (note)
38. *CCR* 2, pp 169–70
39. *CCR* 29, Pt I pp 869–71
40. *CCR* 1, p 162
41. *CCR* 11, p 584

CHAPTER TWO

Some grammar schools and their problems

With Stafford we are approaching the large group of middling grammar schools which tried to maintain their classical teaching and, so far as they could, to broaden their scope. This is an unglamorous and unremarkable group but probably the most typical. These were the schools which avoided scandal or major litigation, which struggled on with resources which were often insufficient, and which by their very ordinariness illustrate most clearly the problems which the grammar schools had to face. I have chosen four examples from different parts of the country: Penrith in Cumberland, Warrington in Lancashire, Brewood in Staffordshire, and High Wycombe in Buckinghamshire. The revenues of Penrith School were tiny – £25 13s. 9d. in 1825[1] – though its standards must have been high because pupils were several times successful in winning a Lady Elizabeth Hasting's exhibition at Queen's College, Oxford, the blue-riband award for northern grammar schools.[2] There is a conflict of evidence about numbers at the beginning of the period. The Register Book lists 114 pupils for 1816, but the Charity Commissioners (1821) gave 34 only and Carlisle (1818) 30.[3] The discrepancy may be explained by one set of figures relating to foundation boys and the other to boarders and pay-scholars as well, but even so it seems extreme, since in 1825 the governors adopted regulations that not more than fifty scholars were to be admitted at any time without their permission. The same regulations provided that foundation boys should be admitted to learn Latin and Greek on payment of 'Five shillings Cock Penny yearly at Shrovetide, as heretofore'. Higher charges were to be made for English, geography, writing and arithmetic.[4] In 1831 Edward Nicholson was appointed headmaster, and it looks as though he was not a success. In September

1831 twelve boys had been admitted. In 1836, there was one admission, in 1837 two, and in 1838 one. In 1839 the governors were considering complaints from parents about the master absenting himself, though he did not resign until 1845. In the early 1850s an annual examination was being held before the governors – a practice which became very common at that time – and the numbers varied from eleven in 1851 to twenty-four in 1853. In 1857–58 the school was rebuilt, but in January 1862 the numbers had sunk to fourteen. The school began to prosper in the late 1860s with the appointment in 1865 of a new master who clearly stimulated new activity. By 1870 there were forty-four boys, thirteeen of them boarders. It is interesting to note that the new man was a layman and a graduate of the University of London.[5]

Warrington unlike Penrith had a substantial income. The Charity Commissioners in 1828 returned a figure of £551 18s. 0d. exclusive of payments made for coals. In 1826 there were two such payments of £285 11s. 1d. and of £195 6s. 11d. The master's salary was £300, plus the use of the school house.[6] New rules had been made for the school in 1820 by the Court of Chancery. The instruction given by the headmaster was entirely classical. There was no usher but there was a master who taught writing and accounts. At the time of the commissioners' visit there were twenty day boys who were taught free and two boarders, though the school house had accommodation for twenty-five to thirty. Clearly the headmaster was unpopular, and the commissioners attributed this to bad feeling arising out of the Chancery suit. The Trustees' Minute Book fills out the picture. There were difficulties with Mr Bordman, the head, about attendance, about punishments, about preferences given to some boys above others, and finally in 1827 he resigned, being given an annuity of £150 and a cash payment of £400.[7] In effect he was bought off. The commissioners in their report had expressed their doubts about the payment of the annuity because it must affect the financial position of the new master, though they agreed that, in the interests of the school, it was essential to get rid of Mr Bordman.[8]

Under the new headmaster, Mr Bayne, the number of free scholars was generally about twenty-five to thirty. Some doubt is cast on their standards of attainment by the fact that in 1839 one of them was given leave of absence 'that he may be taught to read'.[9] In 1828 a new schoolroom was erected. Since this was to cost nearly £500 and the trustees (perhaps embarrassed by their dealings with Mr Bordman) were unable to find all the money, Mr Bayne offered to make up the balance, to be repaid at £40/50 a year without interest.[10] It is clear that there was local pressure for a wider curriculum. In 1821 the trustees had considered making an application to Chancery for power to build a schoolroom in which an usher might teach elementary subjects, but they gave the idea up because counsel had advised them that the court was unlikely to accept it.[11] In 1836 the trustees decided that 1½ hours each day should be devoted to teaching writing and arithmetic. Only a few months later, in reply to a complaint that writing was not sufficiently taught, they resolved that, though they understood the importance of giving more time to commercial subjects, they were unable to adapt the curriculum in any way which would interfere with 'the original foundation of the School as a Free Grammar School, for the teaching grammatically the learned languages'.[12] In answer to further complaints, the writing master stated in 1838 that each boy had ten hours a week in 'writing geography arithmetic algebra Euclid (according to his age and abilities)'. In his view the free scholars were 'equally if not better educated in those branches than in other similar establishments'.[13]

In 1842 Mr Bayne resigned and in 1843 his successor, Mr Bostock, drew up a new scheme which the governors accepted. This was still basically classical, but it also included mathematics, writing, French, history and geography.[14] However, extending the curriculum was expensive. In 1849 the governors had to ask for parental contributions towards the salary of the usher who had been appointed to teach the new subjects, though two years later, since the financial position had improved, the governors did not need to make any further calls on parents for this purpose.[15] In 1851 forty-nine boys were examined in mathematics and fifty-two in classics,[16] but during the 1850s there was a serious drop in numbers – a fall which seems to have occurred in many schools like Warrington. The examiner's report for 1854 picks out one reason which will be developed later. Now that more boys were able, it was argued, as a result of easy travel, to go to the great public schools, more boys would come to Warrington who were intended for commercial pursuits and who needed an education designed for that objective.[17] The 'classical' boys could now travel by train to Rugby or to Rossall. The 'non-classical' boys did not find what they wanted in a traditional grammar school, even though something had been done to broaden the curriculum.

Some radical changes were clearly necessary by the late 1850s, though it was always easier to introduce changes on paper than to make them operate successfully in practice. In 1857 Mr Bostock sent the trustees a memorandum recommending that Greek might cease to be compulsory, that more should be done for the study of French, and that drawing should be introduced. The curriculum would then embrace divinity, Greek (optional), Latin, French, mathematics, drawing, writing, arithmetic, geography and history.[18] The trustees then applied to the Charity Commissioners,[19] the Town Council expressed their views, and finally in 1859 the Master of the Rolls confirmed a new set of rules.[20] A future headmaster's salary was to depend partly on capitation fees – a standard mid-Victorian prescription for encouraging personal effort. In the lower school pupils were to learn religious knowledge, English language, history and geography, writing, arithmetic with bookkeeping, elements of natural philosophy, French and Latin. In the upper school to these were to be added Greek, German and mathematics. Other subjects might be added if finances allowed. The scholars were to pay capitation fees: 21s. per quarter in the lower and 42s. per quarter in the upper school, with power to admit scholars to the lower school at a reduced fee on grounds of poverty. As in many schools, the introduction of a revised curriculum meant the end of free education, since the more subjects which were taught the larger the staff which was needed.

When the new division into upper and lower schools was implemented, there were nine boys in the former and seventeen in the latter.[21] By 1861 the numbers had fallen to thirteen and the trustees complained to Mr Bostock that he needed to show 'greater activity and exertion' if matters were to improve.[22] It seems as though his health was not good, and he had been headmaster for nearly 20 years. In September 1861 he resigned and was allowed a pension of £120 a year from April 1862. Notice was given to other masters to terminate their appointments on the same date.[23] After Mr Bostock's resignation matters seem to have improved, though the story need be carried no further here. The story of Warrington School is interesting through its very ordinariness. There were no scandals, no expensive lawsuits, though Mr Bordman's pension must have imposed a drain on the finances, since he did not die until 1845. The traditional grammar school curriculum did not meet the needs of the town, and some attempt at least was made to introduce modern subjects. Yet little success was achieved. Perhaps it was difficult for the clerical headmaster with his traditional training to promote the new subjects actively. Perhaps the townspeople simply felt that they could do better for their sons in private schools. Whatever the reasons may be, the result was a record of more failure than success.

Brewood in Staffordshire had a smaller income than Warrington – £412 5s. 2d. in 1821, £501 10s. 6d. in 1856.[24] In 1820 there were thirty-six boys in the upper school, twenty-five of them boarders in the master's house, five out-boarders and the rest living in the town. There were twenty-one boys in the lower school, though it is not recorded how many of these were boarders.[25] The Governors' Minute Book throughout is beautifully kept, and great care was clearly taken over the financial management of the trust, a duty which in this as in many other cases could be very expensive. In the 1850s, for example, the Willenhall estate was sold for £4,560. The cost of the necessary parliamentary bill and other legal expenses came to £953 5s. 6d. According to rules adopted in 1810 the master was to teach Latin and Greek, the usher the Latin rudiments as well as 'the English language, Geography, Writing and Arithmetic as usual',[26] and the same kind of curriculum profile was used when the trustees advertised for an usher in 1840.[27] In that year it had been agreed that there should be an annual examination of the school by an external examiner,[28] and a number of examiners' reports are thereafter entered in the minute book. In 1842 the report was very favourable, though 'the youth of the boys at present in the school' was commented on,[29] which makes it unlikely that boys were being sent to universities. In 1843 and 1846 the top class was reading Sophocles, Caesar's *Gallic War*, Horace and Cicero, Euclid books I–VI, algebra, the history of Greece and Rome and of Tudor and Stuart England, and in the latter year there were twenty-two boys in the upper school (eleven of them boarders) and twenty-four in the lower school.[30]

During the 1850s the examiners' reports continued to be favourable, though the boys were still quite young. The top boy in 1856 seems to have been 16,[31] and in the same year a note is entered in the minute book about the careers of the boys who left the school in the 6 years ending 31 June 1856.

Left for Cambridge	1
Left for business	50
Left for illness	5
Left for removal from the neighbourhood	8
Left for father's failure	1
Left for unable to pay	7
Left for residence in Paris	3
Left for private tutor	1
Left for cause unknown	1
Left for other schools	*16

* Of these 3 have gone to the Wolverhampton Grammar School and most of the others left to avoid Latin

It is easy enough to find material about the careers of individual boys, but this kind of detailed evidence for a whole group of leavers is very uncommon and therefore particularly interesting (see pp. 66-8). At the end of the 1850s the fortunes of the school took a sudden dive; in 1859 there were only seven boys in the upper school and seven in the lower. The principal cause of the difficulty seems to have been the financial embarrassments of the master, a not uncommon problem when masters acted as private contractors so far as their boarders were concerned, and in 1860 the trustees required Mr Brown, the master, to resign.[32] His successor had been headmaster of a private school and vicar of St Anne's Birkenhead.[33] The situation must have picked up quickly because at Christmas 1860 about fifty boys were examined.[34]

High Wycombe had a much smaller endowment than either Warrington or Brewood – only the schoolmaster's salary of £70, which included a fairly recent benefaction (1790) of £30 for teaching reading, writing and arithmetic to boys between the ages of 9 and 14.[35] The school, originally governed by the corporation of the town, was administered after 1838, along with other charities, by the municipal trustees set up under the Municipal Corporations Act of 1835. In 1841, after the master had resigned, the trustees set up a committee 'to extend the system of education so as to meet the altered state of society'[36] and the committee, considering that it was not desirable to limit the instruction given in the school to Greek and Latin, recommended an extensive new curriculum which was likely in practice to be far beyond their resources to implement. They recommended that the master should be paid £80, the most that they could afford, and that he should be allowed to take ten boarders, 'they being of opinion that without such additional advantage no person of sufficient standing in society, ability and learning could be procured to fill the office'.[37] The trustees accepted the recommendations of their committee. The school was to consist of thirty boys, sons of inhabitants of the borough and between the ages of 8 and 16, and the master, for his £80, a house and permission to take ten boarders, was to teach 'the Greek Latin French and English languages – Writing and Arithmetic with commercial accounts – the Elements of Mathematics, Geography, History (ancient and modern), the Elements of Natural History and Philosophy and Linear Drawing'.[38] He needed to be a polymath indeed!

The minute book says little about what happened for the rest of the decade, although it is noticeable that on several occasions there were more vacancies than applications to fill them.[39] However in the 1850s the school was considerably affected by the growing movement towards the reform of educational endowments (see Ch. 6). In January 1852 a new master, Mr Poulter, was elected. Only a few months later the vicar of High Wycombe, the Rev. H T Paddon, wrote to the trustees suggesting that a committee composed of the trustees and of other inhabitants be set up to look into the affairs of the school, particularly since the funds of the charity were likely to increase. 'You must be aware', Mr Paddon wrote, 'that investigations of charities have been forced upon public attention, and that they have become and are becoming matters of general interest and legislative enactment.'[40] The trustees, as is the way with such bodies, tried to stall, until in the New Year of 1854 they met to consider a letter from the newly established Charity Commission.[41] The commissioners raised questions about the grant of leases of the property and queried the distribution of income between the school and the almshouses. More money had been spent on the poor and the expenditure on the school had not increased in proportion. In a later letter the commission pointed out that in 1852 the income of the charity was £355. The almspeople received £221 1s. 5d. and the school only the master's salary of £70. In their view the number of almspeople should be reduced, the schoolmaster should be paid more, and there should be a new scheme to extend the usefulness of the school.[42] The trustees did their best to defend themselves, but in June 1854 the case was referred to the Attorney-General under the provisions of the Charitable Trusts Act of 1853. In one of their letters the trustees commented that they would like to know the name of their accuser and to answer his accusations directly. The prime mover was probably the vicar of High Wycombe after his own initiatives had led nowhere.[43]

Two years later new trustees were appointed and a new scheme made for the management of the school and the almshouses.[44] This provided for the enlargement of the schoolroom and for the payment to the headmaster of a salary of £120 (plus £30 from Mrs Bowden's gift) and to the usher of a salary of £70. The headmaster might take ten boarders. A capitation fee of between two and four guineas was to be paid for each boy, except that boys whose parents could not afford to pay might be admitted free – fifteen of them until Christmas 1856 and ten after that time. Boys were to be admitted between the ages of 8 and 17 years and they were to be taught the 'Principles of the Christian Religion, the Greek Latin French and German languages, Mathematics Science and the English subjects'. When the funds permitted a university exhibition of £30 a year was to be established.

The new trustees at once asked the headmaster for a report on the condition of the school, and Mr Poulter's report is of great interest.[45] He began by pointing out that, under the existing arrangements, the boys learned mathematics and English subjects as well as Greek and Latin. There were twenty-seven boys in the school, the oldest was 15, the youngest 9 and most of them were between 12 and 14. Three boys were reading the Greek *Delectus*.[46] The first class in Latin contained eight boys who were reading Virgil and Caesar's *Commentaries*. There were seven boys in the first French class, reading the *History of Charles XII* and *Gil Blas* and Hamel's French exercises. Six boys were studying single-entry bookkeeping, and among the mathematical subjects were conic sections, land surveying and mensuration, as well as arithmetic. Natural philosophy was studied from Chambers's *Matter and Motion* and *Introduction to Sciences*. Mr Poulter also mentioned religious knowledge, English grammar, geography, history, drawing and spelling. He was satisfied with the conduct of the school, but very critical of the standard of attendance. The entrance standards cannot have been high since he pointed out that it was essential for children to be able to read before they were admitted.

A glance at the multiplicity of subjects above, will serve to shew that we have no time to teach children to read. We have such, and as they cannot improve here as they would elsewhere, the school becomes an injury to them and they become impediments to others.

The report concludes with a request for a pair of globes and some maps and diagrams, 'the want of which makes the naked walls of the Grammar School contrast very unfavourably with those of the British School'.

As was so often the case, it was much easier to draw up new schemes than to put them into practice effectively. To judge from the minute book the new trustees seem to have started off with considerable enthusiasm, but within a few years the number attending meetings fell. The new scheme had made the usual provisions about the appointment of an external examiner, and their reports comment that the boys were young and the standard of work consequently low. Nor did the number rise. At Midsummer 1861 there were fifteen boys paying capitation fees, three boarders and seven free boys.[47] In the same year Mr Coombes the usher asked for an increase in salary and when the trustees refused it through lack of funds he resigned. His statement of his case has survived.[48] He had, he explained, been prepared to teach a wide range of subjects at a low salary because he had expected that the new scheme would attract the sons of professional men who would stay longer so that the income of the school would rise and his own salary would rise with an increase in the capitation fees. These hopes had not, however, been realized.

> There appear to be certain prejudices of class in existence in Wycombe which deter gentlemen from sending their sons to a school where they may possibly meet others who are below them in the social scale, and under the influence of such a feeling, they seem to be blind to the fact that the education which we give is exactly suited to their requirements.

Mr Coombes's letter pinpoints one of the major dilemmas of the middling grammar school as the education of different social groups grew more sharply differentiated.

The four selected middling schools – Penrith, Warrington, Brewood, High Wycombe – had all experienced difficulties, but they had all adapted more or less successfully. Many schools had succumbed altogether for longer or shorter periods, or were educating so few boys as to be quite ineffective. The Charity Commissioners' reports give far too many examples to quote them all, and I have chosen only a few, trying once again to present cases from different parts of the country. In 1837 the commissioners reported on Cornwall, a county with few grammar schools and all of them poorly endowed. They list six schools. Four of them had been discontinued, at the fifth the endowment was applied to other educational purposes, and only the sixth – Truro – operated as a grammar school.[49] Carlisle twenty years earlier had called it the Eton of Cornwall.[50] At Somerton in Somerset in 1824 the affairs of the charity were in the greatest confusion. Few if any boys were being educated in the school, 'and it is very obvious that the master has not a sufficient remuneration'.[51] In Surrey no school had been kept at Farnham since 1809 when the commissioners went there in 1824.[52] At Croydon the schoolmaster of Whitgift's hospital also acted as chaplain. He had never had any free scholars, though he had formerly taken private pupils. As he had ceased to take them for several years, he performed no duty whatever and the school house was used by the pupils of the National School.[53]

Several schools had closed in Lancashire. In Liverpool the grammar school had closed in 1803, though in 1825 the corporation had spent considerable sums on establishing two National Schools.[54] At Eccleston in the parish of Prescot the trustees had appointed a master in December 1828, the school having been discontinued for upwards of 50 years previously and the premises let.[55] At Warton in 1826 it was noted that no schoolmaster had been appointed since 1808. There was an usher who taught elementary subjects, but he had received nothing from the endowment since 1815.[56] One extra-ordinary case was that of Kirkleatham in the North Riding of Yorkshire which was examined in 1822. The endowment was quite considerable – £350, though for many years no boys had been educated. It was suggested that the squire of the place had discouraged the school because the building was close to the manor house. However, a master and usher had been regularly appointed and paid their salaries. The only contribution made to education consisted of small grants to local village schools.[57]

Some of the instances cited are schools in remote places, where control might prove difficult, but the same problems occurred in Coventry, a considerable city, where the rental in 1832 was £890 4s. 5d., a much higher figure than in many successful schools. When the inquiry took place in 1833, the master, Mr Brooks, was 82 years of age and had held office since 1779. The usher, Mr Paris, had been appointed in 1794. Mr Brooks had been a successful master, but he and the usher had quarrelled and the school had declined as he got older. When the commissioners came, there was only one boy left. Almost every problem seems to have confronted the foundation. The bailiff who retired in 1831 owed large sums of money to the masters. The headship was united with the city parish of St John Bablake, which made it more difficult to arrange for the master to resign. There was a threat of litigation over a new scheme of management made by the corporation, and when Mr Brooks died in October 1833 the school had been filled up by the usher with boys from the city who, the commissioners thought, were obviously not of a standard to receive a grammar school education.[58] The dilemma of the master who had grown too old for his work and who was either unable or unwilling to retire from it was a common problem. So was the harm done to a school by the bad relations between master and usher, left to grow more and more embittered by the passage of years.

The Charity Commissioners frequently commented that, in a former period, a school had been more prosperous and that the master had attracted boarders to it. Some of this may have been mere local hearsay, and such statements are not always to be taken at their face value. What had certainly happened in the early nineteenth century is what might be called the drift from locality, as part of the differentiation between schools which has already been discussed. At the Bury St Edmunds tercentenary commemoration the headmaster spoke of the importance for local boys of having a good school in their own area, which could combine 'the regular discipline of a public school' with 'the inestimable benefits of parental superintendence'.[59] Dr Donaldson's comment was outdated when he made it. For many centuries local communities possessed a strong coherence, travel was difficult, and the local gentry tended to send their sons to local schools. By the nineteenth century fashions were changing, and the upper classes were more likely to educate their sons in a few major schools. One important change which facilitated this social transformation was improved transport. The influence of the railways has often been noted. How far, one might ask, was Arnold's success secured when Rugby subsequently became an important railway junction? But turnpike roads and stage-coaches had begun the process a couple of generations before the railway age. To pursue the Rugby example, Tom Brown arrived at Rugby on the Tally-Ho coach, having travelled from his Berkshire home via London.

The patterns of an earlier age can be traced in some papers relating to the grammar school at Houghton-le-Spring in County Durham.[60] When the Charity Commissioners went there in 1837, there were six free scholars and about sixty pay-scholars, including boarders, so for that day it was quite a flourishing school.[61] In the early 1840s a considerable sum of money was collected to found a university exhibition, and the list of donors, most of them old boys, has survived. The old boys on the list comprise twenty-four 'esquires' (a fairly specific term in the early-nineteenth-century usage for a man of social position), seven clergymen including the headmaster, three men with military ranks, one Queen's Counsel, and one viscount who was also an MP. The list is dated 1845, so it would be reasonable to assume that most of these men would have been at the school 20–30 years earlier. The fact that they had been at Houghton-le-Spring School does not necessarily mean that they would have completed their schooling there, for it was quite common for boys to go to the local grammar school for two or three years and then to go on to a major public school later. But even allowing for that the list is an impressive one for such a school, and it is unlikely that a similar institution could have capped it by mid-century. J G Fitch, reporting on the West Riding for the Taunton Commission in the 1860s, wrote[62]:

> Locomotion is now so easy, that practically, Rugby or Westminster is as accessible to the son of a Yorkshire squire as Leeds or York. In fact the more distant place of education seems to be invariably preferred. It is the object of the father, as a rule, to withdraw his son from local associations, and to take him as far as possible from the sons of his own neighbours and dependants.

It looks as though nineteenth-century society was becoming more not less socially stratified. Probably two changes were at work here. The first is the tendency for local community isolation to break down and for social institutions to be related more to national patterns. Prominent families tended therefore to look away from their area towards London, or, in the case of education, towards the few schools which had acquired national standing. Secondly the fact that so much new wealth was being made and that so many people were moving up socially because they were richer meant that society in general was more, not less, concerned about class distinctions. In the old stable rural society the natural leaders had a position so secure that they did not need to concern themselves about it. Their position was not threatened because they sat on the benches of the local grammar school with boys from much humbler homes. The more new money was made, the more rivalries developed between land and industry, the more important it seemed to withdraw into the company of your own kind at school as in later life. As we shall see in Chs 7 & 11, this process had an even more profound influence on private schools than on the grammar schools, but for them it was serious enough. The traditional grammar school had – to some extent at least – coped with the demands of widely differing social groups. By the time of, say, the Great Reform Bill of 1832 that synthesis had largely broken down.

NOTES AND REFERENCES

1. Register Book of the Free School of Penrith (Cumbria RO), 1825
2. In 1819, 1824, 1834, 1839, 1844 and 1854
3. *CCR* 5, p 159; Carlisle, Nicholas 1818 vol II p 192
4. Register Book, Penrith, April 1825. The subsequent information about the school all comes from this source
5. See James Gordon's Commonplace Book (Cumbria RO); Leech W H B 1932
6. *CCR* 20, pp 176, 178, 179
7. Warrington GS, Trustees' Minute Book 1820-40, 20 Aug 1827 (Ches RO)
8. *CCR* 20, pp 179-80
9. Warrington Minute Book, 21 Jan 1839
10. *Ibid.* 27 Oct 1828
11. *Ibid.* 9 Nov 1821; 29 Aug 1825
12. *Ibid.* 1 Aug 1836; 30 Jan 1837
13. *Ibid.* 29 Jan 1838
14. *Ibid.* 21 Aug 1843
15. *Ibid.* 18 Dec 1849; 23 Jan 1850; 23 Sept 1850; 23 Sept 1851
16. *Ibid.* 27 Jan 1852
17. *Ibid.* 29 Jan 1855

18. *Ibid.* 21 Sept 1857
19. That is, the body set up under the Charitable Trusts Act of 1853, not the 'Brougham' Commissioners
20. Warrington Minute Book, 12 Sept 1859
21. *Ibid.* 5 Dec 1859
22. *Ibid.* 21 Jan 1861
23. *Ibid.* 28 Sept 1861
24. *CCR* 5. p 555; Brewood School Minute Book 1801–77 (Staffs RO), 4 Nov 1856
25. *CCR* 5, p 559
26. Brewood Minute Book, 15 Feb 1810
27. *Ibid.* 2 Oct 1840
28. *Ibid.* 7 Aug 1840
29. *Ibid.* 5 Aug 1842
30. *Ibid.* 4 Aug 1843; 5 Oct 1846. The books and subjects mentioned are taken from the two lists; not all the topics appear in both lists
31. *Ibid.* 3 Nov 1856
32. *Ibid.* 21 Jan 1860
33. *Ibid.* 12, 25 May 1860
34. See the printed examination list for Christmas 1860 (Staffs RO)
35. *Digest of Grammar Schools* p 4; Trustees of the Wycombe Charities, Minute Book 1838–65 (Bucks RO), 30 Jan 1839. For a modern account of the school, see Ashford L J, Haworth C M, 1962
36. Wycombe Charities Minute Book, 17 Feb 1841
37. *Ibid.* 15 May 1841
38. *Ibid.* 4 Aug 1841
39. *Ibid.* 10 Feb 1848; 14 Feb 1849; 24 Dec 1851
40. *Ibid.* 27 May 1852
41. *Ibid.* 5 Jan 1854
42. *Ibid.* 11 May 1854
43. On 4 Oct 1856 Mr Paddon, in declining to act on a property committee, wrote: 'As I have now seen my endeavours crowned with success in our possession of a New Scheme and in the appointment of New Trustees I feel it right to leave to others the carrying out of matters chiefly of temporal importance.' (*Ibid.* 16 Oct 1856)
44. See '*Attorney-General* v. *Harman.* Analysis of scheme' (Bucks RO, CH1/AP13/15)
45. Wycombe Charities Minute Book, 2 Oct 1856. Another paper by Mr Poulter (Bucks RO, AP 10/31) gives the boys' ages
46. *Delectus*: a selection of passages for translation
47. See the report for 1861 (Wycombe Charities Minute Book, 7 Aug 1861)
48. Bucks RO, CH1/AP/14/96
49. See *CCR* 32, Pt I. The four closed schools were Bodmin (p 502), Launceston (pp 404–5), Penryn (p 431) and Saltash (p 422). The endowment was applied for other educational purposes at Probus (p 474)
50. Carlisle, Nicholas 1818 vol I p 148
51. *CCR* 11, pp 449–50, 457
52. *CCR* 12, p 583
53. *CCR* 31, pp 879–90

54. *CCR* 20, p 91
55. *CCR* 21, pp 241, 243
56. *CCR* 15, pp 309–10
57. *CCR* 8, pp 744–6
58. *CCR* 28, pp 127–32
59. *Record of the tercentenary of the foundation of King Edward VIth's Free Grammar School, Bury St Edmunds: containing the lord bishop of London's sermon; the head master's retrospective address; the proceedings of the day*, p 34
60. Houghton-le-Spring parish records. Prospectus of the Kepier Grammar School Scholarship Fund 1845 (Co. Durham RO)
61. *Digest of Grammar Schools* p 27
62. *SIC* IX, p 148

CHAPTER THREE
The grammar school as a legal entity

The purpose of the ensuing chapters is to look in more detail at the conduct of these schools, examining firstly the external management – property, trustees, local controversies – and secondly the internal management – particularly the curriculum. The division is not perfect, and some topics, for example the position of the headmaster, come into both areas, but as a broad means of attack this will serve well enough to simplify a complex mass of material.

The question of external management looms largest in records like school minute books and the reports of the Charity Commissioners, because their primary concerns were official and legal. Since the grammar schools were corporate bodies which, individually and collectively, owned a great deal of property, it is property and in particular landed property which dominates the records. The first point to make is that the hundreds of grammar school foundations varied from the very rich to the very poor. Some of the rich foundations were poorly managed, but as a broad generalization it is true to say that the rich schools were the most successful because they possessed the resources to innovate. Such innovation, as we shall see, demanded a new Act of Parliament, and the passage of Acts of Parliament involved great expense. A good example of a well-administered foundation was the grammar school at Birmingham which was very wealthy and which could afford to diversify.[1] Often the most serious problems arose when foundations were very poor and these problems were exacerbated as pressures grew to teach more subjects. A wider curriculum demanded more teachers. To pay for those teachers meant higher fees which caused local resentment and sometimes sharper social differentiation among the pupils.

The finances of Blackburn Grammar School in Lancashire provide a good example of these difficulties. In 1819 the governors raised a subscription to make up the arrears due to their treasurer and in the same year they appointed only a single master, leaving the usher's post vacant because they could not afford to pay for a second post. The new master's salary was to be £90 without a house, the total income of the foundation amounting, according to the Charity Commissioners' Report of 1826, to rather less than £120 a year. In 1825 the governors appointed a writing master and in the following year they ordered that since the school was a grammar school, no pupils should be permitted to attend purely in order to learn the elementary subjects. In the following year they had to rescind that regulation in order to make up the number of the writing master's pupils because the stipend allotted to him was so small. In the 1840s money was collected to build a house for the master, and when Mr Atkinson, the master appointed in 1819, resigned in 1845, his successor was allowed £100 plus a house.[2] There were many foundations even poorer than Blackburn, but the example shows how narrow was the margin of security provided by many endowments, and how difficult it was to broaden the range of subjects taught.

At another Lancashire school, Bury, a much richer foundation than Blackburn, the total expenditures in 1843 amounted to £508 8s. 3d. Of this £366 18s. 6d. was salaries. The headmaster received £200 and two other masters £100 and £55 respectively, while £11 18s. 6d. was spent on 'teaching the girls'; £64 8s. 11d. was spent on a wide variety of miscellaneous payments, including books for the library, the salary of the steward, insurances, and the hire of a 'sociable' used on rent day; £29 10s. 3d. was spent on what appear to be estate repairs and £4 18s. 7d. on repairs and other payments at the school; finally £42 12s. 0d. covered a number of small payments, the most important of which was the law bill of the clerk to the governors for drawing leases. On the credit side rents of property 'including tithes and boons' amounted to £467 4s. 9d. There was a small balance of 19s. 0d. on the previous year's entertainment, bank interest and dividends on 3 per cent. Consols came to £36 1s. 10d., other small receipts to £20 9s. 0d., and there was a balance in hand from the previous year of £306 5s. 2d. The total received amounted to £830 19s. 9d., leaving a balance in hand of £322 11s. 6d.[3] The position in that year was a healthy one, but it must be remembered that such a balance could rapidly be swept away by heavy repairs on the estates or by the not infrequent expense of legal proceedings. In 1827–28 the expenditure of Bury St Edmunds School in Suffolk, one of the leading grammar schools of the day, was £521 2s. 7d. Of this the headmaster's salary amounted to £217 15s. 0d.

and other salaries to £44 15s. 0d. Exhibitioners at the universities received £98 15s. 0d., leaving the balance (£159 17s. 7d.) to be spent on tradesmen's bills and a wide variety of small payments.[4]

The traditional system of letting land and houses had been by leases for lives, granted in return for a fine calculated on the basis of the estimated annual value of the property. How this worked can be seen from the Trustees' Minute Book of Wotton-under-Edge Grammar School in Gloucestershire. In 1804 the trustees granted a new lease of a house and premises in the town

> for one life in Revertion of the two lives now in being and for two other lives in Exchange of those two in consideration of a Fine of sixty six pounds and three shillings, being one Year and one Half's purchase for the life in Revertion and two years purchase for the lives exchanged.[5]

As the century went on, this system was gradually replaced by the practice of letting properties at a regular annual rent, which avoided the irregular returns produced by the leases for lives system. The change can be seen from the Charity Commissioners' account of Ilminster in Somerset, which seems to have been a well-managed endowment. About 20 years before their report the decision had been taken to replace leases for lives by leases 'upon short terms of years at rack rent'. As this change had been made, the rents had been steadily increased. When an estate had fallen in, it had been re-let by tender. When the lease had then expired, the tenant had been asked to make a new offer and if this had not proved acceptable, the property had been put out to tender again. The master had a fixed salary of £50, which was increased by a capitation fee of £5 for each foundation boy up to ten in number. The trustees paid the rent, taxes and repairs of the school house, and provided the school furniture. In addition the master had about forty private pupils who boarded with him. Since the trustees had revenues in excess of what was needed to maintain the grammar school, they had established another school for elementary subjects, finding the master a house and a salary made up partly of a fixed sum and partly of capitation payments. The trustees also paid for girls to come to this school in the evening to learn reading, writing and arithmetic, and they maintained a third school for teaching small boys and girls to read. They also contributed £15 per annum towards two Sunday Schools, one Church of England, one Dissenting, and they devoted any final excess of income, according to the original grant, to the repair of highways and bridges.[6]

The sources contain many examples of new statutes or of less formal regulations made for the schools during this period. There are individual differences between them, but in general they conform to a common pattern. Often such statutes and regulations were made by the Court of Chancery after the affairs of a charity had been through the court. The rules made by the court for Warrington have already been briefly mentioned (see p. 19). These provided that the master of the school, appointed by the hereditary patron, should teach the scholars 'grammatically the learned languages'. If the trustees thought that he needed assistance, he might appoint an assistant to teach the same subjects, and also a master to teach writing and arithmetic 'at such hours as would not interfere with their grammatical learning'. The master was to be paid £300 per annum, plus an additional sum, to be fixed by the trustees if there were more than thirty free scholars, and salaries were also settled for the usher and writing master. The master was given power to direct the work of the other teachers and to remove them for neglect of duty or other reasonable cause. In similar cases of misconduct by the master the trustees were given power to complain to the patron so that he might take action according to the terms of the foundation deed.

It was provided that the free scholars should be taught in the schoolrooms and that the trustees might have power to enlarge these if the number of the scholars made it necessary. Rules were laid down about holidays and hours of attendance. The school day was to begin and end with prayers and the children were to be taught 'the principles of the Christian religion, according to the Liturgy of the Church of England' and the Church catechism. No boy was to enter the school under 7 years old, and pupils were to pay no entrance money or fee 'except the four-pennies mentioned in the original foundation deed'. The master was to keep a register and to ensure that all boys came to school clean, decently dressed and free from disease. He was allowed to occupy the school house and garden rent free, though he was responsible for 'tenant's levies and taxes', for interior decorations, and for the whitewashing and cleaning of the school-rooms and for maintaining fires in winter.

Provisions were then made for the management of the trust property. This was to be let at the trustees' discretion 'for terms not exceeding eleven years'. The income might be spent on repairs and improvements to the estates and to meet taxes and other charges, and power was given to retain in the hands of the receiver of rents 'such a sum as they should think necessary to answer the current expenses of the trust'. The trustees were required to keep accounts and to make proper provision to preserve their deeds and other documents. They were required to hold an annual meeting, to approve the accounts and payments to the master and to do other necessary business. Their balances were to be invested 'in some of the public funds'. They might also hold special meetings when necessary. Finally they were not permitted to do anything 'which might in any manner alter or defeat the foregoing rules, or any of them or the original constitution of the said school, as a free grammar school, for the teaching grammatically the learned languages, as declared in the decree of the said Court of Chancery'.[7]

There are too many available examples of similar schemes to cite them all, but some other points are worth emphasizing. Sometimes the master was required to sign a bond that he would perform his duties efficiently and give up possession of the school if required to do so. Thus at Brewood in Staffordshire in 1810 it was provided

That the Head Master and all future Masters shall upon the acceptance of their respective offices, give Bonds in the penalty of one thousand Pounds each, to resign their appointment upon being discharged therefrom by a Majority of the Visitors and Trustees present at any General Meeting, for Immorality, Neglect of Duty, or other sufficient cause of complaint, the same having been first duly proved to the satisfaction of the said Visitors and Trustees.[8]

Getting rid of inefficient masters was a major problem to trustees. It could lead to bitter disputes and, even more important, to very expensive lawsuits. The bond was an expedient for providing against trouble before it arose.

The statutes and regulations often differentiate between the classical languages, sometimes defined as the headmaster's primary responsibility, and the mathematical and English subjects, more particularly the responsibility of the usher. This kind of differentiation seems to be more common in the later than in the earlier examples, since as time went on it became more usual for grammar schools to provide both classical and modern courses. The 1848 statutes of Kinver Grammar School in Staffordshire[9] provided that no boy was to be admitted under the age of 7 or until he could read the New Testament 'with fluency', nor might he remain after the end of the half-year in which he had reached 18 years. The school was to be divided into two parts, classical and commercial. The headmaster was to teach 'the higher branches of education', that is the Greek and Latin classics, while the usher taught 'English Reading, English Grammar, Parsing, Geography, Church Catechism or explanation of it, Writing, Arithmetic, and the keeping of Accounts'. The Kinver statutes provided that classical education in the senior division was free, but that boys in that division should pay for learning other subjects and that all boys in the lower division were to pay a quarterly fee. In general, where tuition was free, it was only Greek and Latin which were so taught. It was common also to distinguish between local boys and 'foreigners'. The Bradford Grammar School governors' rules of 1835, like the Kinver statutes, allowed free tuition only in Greek and Latin, and only to boys born in the parish or whose parents qualified through residence or the leasing or purchase of property there. All boys, resident or not, had to pay a quarterly fee for 'other branches of literature, writing, English reading and grammar, history, geography and the use of the globes, arithmetic and mathematics'.[10] Curriculum will be discussed in Ch. 5 but these rules of the 1830s and 1840s do show that attempts were being made to enlarge the range of grammar school study.

The Kinver and Bradford regulations raise the question of what was meant by a 'free grammar school', the term so often used at the time and so often quoted in later controversies. In what sense were grammar schools 'free'? The argument that the poor had been excluded by the rich from educational advantages which they were entitled by law and custom to enjoy goes back a long way. It has been argued by Brian Simon that the reformers of the Taunton Commission era carried the process much further, and through the general introduction of school fees turned the schools into middle-class preserves.[11] It is impossible, I think, to lay down a single definition of what was and what was not taught 'free' in grammar schools because there were almost as many variations as there were schools. It is broadly true that the Greek and Latin classics were taught free, as the original purpose of all the foundations, though that statement needs a large number of qualifications about the number of pupils to be taught and the amount expected in supplementary payments other than fees. Manchester may be taken as typical of the larger and wealthier foundations. It had a large endowment (£4,408 17s. 1½d. gross in 1825). It had strong university connections and it also educated a large number of boys who went into local trades and industries. The Charity Commissioners described it as a 'free grammar school'. All the boys received a classical education free, but they were charged for writing, arithmetic and mathematics.[12] In the very different circumstances of a village grammar school in the same county similar rules applied. At Widnes the commissioners found about twenty boys, half of whom were learning Latin. They reported[13]:

The school is considered free to the children of the chapelry, for instruction in English reading and classics; but for teaching writing and arithmetic, mathematics and geometry, the master is allowed by the trustees to make certain charges, varying from 10s. to £1 11s. 6d. per quarter.

It would be a mistake to think that the grammar schools which had become elementary schools taught children free because of that change. The point has already been made that such schools were common in the remoter areas like Cumberland, and in these Cumbrian schools fees were commonly charged. At Hycemoor Grammar School, Bootle, for example, different quarterly payments were levied for different subjects, and these were generally laid down when a new master was appointed. In 1827 the quarterly sums were to be 4s. for English, 5s. 6d. for 'writing, the first four rules of Arithmetic, the Rule of Three and Practice', and 7s. 6d. for 'Classics and the higher parts of Arithmetic, or either of them'. At that time six poor children were to be taught free, but by the 1860s there is no mention in the minute book of free tuition, and indeed the specific mention of fees for 'labourers' children' suggests that everyone paid.[14]

Where free tuition was provided, there were often severe limitations to the right. Sometimes the master covenanted only to take a small number of free boys: three at Bideford in Devon in 1815,[15] two at Plymouth in 1810 in consideration of the corporation raising the master's salary from £30 to £50.[16] At Catterick in the North Riding classics were not taught. Of the sixteen children at the school twelve were taught free, the number of free scholars being determined by agreement between the schoolmaster and the vicar and church-wardens.[17] At Yarm there were six free boys who were taught the basic English subjects and learned no Latin. They had to be 10 years of age when admitted and they were allowed to remain only 3 years in the school.[18] At some schools far more prominent than these the right of pupils to free tuition was in practice of limited value. At Bristol in 1821 there were four or five free scholars and the numbers had not generally been higher, though there was no specific limitation. In the usual way the foundation provided only for instruction in the classics. The master also had a number of boarders and paying day scholars, and he told the commissioners that to put 'the foundation boys upon a footing with his private pupils as to all branches of education' cost an additional sum of £16 16s. per annum. Foundation boys paying this fee paid an admission fee of two and a half guineas; otherwise they paid £4.[19] It was not likely under such circumstances that Bristol Grammar School would be very attractive to the sons of poor freemen. A similar situation existed at Beverley in the East Riding, a school of considerable reputation. Legally this was a free school but because of the very small endowment it had been usual for the free scholars to make a quarterly payment. This, the commissioners reported, had reached the sum of £2 per annum for the son of a burgess, and this charge had led to complaint.[20]

If all these limitations – about subjects taught, numbers admitted, entrance fees and other payments – are taken together, the amount of free education provided by the early-nineteenth-century grammar school was severely limited. Moreover social and educational changes were making free education in the classics, which alone was the traditional privilege, less and less what parents required, and there was generally no legal right to anything else. The case of two West Riding schools is interesting here. At Hipperholme complaints were made to the commissioners that the free scholars were not taught writing and arithmetic without payment. The commissioners' reply was that the school had always been conducted as a grammar school and that the master could not therefore be required to teach other subjects free.[21] At Hemsworth the problems were even greater. Classics had not been taught for many years. The master himself did not teach but appointed a deputy who taught the basic English subjects in the schoolroom, though all the children so taught paid a quarterly fee. Once again the commissioners reported local dissatisfaction because there was no free education. They admitted that a grammar school was not needed in the neighbourhood and that the existing school was of little benefit to it. However, since the founder's object had been to establish a school to teach the classical languages, they could not admit that children had any right to be taught the basic subjects without charge. They urged, however, that, if all the parties could agree to establish a free school 'in the ordinary branches of an English education' as part of the foundation, such a change would be very desirable.[22]

Hemsworth had a substantial and increasing endowment. The problems there did not concern lack of money, but rather the fact that it was impossible to spend the money in the ways most appropriate to local needs. Very often fees were introduced or increased, because this was the only way of creating a more effective school. At Lancaster prior to 1824 the grammar school had always been open to boys of the town and neighbourhood without restriction, no payments being made 'except a gratuity at Shrovetide, under the name of a cockpenny'. The school had been maintained by the corporation out of their general funds and there was a small endowment for the usher. In 1823–24 the corporation drew up a report on the state of the school. This recommended an increase in the salary of the master and usher and the introduction of regular quarterly payments for all boys. Free education was to be ended, 'there being ample provision for that kind of education, in the National and other schools'.[23] Clearly the corporation wished to raise the standard of the school, and they saw the introduction of fees as a means of achieving this. What the sons of many poorer people wanted was an education in the basic subjects. With the foundation of National and British schools, institutions were being created for that specific purpose. If the grammar school was to become distinctively a secondary school, it needed the kind of specialization which was bound to cost money. In the case of all but a few rich foundations this meant the introduction of or a considerable increase in fees since there was no likelihood of support from public funds. As the nineteenth century went on the traditional concept of the 'free grammar school', as I have tried to define it, came more and more under attack, not least because of its own inherent contradictions.

Whether a school was or was not well managed was ultimately the responsibility of the headmaster and of the trustees. No school was likely to be efficient unless there was good co-operation between these two parties, and good co-operation also between the head and the usher or other assistant masters. Frequently these good relations did not exist, and the records are full of quarrels, some serious, some bizarre, some laughable, between men who often had to endure years of friction on a small stage where they were brought into constant contact with one another. Mr Spurdens, headmaster of the Paston Grammar School at North Walsham, wrote on 20 March 1821 a long letter to the treasurer of his governing body, complaining about the school-house pump. He concluded[24]:

> It must either be that they (the governors) do not understand how I am circumstanced; or have never given their attention to it: for I should be very unwilling to think (what I understand is thought by some) that a system of annoyance is practised, in order to drive me from the Mastership.

Many other headmasters must have harboured similar thoughts, and it is not difficult to detect this kind of tension behind the entries in many governors' minute books. Often the head found the trustees cheese-paring and oblivious to his hard work, while the trustees found the master neglectful of his duties and unwilling to teach the subjects which they thought that the children should learn.

I shall discuss the headmasters at length in Chapter 4, when looking at school life from the inside. In external affairs the trustees reigned supreme – at least in theory and if they took the trouble to exercise their powers. First of all, what kind of people were they? In corporate towns schools were often administered by the corporation or after the Municipal Corporations Act of 1835 by the municipal trustees set up under that Act. At High Wycombe an agreement executed with a new headmaster gives the occupations of the municipal trustees. Two were described as 'gentlemen', a term which is very difficult to define but which probably means at least some distance from immediate involvement with trade or business. The others were postmaster, grocer, chemist, baker, draper, maltster, fellmonger, surgeon, millwright[25] – a group which would be reasonably typical of the business/professional group of a small town like Wycombe. Sometimes the group was distinctly more landed and aristocratic. At Brewood in Staffordshire in 1841 out of sixteen trustees the chairman (Lord Dartmouth) was an earl and six others were peers.[26] Sometimes power resided in the hands of a hereditary patron, or, as at Houghton-le-Spring in Co. Durham, in two governors, nominated by Lady Londonderry and the rector of the parish as representatives of the founders. In 1860 both these governors were peers.[27] Like so much in this story it is difficult to generalize, but, whether in town or in country, the trustees of schools belonged to those groups holding political and social power.

Some governing bodies were assiduous and efficient. It is interesting here to compare minute books, and it is at least an intelligent guess that a well-kept book means a well-administered trust. The fact that governing bodies represented leading local power groups means that they were embroiled in all the quarrels and rivalries which existed between these groups, and, as we shall see, there were many bitter quarrels and conflicts of interest between trustee and trustee, and trustee and headmaster. There is some evidence of actual corruption in the sense of trustees enjoying benefits as individuals from corporate property with which they had a fiduciary connection. Some of these cases will be considered below, but my impression is that such corruption was rare. On the other hand there was a good deal of plain neglect to ensure that schools and their properties were capably managed.

Commonly governing bodies met once a year to audit their accounts and to do other business, but sometimes years passed without meetings taking place. The Charity Commissioners found many such examples. One extraordinary case was at Great Blencowe in Cumberland (1821) where the trustees had not met for 30 years and where no accounts had been kept since 1797. The management of the property had been left to the schoolmaster – a not uncommon arrangement – and though in this case he had carried out his duties efficiently, the principle, the commissioners argued, was a bad one[28]:

> We apprehend, however, as a general rule, that the schoolmaster for the time being ought not to have the property given up to him. His interests and the general interests of the school, may not be the same, and the trustees are placed in their position, purposely to superintend.

Several examples can be given of gaps of 4–5 years between meetings – not as gross a neglect as at Great Blencowe, but serious enough. At Uffculme in Devon (1820) there had been no audit since 1815. A banker in London had delayed the payment of dividends, and the absence of one trustee from England had made it necessary to apply to the Court of Chancery for a power of attorney to enable the others to act.[29] At Blackrod in Lancashire (1828) there had been no meeting since 1822 and the whole management had been left in the hands of a solicitor in Wigan who for the previous 4 years had only entered the accounts in pencil.[30]

At Wirksworth in Derbyshire negligence had produced more definite abuse. Loss had been suffered because a former trustee had occupied land for which he paid no rent. The receiver had not kept separate accounts of the trust's income and of the income of a private estate. A new school had been built without a proper estimate being obtained and without ensuring that extravagant decoration was avoided.[31] In a few cases trustees had benefited directly from the income of trust property. At St Bees in Cumberland a lease had been granted in 1742 to the great local magnate, Sir James Lowther, of the school's collieries in the lordship of Kirkby Beacock. Lowther was a governor of the school and his coal agent was also a member of the governing body. In the Charity Commissioners' view the validity of the lease should be examined by the Court of Chancery since it had been granted to a trustee and since the rents, estimated at 3d. per ton, would, for the coals already raised, 'greatly exceed the amount of the rent reserved for the whole term'.[32] Clearly the Lowther family had enjoyed a very good bargain from a transaction which should never have occurred in the first place.

Cases like St Bees were, I think, unusual. Most governing bodies administered their trusts honestly enough, and my general impression is that the general standard of probity and effectiveness was rising during the first half of the nineteenth century. Nevertheless

The grammar school as a legal entity

school trustees, however well intentioned, faced formidable administrative problems. The safe custody of trust money could not always be guaranteed. Sometimes funds were paid to trustees who then became bankrupt,[33] or the endowment itself was lost through the financial failure of a descendant of the original donor. This seems to have happened in remote places where the safe keeping of money was not easy to arrange. At Saddleworth in the West Riding the original endowment had remained in the hands of the descendant of the testator's executor until he went bankrupt in 1826. The master, after he ceased to receive the interest, had closed the school, though he still claimed to occupy the school house.[34] Much more common were losses due to the failure of bankers or the negligence of agents. At Cockerham in Lancashire the trust's balances had been paid in 1821 to a Lancaster banker who failed the following year. At the time of the commissioners' inquiry only 5s. in the pound had been paid but another 2s. 6d. was expected.[35] Nor did financial mismanagement occur only in the small rural schools which have so far been mentioned. Mr Samuel Carter had been bailiff of Coventry Grammar School from 1806 to 1831. His accounts were never submitted to the corporation, nor until 1830 did any individual member look at them or enquire about them. When he retired he owed money both to the master and to the usher. The usher had subsequently been paid, but at Lady Day 1831 the master, Mr Brooks, was owed 896l. 8s. 'of which Mr Carter subsequently paid 60l. on account. We are informed that Mr Brooks who died in October 1833, had in his lifetime agreed to accept 10s. in the pound in the sum due to him, but no settlement had taken place with his representative at the date of this report.'[36] The sum owed to Mr Brooks was in excess of 2 years' average salary.

Once the rents and dividends had been safely received there were frequent difficulties about their proper apportionment since many trusts had a number of objectives. One particularly common combination was that of a grammar school with a hospital or almshouse. Sometimes one side was generously treated, sometimes the other, and not infrequently there was no formalized division of the endowment between the parts. At Bath, for example, the commissioners found that the endowment of such a school/almshouse charity had become confused with the general property of the corporation. After their visit in 1822 the corporation passed resolutions for defining the property of the school and of the Black Alms Hospital for the relief of ten poor women, and providing that separate accounts should be kept for both and for other charities administered by the corporation. Here there seems to have been no

43

question of financial abuse, for the commissioners were careful to state that the corporation had expended on the charities as much as, or even more than, they were legally obliged to do.[37] The principle of formal accountability was, however, important, and it is worth noting that in this case the commissioners' visit was quickly followed by reforms, though I have no evidence how effectively the new arrangements were carried out.[38]

The problems at Bath were of a fairly common type where both schools and almshouse existed together. Sometimes trouble was caused by the fact that the schoolmaster had also to perform clerical duties. At Highgate in Middlesex there was both a school and a chapel of which the master was the reader. The school had simply become an elementary school. The master did not teach in it, though he did prepare pupils privately for the university, but much of his time and interest, and the income from the endowment, went into the chapel and its services which had claimed too much of the governors' attention and pushed the school into the background. Since the income was increasing the commissioners urged that more should be spent on developing the school in an area where population had greatly increased.[39] At Wakefield the grammar school governors had to cope with multiple problems. Since they administered a number of trusts, the management was very complex, and difficulty had been increased by frequent exchanges and sales of property. Moreover they had had serious trouble with their agents. An agent who left office in 1811 owed them over £600, on which only 10s. in the pound had been received when he went bankrupt. The next agent who was discharged in 1824 managed to put off for some time the examination of his accounts. Eventually it was found that he owed over £900. Major legal expenses had been incurred in the case, but at the time of the commissioners' report no dividend had been received. These sums should be related to an annual income for the grammar school in 1825 of £326 11s. 0d.[40]

Even conscientious and efficient trustees faced major problems; indeed these managerial difficulties may have been an important cause of the poor condition of many schools. Each foundation stood on its own. There were no state administrative services to give guidance and make reform possible at moderate cost. The only way to make changes lay through legal action, either in the Court of Chancery which was expensive and slow, or by private Act of Parliament, a measure contemplated only by a few schools. Clearly many governing bodies could not depend on their local agents; receivers went bankrupt, banks failed, some trustees themselves were unable to account for endowment monies. At any time trustees might find themselves involved in harmful publicity and heavy expense, and when this occurred, it often resulted from a conflict with the schoolmaster. Their respective interests often clashed and when they did, recourse to law was the only remedy. Events at Atherstone in Warwickshire provide a good example of the way in which trouble developed. In 1817 the Rev. William Bradley was appointed master and executed an agreement whereby, in return for an agreed salary and the occupancy of a piece of land, he covenanted to teach the school, to receive boarders into his house, to make certain payments for the school house and other land, and to give up his office if he ceased to reside or gave up teaching. Bradley did not in this case pledge a financial surety of the kind already mentioned and which was a common feature of such agreements[41] (see p. 36). Soon after Bradley's appointment complaints began that he neglected and ill-treated the boys, and in 1819 two indictments for assault were brought against him at the Lent Assizes. The matter then went no further because his professional adviser paid a sum in compensation and met the costs. But soon afterwards the master gave up the 'English' or elementary school, the free boys learning Latin were withdrawn, and as Bradley obtained some Church preferment, he ceased taking boarders. 'His office', the commissioners reported, 'was reduced to a sinecure, the only boys taught in the school for about eleven years previous to our inquiry being two of his own children.'[42]

In March 1822 Mr Bradley applied to the governors for the payment of the whole residue of the school endowment (instead of the agreed salary which he had accepted in 1817) and later in the year he refused to make the payments specified in the original agreement. The trustees then withheld his salary, and in June 1823 he filed an information in Chancery, praying that he might enjoy the whole rents of the estate, deducting what was due for repairs and management, and that the agreement he had made on his election might be cancelled. The case, like many another, then began a long progression through the byways of the Court of Chancery, the details of which need not be examined. In his judgment of 8 August 1834 the Lord Chancellor agreed that the governors had the power to decide upon what was a reasonable salary for the master, 'but that it ought to have been done by a general regulation, and not by a special bargain made upon the appointment, a practice open to abuse, and highly to be discouraged'. He further required that means should be taken to place the suspension and removal of the master in the hands of the governors and the bishop of the diocese, acting jointly. The Charity

Commissioners, in their report, referred to 'an establishment so liberally endowed, rendered utterly useless for the purposes of its foundation by want of a superintending power'. The school had been useless to the inhabitants of Atherstone for a decade or more. Between the master and the governors there was stalemate; it was the boys of the town who failed to get the education which the founder had intended them to enjoy.

When the governors wanted to get rid of a master, they sometimes resorted to buying him off. At Blackburn in Lancashire there was a direct clash between the master and governors and parents over the question of the school curriculum. The headmaster, Mr Bennett, appointed in December 1845, wanted a classical course; the local people wanted to extend the commercial subjects and to appoint a master to teach them. By Christmas 1848 the governors had set up a committee to collect subscriptions and to take steps for removing the master. They soon found that though local people and old boys had been vociferous in complaining, they were not prepared to contribute any money towards the necessary costs of removal. Attempts were then made to make terms with the headmaster, but he withdrew from the negotiations, and in September 1849 no second master could be appointed because too few governors attended to form a quorum. By 1850 there were no boys in the school. 'So high did feeling run that there are people living today [1909] who can remember the figure of the Master opening the doors of the school for boys who never came.'[43] Finally in 1855 an agreement was made with Mr Bennett that he would resign if he received £700 – he had originally demanded £2,000. By the autumn the money had been raised, and the new master, Mr Ainsworth, had undertaken to pay £250 towards the subscription sum of £700 'in the event of his being appointed Head Master of this institution'. The governors really had no alternative but somehow to get rid of Mr Bennett. It was surely quite extraordinary and irregular for his likely successor to contribute to the cost of so doing.[44]

By the 1850s standards were rising and more was being demanded of schools and of heads. Consequently the Blackburn situation appeared a more flagrant abuse than it would have done 30 or 40 years earlier, when cases of dereliction of duty and gross neglect were not uncommon. The Charity Commissioners had uncovered some extraordinary cases. At Sudbury in Suffolk the patron had in 1827 appointed his son, who was an undergraduate at Cambridge, to the mastership, while an assistant lived in the school house and taught the scholars.[45] At Hampton Lucy in Warwickshire there had been no resident master between 1810 and 1817 and part of the endowment had been applied by the patron towards the discharge of a debt due to his own family.[46] At Guisborough in the North Riding there were no scholars in the school, the master having lived from 1819 to 1821 on a curacy at Malton thirty miles away, though he had later returned to Guisborough and was ready to resume his duties. The wardens of the trust had been anxious to get rid of him, but they had been advised that the master could not be charged with neglecting his scholars, because he did not have any![47]

Two issues in particular caused serious problems: the conflicts of duty and interest when a man held several offices, and the tendency to delegate duties to subordinates. Pluralism was a common feature of eighteenth- and early-nineteenth-century life, and it is not surprising that schools suffered from the problem of masters holding more than one office. Even more serious was the fact that one office might involve duties of superintendence over the other – and a single individual was the holder of both. Again the Charity Commissioners gave many examples in their reports. At Dovenby in Cumberland the schoolmaster had always been master of the hospital. The existing master was also vicar of Bridekirk, and there were complaints that his parish duties took him away from the school. The combination of offices was also undesirable because the vicar was one of the visitors of the hospital. The commissioners commented[48]:

> For this reason, as well as that in point of fact, they are found to conflict with, and to be inconsistent with each other, we think that in this parish, the duties of vicar and schoolmaster ought not to be entrusted to the same person.

The evils of so doing are clearly shown in the case of Wotton-under-Edge Grammar School in Gloucestershire, where the Rev. B R Perkins was both vicar and schoolmaster from 1839 to 1882. In 1839, having been vicar of the parish for 10 years and as such an ex officio trustee, he was appointed master by the patron. The school did not flourish under his rule, and the oddity of the situation is clear from the school accounts which show Perkins receiving, as schoolmaster, a salary and other payments to meet the foundation boys' accounts, while he signs the same accounts as vicar and trustee. In 1853–54 an agitation began in the town against the management of the school, which resulted in an appeal to the Charity Commissioners and the framing of a new scheme drawn up in 1860. This new scheme does not seem to have brought about any improvement, and Perkins remained in office for another 20 years – until 1882.[49]

In many of these cases the master simply handed over the work to a deputy, and they divided the emoluments according to their mutual convenience. One such Pooh-Bah was the Rev. J H Hall, who was appointed master of the school at Risley in Derbyshire in 1811. He was also lord of the manor, 'and as such lord of the manor signed in the book of the charity an approbation of his own appointment'. At about the same time he was also appointed to the curacy of the chapelries of Risley and Breaston. He lived in his own house, and all the duties of the school were carried out by a deputy and an under-master, though Mr Hall retained a considerable slice of the master's income. The commissioners pointed out that the founder had clearly expected the headmaster to receive the income in return for performing the duties, while it was improper for the lord of the manor to be the headmaster since he had under the trust certain supervisory duties over him.[50]

The commissioners found several examples of masters, sometimes incumbents of the parish, who did not teach, but handed over their duties to an assistant, who was sometimes also the curate.[51] One such case which gained a good deal of notoriety because of the sums of money involved in it concerned the school at Brentwood in Essex. The endowment was considerable. The commissioners returned the rents in 1823 as £1,452 7s. 0d., though it was expected that this total would be reduced when the properties were re-let.[52] The patrons of the school and almshouse trust were successive members of the Tower family, who had purchased the estate to which the patronage was attached in 1752, though their rights were disputed by another claimant, and the question was not finally settled in their favour until 1831 after expensive litigation. The owner of the estate had clearly used the mastership of the school as a means of providing for members of his own family. In 1803–6 the mastership was held by the Rev. Shirley Western, who did not himself teach, on condition that he should resign for Charles Tower (1806–25), who was succeeded on his death by his brother, William (1825–47). Both Charles and William Tower exercised some general superintendence, but the teaching was done by a succession of assistants. The commissioners found about 100 boys in the school, about 80 of them receiving only an elementary education, it having been Mr Tower's purpose 'to render the school more extensively beneficial to the desire of the parents of boys in the vicinity'. Most of the parents were farmers and tradesmen, and some were labourers and mechanics. In 1823 Tower's usher, Edward Edwards, who had been dismissed, wrote a pamphlet attacking the management of the school and claiming that Charles Tower received from the endowment £1,563 per annum and that he expended only £280.[53] Edwards' figures were exaggerated. The Charity Commissioners at about the same time estimated Tower's annual expenditure at about £500 per annum, which still left him about £900 in pocket – a generous reward for his superintendence of the school.

The commissioners criticized the system of elementary teaching and considered that the school should be managed as a grammar school, arguing that the ample funds available would enable this to be done successfully. The curriculum changes they suggested were duly made, and the numbers fell drastically in consequence – in the mid-1830s there were only about thirty-five boys. The commissioners also recommended that the affairs of the school should be referred to the Court of Chancery. Legal proceedings duly began and took their usual deliberate course, but it was not until 1851 that the affairs of the school were settled by the Brentwood School and Charity Act. It is very difficult to make a fair assessment of the whole position at Brentwood. Charles and William Tower inherited a bad system. Charles Tower had provided the kind of education for which there was a local demand, and in the 1830s a grammar school curriculum attracted only a few pupils. After the decision to change the curriculum had been made, William Tower maintained a National School in the town at his own expense. Yet it was surely wrong for so much of a large endowment to go into the pockets of a gentleman whose sole claim to receive it was that he was a relative of the patron. A collection of newspaper cuttings about the case has survived. In 1828 the *Kent and Essex Mercury* reported the proceedings in *Attorney-General* v. *the Master and Wardens of Brentwood School*, and commented[54]:

> It was a great abuse that so large a sum as 100 l. a year should migrate into the pocket of a non-effective schoolmaster, who did nothing more than walk in and out when he thought proper.

The figure of £1,000 may be somewhat exaggerated, but the general point is impossible to rebut.

Lawsuits like the Brentwood case wasted the time and energy of all the participants. Above all they cost a great deal of money which normally had to be met out of charity funds. One of the most spectacular of these cases, worthy to rank with Dickens's *Jarndyce* v. *Jarndyce*, concerned the grammar school at Witton (Northwich) in Cheshire.[55] In December 1822 the Rev. Charles Hand was appointed master, the office having been vacant since 1819. At the time of his appointment there was also an usher, Mr Hayward, who ran an

'English' school largely independent of the master but taught in the same building. Very soon Hand complained that the existence of the English school damaged the grammar school and in October 1823 Mr Hayward was dismissed. New regulations were adopted which practically ended free education, and the school went on according to this system until 1832 when the trustees appointed another usher, Mr Thomas Jones, who taught grammar free and other 'English' subjects for payment. Jones attracted about 120 children and Hand complained bitterly of the harm done to the grammar school by the admission of large numbers of poor children of a lower class. Eventually Hand locked Jones out. However these measures did not lead to a recovery in the number of classical scholars, and by Christmas 1835 there were no scholars at all in the school.

In January 1834 Hand began a suit against the trustees on three basic issues. First of all he argued that he had not been paid the proper salary. Secondly he raised the question of the relationship between classical and English teaching, claiming that the introduction of children to learn the basic subjects had harmed the foundation as a grammar school. Thirdly he stated that the trustees' management of the property had been negligent. A new scheme was not finally agreed until 1853, nor the costs settled until 1855.[56] The total costs, including arrears of Hand's salary, were almost £2,000. The 1853 scheme included a retiring pension of £80 a year for Hand, and the trustees had to sell some of their Chester property to meet their liabilities. The modern historian of the school sums the matter up very well[57]:

> The case of the Attorney-General, at the relation of Charles Hand, v. John Barker and his fellow trustees ate twenty years out of the life of the school. It absorbed a crippling proportion of the school's income, made inroads into its capital, and can have profited nobody in the community of Witton and Northwich except the solicitors who managed the trustees' case. The community as a whole suffered from the divisions arising out of the case, for local feeling ran high.

The Witton case sums up all the problems with which this chapter has been largely concerned – the relationship between classical and 'English' teaching, the proper emoluments of schoolmasters, the clashes between master and trustees, the long-drawn-out and expensive nature of legal process. It is clear that as the century went on practices which would have been accepted in an earlier age were more and more sharply criticized. There is, for example, an interesting contrast between the two reports of the Charity Commissioners on Lewes Grammar School in Sussex.[58] In the first (1819) they painted a favourable picture of the relationship between the foundation boys and the master's private pupils and of the master's conduct generally. In the second (1836) a different master was said to devote his chief attention to his paying pupils. The trustees exercised no control over him and used the nomination of the foundation boys simply as a matter of private patronage. There were, for example, no boys from Southover in the school before 1832 because their fathers had had no votes. The commissioners urged that the number of foundation boys should be increased. There may, of course, have been differences in policy between the two heads, but it is also possible that the much more critical tone of the second report reflects the temper of the new age of reform which had begun after 1830. The grammar schools were affected by it like all other institutions. The remarkable fact is that changes in the schools still came about so slowly.

NOTES AND REFERENCES

1. *CCR* 20, pp 647-94
2. Blackburn GS, Governors' Minutes and Accounts 1808-67 (Lancs RO), miscellaneous entries 1819-45; *CCR* 15, pp 12-13
3. Bury GS Trustees' Minutes and Accounts 1840-67 (Lancs RO)
4. *CCR* 23, p 676
5. Minutes of the meetings of the Trustees of Wotton-under-Edge GS, 1726-1858 (Glos RO), 24 July 1804. There is an interesting note in the minute book about the system used: '1809 Conditions upon which the Trustees now grant Leases upon Lives, of the Charity & School Lands in Wotton Underedge; the annual value of the Premises being ascertained at the time of granting the Lease either by view of the Trustees or their Surveyor.
   One Life in Reversion of Two - One & a half years' purchase
   Two Lives in reversion of One - Six years' purchase
   Three Lives in Possession - Twelve years' purchase
                        Exchange of Lives
   One in exchange of One - One years' purchase
   Two for two - Two years' purchase
   Three for three - Two years' purchase
6. *CCR* 15, pp 335-7
7. *CCR* 20, pp 171-3. For similar examples, see *CCR* 32, Pt II pp 811-12 (Pontefract, 1792); *CCR* 7, pp 826-8 (Richmond, 1796); *CCR* 12, p 106 (Holt, 1821); *CCR* 29, Pt I pp 866-7 (Thetford, 1825)
8. Brewood School Minute Book 15 Feb 1810 (Staffs RO). See the very similar provision at High Wycombe (Wycombe Charities Minute Book, 4 Aug 1841 (Bucks RO)
9. *Statutes and Orders to be observed by the Master and Scholars of the Free Grammar School of Kinver in the County of Stafford*, 7 Dec 1848 (Staffs RO)

10. *CCR* 32, p 809
11. Simon B 1960 ch VI
12. *CCR* 16, pp 118–20
13. *CCR* 21, p 248
14. Hycemoor GS, Bootle, Vestry Minutes 1807–1931 and Minutes of Meetings of Ratepayers and Trustees of Bootle School 1811–1910, 7 Feb 1827, 16 Feb 1861, 19 Oct 1863 (Cumbria RO)
15. *CCR* 9, pp 130–1
16. *CCR* 5, p 238
17. *CCR* 6, p 620
18. *CCR* 8, p 751
19. *CCR* 6, p 490
20. *CCR* 10, p 677
21. *CCR* 18, pp 577–8
22. *CCR* 19, pp 554–5
23. *CCR* 15, pp 263–4
24. Paston Grammar School, North Walsham. Correspondence relating to the Rev W T Spurdens, 1817–25: Spurdens to John Petre, treasurer, 20 March 1821 (Norfolk RO). For Mr Spurdens see also p 79
25. Wycombe Charities Minute Book, 20 Jan 1844 (Bucks RO)
26. Brewood School Minute Book, 25 Oct 1841 (Staffs RO)
27. Correspondence relating to Houghton-le-Spring Grammar School (Co Durham RO). Most of this consists of letters from the rector the Hon and Rev J Grey
28. *CCR* 5, p 139
29. *CCR* 3, p 49
30. *CCR* 19, p 189
31. *CCR* 21, pp 20–3
32. *CCR* 3, p 18
33. *CCR* 15, p 141
34. *CCR* 19, p 294
35. *CCR* 15, p 251
36. *CCR* 28, p 128
37. *CCR* 4, pp 282–3; *CCR* 8, p 573
38. *SIC* XIV, pp 175–80 says that the school was not flourishing, but makes no reference to the issues mentioned above
39. *CCR* 2, pp 104–5
40. *CCR* 17, pp 684–5, 690
41. For other examples of bonds given by masters see *CCR* 29, Pt II pp 986–7 (Nuneaton); 1036 (Coleshill); *CCR* 7, pp 280–1 (Rugeley); *CCR* 19, p 223 (Bury); *CCR* 20, p 205 (Ashton-in-Makerfield)
42. This account of Atherstone School is based on *CCR* 29 Pt II pp 961–4
43. Stocks G A (ed) 1909 **66:** xxi; **68:** 389
44. The whole story is in Blackburn GS Governors' Minutes, 18 Dec 1845–23 Nov 1855 (Lancs RO)
45. *CCR* 20, p 576
46. *CCR* 15, pp 533–5
47. *CCR* 8, pp 729–30
48. *CCR* 5, p 62
49. See Minutes of Meetings of the Trustees of Wotton-under-Edge GS

1726-1858 (Glos RO); *VCH Gloucestershire* vol II (1907) pp 408-9 (by A F Leach); Lindley E S 1962 pp 233-6

50. *CCR* 17, p 230. Compare the very similar remarks made about the situation at Coxwold in the North Riding, where the perpetual curate of the parish, who did not teach himself, had accepted the mastership in order to enjoy the use of the master's house (*CCR* 6, pp 394-5)
51. *CCR* 17, p 789 (Worsbrough); *CCR* 12, p 658 (Snaith); *CCR* 22, p 237 (Bungay)
52. The following is based on *CCR* 11, pp 213-16; Lewis R R 1981
53. Edwards E 1823
54. Essex RO, T/B/223/4
55. For the following see *CCR* 31, pp 446-54; Cox, Marjorie 1975 ch X
56. For the scheme of 1853 see *Order of Vice-Chancellor Stuart on the suit instituted by the Rev Charles Hand, the headmaster of the free grammar school of Witton, in the County of Chester, against the Trustees of such School* (1855) (Ches RO: subject file, Witton). The Master in Chancery's report of 1850, which is also in Cheshire RO, says that the annual gross rental was £366 5s. 0d.
57. Cox, Marjorie 1975 p 200
58. *CCR* 1, pp 235-6, 398; *CCR* 30, p 715

CHAPTER FOUR

The grammar school in a competitive market

So far the grammar school has been studied as a legal entity, a property-owning institution. This is important, but it is not the whole story. The daily life of a school revolves around its teaching and how effective that is. In the early nineteenth century the fortunes of individual schools went up and down much more than they do today. Very few schools enjoyed long periods of success. Their position depended in most cases on the reputation of an individual master. When he was young and vigorous, the school flourished; as he grew old, it was apt to decay. If he moved to another school, many of his pupils might accompany him. If he failed, his failure could, as we have seen, involve the closure of the school. The most crucial questions headmasters had to face were concerned with the curriculum. There was a growing demand for the introduction of modern subjects, something which was difficult to reconcile with the teaching of the learned languages enshrined both in law and in tradition. Arrangements were made, in many cases by private Act of Parliament, to introduce modern subjects, though it often proved very difficult to teach them effectively after the formal provision had been established. These changes also involved important questions of status and prestige. Masters wanted to attract private pupils – particularly private classical pupils – because it was in their financial interest to do so. They often wished to exclude the local boys who wanted to learn the English subjects because these boys were generally of a lower social class than the private pupils. The presence of the local boys would, as the heads saw it, lower the tone of the school, and keep away boarders and paying pupils. From the point of view of local inhabitants the headmaster's social and academic ambitions meant sacrificing the interests of boys from modest homes who were entitled to share in the benefits of the endowment. Marjorie Cox, in her account of the Witton/Northwich controversies which were discussed in Chapter 3, made the point that there was little demand for an advanced modern education. What the trustees and the local people wanted was an elementary education with the status of belonging to the local grammar school.[1] The same point might be made about many other places.

The main themes of this chapter will therefore be what was taught in the schools, the position and duties of the headmasters, and the pupils and their subsequent careers. The first questions to be asked are statistical: How many schools are being considered? How many pupils were receiving a classical or an English education? How many were being educated as private pupils? There are no general statistics until the middle of the century and all that can be done for the earlier period is to provide what engineers call an 'order of magnitude', a general estimate of what is involved. The Charity Commissioners' Reports frequently, though not always, give numbers which are summarized in the *Digest of Grammar Schools* of 1842, and the material which follows is largely based on this, with some supplementation from Carlisle's *Concise Description of the Endowed Grammar Schools* of 1818. These figures are of limited value only. First of all, there are many schools for which there are no figures; no attempt has been made here to include schools for which general statements like 'with boarders and day scholars' are made. Secondly, the reports cover a period of about 20 years and so there is no common date basis.

It is probably a reasonable guess that over such a period of time the amount lost by some schools and gained by others would be roughly equal. The best way to display the figures seems to be to show them in three columns: (I) foundation pupils, classical and (II) non-classical, (III) boarders and fee-payers (Table 1). Many schools will appear in two of these colums and some in all three. Consequently each set of figures refers only to the number of schools quoted in that column, and the number of schools in all three colums cannot be added up. Finally the figures include some girls, predominantly in columns II and III. *The Digest of Grammar Schools* of 1842 gives a few separate figures for girls' schools, but these are too few to be of much use and they have therefore been excluded. If all these cautionary points are borne in mind, the figures still suggest some interesting conclusions. These, of course, are not total figures because the *Digest* does not give numbers for all schools, and many schools like the major public schools and the schools with special visitors were exempt from

Table 1 Numbers of pupils in grammar schools from Charity Commissioners' Reports, 1819-37

			Foundation scholars			
	I, classical	No. of schools	II, non-classical	No. of schools	III, boarders and fee-payers	No. of schools
Bedfordshire	33	1	22	1	72	3
Berkshire	9	2	10	2	10	3
Buckinghamshire	37	4	172	3		
Cambridgeshire			190	2		
Cheshire	109	7	756	16	289	8
Cumberland	72	6	256	8	933	17
Derbyshire	69	9	541	9	184	8
Devon	105	11	20	1	367	11
Dorset	68	2	49	3	164	5
Co. Durham	23	2	96	6	400	7
Essex	71	7	496	9	114	6
Gloucestershire	56	5	92	5	64	3
Herefordshire	75	2	174	4	60	2
Hertfordshire	42	5	206	6	92	7
Huntingdonshire	70	2	123	2	86	2
Kent	64	10	170	7	409	9
Lancashire	498	21	2,175	50	990	26
Leicestershire	49	7	772	13	72	8
Lincolnshire	327	12	589	10	178	7
London, City of	1,406	5	37	2	18	1
Middlesex	20	1	409	8	46	3
Norfolk	58	5	283	8	271	10

Table 1 Continued

	I, classical	No. of schools	II, non-classical	No. of schools	III, boarders and fee-payers	No. of schools
			Foundation scholars			
Northamptonshire	32	3	252	9	143	5
Northumberland	85	6	666	6	41	3
Nottinghamshire	95	4	129	7	46	5
Oxfordshire	8	2	166	6	86	3
Salop	169	9	125	4	299	6
Somersetshire	57	6	115	4	239	7
Co. Southampton	21	3	160	7	10	1
Staffordshire	152	11	728	17	169	5
Suffolk	70	6	226	13	183	8
Surrey	153	5	225	4	7	2
Sussex	32	4	201	3	83	3
Warwickshire	168	8	300	7	7	2
Westmorland	185	11	752	26	769	23
Wiltshire	23	3	162	5	139	6
Worcestershire	59	6	275	9	38	4
Yorkshire:						
East Riding and York	45	6	96	4	164	4
North Riding	86	9	585	15	160	9
West Riding	502	21	881	25	877	25
	5,203	249	13,682	346	8,279	267

Source: Figures from *Digest of Grammar Schools* (1842). I have excluded the Welsh counties and Monmouthshire. There is very little information for Cornwall and Rutland, and so I have excluded them also.

inquiry. Nor would it be profitable to average the figures in each column because the very wide variations in school sizes make averages meaningless. The most striking point to emerge from the schools for which precise figures are given is the small number of foundation scholars receiving a classical education – 5,203 in 249 schools. In reality, the general position of the classics was even worse than it appears because 1,148 of the total were pupils at Christ's Hospital in the City of London, leaving about 4,000 for the remaining schools. Many of the boarders and fee-payers were also learning classics, but classical pupils form only a part of the 8,279 listed in column III. Many of these were children whose parents were paying school fees for an elementary education; for example, the large totals for Cumberland (933) and Westmorland (769) were very largely under this head. The same is true of column II. Some of these 13,682 children in 346 schools were in the lower departments of classical grammar schools, but many of them were being taught the basic subjects in what were really elementary schools.

Finally the figures for a single county help to build up a more detailed picture (Table 2). I have chosen Kent because the returns are full and almost all of them date from the same year (1819). The two cathedral schools at Canterbury and Rochester were exempt from inquiry. Carlisle (1818) says that there were seventy pupils at Canterbury. He describes Rochester, which we shall meet again in Ch. 6, as 'a perfectly private institution', but gives no numbers for it.[2]

The Charity Commissioners' figures underline two major points which have already been made. The first is that there was in 1820–30 no clearly defined concept of 'secondary education'. A grammar school in the commissioners' terms was not necessarily a secondary school in the modern sense. The schools listed by the commissioners range from Shrewsbury and St Paul's with their strong university links at one end of the scale to a host of village elementary schools at the other. Secondly, numbers receiving a classical education were comparatively small, though here the way in which the figures were drawn up made the situation of the classics appear even worse than it was in reality. The commissioners had not examined cathedral schools, schools with special visitors, and the six public schools. The cathedral schools will be considered in Ch. 6[3] (see pp. 92–3). They contributed something to classical studies, as did other exempt schools like Merchant Taylors' in London. It was, however, the six public schools which were the classical schools *par excellence* and which trained many of the national leaders of the future. Carlisle gives numbers for all of them except Eton. Charterhouse had 42

The grammar school in a competitive market

scholars and 170 other boys; Westminster and Harrow about 300 each; Winchester about 200; and Rugby 381.[4] In 1823 Eton, the largest of the 6 schools, had 510 boys.[5] The fact that these schools were almost entirely classical must not obscure the fact that, in most of the other grammar schools of the country, the panoply of classical studies was stretched very thin.

A considerable amount of information exists about numbers in individual schools, though it is much fuller for foundation scholars than for fee-payers and boarders, who were largely the private concern of the masters. Once again examples will be offered from different regions of the country. In all of them it is clear that the average period of attendance of a grammar school boy was short, though the averages

Table 2 Numbers of pupils in grammar schools in Kent, 1819

School	Foundation scholars		Boarders/ fee-payers	Notes
	Classical	Non-classical		
Ashford	3	—	40	—
Biddenden	—	10		
Cranbrook	2	—	31	—
Dartford	6	—	14	
Deptford, Dr Breton's	—	17	—	—
Feversham	22	—	—	'Some boarders'. Carlisle, Nicholas 1818 vol I, p 575 says 15
Goudhurst	—	7	—	—
Lewisham, Colfe's	2/3	—	16	These are 1823 figures (*Digest* 1842, p 43)
Leybourne	—	—	50	—
Maidstone	6/7	—	18/19	—
East Malling	2/3	50	—	—
Sandwich	—	—	6	—
Sevenoaks	7	—	38	—
Sutton Valence	1	30	23	—
Tenterden	—	6	180	The 180 are children in the National School
Tonbridge	10	—	32	—
Wye			10	'No free scholars'

Source: CCR 1 and 2.

conceal wide differences between individual cases. The commissioners visited Eggar's Free School at Alton in Hampshire in 1824 and reported that twenty-eight free boys were being taught reading, writing and arithmetic. The *Digest* of 1842 says that instruction in Latin was not applied for.[6] The school minute book shows that in 1825 there were twenty-five free boys, aged from 12½ to 7 years, the most senior of whom had been at the school for 7 years. Twenty years later in 1845 there were eighteen free boys aged from 12¼ to 8¼, the longest stay being 6 years.[7] Comparable figures exist for the non-classical school at Odiham in the same county. Between 1823 and 1829 the average length of school life there was 4 years, children entering between 6 and 9 years. Twenty years later the entry age remained about the same, and the average period of attendance was about 4½ years.[8] The resemblances between the two schools, though they stand on different sides of the 'grammar/non-grammar school' divide, are quite close.

A group of three schools in the north-west – the King's School, Chester and Warrington and Blackburn in Lancashire – provide a rather similar picture, though many boys in the last two schools stayed only a very short time. King's School, Chester, as part of a cathedral foundation, was exempt from the Charity Commission inquiry. The Cathedrals Commission of 1852 reported that there were twenty-four foundationers, aged between 9 and 15, fourteen day boys and two boarders.[9] Very little is known about the fee-payers, but a nineteenth-century antiquary, Thomas Hughes, who was himself an old King's scholar, compiled a list of foundationers which tells us a good deal about them.[10] Up to 1850 the boys were nominated by individual members of the chapter; after that date they were admitted by examination.[11] The figures on p. 61 show the age of entry and of length of school life for three years in each of the decades from 1810 to 1850.

It is evident from the Chester figures that almost all the boys, with very few exceptions, stayed for at least 2 or 3 years. At Warrington and Blackburn the school populations seem to have been more mobile. Perhaps this marks the contrast between a settled county capital with its established trades and the more fluid society of the new industrial towns which offered plenty of job opportunities to boys. The Warrington admission register lists forty-one boys who were 'presented' in 1822, their ages varying from 7 to 14. Fifteen of these had left within the half-year. The average stay of the remaining twenty-six was 2.3 years, though one boy stayed for 8 years and another for 6.[12] The figures for later years give much the same picture.

	No. of entries	Average age in years	Length of school life (to nearest full year)
1815, 16, 17	19	9.6	3.7
1825, 26, 27	23	9.3	4.4
1835, 36, 37	25	9.4	3.1
1845, 46, 47	21	9.3	4.0
After 1850 with the change in the system of entry, the age of entry was higher and the length of school life shorter.			
1855, 56, 57	19	11.7	3.1
1865, 66, 67	25	12.7	2.3

In August 1843, there were forty-one boys, the oldest 15, the youngest 7, the average age being 11.02 years. In the 1850s the boys seem to have come to the school rather older and to have stayed rather longer. Between 1851 and 1858 the average age of entry was 10.7 years and the average length of school life was about 4.4 years. By 1860, the final year of the register, there were only four boys in the upper school. Of one there is no record except his name. Of the other three one was 17 and had been 7 years in the school, one was 14 and had been there 4 years, and one was 14 and had been there 2 years.

A volume of registration slips, which has survived for Blackburn Grammar School for the years 1820–42, tells a rather similar story.[13] It is an incomplete record because clearly many names were not entered, and, as it breaks off in February 1842, it is impossible to be certain how long the fifty-nine boys who were then at the school remained there. Between 1820 and 1829 thirty names are recorded. The average age of entry was 12.4 and the average length of school life 3.5 years. Between 1830 and 1835 seventy-seven names are recorded, with an average age of entry of 9.5 and a length of stay of 3.3 years. Between 1836 and 1839 the average age of entry was 9.6 and, although the length of school life for this period is, as already explained, difficult to calculate, it probably works out once again at about 3 years. One striking feature of this Blackburn record is the very short period for which many boys stayed, a period in many cases so short that it is difficult to understand why these boys were sent at all. The pattern varied from year to year, but in 1838, of thirty who entered, fourteen left in a year or less. The early nineteenth-century parent had little compunction about moving his children from school to school.

The register of Colchester Grammar School is interesting because it specifically differentiates between foundationers and paying pupils.[14] Between 1845 and 1850 twenty-eight boys were admitted: the average age of entry 11.3 years, average length of stay 2.6 years.[15] In 1851 the school was closed and in February 1852 the new headmaster entered a list of scholars in the register. There were twenty foundation boys, 'the total admissible by statute'. They varied in age from fifteen to eight, the oldest boy being removed at Michaelmas 1852. Two were the sons of professional men (clergymen and deputy town clerk). Sixteen were the sons of tradesmen (brewer, bricklayer, chemist, draper, watchmaker, bookseller, fruiterer, publican, auctioneer, coachmaker, fishmonger, baker (2), grocer, paperhanger, tailor), one was the son of a schoolmaster, an occupation very difficult to place socially and financially, and one was the son of a widow. There were eight 'oppidans', which means, I think, fee-paying day boys. Their ages ranged from 15 to 9, and they were the sons of a clergyman, two medical practitioners, a woolstapler, a solicitor and three 'esquires'. Finally there were six boarders, aged between 15 and 13. Two of their parents are described as 'esquire', two were bankers, one was an ironmaster and one was a major-general in the service of the East India Company. None of the boarders came from East Anglia or the Home Counties, the school's local region.

The parents of the foundation boys at Colchester seem to have been a fairly typical social group for a school in a country town, and a study of the foundation boys from schools in three other schools in country towns of differing sizes – High Wycombe, Wotton-under-Edge and Chester – produces a rather similar group of tradespeople with a sprinkling of professional men. The social pattern of these schools will then be compared with that of two schools in large manufacturing cities – Leeds and Manchester. A list has survived of the applicants for places as free scholars at High Wycombe in 1858. It contains the names of twenty boys, aged from 8 to 15. Most of them were the sons of shopkeepers, together with the sons of a solicitor's clerk, a stonemason, a coachbuilder, a manservant and two widows.[16] The Wotton-under-Edge list covers a long period of time (*c.* 1830–60),[17] and the foundationers came from a wide range of social backgrounds. There were several clergymen's sons, including the children of Mr Perkins the vicar/schoolmaster (see p. 47), several surgeons' sons and the sons of men described as 'gentleman' or 'esquire'. Other occupations included clothier, cloth-worker, dyer (the school was in a cloth-making area), the usual range of shopkeepers, and a number of craftsmen (paper-maker, card-maker, cabinet-maker, plumber and glazier, stay-maker). The only parent who sounds like a manual worker is a blacksmith; a shoemaker may have worked with his own hands or he may have employed others.

Thomas Hughes' list of the King's School Chester foundationers, already referred to, contains an almost complete list of parental occupations which has been analysed for three years of each decade from 1810 to 1870.[18] On the whole the Chester list runs on very similar lines to those already cited. There is the usual sprinkling of professional men – a lieutenant, RN, a few 'gentlemen', the editor and proprietor of the *Chester Herald*, though – strangely for a cathedral city – the sample years contain only one clergyman's son. It seems that in the 1860s the social status of parents was rising. For example, the 1867 entry were the sons of a staff officer of pensioners, an architect and surveyor, an engineer, a hatter, a railway goods manager, a lithographer, and two clothiers. A number of the entries reflect the characteristics of the city. There are several 'vergers', probably from the cathedral itself, several 'merchant captains', for the sea is not far away, a number of 'writing clerks', for Chester as a regional capital will have had several banks and many attorney's offices, and some 'commercial travellers', who would be found there for similar reasons. There are tradesmen like 'carpenters' and 'upholsterers', whose precise social position it is impossible to determine, but there is a minority who sound like working men – letter carrier, ostler, labourer and earthenware dealer, pensioner and bootmaker, porter. Indeed, although these form only a small group, they are more prominent here than in the other lists which have been examined.

Manchester and Leeds were both considerably larger schools than those which have been discussed. During the 30 years of Dr Jeremiah Smith's high mastership at Manchester (1807–37), an average of fifty-one boys per year were admitted, though the numbers fluctuated a good deal from year to year.[19] The registers give no figures for the length of school life, but A A Mumford in his history of the school estimates an average of slightly under 4 years, with a variation from 2 years at the bottom to 7 years in the case of boys going to university. During the headship of Dr Smith there were a considerable number of boarders, though an agitation against the general management of the school began in the mid-1830s, and in 1848 a report by a Master in Chancery abolished the system of boarders altogether.[20] The boarders came mostly from the neighbouring counties, and many of their fathers were clergymen or 'gentlemen'.[21] The occupations of many parents reflect the concerns of 'Cottonopolis': cotton spinner, yarn merchant, dyer, warehouseman, fustian cutter, muslin manufacturer, and there are many merchants and cotton merchants. In general the social and financial level is higher than in the schools already analysed, though it must be remembered that the earlier lists were on the whole lists of foundationers while the Manchester list is a list of total admissions. Predominantly the Manchester parents seem to have been people of mercantile and manufacturing backgrounds, with a considerable number of professional men, such as clergymen, attornies and surgeons. There are many publicans, but fewer shopkeepers than in the earlier examples, and my general impression – though it can be no more positive than that – is that over the 30 years the social level was rising, and the school therefore becoming more socially exclusive. The social origins of the boys can be illustrated by analysing a specimen year (Table 3).

Over Dr Smith's thirty years there were a few boys from humbler backgrounds – some mechanics and coachmen, several excisemen, a few porters, a beadle, a lamplighter, a waiter, even in 1829 a labourer, but there were not many of them, and it is impossible to tell how long they stayed. We do know that the future Radical propagandist Samuel Bamford, the son of a weaver who became governor of the Manchester workhouse, entered the lowest class in the school in the later 1790s but was soon removed because his father did not wish him to learn Latin.[22]

An examination of the Leeds registers from 1820 to 1845[23] suggests much the same mix as at Manchester of boys from business and professional backgrounds with a few from much humbler homes. Perhaps in the Leeds case the social level was falling slightly in the 1840s. If this opinion is correct, it may be linked with the fact that at that time numbers were growing fast. In January 1820 there were 85 boys, in August 1832 109; by August 1845 there were 211. The school always sent its quota of boys to the universities and into the professions, but throughout the whole period the numbers in the upper school remained very small. In August 1832 there were 19 boys in the upper school out of a total of 109. In August 1845 there were still only 23 upper school boys out of the total of 211. Of the remainder 27 were in the middle school and 161 in the lower school. In other words, the average length of school life was short – more like Warrington and Blackburn than Manchester if we are able to accept Mumford's estimate of just under 4 years for that school. The editor of the Leeds register worked out the figures for the 2 years 1837 and 1838.

Table 3 Admissions to Manchester Grammar School, 1835 (63 boys (5 boarders), average entry age 11.6 years)

Gentleman	4
Clergyman	2
Solicitor	5
Surgeon	7
Keeper of Chester Castle	1
Army assistant surgeon	1
Schoolmaster	3
Music master	2
Bookseller	2
Methodist preacher	2
Cabinet-maker	1
Stay-maker	1
Stiffener	1
Cotton spinner	1
Fustian manufacturer	1
Merchant	4
Flour merchant	1
Cotton merchant	1
Timber merchant	1
Slate merchant	1
Brewer	2
Machine-maker	1
Potmaker	1
Publican	3
Warehouseman	3
Bookkeeper	2
Overseer	2
Collector	1
Druggist	1
Carrier	1
Tailor	1
Mechanic	2
Butler	1

Source: Smith J F (ed) 1874.

In 1837 there were forty-three entries for ten of whom no details are given. Of the remainder, thirty stayed 3½ years or less, one stayed 7 years, one 10¼ years and one 10¾ years. Of the thirty staying less than 3½ years, twenty stayed less than 2 years. The 1838 figures are very similar.[24] If the admissions from 1833 to 1842 are compared with the numbers in the school during the same period, the average length of school life works out at about 2½ years, though as we have seen in this and other cases the average conceals very great individual variations. Again the problem remains why so many boys were sent to Leeds Grammar School or to the other schools for such a short time.

Some of the sources which have been used provide a great deal of information about boys' future careers. Mumford in his history of Manchester Grammar School says that of 1,500-odd boys whose names appear in the registers under Dr Smith, 145 took holy orders, 111 went into the law, most of them becoming attorneys, 52 entered the medical profession, many of them through the schools of medicine in Manchester. Twenty entered the army, navy or Indian Civil Service, and eight became architects, surveyors or civil engineers.[25] It is always comparatively easy to get information about the professions named, and what is really interesting is to look at the other careers which boys took up and which are much less well documented. For many, of course, there is no record, but Dr Smith's son, J F Smith, who edited the register, did provide much other valuable information. Not much is recorded about boys who went into retail trade. Many became cotton merchants, cotton spinners and manufacturers, silk manufacturers, bankers, directors of railway companies. The international connections of Manchester are brought out by the large number of foreign merchants – from Hong Kong to India and Ceylon, the Southern states of the USA and the countries of South America. Other old boys settled in Australia and in Canada.

The Leeds register provides a similar list of clergymen, lawyers and medical men. The international aspect is much less pronounced than at Manchester, but more information is given about the retail tradesmen and small manufacturers who must have formed the great majority of grammar school old boys. Among the trades mentioned are grocer, publican, drysalter, letter carrier and broker, printer, ironmonger, seed crusher and oil merchant, gunmaker, draper, maltster, watchmaker, fruiterer, bootmaker, plumber, and egg merchant in the central market. All these are mere names; the rare chance to put some flesh on to a figure in this important social group comes from the King's School, Chester papers. Born in 1823, Edward Thomas was a King's scholar from 1832 to 1836, when he was apprenticed to his father who was a printer and publisher. He later succeeded his father in his business, and later still qualified as a homeopathic chemist. He was a teetotaller and active temperance worker, interested in Welsh societies, an overseer of the poor, and founder of the Chester Glee and Madrigal Society. In politics he was a Liberal.[26]

The point has been made many times that grammar schools provided for many different social and educational needs. At one end of the spectrum stood a school like Bury St Edmund's which, under the headship of Dr Malkin (1809–28), stood very close in status to the major public schools. The school list of 1817 contains 128 names, 41 'royalists' or town boys and 87 'foreigners'. There is no information about the future careers of fifty-seven of these boys. The remainder are recorded in Table 4. It is a reasonable guess that many of the unrecorded old boys were engaged in commerce or in farming like those in the second column of Table 4. Bury was definitely a classical school.

Table 4 Careers of old boys of Bury St Edmunds Grammar School

Died young	7	Medical men	3
Graduated (nothing noted		Wine merchant	2
except their degrees)	4	Upholsterer	1
Clergymen	28	Farmer	1
Army/navy	9	Governor of gaol	1
Civil Service	1	Fishmonger	1
East India Company	1	Glass and china merchant	1
Solicitors	10		
Business in			
London/Director of			
the Bank of England	1		

Source: Biographical List of Boys Educated at King Edward VI Free Grammar School, Bury St Edmunds. From 1550 to 1900 (Bury St Edmunds, 1908) is a compilation arranged alphabetically by names. But the original lists survive for some years between 1817 and 1828, and I have analysed the lists for 1817 and 1826. The year 1826 contains ninety-six boys. Forty-two are unidentified, and the general breakdown of the remainder is very similar to that of 1817.

For a period, as we have seen, most of the boys at Brentwood School were receiving an elementary education, and a list of fifty-seven former pupils of that time (1819–23) has survived. The occupations recorded on this list are given in Table 5. Most of these Brentwood boys seem to have stayed very much in the social rank to which they had been born, though perhaps the boy who 'went to college' became a clergyman. The Manchester lists suggest in a few cases that boys from modest homes made good careers, and their education must have been one factor which made this possible. For example, two sons

Table 5 Former pupils of Brentwood School, 1819–23

Baker	5	Farmer	5	'Settled in Canada'	1
Blacksmith	1	Gardener	1	Shoemaker	1
Butcher	1	Groom	1	Stonemason	1
Captain of		'Into the		Tailor	2
a ship	1	law'	1	Usher	1
Carpenter	3	Manservant	1	'Went to college'	1
Coachman	3	Painter	1	Whaler	2
Cook	1	Pig jobber	2		
Corn dealer	1	Publican	1		

Source: Brentwood School: List of fifty-seven former pupils 1819–23 (Essex Record Office, Microfilm T/B 223/3).

of Holland Hoole, a Wesleyan shoemaker, entered in 1809. One, Elijah, left school to help his father in his business, entered the Wesleyan ministry, and became general secretary of the Wesleyan Missionary Society. His brother, Holland, became a cotton manufacturer, an advocate of factory reform and free trade, and borough reeve of Salford.[27] Henry Howarth (1810), son of a bath-keeper, was a school exhibitioner who became a fellow of St John's College, Cambridge, and rector of the fashionable London parish of St George's, Hanover Square. William Blundstone of the same year, who became a surgeon, was the son of an exciseman.[28] Of course, social mobility could be downwards as well as upwards. The Manchester register records another surgeon who gave up his profession, tried unsuccessfully to earn his living as a singer, and 'after passing through various stages of intemperance and poverty, he became an inmate of the workhouse, and died ... some years ago'.[29]

NOTES AND REFERENCES

1. Cox, Marjorie 1975 p 215
2. Carlisle, Nicholas 1818 vol I pp 567, 591. For the Rev Robert Whiston and his battles with the Dean and Chapter of Rochester, see p. 93
3. Carlisle gives some statistics: Gloucester, 8 choristers and 25/30 private pupils (vol I p 450); Hereford, 11 foundation boys and nearly 100 pupils (half of them boarders) (vol I p 493); Peterborough, 33 boys (vol II p 220); Chichester, Prebendal School, about 40 boarders and day scholars (vol II p 593
4. Carlisle, Nicholas 1818 vol II pp 13, 15, 109, 146, 461, 679
5. Maxwell-Lyte H C 1875 p 405 n 1
6. Digest of Grammar Schools (1842) p 100

7. These figures come from Eggar's Free Grammar School, Alton, Minute Book vol II (1806–79) (Hants RO)
8. Odiham GS, Trustees' Minute Books and Accounts 1789–1874 (Hants RO)
9. *CathC* 1st report, pp 84, 739
10. The list was compiled from the Dean and Chapter records. See 'The King's School, Chester. List and Index of King's School Scholars', by Thomas Hughes, revised by G D Squibb
11. A list of (?) 1812 survives at the school. It gives the names of 7 choristers, of 6 boys nominated by the dean, and of 3 nominated by each of the 6 canons
12. These and the following figures are taken from 'List of scholars presented or admitted to the Warrington Free Grammar School commencing 21 January 1822' (Ches RO)
13. Blackburn GS, Volume of registration slips relating to scholars 1820–42 (Lancs RO)
14. Colchester Free Grammar School, Register 1637–1892 (Essex RO, microfilm TB 217)
15. Of this 28, 21 names are marked '†'. I conjecture that these were foundation boys
16. Royal GS, High Wycombe. Applications for places as free scholars, 1856–68 (Bucks RO)
17. Trustees' Minutes, Wotton-under-Edge GS (Glos RO). The admissions of foundationers are separately noted at one end of the book
18. 1815–17; 1825–27; 1835–37; 1845–47; 1855–57; 1865–67
19. The following passage is based on Smith J F (ed) 1874. In 1811 there were 63 admissions; in 1825, 36; in 1837, 64
20. Mumford A A 1919 pp 261, 269, 287-8
21. Boarders as such are not listed, but I have assumed that boys whose homes were outside a radius of about 10 miles from Manchester would have been boarders
22. Bamford, Samuel (n.d.) pp 80-9
23. The following is based on Wilson, Edmund (ed) 1906
24. *Ibid.* p xviii
25. Mumford A A 1919 p 261
26. King's School, Chester. Letters and papers found in the register of foundation scholars *c.* 1812–1969: obituary from the *Chester Courant* 26 Dec 1906
27. Smith J F (ed) 1874 pp 44, 46-7
28. *Ibid.* p 54
29. *Ibid.* p 105 (George Henry Hudson, 1814)

CHAPTER FIVE

Curricula and headmasters

All these men, whether their careers had or had not been successful, had been through the routines of the grammar school curriculum, and we need now to examine in more detail what those routines involved. Again it is best to use specific examples. Louth in Lincolnshire was a well-regarded classical school, and its entry in Carlisle includes a full description of the system of classical studies there.[1] The teaching was based on the Eton Latin and Greek grammars. The boys began with the rules of grammar, using Valpy's Latin *Delectus*, and at this stage they spent two hours a day in spelling and reading English, writing and arithmetic. The first text to which they were introduced was the Fables of Phaedrus, followed by Caesar, Virgil and Horace, Cicero, Livy and Tacitus. When they had learned the rules of prosody they were introduced to Latin verses, working through nonsense verse and imitations of English poets to original composition. They began Greek at 11 years old or sometimes earlier, and followed a similar course through the rules of grammar to the authors – Xenophon, Homer, the tragedians, Demosthenes, Pindar, Herodotus and Thucydides. Each day began with Bible reading in Greek, Latin and English, according to the boys' proficiency, and the senior boys read prayers morning and evening. Preparation involved a great deal of learning Greek and Latin authors by heart, as well as writing compositions and 'double' translations – from the original language into English and then back again into Greek and Latin.

> Every lesson, except in the first class, is construed twice over, and is parsed very carefully. On one day of the week, the work done in the week by each class, is again construed to the Head Master; in the last Month of the Half-Year, the whole work of the Half-Year is again

gone over, – All the lines also are again repeated, – and afterwards
repeated at one Lesson, – in this manner a *book* of Horace, or Virgil,
is repeated by a Class at *one Lesson*, without much apparent exertion.

Emphasis was also laid on elocution. The higher classes gave weekly
speeches from English authors, and once a year there were public
speeches in Greek, Latin, French and English.

An example from the 1830s of a school with a more modest classical
programme is Bury in Lancashire. At Christmas 1835 there were two
classes in the upper school, each containing eight boys. They were
examined in the following subjects:

First Class
Latin verses and prosody   Greek Testament   Scripture questions
Virgil bk. 9   Questions in Geography and History   Livy bk.
22   Euclid & Natural Philosophy   Arithmetic
Second Class
Latin Grammar   Watts' Scripture History   History   Ellis' exercices
Caesar   Geography   Arithmetic
Maps from the First Class of France Italy Greece & Palestine
Theme – Scientiâ nulla res est praestantior
Second class – a letter on the studies of the half-year[2]

The classical curriculum was familiar territory with centuries of
experience behind it. Modern curricula, as we shall see, were often
over-ambitious in their scope and claimed to achieve results which
could not have been reached in the time available. The following
programme for the first class of the commercial department at
Brentwood (*c*. 1820) sounds fairly well related to the boys' likely ages
and abilities. They studied English grammar; geography; an
introduction to arts and sciences; history; geometry, mensuration and
arithmetic; reading; the use of the globes; merchants' accounts;
writing and 'Roman print German text Engrossing', which presumably refers to the specialist scripts used in attorneys' offices. There
were provisions for examination, for prayers at school, and for
attending church. It is interesting that this Brentwood programme
contains no languages other than English.[3]

The Charity Commissioners frequently commented on the schools
where there was little demand for classical education. At Honiton in
Devon in 1820 they found no free boys, remarking that 'a classical
education is probably not considered an advantage by the parents of
such children as would be proper objects of the charity'.[4] In the
manufacturing districts the pressure towards modern studies was
even greater. At Sheffield in 1828 the commissioners noted that the
grammar school had declined. 'Its present reduced condition is rather

to be ascribed to the preference given by the inhabitants to a mercantile education, than to any neglect or inattention on the part of the teachers.'[5] There are echoes of the same point in school minute books. At Bury in Lancashire in 1855 the trustees were discussing the unequal numbers in the upper and the lower schools and resolved to move boys up so as to keep the upper school full. 'Those boys whose Parents wish them to have a mercantile education shall not be compelled to receive the same amount of classical teaching as those who are intended for the Universities.'[6]

In the earlier part of the century any group of trustees was confronted with serious difficulties if they wished to alter the curriculum to meet these new demands. The legal purpose of the grammar school was the teaching of the learned languages, and there was always the chance of legal action if this objective was departed from too widely. The nature of the problem is set out in the commissioners' report on Wolverhampton (1820).[7] This was a large endowment with a rent-roll of £1,168 5s. 0d. The trustees had appointed a large staff. There were at the time of the report a headmaster, usher, writing and arithmetic master, French and German master, and a drawing master, but there were only fifty-four boys, eighteen of whom were boarders. There was a good deal of local discontent with the curriculum offered and demands for the development of courses which might be more useful to the locality. In the commissioners' view the trustees had some discretion to add to the school establishment and they had properly exercised that discretion, given to them by the charter, to widen the basis of training in the school. 'But we can scarcely think that they would be authorized, without the sanction of the Court of Chancery, in applying any part of their funds to the establishment of a course of education, wholly distinct from the grammar school, and in great measure incompatible with it.' In fact, the commissioners thought, the school curriculum had already been much broadened.

The decision which, according to persistent tradition, immobilized the process of curriculum change was Lord Chancellor Eldon's decision (1805) in the Leeds Grammar School case. The trustees and the master, Joseph Whiteley, had been at odds over the introduction of modern subjects. The Master in Chancery had found for the trustees, but Eldon defined the purpose of the charity as being 'for teaching grammatically the learned languages'. In fact, though Eldon ordered the parties to agree on a scheme, the case was never finally decided. After Whiteley's death in 1815, the trustees appointed a master to teach mathematics, and the Charity Commissioners in

1826 noted that the number of boys in the school had increased as a result.[8] A recent article[9] has denied that Eldon's decision was designed to prevent the teaching of subjects other than the classics or that the case had that general effect on the grammar schools. What Eldon was doing, it is claimed, was defining the primary purpose of the foundation; he was not denying that this purpose might be modified by the introduction of new subjects such as mathematics.

The Charity Commissioners' reports make it clear that substantial curriculum changes had been made in many schools, though there was sometimes doubt about the legal position. The general picture which they give supports the view that, provided the main purpose of the school continued to be the teaching of the classical languages, new subjects could be introduced. A good example of this is Giggleswick in the West Riding which possessed a wealthy endowment. New statutes made by the governors in 1795 and confirmed by the Archbishop of York had allowed the appointment of an assistant to teach writing, accounts, mathematics 'and different branches of literature'. The commissioners reported in 1825 that the assistant taught grammar school boys and other boys as well. Most of the governors were in favour of the change, though doubts were expressed, both about the legal position and about the presence in the schools of boys of a lower class than those who came to learn grammar. The commissioners supported the maintenance of the English school 'so far as it tends to promote the objects and increase the utility of the original foundation as a grammar school'. It was likely to do this, they argued, 'as the want of due provision for instruction in the lower departments is frequently advanced as one of the causes to which the declension of similar institutions for grammatical learning is ascribed'.[10]

The most secure way to make such changes was to obtain a private Act of Parliament, though this was expensive and was therefore an option open only to the wealthier foundations. Such Acts sometimes formally incorporated the governing body, and gave them powers to sell or exchange property. Often power was given to introduce the teaching of modern subjects into the school. Macclesfield in Cheshire obtained such an Act permitting modern subjects to be taught in 1774. In 1824 another Act enlarged the governors' powers to grant leases and an Act of 1838 enabled them to establish a 'Modern Free School'.[11] At Bedford a new governing body had been established by Act of Parliament in 1764, one clause providing for the appointment of a writing master. Further Acts followed in 1793 and 1826.[12] The Act of 1793 laid down that the master and usher of the grammar school were to be appointed by New College, Oxford, and the writing master and his assistants by the school trustees. Children born and resident in the town were to be taught free, and there were to be three university exhibitions at any one time. A large part of the endowment was set aside for apprentice fees, marriage portions, for the maintenance of poor children and for almshouses and other charitable purposes.[13] The so-called 'English School' had about 100 pupils by the 1830s, and moved to a new building in 1834.

Where money was available considerable efforts were made to meet new needs, either within the original school or by establishing new elementary schools. St Olave's Grammar School in Southwark was described in 1819 as consisting of three schools taught by seven masters. There was a classical school, a writing school and a reading school. Boys were admitted to the last and then went on to the grammar school if their parents so wished. All the boys in the classical school and many in the reading school also attended the writing school, where arithmetic was taught.[14] At Birmingham, an even richer foundation than St Olave's, the trustees had ordered the appointment of four masters and mistresses to give English instruction to boys and girls of the town in 1751. When the commissioners went to Birmingham in 1828, the charity lay under the examination of a Master in Chancery and in consequence of this the trustees had kept open only one of the eight 'smaller' schools which had recently been in existence. Acts of Parliament were obtained in 1831 and in 1837 for the regulation of the charity, and under their provisions four branch schools were established 'for the free education of boys and girls of the humbler classes'.[15]

The point has already been made that it proved much easier to draw up new schemes than to make them work effectively (see p. 25), and this is well illustrated by the history of Macclesfield School, which had been very early (1774) in getting powers to enlarge the curriculum.[16] The school was quite wealthy, and it seems to have maintained an even and fairly prosperous course. The minute book records the appointment of a writing master in 1813 and of a French master the following year, but the commissioners observed in 1837 that not much had been done to carry out the objects of the Act of 1774. No language had been taught other than French and no branches of science other than mathematics. The governors, they noted, were considering the establishment of a second school for modern subjects, though to do this would probably require another Act of Parliament. No consideration had been given to 'a more extended plan of education' in the grammar school. 'The opinions of the head master are decidedly opposed to such an arrangement.'[17] The governors had in fact set up a committee in December 1833 to consider a more extensive scheme for the school since their income was increasing. The committee's report proposed that the grammar school should remain unaltered and that four university exhibitions should be established. A separate 'modern school' should be set up to teach writing, arithmetic, mathematics and the modern languages with a master or masters to run it. A French and a writing master should be appointed to teach at both schools.[18] This report was accepted by the governors and, after the Master in Chancery had reported favourably on the scheme, the necessary Act of Parliament was passed in 1838. In October 1843 the governors resolved that the 'Modern Free School' should be opened after the ensuing Christmas vacation and that an advertisement be put out for the mastership.[19]

The post attracted 138 candidates, and the governors decided to ask for the assistance of an inspector of schools in making the appointment. The Rev. F C Cook, HMI, set examination papers to three short-listed candidates and recommended the appointment of Mr Oram, third master at Huddersfield College, a proprietary school. The governors' minutes make few references to the new school, though in 1852 they applied to Chancery for permission to increase the annual sum they were allowed to spend on it. The appointment of an examiner specifically to examine the Modern Free School (1856) and the setting up in the following year of a committee to look into the scheme of education there may suggest that all was not well. In October 1859 the governors considered the fact that they had received four unfavourable reports (in 1856, 1857, 1858 and 1859), and they dismissed Mr Oram. Under his successor, Mr Chadwick, the minutes record much more activity – requests for scientific apparatus, for drawing boards and models, for a grant towards the expenses of boys taking the middle-class examinations. When Chadwick resigned in 1865 the governors minuted their appreciation of his services and their hope that 'he may reap the reward of his industry and talents in his future sphere'.[20] It is impossible to say what had gone wrong under Oram. Perhaps he lacked the personal qualities necessary to make a new venture successful. Perhaps he was not interested in the curriculum which such a school required. Perhaps he lacked sympathy with the boys who were likely to attend it and with their parents. It is not evident that the governors were niggardly or unsympathetic.

The contrast between Mr Oram and Mr Chadwick illustrates the crucial importance in all schools of the personality and abilities of the headmaster. So far the head has often appeared in these pages as a figure of controversy like Mr Bradley of Atherstone or Mr Hand of Witton (see pp. 45–6, 49–50). Only a few men got entangled in such bitter disputes; the problems and preoccupations of most of them were much more mundane. They sometimes had difficulties with their ushers. Frequently the upper and lower schools worked as distinct units,[21] and there is evidence of tensions over the master's right to control admissions and discipline.[22] Some of the grammar school heads of the period, like Jeremiah Smith of Manchester, B H Malkin of Bury St Edmunds and James Tate of Richmond, are worthy of remembrance. Smith came to Manchester in 1807 from the second mastership of King Edward's, Birmingham, which he had held since 1798. He remained high master until 1837 and he also held various church appointments in Manchester, including the rectory of St Ann's. In politics he was a Tory and a member of the Manchester Pitt Club. He gave evidence at York when Henry Hunt was tried after Peterloo. He was a strong opponent of Catholic emancipation, and he joined in petitioning against the Reform Bill, 'dreading, among other evils, the recurrence of agitation and riot as likely to attend upon elections in a large town like Manchester'.[23] One of Smith's pupils was the novelist Harrison Ainsworth, who in one of his books wrote an interesting description of the school and of the usher and high master, 'Mr Cane' and 'Dr Lonsdale'.[24] Cane the usher was a flogger to rival the great Dr Keate, but, we are told, the high master's

> plan of tuition was very different from that of Mr Cane. His was the *suaviter in modo*, rather than the *fortiter in re*. He aspired to make his pupils gentlemen as well as good scholars. He never used the cane, but his rebuke was greatly dreaded, and his quiet, sarcastic remarks on a mispronunciation or a vulgarism effectively prevented their repetition. Dignified in manner and deportment, and ever preserving an air of grave courtesy, it would have been impossible to take a liberty with him, and it was never attempted. Dr Lonsdale was a spare man, with large thoughtful features, and a fine expansive forehead, powdered at the top. He looked like a bishop, and ought to have been one. His voice was peculiarly solemn, and it was quite a treat to hear him read prayers.

Dr Smith was a distinguished head of what had already, one suspects, become a rather old-fashioned type by the time he retired. Manchester, though it had boarders, was pre-eminently a big day school. Bury St Edmunds, under Benjamin Heath Malkin (1809–28), was largely a boarding school. The numbers had risen to 160 in 1819 (45 royalists, 115 oppidans), though they fell to 96 in 1827.[25] Smith, we are told by Ainsworth, ought to have been a bishop. Malkin was unusual among the heads of his day in being a layman. The Governors' Minute Book gives a picture of him at work. His duty, and that of his assistants, was to 'instruct in good Manners, as well as literature, and teach Royalists with as much care and diligence as Foreigners'.[26] He had agreed on his appointment to receive as many boarders as his house would hold at thirty-five guineas per annum 'which sum is to include Washing and a single Bed to each'. Each foreigner was to pay an entrance fee and a library fee, and the headmaster was to receive from him 'for his sole use twelve guineas per Ann: for Classical Instruction'.[27] Some of the references in the minute book are financial. In 1812 Malkin was allowed to spend £100 on the library. In 1820 he was allowed £350 for alterations and repairs at the school hall, though it was ordered that no repairs were to be done in future without the directions of the governors. A letter which he wrote in 1824, since he was to be away at the time of a governors' meeting, records a typical set of headmasterly concerns. He made recommendations about university exhibitioners. He had paid money into the governors' account for money received from the oppidans for the library, though he regretted that his accounts were not complete, because he had been trying to complete a textbook. Finally he asked the governors to look at the gravel in the playground path to the school. He had laid this down at his own expense, but it was now so worn that more was needed. His servants would be able to do the work.[28]

Bury under Malkin produced some distinguished literary figures – Edward Fitzgerald, the philologist J M Kemble, and James Spedding, the editor of the works of Francis Bacon. Spedding wrote an interesting appreciation of his old master which, though not uncritical, brings out the appeal of Malkin's character. His teaching, Spedding thought, was not always well geared to university success. In his sixth form he trusted to his own judgment and held no examinations, and he was partial to those whom he liked. But he was a good judge of character. He taught his boys to think for themselves and to take their own independent line. He ran the school on an open system which allowed much freedom. Morally the tone was good; fagging was not allowed, and there was little bullying. Spedding's emphasis is very much on free judgment and independence of thought. Malkin liked and trusted boys. It was said of him, as it was said of Arnold, that since he believed what boys told him, they did not tell him lies. Although his pupils criticized him, he had their confidence. 'There was nothing of formality about him, or pedantry, or cant. You were sure he felt all he said.'[29] A recent writer has noted that there were several Burians among the early members of that famous discussion society, the Cambridge Apostles. The thrust of Malkin's teaching fitted closely with the freedom of judgment which that society cultivated.[30]

James Tate of Richmond in the North Riding, who was headmaster there from 1796 to 1833, was pre-eminently a trainer of university wranglers with a long list of Cambridge tripos successes and of college fellowships to his credit. He was also a kind, warm-hearted and generous man whose good qualities, and particularly his keen interest in his old pupils, shine out clearly from his letters.[31] Tate was himself the son of a maltster who entered Richmond School when he was less than eight years old; it was his father's love of books which set him on the road to scholarship. The school under his headship was never very large; the commissioners in 1822 recorded an average of about fifty boys including about seventeen or eighteen free scholars.[32] Tate's own standing, both as a scholar and as a teacher, was high, but he had a large family, and money was always short. Probably his most distinguished pupil was the mathematician, George Peacock, and one of Tate's letters to Peacock when he was an undergraduate at Trinity brings out how dependent the master was upon his pupils' successes[33]:

> My credit as a Schoolmaster is tried every year in that Hall (of Trinity College, Cambridge): on my professional credit depends the *character* of the pupils committed to me, nam numerum nil moror; and on that character depends, to speak grossly, the extent of the charge which I can modestly make on the children of other people, for the maintenance of eight poor unprovided bairns of my own. You see, therefore, my dear lads, what a strong demand is made on your virtue, and what glorious fellows you may be if you will.

The letters reveal many of Tate's avocations. He corresponded with a local squire, John Hutton of Marske, who had been at school and at Cambridge with him. He wrote to Peacock about his *Horatius Restitutus*, published in 1832, hoping that its sale would be promoted by the fact that the second book of Horace's Satires 'is the Latin subject at Trinity this year'.[34] He advised a possible parent about schools for his sons: why not a public school, and in particular Charterhouse or Rugby? He provided a reference for his usher who was a candidate for the headship of Beverley Grammar School. There were few more attractive figures among the heads of his day than James Tate, and his long years of hard work had a happy ending. He had always been a steady Whig, and Lord Grey, when he came into power, made him a canon of St Paul's in 1833. There 'cum otio et dignitate' he lived until he died in 1843.

The point has already been made that there were frequent conflicts of interest between heads and trustees, and many heads, like Mr Spurdens of North Walsham whom we have already met (see p. 40), thought or feared that the trustees were trying to drive them out. W T Spurdens had been appointed to the headship of North Walsham School in 1807. In 1824 the governors decided that, since the number of boys in the school was so small, they would cease to employ an usher, and Mr Spurdens was informed that the usher's salary would be discontinued from the ensuing Christmas.[35] In Spurdens's view he was entitled to the assistance of an usher, and he simply could not manage the school without one. His formal letter of complaint to the governors is an interesting document which brings out very clearly the difficulties facing many heads.[36] First of all, he argued that the usher's salary was inadequate in relation to what he had himself to pay for help in the school. Secondly, he claimed that, when he had been appointed, nothing had been said to him about the obligations to teach forty free boys. The fact that free boys had been introduced had driven away the boarders.

> I had at that time a school of 84 boys; and, at the very next quarter, I received notice of 23 removals; of which 17 alleged as a reason, the admission of the free boys. It appears therefore that, whatever may be the case elsewhere, a numerous boarding school is not *here* compatible with a day school of free boys.

He was entitled, he claimed, to a fair return for his work, and clearly he did not feel that this was being given to him, though the endowment was sufficient to provide it. 'Indeed no class of educated men, in the whole country', he wrote, 'undergo so much anxious and exhausting toil, for so small a reward, as Schoolmasters and Ushers'. Mr Spurdens lost his fight. The governors upheld their original decision, and he resigned a few months later.[37]

Mr Spurdens's problems were certainly not unique. Very few schools could be run successfully and profitably unless the master could attract boarders, which meant in many cases engrafting a separate private school on the old foundation. The fact that masters were prepared to invest large sums of money in improving school accommodation suggests that this was a profitable step to take. At North Walsham Mr Spurdens's successor, Mr Rees, advanced the governors £700 at 4 per cent interest for building work. This is likely to have been a good investment since in 1833 the commissioners found fifty-six boarders and six free scholars in the school.[38] At

Midhurst in Sussex the private investment side was even more pronounced. The endowment was tiny and the master's salary only £20. It was clearly a school of standing at the beginning of the century since John Wooll, who was headmaster from 1799 to 1806, went on to be headmaster of Rugby.[39] The commissioners reported in 1819 that the head, Dr Bayley, had invested £2,000 in building, as well as paying an annuity to the mother of a former master who had laid out considerable sums.[40] Bayley had built up a classical school of seventy boarders and a few day boys. The foundation boys, who should have numbered twelve, had shrunk to six because they had drifted away to other schools in the town.

A head like Dr Bayley was a considerable entrepreneur with a large capital investment in his school, and though there is no record of this in his case, schoolmasters were often accused of discriminating against local boys and of favouring their own boarders.[41] By the 1830s, when the great inquiry was drawing to a close, the commissioners had become more outspoken about this important question of social differentiation. When they went to Cuckfield in Sussex in 1836 they found that the master was charging a considerable fee to foundation boys. He took boarders into his house at a high fee, and he was

> therefore desirous of excluding as much as possible the children of the poor, whose homely apparel might give his school a less respectable appearance, and thus operate as a bar to his readily obtaining that class of private boarders from which his chief income is supplied.[42]

Masters were in a difficult situation. Competition was keen, and it was easy to lose boys, particularly to neighbouring private schools. Whatever a head's personal views may have been, it was difficult for him to avoid a socially exclusive policy if he wished to raise the level of his school. There are some interesting examples from Surrey schools in the suburban areas of London where social distinctions were difficult to maintain and possibly all the more keenly felt for that. The commissioners' reports on Camberwell, on Dulwich College and on St Olave's, Southwark, all make similar points. At Camberwell 'the better persons of the neighbourhood have often objected to send their children to be placed with the children of their own porters'.[43] At St Olave's 'the higher class of inhabitants dislike the mixture of society which their children meet there, and in general decline to send them'.[44] There are examples in the reports too of parents of a higher social class being unwilling to allow their children to accept free education – presumably because of the stigma of pauperism which it might be considered to involve.[45]

The process of differentiation between secondary and elementary schooling took a considerable step forward with the creation, in the second decade of the century, of the National and British Societies. These aimed to provide elementary education, through the monitorial method, for the children of the poor, and they offered a common model, operating under central guidance. Those grammar schools – and there were a number – which adopted the 'national system' were aligning themselves with a new kind of organization and accepting a specifically elementary role. Sometimes the change was linked with the erection of a new building and the opening of subscriptions for the better education of the poor. Sometimes the grammar school endowment was paid over to the new National School and a certain number of children educated free on the proceeds. Some or all of these changes will be found, for example, at Cromer in Norfolk, at Tenterden in Kent, at Battersea in Surrey.[46] Naturally new plans of this kind sometimes led to controversy and to objections from schoolmasters. At Owen's School, Islington, the Brewers' Company complained that the master had only adopted the Madras system partially: 'certainly not to the extent the governors wished'.[47] There is evidence, however, that in some places the changes were popular. At Tenterden, already cited, 'it appears to be the general opinion of the parish, that the present establishment is more beneficial than the old one could possibly be if restored'.[48]

It might have been expected that the commissioners would have discussed, in the cases quoted, the legal difficulties involved in such a radical change in the objectives of the schools, but they did not do so. Perhaps there is a hint about their views in cases of this kind in their report on Hatfield in the West Riding, where there was a plan to convert a number of charitable bequests into a National School for poor children. The scheme was, they wrote, objectionable in principle because the funds had been given for the maintenance of a grammar school[49]:

> but the emoluments are at the present time insufficient for the due
> encouragement or support of a master properly qualified, to keep such
> a school; and if such a school were kept at Hatfield, there is no
> probability of its being resorted to by the children of any of the
> parishioners for instruction in classical learning, and under such
> circumstances, it does not appear to us expedient, to recommend that
> the execution of the design in contemplation should be interfered
> with.

There is certainly one case where the Court of Chancery approved a scheme for a National School at Tetbury in Gloucestershire (1830) in place of the grammar school which had closed in 1800.[50] The correspondence between the solicitors about the proposals has survived. Mr Colley Smith wrote from Lincoln's Inn to the Tetbury solicitor[51]:

> I am quite of your opinion that a school for the teaching of poor children 'reading writing and arithmetic' is preferable to a grammar school for the poor, and I think it not unlikely that we may be able to get the sanction of the Court for the erection of a National school.

Mr Colley Smith turned out to be right. This decision of the court perhaps suggests that, in a case where it would have been extremely difficult to reconstitute a grammar school, the court was prepared to be flexible about a change in the purpose of the charity. The poor did not want a grammar school education; nor did their social superiors think it right that they should have it. The foundation of a National School met the needs of all parties.

Before drawing this review of the grammar schools in the first half of the nineteenth century to a conclusion, there are some other points which must be briefly mentioned. First of all there is little sign of religious dissension. The schools were Anglican foundations, very often under clerical headmasters, but Nonconformist pupils seem generally to have been admitted. At Chard in Somerset, according to the commissioners, the master 'receives the sons of the members of the established church, and the members of dissenting congregations indifferently'.[52] In Lancashire there were two schools, Stand at Pilkington and Rivington, where all or most of the trustees were Dissenters. At Rivington the master had been licensed by the bishop and the usher was a Dissenting preacher.[53] Rivington is also interesting because girls were admitted. They often stayed until they were 14, they were taught with the boys, and they had received classical instruction. The commissioners commented that this practice 'seems inconsistent with the character of a grammar school'. At Blackburn in the same county a few girls' names appear in the admissions register about 1830, including two daughters of the headmaster. In 1833 the governors made an order that no girls were to be admitted without a special vote.[54] In many of the schools which concentrated on English subjects boys and girls were taught together, and money was sometimes paid from the endowment for teaching girls in a separate school, though they received basic elementary education only.[55] It is probable, I think, that it became more and more uncommon as time went on for girls to receive classical teaching.

A boy's chance of going to university often depended on whether his school possessed endowed university exhibitions, and where there were none of these, there was little incentive to stay on. In the case of a school like Bury St Edmunds the governors' minutes show a regular succession of awards year by year, and the same is true of schools like Manchester and Birmingham. In other schools there were awards, but no candidates, or candidates appeared only at rare intervals.[56] When this happened considerable sums might accumulate and be awarded to the lucky man who appeared at the right moment.[57] Many exhibitions were very small in value anyway. At Beverley, for example, at the time of the commissioners' report in 1823, Lawrence Stephenson held a collection of such small awards. His was a typical career for a successful exhibitioner. He went to Cambridge, became a fellow of St John's, and was rector of Souldern, Oxon. from 1835 to 1889.[58] In some cases boys were sent to a school for a short period simply to qualify for an award. At Warwick School there were two exhibitions to Oxford. Both were filled up in 1823 by candidates, one of whom had been at the school for one year and the other for two years.[59] When the commissioners went to Macclesfield in 1837, they commented without much enthusiasm about the governors' plans to establish university exhibitions. 'That the conferring of these exhibitions would enhance the reputation of the head master is probable: that it would be of very great advantage to the town and neighbourhood is by no means obvious.'[60] Certainly at Macclesfield or any comparable school the number of boys likely to qualify for such exhibitions would not be large. Yet without them there was, for the majority of boys, no path from the grammar school to the university.

NOTES AND REFERENCES

1. Carlisle, Nicholas 1818 vol I pp 828-31
2. Bury GS: two books of examination questions (Lancs RO). I conjecture that this book was kept by the headmaster and relates to the upper school. See also on Bury *CCR*, 19 pp 223-6
3. Brentwood School papers (Essex RO). The office hand-list dates this as post-1820
4. *CCR* 4, p 23
5. *CCR* 19, p 577
6. Bury GS, Trustees' Minutes and Accounts, 14 May 1855 (Lancs RO)
7. *CCR* 4, pp 352-6
8. *CCR* 15, p 663. See also *Rules and Orders for the management of the Free Grammar School in Leeds; as appointed by the Committee entrusted*

with its Guidance and Government, at their Court, holden January 20th, A.D. 1819 (Leeds, 1819)
9. Tompson R S 1970: 1–6. For the judgment see Vesey, Francis jun. 1806 pp 241–52
10. CCR 13, p 649
11. CCR 31, pp 519–27; Wilson G E 1952
12. Godber, Joyce 1973 pp 20, 32–5
13. Carlisle, Nicholas 1818 vol I pp 5–22
14. CCR 1, pp 208–9
15. CCR 20, pp 652–3, 679; Hutton T W 1952 pp 37–41, 187
16. The following is largely based on Macclesfield School Minute Books 1773–1859, 1860–88 (Ches RO); Wilson G E 1952
17. CCR 31, pp 526–7
18. Macclesfield School Minutes 25 Oct 1834
19. Ibid. 27 Oct 1843
20. Ibid. 16 Jan 1865. For the middle-class examinations see Roach, John 1971
21. CCR 19, p 208. The commissioners remarked that at Rivington the master, usher and writing master ran distinct schools
22. See Macclesfield School Minutes, 26 Nov, 9 Dec 1844, 1 Aug 1854 (Ches RO); Bury GS, Trustees' Minutes 6 Feb 1856 (Lancs RO)
23. Smith J F (ed) 1874 pp 2–8
24. Ainsworth W H 1858 pp 8–11. 'Mr Cane' was the Rev Robinson Elsdale, usher from 1808 and high master, 1838–40
25. Bury St Edmunds GS, Governors' Minutes 1776–1830 (Suffolk RO, Bury St Edmunds). For the general history of the school see Elliott R W 1963
26. Governors' Minutes, 5 March 1814. The royalists were the local boys.
27. Ibid. 28 Aug 1809
28. Ibid. 7 June 1824
29. Record of the tercentenary of the foundation of King Edward VIth's Free Grammar School, Bury St Edmunds. 'Remarks on the character of Dr Malkin' pp 77–89. The quotation is on p 79
30. Allen, Peter 1978 pp 36–7, 234 n 22
31. Wenham L P (ed) 1965. There is also material about Tate and Richmond School in Speight, Harry 1897
32. CCR 7, p 655
33. Wenham L P (ed) 1965 p 90 (14 April 1810)
34. Ibid. p 103
35. North Walsham School, Governors' Order Book 1769–1839, 31 Aug 1824 (Norfolk RO)
36. North Walsham School, correspondence relating to the Rev W T Spurdens 1817–25. Spurdens's letter is dated 20 Oct 1824
37. North Walsham Governors' Order Book, 21 Oct 1824, 3 March 1825
38. CCR 26, pp 321–3
39. Rouse W H D 1898 p 193
40. CCR 2, pp 175–6
41. See CCR 1, p 96 (Cranbrook, Kent); CCR 3, pp 106–7 (Ottery St Mary, Devon); CCR 5, p 215 (Plympton Maurice, Devon); CCR 31, p 473 (West Kirby, Cheshire)
42. CCR 30, p 696

43. *CCR* 1, Appendix p 374. For Dulwich College in the same parish see *CCR* 29, Pt II p 904: 'the reason why more children are not sent to the college school appears to be, that the rich are not willing that their children should associate with boys of such habits as parish boys usually have ... '.
44. *CCR* 1, p 210
45. *CCR* 3, pp 464–5 (Knaresborough, West Riding); *CCR* 11, p 121 (South Molton, Devon)
46. *CCR* 26, p 211 (Cromer); *CCR* 1, pp 148–9 (Tenterden); *CCR* 3, p 427 (Battersea)
47. *CCR* 2, p 315. See also Dare R A 1963 p 47
48. *CCR* 1, p 149. See also the very similar view at East Grinstead, Sussex, *CCR* 2, p 165
49. *CCR* 18, p 619
50. See *VCH Gloucestershire* vol II p 439 (Leach A F)
51. Letter dated 24 Dec 1828 in Tetbury GS, Miscellaneous Papers (Glos RO)
52. *CCR* 9, p 507
53. *CCR* 16, p 129 (Pilkington); *CCR* 19, pp 205–8 (Rivington)
54. Blackburn GS, Governors' Minutes 20 Dec 1833 (Lancs RO)
55. See, for example *CCR* 11, p 527 (Bradley, Staffs); p 531 (Church Eaton, Staffs); *CCR* 19, p 225 (Bury, Lancs)
56. See *CCR* 1, p 148 (Sutton Valence, Kent); *CCR* 7, p 625 (Gilling, Hartforth, North Riding); *CCR* 28, p 27 (King's Lynn, Norfolk)
57. *CCR* 10, p 630. At Guildford no award had been made between 1809 and 1816, and the balance was then paid to one boy who enjoyed it for 6 years
58. *CCR* 10, pp 679–80. For Stephenson's career, see Venn J A 1940–54 vol VI
59. *CCR* 17, pp 491–2
60. *CCR* 31, p 527

CHAPTER SIX
The slow coming of change

The preceding chapters have shown that there was a steady process of change in the grammar schools which had begun in the eighteenth century and which continued during the first half of the nineteenth, though the process was sometimes maddeningly slow. The twentieth-century observer, conditioned to expect reforms to be enacted by central government, tends to judge the situation as static because there was very little legislation. Change in early-nineteenth-century English society did not necessarily work in that way. Each grammar school had an independent endowment, each board of governors had a good deal of autonomy, and, as we have seen, there was a steady flow of new statutes and regulations, and the occasional private Act of Parliament, to improve the ways in which schools were managed. Standards generally were rising, there was more external criticism, there was more competition from private-school masters, and heads and trustees had to take account of these facts. Nevertheless there was a limit to what local action could achieve, particularly when such action involved the law of charities and brought into play the whole cumbrous and expensive regulatory machinery of the Court of Chancery. There was a crying need for a cheap and simple process for modifying charitable trusts and for bringing them into line with modern needs and this could be done only through the intervention of Parliament.

It was Henry Brougham who first directed the attention of Parliament to the whole question of charitable endowments. First of all in 1816 he obtained a select committee into the education of the poor in London, and two years later Parliament set up, through his initiative, the national inquiry into educational charities which has been used so extensively in this book.[1] Nicholas Carlisle published his description of the endowed grammar schools in the same year as the Charity Commissioners were established. There was an urgent need, he argued, for a public inquiry to deal with the abuses which affected the administration of charities. 'It appears absolutely necessary, that such disorder and misapplication should speedily be abolished by a PUBLIC INVESTIGATION and REFORM of those evils, which is only within the power of Parliament.'[2] 'Speedily' turned out to be an ill-chosen adverb. The commissioners' reports were not completed for 20 years, and, although a select committee of the House of Commons recommended in 1835 that a board of commissioners be set up to superintend the sale of property and to suggest new schemes, no legislation was passed until the 1850s.

By 1835 the reform era had begun, and the idea of a board of commissioners, like the Poor Law Commissioners of 1834, was very much in accord with the practice of the new age. So too was municipal reform. The Municipal Corporations Act of 1835 had come only three years after the Great Reform Act. There was a persistent Radical thread of argument, beginning at that time and running right down to the local schemes considered by the Endowed Schools Commissioners of 1869–72, which claimed that local elected bodies should have a say in the management of school endowments. Governing bodies, as the Radicals saw the matter, were co-opted and therefore unrepresentative. Such bodies tended to be strongly Anglican, while Dissent was powerful among the urban middle class in towns like Leicester and Birmingham. Town councillors felt, in some towns at least, that they, as elected representatives of the people, ought to have say in the way that endowments, given for the benefit of local people, were managed. The governing bodies resisted what they saw as aggression, and asserted their own independence. The Radical claim is set out in J A Roebuck's *Pamphlets for the People*, published in 1835–36. The people, Roebuck argued,[3] should be responsible for their own social affairs, and there should be a universal system of national education.[4] Municipal corporations should be in charge of the public utilities which were in private hands. They should control 'all the public charities – and ... all institutions of education supported by the people'.[5] Francis Place, writing in the same collection of pamphlets, argued that the municipalities ought to administer the public charities, including trusts for hospitals and schools.[6]

In the minute books which have been examined for this study there are a number of examples of pressures being applied – by parents, by other groups, by town councils – to persuade trustees to change the way in which schools were managed, usually by enlarging the curriculum. It would, of course, be absurd to argue that such pressures were stimulated by people who took their ideas from *Pamphlets for the People*. Probably most of them had never heard either of the pamphlets or of Roebuck himself. But the fact that these examples exist, and that so many of them involve a move by the mayor or the town council acting as a body does suggest an increasing tendency to demand closer control of schools by local elected representatives. Such a tendency at the very least runs parallel to Roebuck's arguments. The growth of popularly elected education authorities was very slow, and in secondary education it did not take place until the twentieth century. However the concept of popular control has quite a long history, and there was a feeling in some places that trustees needed to take note of 'consumer-opinion' if schools were to be made more useful to those who did, or who might wish to use them. I have found several examples from the 1830s. At Warrington in 1833 the governors made new rules for the school after they had received a deputation 'from the Town to hear certain complaints' about the management.[7] At Macclesfield four years later, when the trustees were considering the establishment of a modern school (see p. 75) they received a resolution from the town council about the extension of the charity, and they informed that body that the plan for a new school was going ahead.[8] The same desire to be consulted is suggested by the request in 1838 of the town council of Bury St Edmunds, in reply to a memorial from 'a numerous body of inhabitants', to be given a list of governors, a copy of the statutes and regulations, and to be allowed to inspect the charter.[9] The governors' answer was quite conciliatory. They replied that they did not accept that the town council had any right to ask for the production of documents, but they did explain where the documents might be found and they sent a list of the governors.

The later examples which I have found express a more specific desire to broaden the curriculum. At Basingstoke in Hampshire the grammar school had been for some years in a decayed state and when the master died in 1849, a public meeting was held which resolved that the education of boys in grammar schools should afford a preparation not only for the learned professions, but also for trade and commerce,

> and that as regards the town of Basingstoke it would be highly beneficial to the inhabitants if the system of educn and instruction of the Youth and Boys at the Free Grammar School of the Town called the Holy Ghost Grammar School was not confined to the dead

languages but extended to the other branches of literature and science in order to a more substantial fulfilment of the intentions of the Founders and the requirements of the present age.

The meeting also resolved that the town council be asked to petition the Lord Chancellor.[10] Similar initiatives were taken at Wotton-under-Edge (1854) and Warrington (1858) by the town council,[11] at Bury St Edmunds (1855) by the mayor and eleven other inhabitants,[12] at Bury in Lancashire by parents of boys in the school.[13] By the 1860s the concept of local control had influential advocates. Local boards of education were recommended by both the Newcastle and Taunton Commissions.

Local plans and local issues remained predominant for the ten years after the completion of the Charity Commissioners' inquiries in the late 1830s, and there were few national initiatives for change. It is only necessary to mention Sir Eardley Wilmot's Act of 1840, which gave the courts more general powers to change school statutes and to enlarge the range of subjects taught.[14] At local level, however, there was continuing interest in many places in improving the grammar schools, sometimes through the introduction of new schemes of management, sometimes through the erection of new buildings. The 'Brougham' commissioners had often commented that a school performed no real service to its town or district. The fact that many people were taking trouble and spending money to improve their own local school suggests a greater community involvement and a more optimistic view of what schools had to offer than has commonly been allowed.

One example which is particularly interesting because the correspondence has survived and the story can therefore be traced in detail comes from the small Staffordshire foundation of Kinver in the mid-1840s. The Charity Commissioners in 1821 had reported an income of £112, due to be increased by another £20, so the endowment was quite small. At that time the recent history had been chequered. The school had been closed because the master had become old and incapable. The building had fallen into a poor state, and the income had been devoted to repairing it, though at the time of the inquiry a master had recently been appointed and was preparing to reopen the school.[15] Presumably he had been successful because twenty years later the building needed extending. In 1845 the churchwardens, James Foster and Thomas Bolton, issued an appeal for subscriptions to build an additional schoolroom, the plan to be settled by a committee elected by the subscribers to the fund.[16] The circular was sent to thirty-eight people. A local clergyman sent £2, 'which is as much as can be expected from the quantity & quality of the land I possess in your parish'. The Bishop of Lichfield, who was visitor of the foundation, wrote at length. He was doubtful whether the school would qualify for aid from either the National Society or the Committee of Council for Education, but he advised that applications be made and he sent the addresses of the respective secretaries. There were difficulties in getting a reply from Lord Stamford, who seems to have lost a list of the subscribers which had been sent to him. The Staffordshire and Worcestershire Canal Company sent £5, but stated 'their surprise in not seeing the Earl of Stamford Dr. Johnson and several other names in the list of subscribers'. Finally a local ironmaster engaged 'the Collins family' to give a concert which made a profit of £15. The subscriptions from all sources raised £195 15s. 0d. There was one of £50 and another of £20, but all the rest of the money was raised in small sums. The new building cost £200. This was a small venture for a small school, but a considerable achievement for the many people involved, who showed their concern about their local school in the most practical way possible – through their purses.[17]

During the 1850s there are many examples of new building plans and new schemes of management, some of them resulting from complaints lodged long before by the Charity Commissioners. Here an Essex school, Felsted, will be used as an example. Lord Rich's charities at Felsted possessed a substantial endowment – the net annual value for all purposes in 1851 was £1,728. The Charity Commissioners had referred the school to the Attorney-General in 1836, but the case was not decided until 1849, and the headmaster, Dr Surridge, left in 1850 with a generous pension and a large cash payment.[18] In 1851 the Felstead (*sic*) Charities Act dissolved the old corporation and set up a new board of trustees.[19] After provision had been made for the poor of Felsted and of two other parishes the income was to be used to maintain a school at Felsted for both day boys and boarders, 'suitable for the sons of persons of limited means'. The headmaster's house was to be altered to take 100 boarders. The head himself was to have general supervision of this, but the house was to be managed by a steward. Church accommodation was to be provided, and day boys were to attend the parish church on Sundays, but the sons of Dissenters were allowed to attend their own places of worship. The school was to be open 'to Children of parents of all religious tenets', and no boy was to be required to learn the Church catechism. The existing school house and site were to be sold, land purchased and new buildings erected. Instruction was to be given in the principles of the Christian Religion, Reading, Writing, Arithmetic, Book keeping, Mathematics, Land Measuring, Geography, Sacred and Profane History, General English Literature and Composition, and the Greek, Latin, French and German languages, and in such Languages, Arts and Sciences as to the said Trustees may from time to time seem expedient.

The trustees were to appoint a headmaster, who was to be in priest's orders, a second master, and such other masters as might be necessary. They had power also to remove the masters, though in the case of the head only with the agreement of the bishop of the diocese. Boys 'being resident in Essex or born of Essex parents' were to be admitted between the ages of 8 and 19. Capitation fees were laid down, though day boys might still be taught Latin, Greek and the principles of the Christian religion without payment. Provision was made for an annual examination of the school and, if funds allowed, the trustees might make proposals to the Master in Chancery to establish university exhibitions.

Obviously, different schemes differed in detail, but the Felsted scheme of 1851 seems to be typical of the kind of structure which was being laid down for a reformed grammar school in the middle of the century. What is remarkable is that the notes prepared for the first meeting of the new trustees have survived.[20] First of all the financial position was summarized. Out of the total income of some £1,700 about £700 was committed for other purposes, largely for the almspeople and for Dr Surridge's pension. Of the remaining £1,000 about half was needed to pay salaries and insurances, leaving about £500 a year as security for sums to be borrowed for land and new buildings. Among the trustees' first tasks would be to inspect the buildings, to look into the question of purchasing land and to consider how to dispose of the accommodation in 'the existing House' and in the new building. Until this was done it would be difficult to 'shew to candidates for the Masterships what they have to expect'. There were other appointments to be made: a clerk, a banker and a receiver, as well as a new head and an under-master. The trustees had to appoint a house steward and settle the boarding arrangements which, under the Act, were their responsibility. They needed to settle the boarding and the capitation fees, both of which had been limited by the Act. These notes certainly give a vivid picture of the practical problems involved in turning an Act of Parliament into a working scheme.

By the time Felsted had its new scheme, the waters were beginning to move in London. The census of 1851, for example, collected information on schools. Horace Mann's report on education, published in 1854,[21] though it dealt very largely with popular education, did provide statistics both of 'collegiate and grammar schools' and of private schools (see p. 105). He listed 566 'collegiate and grammar schools' supported by endowments, educating 32,221 boys and 3,391 girls. The sources of income were given for 304 of these schools with 17,725 scholars. The total income was £128,693, of which £87,631 came from permanent endowment and £28,000 from payments by scholars.[22] Of the same group of schools 71.5 per cent taught ancient languages, 44.6 per cent modern languages and 67.6 per cent mathematics, almost all of them teaching the basic subjects and geography.[23]

At much the same time as Mann's report appeared came the Charitable Trusts Act of 1853 and the report of the Cathedrals Commission (1854), which investigated one group of schools exempted from the Brougham inquiry. Fifteen of the cathedrals and two collegiate churches had grammar schools, and about the same number separate schools for choristers.[24] The general picture of the cathedral grammar schools given in the report is much the same as that of the schools already discussed. Many, though not all, had foundation boys, and they took in day boys and boarders in the usual way. Many of the cathedral statutes had included provisions for awarding university exhibitions, but these had in most cases ceased to be given. The Cathedral Commissioners in their final report judged that the schools were not in a flourishing state. The assignment by statute of fixed monetary payments had meant that a steadily smaller proportion of capitular income had been devoted to the schools. Masters were insufficiently paid and had to depend upon fees from their boarders and paying day boys. The masters should, it was argued, be guaranteed a set stipend plus a house. The foundation boys should receive a liberal education free of expense and if possible money should be found for exhibitions. Schools should be set up for choristers and preference for admission to them should be given to boys who were likely to go on to the grammar school as foundation scholars.[25]

The headmasters' evidence to the Cathedral Commissioners suggested that some of them faced major difficulties. C. H Lowry of Carlisle complained that none of the three masters in the school 'can be said to earn such a maintenance as our position in society requires'. The school could develop only by taking boarders which meant excluding the free boys to whom it by right belonged. When he got an able boy, he had, if possible, to send him on to a public school because

The slow coming of change

he had no means of educating him.[26] James Harris of Chester had no house and the whole of his salary of £150 went in paying for assistance in the school.[27] John Ingle of Ely thought that the condition of the school there had been greatly improved; when he came in August 1852 he found 'the school in the lowest stage of decay'.[28] At Worcester S P Denning spoke warmly of the desire of the Chapter to promote the school. However the King's scholars had to be 'pauperes' and such boys did not want classical education. If the school was to flourish, the system needed remodelling.[29] One of the heads who gave evidence, Robert Whiston of Rochester, had become a national figure in the years before the inquiry. He had been in conflict with the chapter over the rights of the foundation boys and of the school exhibitioners, and he had written a pamphlet, Cathedral Trusts and their fulfilment (1849), which attacked the mismanagement of cathedral revenues, The Rochester Chapter had twice dismissed him from his office, but after lengthy litigation he had been restored to his headship from January 1853. The case had attracted widespread attention in the press, and Whiston's restoration to office did not end his combativeness. He complained to the commissioners about the houses provided for the masters, about the arrangements made for the award of exhibitions, and about the requirements that his boys should attend the cathedral services. Whiston was a difficult prickly man, but he had a good case when he argued that the Chapter had benefited from long-standing practices which reduced the amount of money spent on the school. His campaign certainly raised important questions about the management of cathedral endowments, and thus about the management of endowments in general, and it is likely to have contributed to the growing pressure during the 1850s for the more efficient supervision of charitable bequests.[30]

In 1853 Parliament finally passed the Charitable Trusts Act.[31] This set up a board of commissioners with power to inquire into charities in England and Wales and to obtain accounts and statements from trustees. Their inspectors might examine witnesses on oath. They could sanction leases, repairs and improvements, and the sale and exchange of land. Their secretary and another officer appointed by the Lord Chancellor were to be official trustees of charitable funds. However, for new schemes to be made, application had still to be made to Chancery or Parliament, and David Owen argues that, until the passing of another Act in 1860, the commissioners' powers to effect reform were limited.[32] The trustees' minute books which have been examined certainly show the commissioners in regular contact with trustees and imposing steady pressure from the centre towards more effective management. Some governing bodies tried to claim that they were exempt from the new jurisdiction. At Blackburn, when in 1857 the commissioners asked for a statement of accounts, the governors resolved that in their opinion the charity lay outside the provisions of the Act, and they were still resisting as late as 1865.[33] At Bury St Edmunds, when the governors were asked for a statement of their accounts, they claimed exemption as 'a free school having a visitor'. However the accounts were quite soon sent in, counsel's opinion having been given that the school was subject to the Act.[34]

One example of the Charity Commission's early activities has already been given in Chapter 2: their intervention at High Wycombe led to the making of a new scheme by the Master of the Rolls in 1856 (see p. 24). A small collection of correspondence from Rivington in Lancashire shows the commission at work in financial affairs.[35] First of all they had difficulty in collecting the accounts for 1854-58 and when they had received them, they asked for further information. In 1859 their inspector, Thomas Hare, announced his intention of visiting Rivington to hold an inquiry into the grammar school and other endowed charities of the township. A later letter from the governors refers to 'a hostile party in Rivington which resulted in the visit of your inspector', so clearly there had been local criticism of the governors' actions. The commissioners took care to see that when property was sold, the arrangements were advantageous, and they would not consent to the sale unless this was the case. A report and valuation was required on some property which was to be sold by the Rivington trustees near Darlington. Public notices had to be posted and when this was done, the incumbent of Rivington protested that the price was too low. Would the purchaser, the commissioners inquired, put the price up? In answer to inquiries from London the governors explained why certain interest had not been paid into their account and why they had spent so much money on a new safe.

All of this, of course, is small beer indeed, but it is important because it shows in practical terms the steady pressure towards accountable and effective management which was characteristic of Victorian administration. No longer were trustees to be their own masters, subject only to the fitful control of the courts of equity. They were to be subject in future to regular administrative supervision, which was alert to prevent abuse. Whiston, in his *Cathedral Trusts and their fulfilment*, was making a very similar point. His agitation stressed the need to ensure that expenditure was reviewed in accordance with changing circumstances. The cathedral chapters were not wicked men, shamelessly lining their own pockets, but they had been themselves unable to ensure that their endowments were regulated for public purposes rather than for private benefit. Such controls on educational endowments could be provided only through the more active intervention of the state. The need for national control was being more and more strongly felt during the 1850s. The foundations were being laid for the more striking and much better known changes of the following decade. The reforms of the 1860s and 1870s had a long pre-history behind them.

One interesting reformer who was active in pressing for change during the whole of this period is the Worcestershire corn merchant, George Griffith. Griffith is a remarkable figure, a maverick outsider who represented no one but himself, though his ideas do carry on the Radical critique which has been earlier outlined. Whiston may have been a trouble-maker, but he was a fellow of Trinity College, Cambridge and he was in priest's orders. By qualifications and background he was a member of the establishment, a critic from within. Griffith was the kind of middle-class man who was not well accommodated by the political and social system of his day. He was a tradesman from Birmingham, a corn merchant who settled first at Bewdley, then at Kidderminster and later at Wolverhampton. Perhaps his travels all over the West Midlands as he went to the markets first made him interested in the grammar school problem.[36] When he went to live at Kidderminster in the late 1840s there was keen controversy in the town about a new Chancery scheme for the grammar school which many townspeople attacked because it favoured the development of a classical boarding school to the detriment of the interests of the town boys. Griffith soon became involved in the agitation.

There is at least some suggestion of personal pique in this because the headmaster had refused to receive Griffith's son as a boarder because he was a tradesman in the town.[37] At the New Year of 1848–49 the townspeople appealed to the Bishop of Worcester as visitor. Their propositions, to which Griffith was a signatory, are typical of what might be called the Radical/townsman line of argument. No charges, they urged, should be made to the sons of parishioners, who should be given both classical and commercial education free. The sons of Dissenters should be admitted on equal terms with the sons of Churchmen. The masters should give their undivided attention to the local boys 'because we find that, under the present scheme, the number of the boarders increase, and the number of town boys decrease'. The plan to create exhibitions should 'under certain events' be revived. The mayor of Kidderminster should be a feoffee ex officio and the accounts of the trust should be published annually in the local press.[38] The bishop found for the trustees and the same group of townspeople then filed an information in Chancery. In his judgment (Michaelmas Term, 1851) the vice-chancellor refused to overturn the existing scheme or exclude boarders, though more liberal arrangements were made for admitting Dissenters. And there the matter rested because the town committee decided to make no appeal to the House of Lords because of the expense involved.[39]

Griffith wrote later that, as soon as the Chancery judgment had been given, 'I made a solemn vow, that I would never, during my life, cease to expose endowed school perversions, wherever I found them existing.' He went on in the same passage to quote an article in a local newspaper – he does not mention the author – perhaps he wrote it himself. Why, the writer asked, should gentlemen's sons learn Latin and Greek free while tradesmen had to pay for their sons to be taught commercial knowledge? There was no need for Kidderminster School to have boarders, because the endowment was sufficient to educate all those who were entitled to enjoy it. Nor would the author of the article accept the vice-chancellor's complaints about agitation got up at public meetings[40]:

> What public abuses have ever been removed except by these means? The corn-laws were extinguished by similar instrumentality. Law reforms have been brought about in this way, and we expect that the abuses of the Chancery Court will not yield except to such potent agency. Surely, when a great majority of the inhabitants of a town prefer a complaint, they are more worthy to be listened to than is the peevish and interested puling of a paltry clique.

Griffith quickly moved on to consider all the endowed schools in the county and his book, *The Free Schools of Worcestershire and their fulfilment*, appeared in 1852, with a dedication to Robert Whiston in the hope, as Griffith wrote, that the contests at Kidderminster and at Rochester might be 'the pioneer of a successful reformation' in all the endowed schools. A large part of Griffith's material was taken from the Charity Commissioners' reports on the schools of the county, supplemented by his own observations. He attacked the abuses of the Court of Chancery, the mismanagement of trustees, the masters' concentration on attracting boarders and their neglect of the free boys, the prominence given to classics in the curriculum. The two schools in the county which illustrate what Griffith approved of and what he attacked were Dudley and Bromsgrove. At Dudley the provision of commercial education had been extended, the capitation fee was very low, and no distinction was made between Churchmen and Dissenters. Since both classical and commercial education were given, the school was full and was highly regarded in its neighbourhood.[41] At Bromsgrove, on the other hand, the interests of the poor boys for whom the foundation existed had been completely neglected.[42] At Christmas 1851 there were six day boys and sixty-five boarders. The school possessed valuable scholarships and fellowships at Worcester College, Oxford, but these were monopolized by the boarders. Since the free boys were not taught classics, they could not compete for them. The boarders came to the school because, for the expenditure of less than £70 per annum, a boy 'could get a scholarship worth £50 per annum, with a title to holy orders, and a fellowship annexed'. Griffith argued consistently throughout his books that endowments had been designed for the benefit of the poor; at least £500,000 a year had been taken from them and given to the rich.[43] At Bromsgrove the free boys were the sons of working men such as nailers, whitesmiths, labourers, gardeners, button-makers, milkmen. The boarders were the sons of 'esquires', army and navy officers, clergymen and other professional people.

Griffith did not, in his survey of the Worcestershire endowed schools, merely amass facts about individual foundations. In the preface to his book he asked the question how what he called a conspiracy on the part of the upper classes to deprive the middling and working classes of their educational birthright was to be defeated.[44] A reforming Act of Parliament was necessary. The Court of Chancery should cease to be responsible for educational trusts and special visitors should be abolished. Trustees should be elected in the same way as town councillors and should elect their own chairmen. There should be county boards representing all governing bodies. The county board should have the power to audit accounts, to hear complaints about school management (with an appeal to the assizes), and to ratify the sale and exchange by trustees of school property. It should meet in open court and all new rules should be published in the local press. The education of scholars should be conducted in accordance with local needs, and 'the boys shall belong to the class and place of residence contemplated by the founder'. Where the funds were sufficient to pay the masters, no boarders should be allowed, and all exhibitions and other awards should be confined to foundation boys 'unless ordered otherwise by the founder'. No clergyman should be a trustee or member of a county board since such membership would interfere with his parish duties.

Griffith's projected Act of Parliament was a remarkable proposal to have come from a corn merchant in a provincial town in the early

1850s, and it incorporates many of the reforming ideas which have been considered in this chapter and which were to be put forward again in the ensuing decade. At the time he was not able to make any progress with his plans, and by 1853-54 he seems to have given the subject up, and not to have returned to it again until the end of the decade[45] (see p. 288).

NOTES AND REFERENCES

1. Owen D 1965 ch VII deals fully with the 'Brougham' Commission and the Charitable Trusts Act of 1853, and I have used his account extensively
2. Carlisle, Nicholas 1818 vol I p xxxv
3. For an account of the pamphlets see Leader R Eadon (ed) 1897 pp 60-1, 75, 78. The pamphlets are paginated separately, and I have referred to them under their independent titles below
4. 'The King's speech, which ought to be spoken' p 3
5. 'A Letter to the electors of Bath ... ' p 7
6. Place, Francis 'The Peers and the people' p 6
7. Warrington GS, Trustees' Minutes, 28 Jan, 4 Feb 1833
8. Macclesfield School, Minute Book, 28 Nov 1837
9. Bury St Edmunds GS, Governors' Minutes, 17 April 1838
10. Basingstoke, Holy Ghost GS, Papers in Chancery proceedings 1850-53 (Hants RO): from the scheme made by the Master in Chancery, 29 April 1850
11. Wotton-under-Edge GS, Trustees' Minutes, 17 Jan 1854; Warrington GS, Trustees' Minutes 13 Sept 1858
12. Bury St Edmunds GS, Governors' Minutes, 3 Aug 1855
13. Bury GS (Lancs), Trustees' Minutes, 18 Feb 1861
14. Adamson J 1930 (repr 1964) p 44
15. *CCR* 5, pp 624-5
16. Kinver GS, papers relating to additions to school buildings, including estimate and committee minutes 1845-47 (Staffs RO). The following section is based on these papers
17. The school was given new statutes in 1848 (see p 36). Presumably these form part of the same movement for reform
18. Craze, Michael 1955 pp 142, 148-50
19. For the following see Round (Birch Hall) Papers (Essex RO)
20. 'Minute for the Trustees as to the position of the Charity preparatory to their First Meeting' (Round (Birch Hall) Papers)
21. Census of Great Britain 1851. *Education. England and Wales. Report and Tables* 1854. Another statistical compilation of the same period is the Educational Register; see Wallis P J 1964. The Educational Register 1851-5 *British Journal of Educational Studies* XIII(1): 50-70
22. *Education Report 1854* Census of Great Britain 1851 pp xlvii, xlviii
23. *Ibid.* p xlix

24. *CathC* 1st Report. The fifteen cathedrals were Canterbury, York, Durham, Carlisle, Chester, Chichester, Ely, Gloucester, Bristol, Hereford, Lincoln, Peterborough, Rochester, Salisbury and Worcester. The collegiate churches were Westminster and Southwell
25. *CathC* 3rd Report, pp 56-7
26. *CathC* 1st Report, pp 734-8
27. *Ibid.* p 739
28. *Ibid.* p 740. For a modern study see Owen, Dorothy M, Thurley, Dorothea 1982
29. *CathC* 1st Report pp 752-3
30. *Ibid.* pp 747-9. For Whiston's controversies with the chapter of Rochester see Arnold, Ralph 1961
31. *Public General Statues* 16 & 17 Vic., c. 137
32. Owen D 1965 pp 202-8
33. Blackburn GS, Governors' Minutes, 21 Dec 1857, 21 Dec 1959, 30 Jan, 17 Feb 1865
34. Bury St Edmunds GS, Governors' Minutes, 12 July, 26 July, 18 Dec 1854
35. Rivington GS, correspondence with the Charity Commission 1858-61 (Lancs RO)
36. See Griffith G 1870
37. *Ibid.* vol I p 254; for the headmaster's reply see p 309
38. *Ibid.* p 360
39. For the vice-chancellor's judgment see Griffith G 1852 pp 293-6. For the decision not to appeal, Griffith G 1870 vol II pp 448-9
40. *Ibid.* vol I pp 436-41. The quotation is on p 440. See also Griffith G 1852 pp 299-302. The article appeared in the *Worcestershire Chronicle* 19 Nov 1851
41. Griffith G 1852 pp 151-62
42. For Bromsgrove see *ibid.* pp 59-70
43. Griffith G 1870 vol I p xxi
44. For the following see Griffith G 1852 pp xxiii-xxiv
45. Griffith wrote of the year 1854: 'the endowed school waited for the expression of public opinion' (Griffith G 1870 vol II p 523)

PART TWO

Private schools of many kinds

CHAPTER SEVEN

The response to parental demand

There was constant interaction between private and endowed schools, and it is a great mistake to view them as existing in watertight compartments. Those endowed schools flourished whose masters were able to attract private pupils. Teachers moved about between schools of different kinds: endowed, private, proprietary. Dr Arnold went to Rugby from a small private coaching establishment at Laleham. In Sheffield G A Jacob came to the headship of the Collegiate School, an Anglican proprietary school, from Bromsgrove Grammar School and later went on to be headmaster of Christ's Hospital. We know something about Jacob's third master, J E Adams, because the prospectus of his private school has survived. He taught at the Collegiate School for 6 years after teaching in a number of private schools, and, in 1853, took over a private school of his own, which had previously been run by a Dissenting minister, Peter Wright.[1] During the first half of the nineteenth century the private schools were growing, certainly in numbers and to some degree in prestige, while the endowed schools fell behind. After 1860 the balance altered again. The grammar schools were reformed, the public schools were expanding, the private and proprietary schools fell back, though they remained important all through the century.

The private schools are much more difficult to analyse than the endowed schools, which formed a recognizable legal entity, because they were of many kinds, and they tended to come and go with the masters or mistresses who established them. As J C Bruce, master of a very successful private school in Newcastle upon Tyne, commented at the jubilee dinner in 1855: 'It is not a usual thing, Mr Mayor, for a school unsupported by public funds to subsist for half-a-century, especially in the same spot.'[2] Broadly these schools fall into four separate sectors, though there was overlap between them. The commonest were those run entirely for private profit by masters or mistresses who owned them. These varied enormously, both in standard and in cost, from the Yorkshire schools satirized in Dotheboys Hall to very reputable institutions like the Hill family's schools at Hazelwood and Bruce Castle which were pioneers in their day. The second group were the schools founded by bodies of proprietors in the 1830s and 1840s to provide a good education for boys in classical and modern subjects, most commonly in towns where there was no grammar school or where the grammar school had ceased to meet the needs of local middle-class families. Many of these proprietary schools were under-capitalized and disappeared quite quickly; some hung on, at varying levels of prosperity, for a long time. A few, the best known being perhaps Cheltenham College, established themselves as public schools.[3]

The third group were the 'religious' schools run with a specifically denominational objective. The Quaker schools like Bootham, Ackworth and The Mount and the Roman Catholic schools run by the many orders of nuns form good examples. All of these were in a sense public foundations, but there was only a narrow line between them and private schools run by clergy and ministers in tandem with their parochial work.[4] Finally there was much concern in the middle of the country about the education of the skilled artisan, the shopkeeper, the clerk, the small farmer. The County Schools, like those established by the Rev. J L Brereton, were founded for the farmers. In some large towns as at Liverpool and Leeds, the Mechanics' Institutes established schools. In London the Birkbeck Schools created by William Ellis and the schools of the Rev. William Rogers provided what might be called a lower secondary education, as did the 'middle' or 'yeoman' schools set up in association with many early teachers' training colleges like York and Chester.

A great deal of material has survived about all these schools, though it is patchy and incomplete and there are so many gaps that a coherent picture is difficult to paint. Between all these many kinds of private school there were major differences. There is, however, one generalization which can be made about all of them. Their clientele divided itself on lines of expense and broadly of class, since, when a free choice was available, no parent wished his children to consort with those who were socially beneath them, nor could he expect, in a free market, to be admitted to the company of those above him. There was a clear distinction here in the first half of the nineteenth century between the private schools and the endowed schools. One of the

The response to parental demand

problems of the latter, as we have seen, was that the public nature of their foundation opened them to boys of differing social rank. In the case of private schools, and particularly of girls' schools, these problems did not arise. Parents and children selected themselves according to what they could pay, what religious denomination they belonged to, what kind of education they wanted.

The point has already been made that, in the early nineteenth century, there was no clear concept of secondary education. Many so-called grammar schools were in fact elementary schools, and many others contained boys at every stage from likely university entrants to those barely able to read. The same was true of the private schools. At one end of the spectrum were the dame schools which often did little more than look after small children. At the other end the private school shaded into the tutorial establishment, preparing a few boys for the university or for the Indian civil and military services. The group with which this study is concerned were sometimes called 'superior day and boarding schools'. They took in children as young as 7 or 8, and they did not normally retain them beyond 15 or 16 because by that age the middle-class parents who patronized them thought that their boys should begin business or professional life and that their daughters had acquired the accomplishments necessary for marriage.

Some statistics of grammar schools have already been given (see pp. 56–7). Though these are imperfect, they are more precise than can be provided for the private schools, where all we can say with certainty is that these schools were very numerous and that most of them were small. However, some attempt can be made to quantify private school provision, partly from contemporary sources and partly from modern sources like the *Victoria County History*. The Education Census of 1851 gave some overall figures, though they are so general as to be only of limited value; 29,425 private schools sent in returns, which were then classified 'according to efficiency'.[5]

1.	4,956	Superior (classical, boarding, proprietary, ladies', etc.)
2.	7,095	Middling (commercial, etc.; teaching arithmetic, English grammar and geography)
3.	13,879	Inferior (principally *dame* schools; only reading and writing taught, the latter not always)
	3,495	Undescribed

If the 'undescribed' group are excluded from the calculation, the 'superior' and 'middling' schools were in number almost half the total of all the private schools. Thirteen years earlier in 1838 Thomas Sutton, the vicar of Sheffield, had investigated the number of 'Private or General Day Schools' in the parish, and his figures were as follows[6]:

	Schools	Scholars
Superior	31	1,273
Middling (day/evening)	22	1,019
Common (day/evening)	27	1,130
Dame schools	46	1,037

The balance in numbers of 'superior' and 'middling' as against 'common' and 'dame' schools (53 to 63) is not radically different from the 1851 Census returns. Sutton's figures also make it possible to give the average size of each group of school in Sheffield:

Superior	41
Middling	46
Common	42
Dame	22.5

The most complete contemporary figures which I have found are those provided in some of the early reports of the Manchester Statistical Society on the 'superior private schools' of Liverpool, Manchester, Salford, Bury (Lancs.) and York (Table 6). The years covered are 1835–37. From these statistics several interesting points emerge. In all five towns the average size of school was very small and each school had only a very small staff (presumably visiting masters and mistresses were not included). Secondly, many boys' schools contained pupils of the other sex and vice versa. Finally there were very few children in the schools over the age of 15 – only 412 out of 5,852 (no age figures are given for the Manchester schools). The York report also cites the percentage of the total number of scholars who were attending superior private schools in the five towns[7]:

	%
Manchester	6.77
Salford	6.85
Bury	3.03
Liverpool	12.30
York	12.80

Table 6 Private schools in Liverpool, Manchester, Salford, Bury and York, 1835–37

	Nos	Teachers	Boys	Girls	Totals	Grand totals Schools	Grand totals Scholars	Av. pupils per school	Under 5	5/15	Over 15
Liverpool											
Boys' schools	53	115	1,887	292	2,179 ⎫				161	3,637	282
Girls' schools	90	167	224	1,677	1,901 ⎬	143	4,080	28.5			
Manchester											
Boys' schools	36	65	1,228	170	1,398 ⎫				(not given for Manchester)		
Girls' schools	78	123	127	1,409	1,536 ⎬	143	3,816	26.7			
Salford											
Boys' schools	9	19	335	76	411				7	384	20
Girls' schools	20	37	47	424	471				23	406	42
Bury											
Boys' and girls' schools (B.2,G.6)	8	11	51	123	174	8	174	21.75	Boys 2	39	3
									Girls 4	117	9
York											
Boys' schools	6	11	216	13	229				—	221	8
Girls' schools	24	40	48	439	487	30	716	23.86	45	394	48

Source: Manchester Statistical Society, *Report, Liverpool* 1835–36, *Report, Manchester* 1834; *Report, Salford* 1835; *Report, Bury (Lancs)* 1835; *Report, York* 1836–37.

Some further light is thrown on particular areas by modern studies, though these generally only give numbers and do not distinguish between the different types. Margaret Bryant pointed out the very large numbers of private schools in outer London suburbia – in 1832-34 at least 95 in Chelsea, in the Islington area 135, in Clerkenwell 144, Hackney 88, Kensington 77, Marylebone 97, St Pancras 57, Stepney and district 123.[8] One estimate records 48 private schools in Leicester in 1846 of which 15 took boarders.[9] Another independent calculation, based on the boys' schools, advertizing in the *Leicester Journal* 1820-39, gives figures for the town and county (Table 7).

In Hull John Lawson wrote of growth in the number of boys' private schools after the 1790s, 'mostly in the new middle class suburbs to the north and west' and of parallel growth of girls' schools.[10] Such isolated figures do no more than suggest a pattern. Large numbers of private schools might have been expected in the London suburbs, but the same development had occurred in provincial towns, large and small.[11] It is noteworthy that, both in Hull and Leicester, the grammar school was in a poor state – indeed in Leicester it had ceased to function by 1841.

During the first 50 or 60 years of the century two processes were going on. The first was a steadily growing demand for 'secondary' education which meant that more schools were necessary. The second was that the private schools were more successful in meeting that demand than the grammar schools, partly because, as we shall see, their curriculum and organization were more flexible. Circumstances naturally varied from place to place; it is probably true that private schools did best where the endowed schools were least effective. The

Table 7 Private schools in Leicestershire, 1820-39

Leicester	27
Loughborough	4
Hinckley	4
Ashby de la Zouch	3
Melton Mowbray	2
Lutterworth	3
Market Harborough	2
County elsewhere	31
Total	76

Source: Simon B (ed) 1968 p 118.

examples of Hull and Leicester have already been cited. Another very interesting example is that of Southampton. There the grammar school, despite attempts at reform, had shrunk to three boys by 1853 and when the master died the following year, it was closed for 6 years until it reopened in 1860 with better premises and a new curriculum. Into the breach moved the private Southampton College opened about 1848 by the Rev. James Duncan, taking both boarders and day boys, and preparing candidates for the universities and the services. Until it closed in 1886 the college remained the most successful boys' school in the town.[12]

Though many individual schools like Mr Duncan's were successful, the private schools as a group were much criticized. There was a growing sense that, while the educational provision being made for the workers was steadily being improved, the schools available to the middle classes were not making comparable advances and were, if anything, falling behind. One example of this very common complaint comes in the evidence given to the Newcastle Commission by the Sheffield educationalist, Samuel Earnshaw: 'Some people think that under the present system of inspection, the children of the workmen have within reach a better and sounder education than children of the employer.'[13]

W J Conybeare, Principal of the Liverpool Collegiate Institution, identified three major problems in 1847: the lack of a 'uniform system of instruction'; the interference by ignorant parents with the subjects taught; and the very short length of school life. It was fashionable to remove boys from school at 14 and they were often sent to school for only a year or two.[14] Twelve years later, in 1859, T D Acland noted some recent improvements. Middle-class parents were ready to accept help, and a number of schoolmasters appreciated the advantages offered by the new University Local Examinations. Textbooks and teaching methods had improved, and the importance of general non-vocational education was more fully recognized. But there were still many defects. More attention should be given, both to elementary training and to the continued education of boys who left school in their early teens. There was need for better teaching of drawing and music and for more emphasis to be given to boys' games and social life. New schools needed to be established and old ones reformed, and there was a particular need for better facilities for educating farmers' sons.[15]

One constant note sounded by many reformers was the plea for some kind of national system providing a general standard to which middle-class schools could work. Thomas Arnold, as we have seen, wanted such a standard to be set by government (see p. 10). The Irish reformer, Thomas Wyse, speaking at the opening of the new Mechanics' Institution in Liverpool (15 Sept. 1837), looked forward to the future achievements of the Institution's new high school. Schools, he commented, were usually set up by individual benefactors. What was wanted was a national system: 'a national guarantee for the education of the nation'.[16] Ten years after this, government was spending considerable sums on elementary education. W J Conybeare wanted some of that state money spent on bursaries for middle-class boys who were intended for business to enable them to stay longer at school. If the state had made grants to the Irish colleges, he argued, why should it not do something comparable in England.[17] The plan for a national reorganization of educational endowments was the central recommendation of the Taunton Commission. The fact that nothing was done until the beginning of the twentieth century can be regarded as a major disaster for English education.

If the failure was disastrous, it is not difficult to understand. The national government had accepted a responsibility to finance elementary education, which became increasingly costly and which left little enthusiasm for a state commitment on behalf of middle-class people who, it appeared, were perfectly well able to look after themselves. Nor did the middle classes want state interference. They preferred freedom and low taxes, and the strong Dissenting element among them had inherited 200 years of suspicion of state activity which had always appeared to work against their beliefs and interests. The teachers were no more anxious for state interference than were their patrons. The efficient private-school master believed that he could do well enough for himself. The inefficient feared that state supervision would show up his deficiencies and take away his livelihood. The grammar-school masters and their trustees were no more enthusiastic. It was fear of state interference which led Edward Thring of Uppingham and his fellow heads to create the Headmasters' Conference in the early 1870s. The movement to organize such a body came, not from the major schools which had little reason to fear an attack on their autonomy, but from the schools of the second grade which were more vulnerable and felt that they had more to lose.

The fact that middle-class schools and schoolmasters, in both the endowed and the private sectors, were resistant to the idea of a national system does not mean that they were also resistant to new ideas. It has already been argued in earlier chapters that by the 1850s, and despite their many weaknesses, the endowed schools had made considerable efforts to reform themselves. Because the private schools had so little formal structure, they were much more open to change than the grammar schools. Any innovator who could attract enough parents to make his venture pay could launch his own scheme. By no means all successful private-school masters or mistresses were innovators, but some of them were, and the new ideas which they tried to implement came from many sources and are of considerable interest.

One school of thought which declined in the first part of the century was that which claimed that children should be educated at home. The case for domestic education had many advocates in the eighteenth century from Locke at the beginning through Rousseau to R L Edgeworth at the end.[18] The case for 'public' as against 'private' education was made by M D Hill of the Hazelwood family in his book, *Public Education* first published in 1822.[19] We learn more, Hill argued, from companions who resemble us the most closely in age and in tastes. Their example has the greatest influence upon us and we are likely to compete with them most effectively. The company of a large number of other pupils makes it easiest to assess the standards which an individual should be able to attain. For similar reasons large schools work better than small ones. The fact that Hill thought it worth while to devote a chapter in his book to arguing the case for public education suggests that the domestic idea was still influential around 1820. Throughout the century, of course, much education was gained in the home and the family. Large families meant that children educated one another. There was a considerable output of children's books and books for family reading. Until the twentieth century many middle-class and upper-class children probably learned at least as much at home as they did at school.[20]

New ideas in education originated both in Britain and abroad. Both British and foreign thinkers laid heavy stress on the importance of education because they believed that the early years were decisive for later human development. One interesting, and now little known, group in Britain were the Phrenologists, followers of the Germans Gall and Spurzheim, who believed that the mental faculties were located in different parts of the brain. The leading British thinker of the school was George Combe, who taught a creed of rational progress and human educability, which demanded universal education and the development of scientific knowledge.[21] Combe was essentially a theorist and, though his ideas may have influenced many progressively minded teachers, it is difficult to provide examples of schools and of teachers whose work was affected by phrenological ideas. More important and more far-reaching in their influence upon the liberal and progressive thought of the time were the Utilitarians. Their doctrines were based on the theory of the association of ideas. Man experiences sensations and gradually forms from them continuous images of the universe. Consequently education is all powerful since the educator can control the environment which shapes the development of the personality. Bentham and his circle were interested in the mutual system of instruction pioneered by Joseph Lancaster and by Andrew Bell. Bentham himself planned the Chrestomathic School with an encyclopaedic curriculum where the instruction was to promote useful knowledge. James Mill wrote an important article on education in the *Encyclopaedia Britannica*. The Utilitarian circle had much influence on the founding of University College and of London University, the model for all the new universities of modern Britain.

The practical schoolmasters who came very near to Utilitarian ideals were the Hill brothers of Hazelwood and Bruce Castle, though they specifically stated that they had not read *Chrestomathia* (1816) before they published *Public Education* in 1822. Certainly, M D Hill presented a copy of the book to Bentham and maintained links with him for some years, while Bentham supported their schools and many Radicals visited them. Whatever the relationship between the two books may be, Bentham and the Hill brothers certainly moved within the same parameters of thought. Michael Sadler, in a perceptive essay, wrote of the brothers in words which might also be applied to Bentham: 'they were men of their time; borne forward by the movement of liberal thought; sanguine in their belief in the virtue of self-government, a little prone ... to over-elaborate the details of organization'.[22]

An account will be given later of the workings of Hazelwood School (see pp. 123–5). Here an attempt is made to place the Hills in the general movement of early-nineteenth-century educational thinking. They emphasized self-government and self-education. They stressed the need for the pupil to appreciate that it was useful to acquire knowledge, and they were anxious that boys should not associate unpleasant feelings with school. Learning – though the words are not theirs – was to rank high on the felicific calculus. There was something very Benthamite too in their emphasis on punctuality and on the muster and roll-call of the boys without any waste of time. In *Public Education* the debt to other educationalists is discussed. They mention R L Edgworth and his daughter Maria. They had not, they said, depended on Bell and Lancaster because the mutual system was too involved with restraint and rigid order.[23] To point out these connections with their contemporaries is not to deny the originality of the brothers and the hard work and long experience which they brought to the elaboration of their system. In the 1820s and early 1830s they certainly represented an important strand of thinking on the Radical side.[24]

Among the authorities quoted in *Public Education* was the Swiss J H Pestalozzi,[25] who, with his fellow-countryman, P E von Fellenberg, was the major foreign influence on English educators during this period. Pestalozzi's distinctive doctrine was the need for the harmonious development of intellect, emotion and will, achieved through the active participation of the pupil in his own development. He is generally remembered as a major force in the development of English popular education, but he also had an influence on upper-class and middle-class schools in this country. The most successful of the English Pestalozzians was Dr Charles Mayo, who had taught at Pestalozzi's school at Yverdon, and who set up his own school in 1822, removing to Cheam in 1826. Cheam was a successful school which produced some distinguished pupils. Basically it was an ordinary English private school, with some boys going on to public schools and others finishing their education there, but there was an admixture of Pestalozzian ideas too. Mathematics and science were particularly well taught by the German Charles Reiner who had been one of Pestalozzi's assistants.[26] Another innovator who ran a school on Pestalozzian lines was Dr Heldenmaier of Worksop in Nottinghamshire. An interesting picture of his school is given in the letters of William Marling who was a pupil there from 1847 to 1849 between the ages of 12 and 14. William's letters say a good deal about school work and games, about music, and about the long excursions to see mills and factories as well as historic buildings which were a regular part of the programme.[27]

Fellenberg, the other great Swiss educator of that day, ran a series of schools at Hofwyl, graded by academic level and social rank. Again, he is chiefly remembered here through the influence of his Poor School master, J J Wehrli, on Kay-Shuttleworth, but he had also some influence on the superior private schools. W H Herford, a pupil of the distinguished Unitarian schoolmaster, J R Beard, who will be mentioned later (see p. 161), went to Hofwyl as tutor to the grandson of Lady Byron. In 1850 Herford opened his own school at Lancaster, making use of some of the ideas he had learned in Switzerland. He gave up the Lancaster school in 1862, though it was continued by his brother-in-law, and had a successful later history. Herford later opened a school in Manchester for young children and did much to introduce the ideas of Froebel to English teachers.[28] Mayo, Heldenmaier and Herford are only isolated examples, and the great mass of teachers in English private schools were quite unaffected by European ideas. However, both the Anglican Mayo and the Unitarian Herford came from within the established English cleric/schoolmaster tradition – they could not simply be written off as foreign eccentrics. Their native roots perhaps made it a little easier for their practice and writings to gain credence and for their ideas to penetrate the rather tradition-bound English scene.

All these schools, conservative and progressive alike, had to attract the parents who paid the fees which enabled them to survive. To conclude this initial survey, something must be said about the costs of private education and the length of time for which parents were prepared to keep their children at school. The complaint was often made that school life was too short, and some figures can be given for private schools of different types. One of the large towns which was most active in educational matters in the first half of the century was Liverpool. Since it lacked educational endowments, the townspeople were forced to create new institutions appropriate for the needs of a great port and major commercial centre. The Collegiate Institution, founded in 1839–40, ran schools of three grades, upper, middle and lower.[29] The Mechanics' Institution, founded in 1825, opened what was to become their lower school in 1835, a high school in 1838, and a girls' school in 1844.[30] W J Conybeare, principal of the Collegiate Institution, claimed in 1847 that the average stay of the boys in the Mechanics' Institution High School was about 1½ years, and that much the same was true in the Collegiate Institution's Middle School. Boys usually came to the Middle School between 11 and 12, and they generally went into business at 14. Conybeare claimed that only 18 per cent of the middle-school boys

> had gone through that course of teaching, to which, theoretically,
> every boy in the School ought to be subjected; and that nearly half the
> numbers of boys who left the School were sent into business with
> knowledge disgracefully below that which ought to be attained even
> by the age of fourteen. Such is the result which naturally follows from
> the habit of sending boys for a year and a half to School; for what can
> be done with a boy of twelve or thirteen, who comes to School scarcely
> able to read, write, or spell, and intends to complete his education in a
> few months.[31]

Ten years later another principal of the Collegiate Institution, J S Howson, gave figures of boys going into business of all kinds in 1856 and 1857 from the Collegiate Institution's three schools, together with the boys' average ages and length of school life.

	Upper	Middle	Lower
Total numbers	47	121	124
Average age (years)	16½	15	14⅙
Average stay (years)	3	2⅝	2¾

For the middle school this represented an advance on Conybeare's figures of about a year in both sections, but Howson still thought that the boys left far too young and stayed too short a time at school. He favoured a leaving age of 18 for commerce and 16 for shopkeeping.[32] Since the early Victorian middle classes were very anxious to get their boys to work, this was hardly a practicable objective at the time.

Comparable figures are not easy to find for the ordinary private school run by an individual master, and the only clues which I have found come from masters' ledgers where these have survived. Since such ledgers record payments made for individual boys and girls, it is possible to calculate how long they stayed at that particular school, though no clue is given, of course, to the quite common situation of a child being sent to more than one school. One such ledger, covering a period of 30 years (1799–1829), has been preserved for a school kept by William Buck at East Dereham in Norfolk. It is an interesting record because Buck taught boys, both boarders and day boys, and day girls. I have analysed the length of school life, as revealed in the school bills, for the children who were in the school in the years 1799–1805 and 1820–25. The material is not always easy to interpret with complete certainty but the following is, I think, broadly correct.

	1799-1805		1820-25	
	Av. school life (years)	No. of entries	Av. school life (years)	No. of entries
Boarders (boys)	2.9	120	2.3	42
Day boys	2.6	77	2.6	85
Day girls	1.6	42	2.3	13

It is to be expected that the girls would be sent to school for a shorter period than the boys, though with such a small sample, it is impossible to say whether there is any significance in the fact that the girls' school life had got longer in the 1820s and the boarders' school life shorter. Clearly in the 1820s day pupils had become more important in the school than boarders. Perhaps, as he got older, Mr Buck did not wish for the work and responsibility entailed by a large boarding side. In both samples the average length of stay for a day boy was about 2½ years. None of the figures provide any information about the ages at which the pupils left the school.[33]

Ledgers have also survived for a school in Wiltshire kept by C E Meyrick.[34] From an analysis of the first 10 years (1802–12) it appears that in 1802 there were seventeen boys in the school, and that sixty-nine entered between 1802 and 1812 (both dates inclusive), or an average of about six per year. In the earlier years of this decade Meyrick noted that a number of boys went to public schools like Eton and Winchester, so he was obviously attracting boys of high social position. Later there are no such notes and the boys seem to have stayed longer, so it is possible that Meyrick changed his policy and tried to retain boys in his own school rather than sending many of them on to public schools. The average stay during the period was 4.43 years, though as usual there were the widest variations. A few boys stayed 8 or 9 years, some for less than 1 year. No general information is given about age of entry; where this is mentioned, it varies from 7 to 12.

For the semi-public foundations some figures are available for the 1840s and 1850s. At Ackworth, a Quaker school founded for the boys and girls of Friends 'not in affluence', the average stay of the boys during the ten years before 1856 had been three years and eight months, though the source gives no figures for the girls.[35] This Ackworth figure is similar to the average calculated from the school list of the Sheffield Collegiate School, an Anglican proprietary school established in 1836. The Sheffield entries for 4 years in the mid-1840s are as follows[36]:

	No. of entries	Av. school life (years)
1843	35	3.81
1844	28	3.24
1845	27	3.61
1846	17	2.30
Average 1843/46		3.24

These two examples, though they show similar averages, are in fact very different. At Ackworth all the boys left at 14 or 15 after a common course. At the Sheffield Collegiate School some boys stayed until they went to university, and thus the average of 3.24 years embraces some boys who stayed for 6, 7 or even 8 years and others who stayed for only 1 or 2. Such variations in length of study must have made school organization very difficult, particularly since the total numbers were small anyway.

There is no shortage of information about school fees because many school bills have survived. Estimates of fees vary from the most expensive boarding academies at from 70 to 100 guineas a year with the cheapest Yorkshire academies charging from 16 to 22 guineas.[37] There were major variations between different schools, and in many cases various extras immediately increased the basic charge. For example, the very reputable Warwickshire girls' school run by the Misses Byerley which educated the future novelist Mrs Gaskell and the feminist Jessie Boucherett, charged in June 1832 £26 5s. 0d. for a half-year's board and instruction. The account for that half-year of Miss Radford shows that to this had to be added payments for subjects such as French, Italian, writing and arithmetic, for accomplishments such as dancing and drawing, and for items like washing and clothes. Miss Radford's total bill amounted to £74 0s. 6d. This did include £7 7s. 0d. for board in the Christmas holidays, but if such vacation payments be excluded, the school's total annual charge was probably about £120–130.[38]

This was distinctly expensive. Several other accounts which I have found show a basic charge of about £20–£25 per half-year. The guardian of a Cheshire boy, P D Finney, was, in the 1830s, paying Mr Cooke of Newark half-yearly bills which, including extras, varied from £25 to £41, though the largest bill included 6 weeks' board in the holidays.[39] In the following decade Mr Charles Sperling of Great Maplestead in Essex had children boarding at several schools. The Rev. William Presgrave of Sevenoaks charged him some £10 per quarter per child in 1848–50 with extras amounting to a few pounds only. One of the children was a daughter who was to be instructed by Miss Presgrave 'in Music, French, Drawing, Italian and Dancing for 40 guineas per ann: including Board and every department of an English Education', though Presgrave explained that this did not include washing: 'It would have been more to my interest to have taken £40 exclusive of washing than 40 gns. inclusive.'[40]

The Dorset poet William Barnes opened a school at Dorchester in 1835. In his advertisement he announced fees for boarders under 12

A History of Secondary Education, 1800–1870

years old of twenty-two guineas and of twenty-four guineas for those over that age. Boarders 'prepared for the Naval or Military Colleges, or Mathematical Professions' were to pay twenty-eight guineas. Day boys were to pay five guineas. By 1844 the boarders were paying £30 and the day pupils £10. In 1845 he had forty-four pupils, half of them boarders. Barnes's modern biographer, Mr T W Hearl, estimates that in the mid-1840s his income from the school was about £1,000 and his expenses which can be calculated, though the list is certainly not complete, were about £400. Of this sum, food and ale cost about £175, rent, insurance, rates, repairs and decorations about £80, coal and gas about £15.[41] Out of the £500 or thereabouts which was Barnes's gross profit on the year, he had to pay his assistants and make any savings he could for his old age. As was the case with many private-school masters, he only rented his school house.

NOTES AND REFERENCES

1. Adams J E 1853; Board M J 1959
2. Williamson J B 1903 p 296
3. See Morgan M C 1968
4. A good example is the excellent school of Dr Lant Carpenter, minister of Lewins Mead Unitarian chapel in Bristol (Carpenter R L (ed) 1842)
5. Census of Great Britain 1851 *Education, England and Wales Report and Tables 1854* p xxxiii
6. Holland G C 1843 p 220
7. Manchester Statistical Society: Report 1836–37 p 16
8. Bryant, Margaret E 1969 in *VCH Middlesex* vol I p 255
9. Martin, Janet D 1958 in *VCH Leicestershire* vol IV p 335
10. Lawson J 1969 in *VCH Yorkshire and East Riding* vol I p 350
11. For some figures of Warwickshire schools see Leinster-Mackay D P 1974: 10–11
12. Patterson, A Temple 1971 vol II pp 130–1; 1975 vol III p 38
13. *NC* vol V (1861) p 188 (Rev Samuel Earnshaw, Chaplain of St Peter's, Sheffield)
14. Conybeare W J 1847 pp 3–6
15. Acland T D 1859: 307–8. For Acland and the movement which led to the establishment of the Oxford Local Examinations in 1857, see Roach J 1971 pp 64–9
16. *Prospectus of the Course of Instruction, terms and regulations of the schools attached to the New Mechanics' Institution, Mount Street, Liverpool* (1837) pp 32–3 in *Liverpool Mechanics' Institution Reports* vol I (1825–38) (Liverpool Central Libraries). For the Liverpool Institute schools see pp 200–1
17. Conybeare W J 1847 pp 7–12
18. See Musgrove, Frank 1958

19. (Hill M D) 1825 pp 277, 281, 287. I have used the reprint of 1894 edited by C H W B (?Biggs)
20. There is an attractive picture of children's lives in a Wiltshire Baptist family in Reeves, Marjorie 1980
21. For a discussion of phrenology and of the ideas of Combe and of James Simpson, see Stewart W A C, McCann W P 1967 pp 280-6
22. Sadler, Michael 1923: 22
23. (Hill M D) 1825 pp 201-4
24. Bartrip P W J 1980: 46-59 argues that by about 1830 Hazelwood had come to represent a kind of 'liberalism' which was becoming out of date
25. On language teaching (Hill M D) 1825 pp 216-19. For the Swiss educators and their influence, see Adamson J W 1930 pp 112-21
26. On Mayo and Cheam, see Stewart W A C, McCann W P 1967 pp 149-50, 169-78. On science teaching, see pp 127-32
27. William Henry Marling's letters from school to his parents, 1847-49, are in Glos RO
28. McLachlan H 1934 pp 136-9. The Lancaster school under Herford's successor, David Davis, was called Castle Howell. On Herford's later career see Hicks C R 1936
29. See Wainwright, David 1960
30. See Tiffen, Herbert J 1935
31. Conybeare W J 1847 pp 6-7
32. Howson J S 1858: 246-7
33. Records of William Buck's private school at East Dereham (Norfolk RO)
34. Accounts of C E Meyrick's private school at Ramsbury, 1802-41 (Wilts RO)
35. Thompson, Henry 1879 p 269
36. (Jacob G A) 1852 *The Sheffield Collegiate School ...* pp 13-14 (Sheffield Local Studies Library)
37. Greenberg E L 1953
38. Hicks, Phyllis D 1949 pp 81-2. See also pp 156-7
39. Papers relating to Peter Davenport Finney III (1824-40) (Ches RO)
40. Sperling papers and correspondence (Essex RO). For the daughter Rosalie, see Mr Presgrave's agreement of 18 April 1849 and letter of 2 July 1849
41. Hearl T W 1966 pp 115, 176, 193, 215

CHAPTER EIGHT
Innovations in teaching

Less homogeneous in their curricula than the grammar schools, the private schools were more open to innovation. Though there were often differences between what appeared in the prospectus and what was actually taught in the classroom, these schools did offer science, modern languages and practical subjects like land surveying and, by so doing, were major agents of change, playing a substantial part in determining the curriculum of the modern secondary school. Most of them have survived only through brief entries in advertisements and directories, and they tend to appear as no more than a name on a list. Such lists have their value and some use has been made of them here, but I have chosen rather to concentrate on those schools about which it is possible to obtain more detailed information. To do this gives a more interesting picture of those schools; the disadvantage of the method is that it lays too much emphasis on the better schools since it is they, on the whole, about which most information has survived. However the better schools were the pacemakers, and to describe them in some detail goes a long way to destroy the claim that private schools were run by dishonest charlatans, anxious only to make money from their helpless pupils. It is not difficult to show that this claim is untrue and that many of the schools were well run with good teaching and innovatory courses. If their difficulties be remembered, it is remarkable that so many of them accomplished so much.

Before describing individual schools something more can be said about particular towns or districts. In Yorkshire both York, the ancient northern capital, and Doncaster, with excellent communications in all directions, had a large number of schools. In 1840 eighteen boarding schools can be traced in York and in 1850 twenty. Only three, which appear on both lists, were clearly boys' schools.[1] At

Doncaster between 1800 and 1850, there seem to have been twenty-nine masters, either keeping boarding schools or taking private pupils to board. Naturally not all were active for the whole period, but, in so far as it is possible to give precise figures, each of these masters was active in the town for at least 12.65 years. During the same period thirty-nine mistresses of girls' boarding schools can be traced with an active life in each case of 9.64 years. These figures are certainly minima so far as the length of teaching life is concerned because, where a master or mistress is mentioned in a source for only 1 year, that period of a single year has been cited, though the school will normally have survived for much longer.[2]

Before the railway age private schools could build up a very strong position in their own districts, especially where these were remote from London. One such area was the north-east, where a good deal is known about two successful schools, that run by the Bruce family in Newcastle and Dr Cowan's school in Sunderland. Both of these had strong Scottish connections. They attracted many Scottish boys, and both Cowan and John Collingwood Bruce had been students at Glasgow University. The historian of Cowan's school pointed out that it had been most successful before the coming of the railway. For many parents the public schools were accessible in 1850 in a way which had not been the case 20 years earlier, and both private schools and local grammar schools lost boys in consequence.[3]

James Cowan, son of a Lanarkshire schoolmaster, came to Sunderland and opened his first school in 1822. In 1830 he moved to the Grange, a property of twelve acres. At the time of the move there were 40/50 boarders and as many day scholars; by 1845 the school was at its height with 161 boarders. Cowan himself retired in 1846, and, after that time, numbers began to fall, though the school was carried on until about 1860. Many of the boys were preparing for Haileybury and Addiscombe, and several old pupils had distinguished careers in the Indian military and civil services. There were prominent representatives of the school in many professions, like Francis Sandford (Lord Sandford), permanent secretary of the Education Department, Edward Macnaughten who became a Lord of Appeal, the politican M E Grant Duff, Tom Taylor, editor of *Punch* and Charles Mackenzie, first Bishop of the Central African Mission. Latin and Greek were prominent in the curriculum but modern languages, English literature, mathematics and drawing were taught as well, and there were many outside activities. A number of plays were produced. Mock parliamentary elections were held. There was a gymnasium, the boys played fives and cricket, and Cowan was fond of football and played it himself. Every September there was an exhibition of fencing, drilling and gymnastics attended by 'the beauty and fashion' of the town.

The Bruces' school in Newcastle was a similarly successful venture which lasted much longer than the Grange at Sunderland. Like Dr Cowan, John Bruce benefited from the fact that 'in the earlier part of this century travelling was not easy'. 'My father', J C Bruce wrote, 'had many scholars of the upper classes who would now be sent to Rugby, Harrow, Winchester, Westminster or Eton.'[4] Like other successful masters of the late eighteenth/early nineteenth centuries the brothers Edward and John Bruce were entirely self-educated. In 1802 they jointly opened a school in Percy Street, Newcastle. In 1803 they wrote a very successful textbook, an introduction to geography and astronomy, which, by the 1840s, had gone through nine editions. Their school in its early days must have been quite a modest establishment, since they charged only one guinea a quarter, plus 10s. 6d. entrance fee, for teaching writing, French, geography and mathematics, and John Bruce, in addition to his school work, taught private pupils as well. In 1806 Edward died, and John moved the school to a larger house and discontinued his private pupils. By that time he was ready to take up to twelve boarders for a fee of £40 per annum and he offered 'English Grammar Writing Mathematics Geography and the Classics'.[5]

John Bruce himself employed masters to teach the classics; he had taught himself some Latin but he had no Greek. He was however a good teacher of mathematics. One of his pupils, the engineer Robert Stephenson, wrote later in life: ' . . . it is to his tuition and methods of modelling the mind that I attribute much of my success as an engineer. It was from him that I derived my taste for mathematical pursuits and the facility I possess of applying this kind of knowledge to practical purposes and modifying it to circumstances.'[6] John Bruce ran the school until he died in 1834. His son, John Collingwood Bruce, who had become a partner in 1831, then succeeded him and went on until he retired in 1859. The Bruce family were Presbyterian though most of the boys were Anglican. J C Bruce had been sent (1818–20) to the Protestant Dissenters' Grammar School at Mill Hill, and then to Glasgow University. He was later licensed as a Presbyterian preacher, but he decided to give up the ministry and join his father in the school. One of the great features of the school under both father and son was the annual public examination of the pupils in their school work. Under J C Bruce who was very interested in teaching history, these occasions included a debate on some historical question. He prepared the speeches and the boys learned them and delivered them. In 1837 for example the subject for debate was 'Did the advantages resulting from the invasion of Britain by the Romans compensate for the evils which attended it?'[7] J C Bruce, like Cowan at the Grange, Sunderland, provided a varied programme. There was a good school library. There were frequent expeditions to Durham and Hexham, to Carlisle and to the Roman Wall. The mathematics teaching was kept up and Bruce gave regular courses on science. In the mid-1830s he announced three courses of lectures 'illustrated by every possible variety of experiments and diagrams' on natural philosophy and astronomy, on chemistry, geology and mineralogy, and on natural history.[8] The school was very successful. Numbers rose to 225, of whom 35 were boarders. Bruce's alertness to new developments can be judged from the fact that in 1858 he took five boys to Oxford to be examined under the new Local Examinations, which he believed would prove a valuable means of testing the efficiency of private schools.[9] After Bruce's retirement the school went on under his partner Gilbert Robertson until it closed in 1881 after a life of some 80 years, and a very respectable record of achievement.

The Bruces' school was a North Country equivalent of some of the prestigious schools in the Home Counties like Dr Mayo's school at Cheam, which has already been mentioned (see p. 113), and Mr J C King's school at St John's Wood, attended by two of Dickens's sons. Mr King had a strong connection among literary and professional people – Dickens was probably introduced to the school by the actor Macready. Frederic Harrison the Positivist, an old pupil, thought King the finest schoolmaster he had known. He was praised for his skill in avoiding mechanical methods. Harrison wrote that at King's school he had learned the classics with delight and had been able 'to enjoy them for themselves'.[10] There was nothing innovatory about a school like this. Mr King was simply doing a traditional job well, but the existence of good schools like those which have been mentioned does raise the question whether the achievements of the Hill brothers at Hazelwood were quite as unique as is sometimes claimed. They were certainly the best-known innovators among private-school masters of their day. Their ideas are still of great interest, but there were others among their contemporaries who were also doing good work along more traditional lines.

The place of the Hill brothers in the general development of liberal education has already been discussed. More needs now to be said about the methods which they used. The founder of the school was their father, Thomas Wright Hill. Born at Kidderminster in 1763, he had little formal education, being apprenticed to a brass founder when he left school at the age of 14. He opened his school at Hill Top, Birmingham in 1803. For the first 10 years the school was not remarkable. T W Hill had some good ideas, but he was muddled and rather unsystematic in what he did – for instance, a great deal of time was wasted in teaching his own system of shorthand. The school began to advance as his large family of sons, in particular Matthew Davenport and Rowland, began to teach in it as they did from an early age. Gradually the brothers took over the management, Matthew improving the teaching and Rowland looking after the organization and accounts. In July 1819 they opened their new school at Hazelwood, and 3 years later *Public Education*, written by Matthew Davenport, Rowland and Arthur Hill appeared, and made their efforts widely known.[11]

Their basic ideas were those of self-education and self-government and of the utility of knowledge.[12] As much power as possible was left in the hands of the boys themselves. Their committee met regularly to control the benevolent fund for charitable purposes and the school fund from which books and instruments were purchased. Offences were judged by the boys in a weekly court with a jury of six, though the principal might mitigate or pardon the sentence. The advantages of the system were, it was claimed, that the boys were taught to assess the weight of evidence as well as to speak in public. Corporal punishment had been abolished, though solitary imprisonment for a limited period was used. Punishments and rewards were awarded through the giving or depriving of marks which formed the general currency of school affairs and which could be bought and sold. The punishments of the court were expressed by fines in marks. Marks were given for good work and good conduct as well as for voluntary work done by boys in their free time. As boys moved up the school, they gained a progressively higher rank which brought increased privileges. The general objective of the brothers' plans was to stimulate them through pleasurable exertion rather than through harsh punishment.

The school had a library, printing press, extensive playgrounds and a swimming bath. For purposes of study the boys were arranged into separate classes for each subject. The school was large enough to make this possible – 120 when *Public Education* appeared, and about 150 boarders by the late 1820s. Great stress was laid on practical methods. In arithmetic boys were to work from concrete objects like marbles before they depended on words and figures. Trigonometry was to be learnt through practical surveying. In learning languages boys should learn examples before rules or general principles. They should, as soon as possible, learn to read a foreign author in the original without first translating the work into their own language. As in many private schools the boys gave regular public exhibitions of their work, which at Hazelwood often included producing plays, the school house being equipped to make this possible.

For some years the school was a great success, and it attracted a number of foreign boys.[13] In January 1825 the great liberal journal, the *Edinburgh Review*, made the school the subject of an article which included the comments of an observer who had recently paid a visit. He noticed the cheerfulness of the boys and their good relationship with the masters. The place had a purposive air – the boys went about their business with a will, and the rigid care for punctuality helped maintain system and good order. He commented favourably on the wide range of voluntary activities and on the general neatness and tidiness. The system had not, he thought, made the boys affected or self-conscious. 'They are still boys, but boys with heads and hands fully employed on topics they like.'[14] This *Edinburgh* judgment is more favourable than that of W L Sargant, a Birmingham business man, who went to Hill Top in 1817 at the age of 7 and who left at the age of 15. T W Hill and his sons were, Sargant thought, able men, though in some areas they lacked knowledge themselves; for example, the Latin teaching was poor for this reason. English and mathematics were thoroughly taught, though he considered that the disciplinary system of courts and marks produced a priggish atmosphere which took away the proper freedom of childhood. Moreover the system was in a continual state of change. 'The school was in truth a moral hotbed which forced us into a precocious imitation of maturity.'[15]

In 1827 the brothers opened a second school at Bruce Castle, Tottenham, which was later directed by Arthur Hill as the other brothers moved into different professional careers. Hazelwood was disposed of in 1833 and later closed, though the family controlled Bruce Castle until 1877 and the school continued there until 1891. The main new development of the years around 1830 was the attempt, which seems to have been largely unsuccessful, to introduce the teaching of science (see p. 132). The comments of an American visitor, A D Bache, on both the discipline and the curriculum of Bruce Castle during the 1830s suggest that the school was continuing to run on much the same lines. He was favourably impressed by the regularity and exact punctuality of the routine and by the encouragement given to private study, though he was doubtful about the power over discipline given to the pupils.[16] By mid-century Bruce Castle had probably become more conventional in its methods; it remained a successful school for many years.

A few samples of the curricula and programmes of work for private schools, of which a fair amount has been preserved, must suffice. They range from Portsmouth to Sheffield, Liverpool and Cumberland. John Shoveller, master of a school at Landport Terrace, Portsmouth, described a largely classical school, though he also stressed the importance of mathematics and thought that a school should possess a collection of apparatus such as a telescope, microscope, electrical machine and air pump for scientific work.[17] A school should not, Shoveller thought, be too large. Forty boys would provide full employment for a headmaster and two assistants. A boy should begin Latin at 7, Greek at 11 or 12. In a boarding school 9 hours should be given to study, 5 to exercise and meals, and 10 to sleep. The pupil should stay at school until the end of his sixteenth year.[18]

Mr J H Abraham of Sheffield opened his Milk Street Academy in 1800, and was for over 40 years an active figure in the scientific and cultural life of the town. He lectured on science and was himself an inventor, being awarded the Society of Arts Gold Medal in 1822 for a device to prevent the inhalation of dust by dry grinders. He was an active member of the Sheffield Literary and Philosophical Society and attended, as the society's delegate, the first meeting of the British Association at York in 1831. In 1805 he republished the prize compositions of his pupils, appending to them an outline of the system used in his academy. The boys began with arithmetic and mathematics from seven to nine o'clock. The girls began an hour later at eight o'clock. After nine o'clock there was English language, reading, writing and spelling, and geography with the use of the globes. On one morning a week time was set aside for learning the arithmetical rules and tables. French and drawing were studied in the afternoons and the account books prepared by the pupils were examined twice a week. There were weekly grammatical exercises for the younger and English composition for the older pupils. On Saturday mornings they repeated pieces 'for the double purpose of speaking properly and strengthening the memory'.[19]

Mr Abraham's curriculum was restricted and business-oriented. Across the Pennines in the 1830s a more ambitious Liverpool school was visited by the American, A D Bache. This was the St Domingo House School, Everton, a boarding school run by Mr Voelcker, who was a follower of Pestalozzi and a Swiss or German who taught for some years in Liverpool. Voelcker desired to create a close relationship between teachers and pupils as a means of promoting moral education. He was opposed to emulation so the boys took no rank in their school work or examinations. The school was organized into five classes, spanning the ages of 6 to 16, each with its own teacher and containing eight to fifteen pupils. The main feature of the curriculum was that French and German were begun before Latin, which was postponed until about the age of 13. This, Bache thought, might be a disadvantage for boys who were intended for the university, but was desirable for those entering engineering or commerce. In the fifth class of the school additional studies were undertaken to prepare boys for the universities, for naval and military schools, and for commerce. Some boys, we are told, stayed on after 16 to prepare for university, but no numbers are given. The commercial instruction in the fifth class was 'accompanied by a kind of practical exercise in the system of banking, in the different operations of trade, in the mode of keeping books, &c, the members of the class being converted into an imaginary community, carrying on supposed operations of this kind under the direction of the teacher'.[20] The commercial demands of a great port are very evident here. One wonders how real these exercises appeared to the boys as compared with the pressures of the real business world which they were soon to enter.

Some interesting material has survived from a school in Cumberland which also attracted Liverpool boys, Green Row Academy at Silloth on the Solway. Green Row was kept by Joseph Saul, who seems to have been a Quaker, but it was not a Quaker school.[21] About 1830 there was only one vacation in June and July, the Christmas vacation having been discontinued some years previously. The boarding fees were about average: twenty-five guineas per annum, though foreign languages and drawing were extras. The prospectus and list of students for 1840–41 pointed out that the school, being near the Solway, was easily accessible by the Liverpool to Carlisle steamers, which pulled in at Skinburness only two miles away. Not only was the school easily accessible from Lancashire, other steamers ran frequently from Whitehaven and Port Carlisle to Ireland, Scotland and the Isle of Man. This 1840/41 list gives a total of seventy-eight boys, and it further shows the subjects which each boy studied (Table 8).

It is difficult in this list to understand the differences between some of the subjects – 'geometry' and 'Euclid' or 'astronomy' and 'lunars' sound very similar – but certain points do stand out clearly. There is a

Table 8 Subjects studied by seventy-eight boys at Green Row Academy, Silloth 1840–41

English	78	Geography	34
Writing	77	Bookkeeping	9
Arithmetic	75	Gauging	18
Classics	25	Algebra	15
French	34	Natural philosophy	14
Spanish	6	Navigation	10
Drawing	30	Spherics	10
Geometry	49	Astronomy	11
Euclid	32	Lunars	11
Trigonometry	24	Use of the globes	9
Mensuration	43	Construction of maps	2
Surveying	37		

Source: Cumbria Record Office, PR/122/98.

wide disparity between the numbers of subjects studied by different boys. Some of this difference must relate to age. For example, a sizeable group were studying only English, writing and arithmetic, and they are likely to have been the 7/8 year-olds who had only just joined the school. Of the remainder some boys are listed for all or almost all of the twenty-three subjects, whereas others are taking only eight or ten of them. Though the school was for its day quite large, this must have made the construction of a coherent timetable very difficult. What this kind of school offered was a long way from the basic secondary curriculum which developed towards the end of the century and which was enshrined in the Secondary School Regulations of 1904. The other point of interest at Green Row is the markedly mathematical emphasis of the curriculum and its strong practical bias. French was studied by nearly half the boys and a few learned Spanish. The classics – not differentiated between Greek and Latin – were studied by only one-third of the whole – considerably less than the numbers taking geometry, Euclid, mensuration and surveying. Something about the practical nature of the work can be deduced from some of the boys' problem books which have survived. One set, belonging to Daniel Jennings, shows the progression of his studies in successive years. He begins with two books on arithmetic, followed by geometry, trigonometry, mensuration and surveying, by solids, conic sections and gauging, and finally by algebra. Some of these and other books contain straightforward mathematical problems, but much of the emphasis is on practical application. For example, a volume on *spherics, astronomy and lunars* begins with the chief properties of the sphere and goes on to nautical astronomy and navigation. A book on practical geometry leads through mensuration into land surveying. There is work on the measurement of area, on practical examples of artificers' work, on the measurement of haystacks, timber and embankments. 'Gauging' is defined as 'the art of finding the capacities or contents of all kinds of vessels used by Maltsters, Brewers, Distillers, Wine Merchants, Victuallers &c'.

These Green Row examples emphasize a side of private-school learning which was important and which has been too little stressed. Charles Pritchard, who was later head of the very successful Clapham Proprietary School in South London, described how he learned mapping and architectural planning at the private school which he attended after he left Merchant Taylors'[22]:

> Very many of us could use the theodolite, and could survey and plot an estate. Our practice ground was mainly in the Isle of Dogs, at that time an all but unoccupied waste, and I well remember how, at the age of less than sixteen, I earned two guineas for indoctrinating an intending colonist in the art of field-surveying. I did not leave him until we had completed the plan of Kennington Common, and had calculated its acreage.

Another boy, who went to the Quaker school, Ackworth, in 1819, recalled being taken out on to the farm 'to have practical lessons in [land surveying], carrying with us the "Rod" or "Pole" staff and "Gunter's" chain of 700 links, with other paraphernalia for accomplishing our work which we made notes of and then had to enter in our Ciphering Books ... '.[23] Perhaps these were similar to the Green Row books which have survived.

This interest in practical science sometimes led to the creation of specific 'science' schools. There were several in Middlesex, like the Islington School of Science and Art, established in 1852,[24] but these were, I think, uncommon. However the number of ordinary private schools which taught science does show that these schools were a long way ahead of the public schools where science does not appear until the 1860s with pioneers like J M Wilson of Rugby. Musson and Robinson, in their study of science and industry in the late eighteenth century, argued that there were at that time schools in many towns where mathematics and science were effectively taught. If this were so, they argued, it might be necessary to modify the traditional view that industrial innovation was the work of practical craftsmen. There was a real contribution from organized scientific knowledge, some of it acquired in the schools.[25] It is very difficult to estimate exactly what the many references to the natural sciences in school prospectuses and similar literature really meant. Many schools claimed to possess scientific instruments, though one suspects that these were mainly used in demonstrations, and that the bulk of science teaching consisted of lectures by the master with some kind of note-taking by the pupils. The interest in subjects like land surveying was valuable because it had a strong practical side. The commonest kind of scientific study is probably outlined in this description, by his daughter, of the methods of the Dorchester schoolmaster, William Barnes[26]:

> - in turns botany, natural history, physics, chemistry, electricity and geology were all discussed. The lecture (which combined dictation, orthography and composition, in such a way as to make them all interesting) began with a short dictation; if on botany or natural history, the distinctive marks of an order or class formed the subject. Then some flowers or specimens were shown, and the boys had to find the distinctive marks of the class, or to reject the specimen as not apposite. This trained their discrimination, the master then gave a lecture on the subject and the boys were required to take notes, and write them out in a clear form as a composition for one of their daily tasks.

The value of these studies probably varied greatly from school to school, as the reminiscences of old boys suggest. The historian of the Congregational School at Silcoates near Wakefield speaks of its head in the 1840s giving an occasional science lecture, 'which would be laughed to scorn by a School Board lad of the 5th or 6th standard'.[27] On the other hand Bootham, the Quaker School in York, had established a Natural History Society in 1834, and the standard of the science teaching 30 years later was praised by the Taunton Assistant Commissioner. Lectures were given on chemistry, physics, mechanics, hydrostatics, anatomy and physiology, and there was a particularly successful course, with working models, on the steam engine. The difficulty was - and this was a common problem of the day - that science was not yet organized as a regular part of the curriculum. The lecturer at Bootham had the whole school - staff and pupils - in front of him. 'The lectures were in fact organized on the basis of discourses before a philosophical society, more even than of a professor to his students.'[28] Once the charm of novelty had worn off, most of the boys must have found it all difficult to follow. However some teachers were successful. Charles Pritchard at Clapham, himself a Cambridge

Wrangler and later an astronomer of distinction, gave a weekly lesson which covered at different times heat, hydrostatics, mechanics and optics, electricity and chemistry. One of his pupils, G G Bradley, later a public-school headmaster and head of an Oxford college, wrote that these lessons were eagerly awaited. Perhaps the boys did not learn a great deal of science, but they did learn 'a sense of the greatness and importance of the world of science, whose door was at least set ajar for us, a sense that once given us nothing could efface'.[29]

One particularly interesting school was Queenwood College in Hampshire under the Quaker George Edmondson. Edmondson's prospectus shows that the school taught the usual mixture of classical and modern subjects, together with 'Book-keeping, Surveying, Geometry, Algebra, Mechanical Drawing, the elements of Chemistry, Botany, Geology and Mineralogy' in the highest division.[30] Edmondson also taught a group of older students about 18 years of age who, as he wrote to a correspondent, 'are here for the study of particular branches, such as Chemistry, Civil Engineering, Agriculture &c in all of which branches I have competent assistants'. The school was therefore a mixture between an ordinary private school and a technical college for young men. Some of Edmondson's 'competent assistants' were to become scientists of distinction, especially the physicist John Tyndall, professor at the Royal Institution, and the chemist Edward Frankland of the Royal Colleges of Chemistry and of Mines. In 1848 they were lecturing on chemistry (organic, inorganic and agricultural), on botany and vegetable physiology, and on the steam engine and railways. A few numbers of the school magazine have survived. Much of it consists of the usual collection of general essays and accounts of school visits, but some interesting light is also thrown on the science work. For example, there is an account of Dr Fox's course on physiology. Among the questions he asked were 'Name the two grand divisions of the kingdom of nature and give some of the distinguishing characters of each class', and 'How do you account for the fact of a man being able to swallow while standing on his head?' The answer expected to the latter question was that food does not descend by gravitation, but by the action of the muscles of the gullet which drive the food downwards until it reaches the stomach. The school had a laboratory, printing office, carpenter's and blacksmith's shops. The boys did practical chemistry and particularly chemical analysis, and there are accounts of surveying work similar to those already quoted. Edmondson ran Queenwood until his death in 1863, but the earlier years up to about 1855 saw the school's most interesting work in science teaching.

Few schools had such a developed science programme as Queenwood, but there are a surprising number of other references. Of the schools and masters already mentioned, J C Bruce at Newcastle gave regular science courses, and the Pestalozzian Dr Heldenmaier of Worksop maintained a chemistry laboratory and a natural history museum.[31] At Cheam Charles Reiner taught science and in particular chemistry.[32] The Hills appointed E W Brayley to teach science in 1829, and both Hazelwood and Bruce Castle had laboratories. The teaching consisted both of lectures with demonstrations given to the whole school and of class lectures to fifteen/twenty boys, based on work from a textbook. Brayley announced a most ambitious and comprehensive course which was never put into effect, though in 1830 lectures were being given at Bruce Castle on combustion and on vegetable and animal chemistry. However these plans were never fully realized. The project of introducing science into the regular instruction had to be given up, and the teaching was limited to occasional lectures for pupils who wished to take them.[33]

Science teaching appeared too in some of the schools run by religious bodies. Bootham has already been mentioned. At Methodist Woodhouse Grove Samuel Parker, who became head in 1816, gave a weekly science lecture,[34] and at another Methodist school at Taunton, opened in 1843, the first head, Thomas Sibly, taught science as a regular subject.[35] Finally, among private-school masters, the Nesbits, father and son, make an interesting pair. The father, Anthony (1778–1859), had a school in Manchester and later moved to London. He wrote a number of books, in particular a work on land surveying which went into many editions. The son, John Collis (1818–62), helped his father to run the school in London, 'being one of the first to introduce the teaching of science into an ordinary school course'. He laid particular stress on chemistry and each pupil did practical work in the laboratory. Later the school was converted into a chemical and agricultural college, and J C Nesbit built up a large practice as an analytical chemist.[36]

Too much must not be claimed for private school science. No doubt many of the lectures announced in school prospectuses were very superficial, and even successful schoolmasters like the Hills failed to make science a part of the regular school course. There were no trained teachers and no developed curriculum skills. Yet the examples which have been given do show that something was being achieved by the science teaching of private-school masters. Their efforts show both the extent of the demand and their readiness to experiment with new ideas.

NOTES AND REFERENCES

1. Benson, Edwin 1932. There are statistics of schools in York in *SIC* IX, pp 333-5
2. These estimates are based on the work of Harrison J A 1958-69; for the individual schools see Parts V and VI. The total number of mistresses will have been slightly greater than this because in several instances a school was kept by 'the misses', but we are not told how many sisters there were. I have reckoned only one mistress per school in these cases
3. Collingwood C S 1897 p 140. This book is the source of my information about Cowan's school
4. Quoted in Bruce, Sir Gainsford 1905 p 7
5. Williamson J B 1903 pp 91-2
6. *Ibid.* p 241
7. Bruce, Sir Gainsford 1905 p 68
8. Leinster-Mackay D P 1972 reproduces (Appendix 10): 'An Outline of the system of education pursued in the Percy Street Academy, Newcastle on Tyne under the direction of John Collingwood Bruce, A.M.'
9. Bruce, Sir Gainsford 1905 pp 72, 74
10. Quoted in Collins, Philip 1963 pp 30-1
11. On the family in general see Dobson J L 1959-61 II (10): 261-71; III (11): 1-11; III (12): 74-84. Sadler, Michael 1923: 15-25. Hey, Colin G 1954
12. The following section is based on the brothers' book, *Public Education*
13. C G Hey says that 10/15 per cent of the roll in the 1820s were foreign boys
14. Public Education - Hazelwood School 1825: 315-35. The quotation is on p 333
15. Sargant W L 1870 vol II, p 191. The whole passage on the school is on pp 185-92
16. Bache, Alexander Dallas 1839 pp 409-16
17. Robert Goodacre's Standard Hill Academy in Nottingham possessed in 1808 a microscope, electrical machine, air pump, a prism, barometer, thermometer, quadrant, an orrery, and instruments for land surveying (Wadsworth, F Arthur 1941: 66)
18. Shoveller, John 1824 esp. pp 46/7, 51, 67, 124, 130
19. Abraham J H 1805
20. Bache, Alexander Dallas 1839 pp 402-9. The quotation is on p 407
21. The following account is based on papers about Green Row Academy in the Cumbria Record Office, Carlisle
22. Pritchard, Ada 1897 p 28
23. Hunt, Harold C 1942: 183-4
24. *VCH Middlesex* vol I p 273
25. Musson A E, Robinson, Eric 1969 Science and industry in the late eighteenth century *Science and Technology in the Industrial Revolution.* pp 87-189
26. Hearl T W p 182
27. Oakley H Hislop 1920 p 26
28. Pollard F E (ed) 1926 pp 141-2
29. Bradley G G 1884: 455-74. The quotation is on p 461
30. For a general account of the school under Edmondson, see Thompson D 1955: 246-54. The material about the prospectus, the magazines and

A History of Secondary Education, 1800–1870

Edmondson's letters comes from a small collection of papers in the Hants RO

31. For Heldenmaier, see Leinster-Mackay D P 1980: 214–15
32. Stewart W A C, McCann W P 1967 p 175
33. Hey, Colin G 1954 ch 7
34. Gregory, Benjamin 1903 p 91
35. Sibly gave evidence to the Taunton Commission, *SIC* V, pp 337–45. See also Pritchard F C 1949 pp 168–9. This school is now known as Queen's College Taunton
36. *DNB*: Nesbit, Anthony; Nesbit, John Collis

134

CHAPTER NINE
Some teachers and their pupils

The fate of any nineteenth-century school depended very much on the personal qualities of the teachers who ran it. Something has already been said about the masters of grammar schools. The masters and mistresses of private and proprietary schools were a less homogeneous group. Most grammar-school heads were clergymen. The principals of private schools came from many trades and professions, and some of them moved out of teaching as readily as they had moved into it, if better opportunities offered. Some private-school masters prospered, but many of them struggled along on the margin of success and failure. Their calling lacked prestige and professional status. They were too much at the mercy of charlatans within their own rank and of pressure from parents who preferred the meretricious and the showy to the solid fruits of scholarship. They were expected to achieve too much with boys and girls who were sent to them for too short a time.

Teaching often seems to have been a family occupation as it was in the family of the sociologist Herbert Spencer. His father began teaching as a boy in the school of his own father. At the age of 17 he began giving private lessons, and he continued to do this after his marriage, while he was also running his own school and acting as honorary secretary to the Derby Philosophical Society. He overworked himself as a result, and moved from Derby to Nottingham, where he tried unsuccessfully to enter the lace manufacture. Later he came back to Derby to take private pupils. His son Herbert was at first sent to a day school conducted by 'a very ordinary mechanical kind of teacher who had no power of interesting his pupils in what they were taught'. When he was ten, Herbert was sent to a school conducted by his uncle William, who had inherited his own father's school and had managed it for some years until his health broke down. After he recovered he started teaching again and Herbert was one of a small number of pupils. At William Spencer's school Herbert learned little Latin and Greek but he learned to draw and he did 'experiments with pulleys and levers' which gave him a basic understanding of physical science. Later he spent three years with another uncle, Thomas, a clergyman with a living near Bath who prepared pupils for the university, though Herbert was only 13 when he went there. He learned, he says, a fair amount of mathematics from Thomas Spencer and though the education offered was narrow, he benefited a great deal by being made to apply himself to his work. In 1836 when he was 16 he came to home to Derby and taught for a year in the school of his first master. In November 1837 he was offered an appointment under an engineer of the London to Birmingham railway, who had been a private pupil of his father's.[1]

Spencer's account brings out the strong family connection among many teachers, something of the strong and weak points of what private school teachers could offer, and the importance, when he is offered an engineering appointment, of private connection at a time when career opportunities were much more personal and much less institutionalized than they later became. It is noteworthy too that two of the Spencer brothers had to give up teaching for a time through overwork. A successful private-school teacher had to work very hard, and though some were very successful, they lived very near the line of bankruptcy and failure, and a serious epidemic among the pupils, a major accident, a hint of personal scandal, the onset of old age or illness could all too easily push a school over that line.

The private-school master or mistress lacked the cushion provided for the grammar-school master by his house and endowment income, and he or she was completely at the mercy of the parents, who might or might not pay their bills. The account books of a south Midland schoolmaster, Joseph Randell, illustrate the problems. He seems to have had a school at Brackley (Northants) from 1817 to 1820 when he went bankrupt. From 1820 to 1824/25 he had a school at Bicester (Oxon.), and in 1829 he opened another school at Brill (Bucks). The Brill school was not short of pupils. In 1830–33 he had an average of fifty-two – both girls and boys and some boarders. The returns were not likely to have been very high because the school gave only basic elementary instruction, but the account books show a steadily increasing burden of debt. A considerable and increasing sum was carried forward from quarter to quarter on the income side, which was presumably fees owed to him but not paid. It was little use attracting pupils if the parents did not pay their bills. The final entry in the ledger is for Midsummer 1833 after which it seems likely that bankruptcy followed.[2] The master paid the price too when numbers fell, even in a denominational school with a semi-public foundation. The Rev. W J Hope was head of the school for the sons of Congregational ministers at Lewisham in South London from 1823 to 1852. The financial circumstances of the school were difficult. In 1835 Hope had been given a salary of £200 without any allowance for a house, a sum which he regarded as barely sufficient to maintain a large family, and in 1852, after nearly 30 years' service, his salary was cut from £200 to £100 per annum. He saw no way of making ends meet under the new arrangement and decided to emigrate to Australia. His letter of resignation strikes a note of genuine pathos[3]:

> Finding it will be impossible for me to maintain my family with the salary allowed by the new arrangement, seeing little probability of adequately augmenting it by private teaching, and not much relishing the idea of a residence in the Poor House or in the Queen's Bench, I have come to the determination to emigrate to Australia and cast myself with family on a gracious Providence, trusting that He at least who has helped us hitherto will not now forsake us.
> ...
> May it never fall to the lot of any member of the Committee to experience in his sixty-fifth year such a trial as has befallen the master of the Congregational School.

If the position of the masters and mistresses was in many cases so unfavourable, the position of their assistants was even worse. Resident assistants in boarding schools were underpaid and were often treated like servants. An article of 1838 divided up the assistants in several groups.[4] Some were very young, a kind of apprentice receiving no salary; others received their board and lodging and a small gratuity; a third group were men from 20 to 30 years of age receiving a salary of £20–100 per year. Many of them were preparing for college, others hoped some day to keep schools of their own, others had no such expectation – 'men who go on from year to year spending all they get ... men of no character whatever'. All teachers, whether masters or assistants, were very much at the mercy of the agents through whom posts were filled and in whose interest it was, since they were paid on commission, that assistants should not remain very long in the same post. Assistants moved about too because of the reluctance of masters to increase their assistants' salaries since 'the public are not ready to pay large sums for instruction'. In a highly competitive market masters often remained in business by exploiting those who helped them to run their schools. The position of the women was even worse than that of the men. In an age of industrial and commercial expansion a man of character and personality could find other openings. For a lady of education, teaching, whether as a governess in a private family or as an assistant in a school, was the only opening available. The wretched position of the governess was one of the hardest worked of Victorian literary conventions. It would be highly desirable, wrote a woman author in 1838, to provide other career opportunities for women, many of whom were quite unfitted for teaching work. 'The prejudice against ladies being employed in various other occupations seems to be inveterate.'[5]

The careers of a few individuals can be traced. Robert Whitaker became superintendent of the Quaker School at Ackworth in 1805. Born in Lancashire in 1766, he had been educated in local schools and had been taught classics and mathematics by a clergyman. At 18 he was appointed master of the Friends' school at Crawshabooth and later of a Friends' boarding school at Llanidloes in Montgomeryshire. After 4 years there he was appointed bookkeeper and assistant in the school at Ackworth in 1796. He remained superintendent from his appointment in 1805 till 1834.[6] Some 20 years later in 1853 the testimonials offered by J E Adams when he started his own private school in Sheffield make it possible to reconstruct his curriculum vitae.[7] He had, he claimed, 'been regularly educated and brought up to the Scholastic Profession' and he had 23 years' experience. He had been educated at the school in Poland Street, Oxford Street, London, where he had been the chief assistant for several years. He had taught at schools in Romford, Edmonton, Milton (near Gravesend), Margate and Kelvedon (Essex), sometimes remaining in a post for only a few months. In January, 1847 he had become third master at the Sheffield Collegiate School where he had been in charge of the writing and arithmetic teaching and had taught the lower classes French, Latin and Greek. During this period of 6½ years he had, wrote the principal Dr Jacob, 'continued to discharge the duties of his mastership much to my satisfaction'.

Among his testimonials Adams included his certificate as Licentiate of the College of Preceptors to which he had been admitted in January, 1847, at the first examination held by the college.[8] Teachers in private schools were poorly paid, poorly qualified and lacking in social status. The foundation of the College of Preceptors was a brave attempt by private-school masters themselves to raise the standard by providing a system of training and examinations which would in the end produce a better qualified teaching force. Mr Adams, for example, was examined in 'Bible History, the Theory and Practice of

Education, Classics, Mathematics, Commercial Education and French Language'. The scheme was a very ambitious one, aiming at professional qualifications controlled by teachers themselves. Initiated in 1846 by a group of private-school masters at Brighton, the college received a royal charter in 1849. Its objectives and some of the difficulties in the way of achieving them were explained a few years later in papers read to the Social Science Association. In 1857 E R Humphreys looked forward to the college providing a central board with government sanction and enjoying 'the power to admit into or exclude from the profession all candidates whatever. Such board to consist chiefly or entirely of men who had proved their scholarship and their ability as teachers.'[9] In 1862 Dr Jacob (of Sheffield) pointed out what had been achieved in examining both teachers and pupils, though there were many problems in providing training of which teachers in middle-class schools could avail themselves, particularly when posts could be obtained without any training at all. There was a need, he argued, for an Act to register qualified teachers.[10]

The high hopes of the early days came to nothing. Very few teachers came forward to be examined. Payne, lecturing in 1868, said that the average of the past 7 years had been four. Since the diplomas were not necessary in order to obtain work there was no incentive to take them, and there was no likelihood of Parliament giving the college any formal powers. Moreover its qualifications lacked standing because they were awarded on easy terms to people with small claims to enjoy them. The college's only success was in providing examinations for schools, a field which it entered in the early 1850s. These examinations, though they filled the college coffers, perhaps distracted it from its original objective of creating better-trained teachers. Under the conditions of the day that was a very difficult objective to achieve because the private schools were not capable of organization; in an individualistic society it was every man and woman for himself. There were, however, some more modest attempts at training which ought to be mentioned. One major objective of F D Maurice and the other founders of Queen's College, opened in 1848, had been the better education of governesses (see p. 296). The training of teachers for their schools was a particular concern of the Quakers. At Ackworth apprentices who were articled for 6 or 7 years had been engaged since 1782. At the girls' school, The Mount at York, in 1835 the committee decided to admit (at lower fees) four or five girls at a time who were to prepare as teachers.[11] By 1856 fifty-four young women had been thus assisted, more than half of whom were still employed in Friends' schools or families.

'Inadequate as is the present supply of competent teachers in the schools and families of Friends, the deficiency must obviously have been still greater, but for the provision thus made; a provision which York Quarterly Meeting is now desirous of enlarging.'[12] For boys over the age of 15 and older students the Flounders Institute had been opened near Ackworth School in 1848 as the result of a bequest for the training of teachers. At the time of the Taunton Commission inquiry (1864) the course lasted for 3 years and the students were encouraged to take London University examinations.[13]

The creation of a better-trained and better-educated body of teachers was a very desirable change which happened all too slowly. It did, however, make it difficult or impossible for school-keeping to provide a means of social advancement as it had clearly been at the beginning of the nineteenth century. It is remarkable how many of the successful private-school masters who have been mentioned here were men of little formal education. Thomas Wright Hill, founder of the Hazelwood family, had left school at 14 to be apprenticed to a brass founder. Both John Bruce of Newcastle and his brother Edward were self-educated. A draft letter has survived, written by them to a professor at Edinburgh, enquiring whether there was any prospect of finding employment there and at the same time attending lectures in the university.

> We may say with propriety ... that the whole of our life has been employed in teaching others and instructing ourselves. For having no other means of accomplishing the latter than by attempting the former we commenced teachers at a very early period. To a man of science it will be needless to point out the difficulties we have encountered, when after experiencing the lassitude and fatigues of a common school, and frequently of an evening school, we had to devote the remaining hours of the day, and sometimes part of the night to the study of mathematics, which was always our favourite pursuit.

Many years later John's wife, encouraging their son to persevere with his algebra and mathematics, cited her husband's example of determination, without which 'how very inferior a rank in society he would have been able to fulfil to what he now does, and how very differently he must have brought up his children to what he now hopes to do ... '.[14] Another successful schoolmaster family like the Bruces were the Goodacres of Standard Hill Academy, Nottingham. The first of them, Robert, had been a journeyman tailor who became assistant to a master at Mansfield and then opened his own day school in Nottingham in 1797.[15] The examples which have been given are all early – around 1800. Later in the century the Dorset poet, William

Barnes, who for a number of years ran a successful school in Dorchester, was another master whose formal schooling had ended at 13. In the end, after his wife's death, the school failed, and by 1860 there were few pupils left. There may have been many reasons for Barnes's eventual failure, but his recent biographer, Mr T W Hearl, suggests that one reason may have been his unwillingness to adjust to the norms of middle-class society.[16] Certainly by the 1850s there was keen competition between schools which made it more difficult to survive.

Throughout the period the line between a man who took private pupils in his own house and the man who ran a small school was difficult to draw. The point has already been made that it was common to move children from school to school. One identifiable form of movement was from the local school (grammar, private or proprietary) to one of the major public schools. Another was the tendency to send boys from school to a private tutor who would prepare them for university or for professional employment. The ledger of C E Meyrick's school at Ramsbury (Wilts.) show that a number of his boys went on to Eton, Winchester and Charterhouse; in other words the school was providing the service offered by preparatory schools later,[17] though many of the boys stayed there for much longer periods. Sometimes boys went from proprietary schools to a public school for the last 2 years or so of their schooling. Thus the Bowen brothers, the Harrow housemaster and the Lord Justice, went from Blackheath Proprietary School to Rugby (1850 and 1851),[18] and Henry Jackson, later Regius Professor of Greek at Cambridge, from Sheffield Collegiate School to Cheltenham (1855).[19] An extreme example of this tendency to move schools is the case of A J C Hare. At 9 years of age he went to a very Evangelical private school in Wiltshire. This was followed by a year at Harrow (1847–48), but he was taken away because he was ill, and sent to private tutors. The first of these proved to be quite unsatisfactory and after two years there he was sent to the Rev. Charles Bradley at Southgate in Middlesex, an eccentric man with whom his personal relationships were often very difficult, but who was an exciting and enthusiastic teacher – 'the only person who ever taught me anything, and that he did not teach me more than he did was entirely my own fault'. From Bradley's tuition he went up to Oxford in March 1853.[20]

Some correspondence has survived which throws light on the relationship between the private tutor and the parent whose son was being prepared for the university. W J Butler prepared two sons of Col. G W Blathwayt of Dyrham Park, Glos. for Cambridge in the early 1840s. The two boys, Wynter and Richard, had previously been pupils at King's School, Bruton. Wynter, Mr Butler thought, had been excellently brought up and had good abilities. However his classics were weak and he had never been taught to read accurately.

> He just wants what I expected, and that is Public School manners and Public School Scholarship. He is rather rough, you will understand what I mean. But even here he is already much improved and I have no doubt that he will go on improving.

Richard, the younger of the two, was docile and well disposed, sharp in matters of ordinary life, and quick at games and exercises. But he was very backward 'owing to a careless disposition on his part and careless teaching on that of his late instructor'. 'Wynter ... used his wits. But Richard no sooner takes up his books than he seems to put his wits off.' Until these faults were overcome 'reading is very toilsome work for both Tutor and Pupil'. Both boys got into Trinity, Wynter in 1843 and Richard in 1845, so Mr Butler's efforts must have been reasonably successful.[21] The tutor/pupil relationship could present problems. The Rev. A W Headlam and Mr Ross took their differences to the arbitration of W C Mathison, tutor of Trinity College, Cambridge because they could not agree about the tuition fee to be paid for Ross's son Edward (1859–60). The agreed fee was £150 per annum plus extras. Headlam claimed that Edward had absented himself and that, if he was not as well prepared for college as his father had expected, this was because of the time he had spent deerstalking and rifle-shooting. The family argued that Headlam had charged fees for 21 months while Edward had been with him for only 13 months and that he had not received the amount of individual supervision which had been promised because Headlam had increased the number of his pupils. There is no record in the correspondence of Mr Mathison's decision[22]; the letters do illustrate very clearly the problems which could arise between a young man and his tutor, who did not possess the sanctions available to a schoolmaster with younger boys.

To any parent whether he was a country gentleman like Col. Blathwayt or a poor clergyman like the Rev. Francis Hall of Greasbrough whom we are soon to meet, efficient preparation for a future career was a matter of great importance. Though middle-class parents were criticized for taking their children away from school too young, it seems likely that, as the generations succeeded one another, rather more education was demanded for the children, both in quality and in quantity. The miller, Mr Tulliver, in George Eliot's *The Mill on the Floss*, is clearly not a man of much education himself, but he is recommended by his friend, Mr Riley, to send his son Tom away to board with a clergyman as a private pupil, and takes the advice. Not only, urges Mr Riley, is a clergyman 'a gentleman by profession and education', but 'he has the knowledge that will ground a boy and prepare him for entering on any career with credit'.[23]

Two important careers of the time were the Indian civil and military services and engineering, into which were recruited two sons of Mr C R Sperling of Great Maplestead in Essex.[24] In 1840 the family were discussing the future of his son, Charles, who wanted to be an engineer. There was discussion about getting an introduction to I K Brunel, but eventually he went as a pupil to Mr Edward Lomax, 2 Queen Sq., St James's Park at a fee of 150 guineas for 2 years with permission to go on at a further fee of 50 guineas per annum. 'The pupil to be maintained by his friends while at my offices in London and Bedfordshire – at all other times, on business, his expenses will be paid by me', (30 November 1840). In the course of the negotiations about the pupilage Lomax wrote to Mr Sperling (26 December 1840):

> I assure you, Sir, I cannot think a father too troublesome, or too careful in a matter of so much importance, as the choice of a profession for his son. I am a father too, and can well understand your feelings. I should be sorry you did not thoroughly satisfy yourself in every particular. The parents of my present pupils are the references I am proud to offer of how I have fulfilled the charge I have undertaken.

Later letters suggest that Charles Sperling worked well with Mr Lomax. The last of them ends: 'We are all bustle with our parliamentary plans, which will turn out well' (19 February 1842). The railway age had begun, and with it much work for civil engineers. About 15 years later in 1855 a younger brother Frederick went to Mr Sherrat of Southlands, Battersea to prepare for the Indian military services. His terms were 120 guineas a year with no extras. In a letter home Frederick wrote[25]:

> I have been working at my Arithmetic and Euclid in wh: they are rather strict at Addiscombe, Roman Grecian and English History – Fortification – French and Latin the two latter I just keep up – as I did a great deal of my Latin with Mr Bell.

Professional preparation of this kind was clearly expensive and within the means of only a few parents. The concerns of a father of much more modest means are revealed in the letters of the Rev. Francis Hall, vicar of Greasbrough near Rotherham in the West

Riding, who had a son, John, at Christ's Hospital in London (1838–43), and other sons in local private schools. In May, 1839 Mr Hall had to find new schools for two of the boys, Frank and Sam, because Mr Langley, their schoolmaster, had been imprisoned for forgery and deceit and Hall himself had, as a result, lost some money (4 May 1839). Eighteen months later efforts were being made to find a situation for Frank. Finally (10 April 1841) Mr Hall wrote to John to report success: 'he is going to be a Clerk at the Thorncliffe Iron Works near Chapeltown. If he is a good and industrious boy the situation will be a good one.' Sam, who was lame, found it more difficult to get an opening; 'we are still without a situation for Sam and trade is becoming worse and worse. The Sheffield Old Bank has stopped payment and almost ruined Sheffield' (23 January 1843). By that time the education of a younger son, William, was causing Mr Hall concern. It was likely, he thought, that Lord Fitzwilliam, who was the great local magnate and who had obtained a nomination at Christ's Hospital for John, would do the same for the younger brother; 'he does not like the Latin grammar – but I will try to make him' (21 September 1842). John Hall left Christ's Hospital in April, 1843 aged 15. Mr Hall would have liked him to stay another year because that would, he thought, have extended his education and given him a better chance of finding a post. 'Situations are very scarce at present. It seems to me that a good situation in London would suit you the best' (3 December 1842). In the end things worked out well for John Hall. There is no evidence about what he did for the year after he left school, but on 1 May 1844 he was apprenticed to a chemist and druggist in Sheffield at a premium of £40, £10 of it paid by Christ's Hospital. Later he qualified MRCS and LSA and in 1856 was applying for the post of house surgeon at the General Infirmary, Sheffield.[26] It is likely, I think, that the medical profession offered a chance of social and professional advancement for some boys, particularly after the growth of local medical schools through which qualifications could be obtained.

The future careers of grammar-school boys have already been fully discussed, and not much can be added to this from the private and proprietary schools, who were serving much the same social group. I have found no information of this kind for the private schools and I doubt whether it exists, though there is material for denominational and proprietary schools. The boys of Woodhouse Grove, established in 1812, were in this period all sons of Wesleyan Methodist ministers. They stayed for 6 years, most commonly from the ages of 8 to 14. Their general social background will not have been very different from that

144

of Francis Hall's sons, one where education was valued, where means were modest and where pressures for professional and business success were strong. The trades and professions of some 600 old scholars up to 1877 are recorded, and they fall into the main divisions given in Table 9.

The careers of some of the old boys of the Collegiate School at Sheffield, admitted under Dr Jacob (1843–52), have been traced. The boys were the sons of the solid middle class of an industrial town, very much the same group as might equally well have been sent to the more prestigious kind of grammar school or private school. A number of the Collegiate-School boys went on subsequently to other schools, but that has been ignored in the list in Table 10. The 101 men

Table 9 Careers of old boys of Woodhouse Grove School to 1877

Methodist minister	153	Banks/insurance	22
C of E clergyman	26	Editor/journalist	8
Congregationalist/			
Baptist minister	4	Printer	20
Chemists/druggists	51	Lecturer/author	12
Medical practitioner	48	Tradesmen	62
Dentist	5	Manufacturers/managers	17
Home and Indian Civil		Merchants/agents	21
Service	8	Accountants/brokers	14
Barrister/solicitor	26	Miscellaneous	
Architects/surveyors	6	(from ship's captain to	
Engineers	21	photographer)	25
Teachers	34	Clerks, etc.	32

Source: Slugg J T 1885 pp 237–325; see also Pritchard F C 1949 pp 91–2.

Table 10 Careers of old boys of Sheffield Collegiate School

Clergymen	26	Medical practitioners	3
Manufacturers (of			
all kinds)	22	Architects	2
Barristers/			
solicitors	13	Engineers	2
Business/commerce	6	University professors	
Merchants/agents	5	(1 Oxford, 1 Cambridge)	2
Overseas (3 of them		Army officers	3
in Australia)	5	Clerks	3
Schoolmasters/		Miscellaneous e.g.	
HMI	4	('gentleman', RC	
		priest, lithographer)	5

Source: Sheffield Local Studies Library, Sheffield Collegiate School 1836–1885. A biographical register compiled by P J Wallis (typescript).

whose careers can be traced break down as shown in Table 10. The list has very much the same make-up as the material from the grammar schools already cited. Clergymen and lawyers are certainly over-represented because they are always very easy to trace. The large numbers of manufacturers reflect the economic concerns of a major industrial town.

NOTES AND REFERENCES

1. Spencer, Herbert 1949 pp 49-51, 53-4, 65-9, 84-9, 115, 122-5
2. Accounts of insolvent debtors 1807-46 (Bucks RO)
3. Stafford, Hugh 1945 · p 53. The school moved from Lewisham to Caterham in 1884
4. For the following, see Resident Assistants in Private Boarding Schools *CSE 2nd Publication* 1838 (reprinted 1968): 199-202
5. Ellis, Mildred The Education of young ladies of small pecuniary resources for other occupations than that of teaching, *ibid.*: 192-8. The quotation is on p 193
6. Thompson, Henry 1879 pp 86-7, 110, 197
7. Adams J E 1853 pp 8-12. For Adams see also p 103
8. Payne, Joseph 1883 On the past, present and future of the College of Preceptors pp 307-27. Roach, John 1971 pp 60-1, 90-1. The college's journal, the *Educational Times*, contains general articles on education and much about the history of the college
9. Humphreys E R 1857: 144
10. Jacob G A 1862: 235-45
11. Stewart W A C 1953 p 97. In 1836 the school was in Castlegate. It moved to The Mount in 1857
12. *York Quarterly Meeting's School for Girls and the training of female teachers* (Hodgkin Papers, 'Society of Friends Schools and Education', Co. Durham RO). The covering note from the committee is dated 3 mo 7th (7 March) 1856
13. *A Declaration of the views of the trustees of the Flounders Institute, relative to the educational trust reposed in them by the late Benjamin Flounders of Yarm* 6 mo 3 (3 June) 1848. (Hodgkin Papers, Co. Durham RO); Stewart W A C 1953 pp 100-1; Shanks R 1956-57: 221-7
14. Williamson J B 1903 pp 27-8, 135
15. Wadsworth, F Arthur 1941: 57-75. Goodacre and Cockayne's school was the first to take the school examinations of the College of Preceptors, December 1850 (Payne Joseph 1883 p 321)
16. Hearl T W 1966 pp 128, 272-4
17. Accounts of C E Meyrick's school, Ramsbury (Wilts RO)
18. Kirby J W 1933 p 47
19. Parry R StJ 1926 p 9
20. Hare A J C 1896 The quotation is on p 298
21. Collection of letters about the sons of G W Blathwayt. Blathwayt of

Dyrham papers, Glos RO. These letters are dated 7 November 1842 and 11 July (no year given). See Venn J A 1940–54, Vol 1, Wynter Thomas Blathwayt, Richard Vesey Blathwayt

22. A W Headlam, collection of letters about unpaid fees for Mr Ross's son, 1861–62 (Co. Durham RO)
23. Eliot, George *The Mill on the Floss* (Daily Express Publications 1933) p 27
24. Sperling papers and correspondence, Essex RO
25. *Ibid.* The Battersea letters are not dated. Addiscombe was the East India Company's military college.
26. Correspondence between the Rev Francis Hall and his son, John, 1838–43 (Sheffield Local Studies Library)

CHAPTER TEN
Girls' schools. Dotheboys Hall and its fellows

Before concluding this survey of the teachers and the private school world, more needs to be said about three groups within it: the preparatory schools; the very bad schools, those which provided the model for Dotheboys Hall; and, most important of the three, the girls' schools. The preparatory school can be dealt with very briefly because it lies on the fringe of secondary education as discussed in this book. The growth of such schools as providing a specific stage in the progress of a boy towards his public school which he entered at the age of about thirteen occurred during the final third of the century. It was linked closely with the appearance of a coherent group of established public schools, itself a late-nineteenth-century phenomenon. As we have seen, pupils moved about a great deal from school to school before 1860, and it was quite common for a boy to attend a grammar, a private or a proprietary school before being sent to Rugby or to Winchester. It has recently been argued that, between 1830 and 1865, a group of 'quasi-preparatory schools' was being formed, concentrating on the teaching of younger boys. One of the best-known schools in this group was Cheam, Dr Charles Mayo's school, which became definitely preparatory under R S Tabor (1855–90).[1] The fuller development of the preparatory school after 1865 lies outside our limits, but the change is an important one because it helped to increase the self-sufficiency of the major independent schools.

The private schools which were inefficient or worse loom large in Victorian writing. Dotheboys Hall does not stand alone. Alongside it can be placed the harshly oppressive atmosphere, the disease and death of Charlotte Brontë's Lowood, and the showy pretentiousness of 'the private adventure schools of the middle class' satirized by

Matthew Arnold. In one of his reports, for example, he contrasted a letter written by a girl in an elementary school in his district, which is plain, direct and vivid, with the showy, convoluted, over-ornate – and obviously dictated – letter written by a private-school boy to his parents. 'To those who ask', Arnold wrote, 'what is the difference between a public and a private school, I answer *It is this.*' In the one school the work was appraised by 'impartial educated persons', in the other by 'the common run of middle class parents'.[2] Arnold was in fact repeating the criticism which has already been noted that in many cases a better education was available to the children of the poor than to those of the middle classes (see p. 109). In the eyes of many critics the greatest weakness of the private schools was that there was no general standard by which their performance could be judged. Matthew Arnold argued that only the state could set such a standard. His father had made the same point in the 1830s, and the same theme is raised in one of the reports of his HMI brother, E P Arnold, on the schools of the borough of Bodmin in Cornwall. Bodmin had a National and a Wesleyan School, seven private schools and seven dames' schools. The standards of the first two could be tested because they were under government inspection, but what guarantee could there be of the character of the education in the others.[3]

J G Fitch, reporting for the Taunton Commission on the West Riding Schools, gave a very balanced judgment. There were, he said, many very good private schools, run with great enterprise, though the examples he gave made it clear that standards varied a good deal. The teaching profession was over-stocked, there were too many schools, and they were often too small. In the eighty-one schools for which he had statistics, the average numbers were about thirty. He found no school like Dotheboys Hall, and the food provided and the general standards of health were good enough. Masters were too much at the mercy of parents, who interfered a great deal, sometimes to insist on special privileges for their sons. 'At present', in his judgment, 'the number of schools in which no attempt has been made to comply with a false shop-keeping view of the purposes of education appears to me to be very small.' He was generally critical of the teaching, particularly of the time spent on activities like mercantile correspondence and making drawings of steam engines, which impressed parents but had little educational value. There was too much learning by heart, too much use of catechisms in all subjects and not enough oral teaching. Very few boys learned Greek and few boys had enough Latin to be able to read an author. A number of boys learned French but very few German. Fitch claimed that he had found four schools where the physical sciences were taught seriously, but elsewhere they were little studied and were confined to learning by heart from a manual. There was some teaching of Euclid and algebra, but little sign that enough of them had been learned for boys to be able to think for themselves about mathematical problems. Like all other observers who have been quoted, Fitch found few boys in private schools over the age of 16.[4]

The subject of the bad school and of the evil and incompetent teacher cannot be left without saying something more about Charles Dickens and the background to Mr Squeers in *Nicholas Nickleby* and Mr Creakle in *David Copperfield*.[5] Dickens's memories of his own schooling did not predispose him in favour of schoolmasters. In a speech of 1857 he criticized one of his schools, the Wellington House Classical and Commercial Academy kept by Mr Jones in Hampstead Road[6]:

> Its 'respected proprietor' was 'by far the most ignorant man I have ever had the pleasure to know', and 'one of the worst-tempered men perhaps that ever lived'. His business was 'to make as much out of us and to put as little into us as possible'. The school was, in short, 'a pernicious and abominable humbug altogether'.

The Yorkshire schools had long been objects of attack before the subject led Dickens to begin *Nicholas Nickleby*. They had a reputation for low fees and harsh treatment with the advantage of keeping boys out of the way in cases where families and friends wanted no close contact. Mr Squeers's advertisement, it is to be remembered, included the words 'No vacations'. William Shaw of Bowes Academy ran one of the largest of these schools with 200/300 boys, and he has been taken as the original of Mr Squeers though that luminary is probably a composite figure. Shaw's school had become prominent in 1823 when it had been attacked by an outbreak of ophthalmia. He was sued by parents of boys who had gone blind in consequence and had had to pay damages. Strangely one personal link with Shaw has survived – the agreement of 1810 in which he contracted to teach the pupils of George Clarkson, whose assistant he had previously been at Bowes, for an annual payment plus board and lodging.[7] There was at the time of the publication of Dickens's novel and for long afterwards keen controversy about the accuracy of the picture which he painted of these Yorkshire schools. In Philip Collins's view there was much truth in it, and he cites other examples like that of Richard Cobden whose 5 years in one of these schools was 'a grim and desolate time, of which he could never afterwards endure to speak ... ill fed, ill taught, ill used'.[8] Moreover Dickens's criticism did something to lessen the evils which he attacked. In many ways his picture of Mr Creakle in *David Copperfield* comes closer than that of Mr Squeers to the central criticisms of early Victorian schools which have been reviewed here. Creakle had come into teaching only when he had failed in trade. He relished cruel punishments. His management of the school was based on snobbery and obeisance to the pretensions of class. As the mother of the rich young Steerforth explained: 'my son's high spirit made it desirable that he should be placed with some man who felt its superiority, and would be content to bow himself before it'.

The powers of class and of personal preference were even more strongly felt in girls' schools than in boys'.[9] Great as were the problems of boys' education, the problems of girls' education were even greater. There were no accepted standards to which girls might work. The teachers were untrained and, even more than in the case of men, many of them had drifted into the work with little enthusiasm because there was nothing else they could do. Since middle-class girls looked forward to no career other than that of marriage there was none of the stimulus provided in boys' schools by the pressures of the job-market and the need to earn a living. Girls' schools were very numerous, though they were mostly very small, and few of them have left much trace behind them. Governesses in private houses were numerous too, but, although they appear a lot in Victorian literature,[10] they have left few traces in the educational records. In one of the Quaker schools, where boys and girls were educated in parallel, its modern historian has noted that much more is known about the boys' lives than the girls'.[11] Though the picture of girls' education in the first half of the century is a rather gloomy one, there were, as we shall see, some good girls' schools. The development of the education of the two sexes is different in the major sense. Boys' education changed through a slow continuous evolution. Girls' education was revolutionized in the 1860s and 1870s and put on a new footing, modelled principally on the education of boys. The revolutionaries were people like Barbara Bodichon, Emily Davies, Dorothea Beale and Frances Buss, whose careful and modest public demeanour must not disguise the fact that they were promoting a major change in the relationship between the sexes. Of course, older patterns died hard. Winifred Knox (Winifred Peck) daughter of E A Knox, later Bishop of Manchester, was born in 1882 and was sent to Miss Quill's academy at Eastbourne, run on lines unchanged from the days of early and mid-Victorian England.[12] Later in her girlhood she was sent to Wycombe Abbey, a girls' boarding school of the new type, so in her own education she bridged the gap between the old and the new.

Here we shall concentrate on the older world of the governess and the private school, since the new girls' education is more easily dealt with in relation to the events of the 1860s. The Taunton Commission report and evidence of that decade bridge the two eras. For the new they argued that girls had intellectual abilities similar in nature to boys and they claimed that girls should enjoy a share in educational endowments. For the old they passed a severe judgment on the schools which they found. Fitch, in his survey of the West Riding, collected information from about eighty schools, most of them very small with an average of about twenty-five pupils. These small schools were wasteful and expensive to run, the teaching was inefficient and the teachers untrained. Young girls were often ahead of young boys, but after the age of 12 the pattern changed. Most of the instruction, Fitch thought, was poorer than in boys' schools. Subjects were not pursued systematically and there was too little mental discipline in the teaching, particularly for the older girls. Too much time was spent on music and on fancy needlework, and, although more French was taught than in boys' schools, it was not taught well. The teaching of mathematics was very defective. As places of instruction, the more expensive schools were not necessarily better than the cheaper ones because of the weaknesses in the teaching. Women teachers had no stimulus to improve their standards.

> Many governesses who are working hard and conscientiously seeking to do their best, are scarcely aware of the stagnation of mind which exists around them, nor of the use which might be made of the materials in their hands if proper methods were employed. They have no standard of comparison. They know little or nothing of what is being done in schools under skilled teachers; and their pupils are subjected to no examination or other tests by which deficiencies might be revealed. The educational theories of a governess are necessarily suited to her circumstances. If she has never studied or taught beyond a certain range of subjects, everything beyond that range seems unnecessary.[13]

In their final report, the commissioners argued that the main obstacle to change was the unwillingness of many parents to take trouble over the education of their daughters, and their apathy, or even opposition, towards measures for improvement.[14]

No doubt many girls' schools of the early Victorian period were inefficient, but their pupils did learn something. What did these schools profess to teach? The curriculum in most of them covered the English subjects, arithmetic, French, geography, history, needlework and accomplishments such as music and drawing.[15] Some schools also offered science and mathematics, classics and other modern languages. This general picture is confirmed by some examples of schools of different kinds. A new school, recently established at Edinburgh in the 1830s, offered 'English and geography, writing and accounts and the languages', 'the ornamental branches – which include music, singing and drawing', and courses in chemistry, natural philosophy, botany and geology.[16] This was clearly quite an ambitious plan. A school run on similar though more modest lines in Liverpool was described by J S Howson to the Social Science Association in 1859. It had been running for three years and had an average attendance of about seventy-seven.[17] An earlier school had been set up in Liverpool in 1844 by the Mechanics' Institution for the daughters of tradesmen, clerks and shopkeepers. In numbers the school was an immediate success. In 1846 there were 291 in the senior school and 52 infants. The course to be offered to these lower-middle-class girls was planned in broad lines with mention of vocal music, drawing, natural philosophy and chemistry. In practice what was offered, in the early days at least, was the English subjects, including geography and history, arithmetic, writing, drawing and needle-work. A few girls also learned French.[18]

It is noteworthy that many of the better girls' schools had a specifically religious or denominational basis. Many of them were 'private foundation schools' (see p. 7). Of the religious schools pre-eminence must be given to the schools of the Roman Catholic religious orders, particularly since their major contribution to girls' education is often ignored. By 1850 there were over twenty orders of nuns in active teaching work, both in parish schools for the poor and in schools for the middle class.[19] Among the Dissenting bodies both the Quakers and the Unitarians were prominent. Some Quaker schools like Ackworth taught boys and girls in parallel. In 1831 the York Quarterly Meeting established a girls' school which in 1857 moved to The Mount, the name by which it is always known. The teaching there in 1860 was thorough but fairly limited in scope. As was so often the case the teachers had little opportunity to prepare themselves for their work.[20]

The Unitarian contribution was personal and private rather than institutional. They wanted women to develop their powers through enjoying the best education possible. In that way women would fulfil their natural role more effectively and promote the general advancement of mankind. Some Unitarian women moved outside the home circle, though it was not generally expected that they would adopt a public role equal to that of men.[21] The conduct of girls' schools among the Unitarians was often closely linked with the ministerial family. Mrs Carpenter and her daughters ran a girls' school at Bristol, which succeeded to the boys' school run by Lant Carpenter until his illness.[22] Mary Carpenter had been taught by her father alongside his boy pupils, like Sarah Beard, daughter of the Manchester schoolmaster-divine, John Relly Beard (1800–76). Sarah Beard's first school, where she began Latin at the age of eight, was taught by two sisters, daughters of another Unitarian minister – 'though Miss Johns was not severe, she insisted on the greatest accuracy in our lessons'. Sarah then went to her father's school where she did the same lessons as her brother until he went to college. Her father, she thought, was a really splendid teacher, and she had always been grateful for the education which he had given her. At 15 her parents sent her away for a year to a boarding school near Warwick, run by the daughter of a minister, William Field, who had for many years run a boys' school in the same house. Here, though she could manage the lessons easily, she was less happy. One of her friends, she thought, had passed a much more useful year at Miss Rachel Martineau's school at Liverpool.[23] Miss Martineau's brother James, who was to become one of the leading Unitarians of the century, had himself been a pupil of Lant Carpenter's at Bristol. This close contexture of family and chapel relationships gave a solid weight to Unitarian efforts in education, though they lacked the institutional structure provided by the Quakers.

A Methodist principal who ran a very successful school was Hannah E Pipe of Laleham, Clapham Park in south London. Born in Manchester into a strongly Wesleyan circle, she was much influenced by W B Hodgson, who in 1847 became principal of a school in Manchester and who had previously been secretary of the Liverpool Mechanics' Institution. Hodgson was very interested in girls' education – he had induced his Liverpool committee to start the school already mentioned in 1844 – and Hannah Pipe joined the classes for girls which he ran in Manchester. Hodgson encouraged her to become a teacher.[24] She opened a school, first in Manchester, and then in 1856 she and her mother removed their school to London, after assuring themselves that their Methodist clientele would be prepared to send their daughters south as boarders. In London there were no day girls. Most of the pupils came from well-to-do Wesleyan families in Lancashire and Yorkshire, homes, as one of her teachers wrote, 'where money abounded but no culture'.[25]

Miss Pipe defined her aims in a letter to an enquirer written about the time that she started her school in London. She explained that she herself taught English, with special attention to poetry and to grammar and composition, ancient and modern history and geography. Each day she took a Bible class in which she aimed to relate religion to the duties of ordinary life and particularly to the duties of girls at school. No use was made, in the management of the school, of prizes, good or bad marks, stated rewards and punishments. Much attention was given to polite accomplishments which ought, she believed, to form an important part of a thorough education. The languages and the sciences were entrusted to other resident teachers and to visiting lecturers. Above all, Miss Pipe wrote,[26]

> My energies and efforts are mainly concentrated in the training of those powers of mind and heart that fit a woman for the thoughtful and intelligent performance of her duties in life, the cultivation of judgment and imagination, the implanting of sound tastes and the formation of sound habits.

It is rare to find a teacher – man or woman – expressing basic objectives with such clarity and vigour. Miss Pipe was not preparing her girls for professional life because such preparation was not required by their parents nor by the social duties which they were likely to fulfil, but, within the context in which she operated, she had a very clear view of the relationship between the education of girls and their life in the world which was to follow it, and there is nothing mean or petty in her aspirations. Clearly her pupils and teachers liked and respected her. She recruited some distinguished men as lecturers like the poet and novelist George MacDonald and the astronomer (Sir) William Huggins. Indeed the teaching of some of these men brought her under the criticism of the Wesleyan authorities, but she overcame these early difficulties and the school became very successful. The numbers were not large. In 1861 there were twenty-six pupils, and the general impression left by Laleham at that time is of a large and cultured household where Miss Pipe and her girls met in the evenings, sang, played instruments, listened to readings from books and newspapers, and got on with their needlework. Miss Pipe's ideas were not always those of the innovators. A letter has survived to Emily Davies in which she expressed herself as being very doubtful about the value of the new examinations for girls.[27] Her school was a very good example of the private school of the older kind. She did not retire until 1890 – and in her later years a number of her girls did go on to Newnham and Girton.[28]

Miss Pipe's school is of particular interest and deserves a lengthy treatment, but shorter sketches can be drawn of several others.

Another successful school with a strong denominational character was that of Miss Jane Procter and her sisters who opened a boarding school for the daughters of Quaker families in Darlington in 1848; the school moved to Polam in 1854. The Procters generally had about forty girls. The girls came down to the schoolrooms by seven in the morning. After breakfast at eight there were lessons from nine till twelve, followed by recreation for an hour and dinner at one. The afternoons were spent sewing, reading or drawing and the older girls used that time to 'prepare for the masters'. Preparation for all was from four to five, followed by tea, bread and butter, with the evening spent all sitting together in the dining room, reading or working. More bread and butter at eight was followed by evening reading and bed. Jane Procter herself was an early advocate of greater independence for women. She was unusual among private-school mistresses in having strong outside interests. She was active in 'First Day Schools', in the Women's temperance movement, and she was on the committee of the Darlington Training College. She died in 1882 while on a visit to an old scholar in Rome.[29]

It is possible, though there is no evidence, that Miss Pipe and Miss Procter sometimes used that great stand-by of the Victorian schoolroom, Richmal Mangnall's *Historical and Miscellaneous Questions for the use of young people*, which went through many editions after its first anonymous publication in 1798.[30] Miss Mangnall was born in 1769 and died in 1820. She went to Crofton Old Hall near Wakefield as a pupil, became an assistant there, and finally headmistress in about 1808 when there were some seventy girls. *The Questions* may have been a response to the demands of her own teaching. Miss Mangnall was probably a successful headmistress because she left £13,000 when she died, though the rights in the *Questions* had earlier been sold to the publishers, Longmans.[31]

At about the same time as Miss Mangnall became headmistress at Crofton, the Misses Byerley opened their school at Warwick (1810). They were well educated, being able to teach Latin, French and Italian, and they went regularly to London to keep in touch with the latest 'accomplishments' which were important to the prosperity of girls' schools. The sisters had financial difficulties in the early days but the school moved in 1817 to more spacious quarters at Barford and then in 1824 to 'Avonbank', Straford-upon-Avon. The two sisters, Maria and Jane, who had continued to run it, finally gave it up in 1840/41. In 1828 the school was said to be flourishing with thirty-nine pupils. The sisters were Anglican and the pupils attended their parish church, but the school also attracted girls from Dissenting families, one of whom was the Unitarian Elizabeth Stevenson, the future novelist Mrs Gaskell, who came in 1822 and left in 1827, when she was 17. Winifred Gérin, in her recent biography, argues that the sisters gave Elizabeth an education which was both balanced and stimulating and which encouraged her imagination. 'Perhaps the quality that she owed most to the teaching of Avonbank was her total absence of false gentility.'[32] To say that is to praise the Byerley sisters highly in the social context of their time.

Most of the girls' schools which have been described drew on a clientele which was well-to-do or of at least moderate means. Elizabeth Stevenson's father, for example, was a civil servant. Many charitable people were concerned with the education of girls from less affluent homes, like clergymen's daughters, who would need to earn their own livings. One such would-be benefactor was the Rev. William Carus Wilson, Charlotte Brontë's 'Mr Brocklehurst of Lowood'.[33] A similar institution, which did not achieve the notoriety of the school at Cowan Bridge, was described by the Cambridge diarist, Joseph Romilly, when he visited Brighton in 1843.[34] During his stay Romilly heard the celebrated Evangelical preacher, H V Elliott (1792–1865) discourse on the profanation of the Sabbath and was taken by him to visit a school for clergymen's daughters, called St Mary's Hall, which Elliott had founded on the same lines as Carus Wilson's school. St Mary's had been opened seven years earlier; the designs had been made gratuitously by Basevi, and the buildings and grounds had cost £10,000. The pupils numbered 100 and the fees were £20 per annum; the whole place, Romilly considered, was very clean and comfortable, as well as having 'an extraordinary air of propriety and decorum'. Each girl had a separate bed divided off from the others in the dormitory by curtains; their uniform was a grey print dress, 'very neat: high gowns, perfectly decorous'. Part of the curriculum consisted of 'Callisthenics', gymnastic exercises with hoops and bars, which Romilly considered to be in general pretty and elegant. He was less certain about one exercise in which 'each girl had a wooden machine (like a racket with the centre part taken away) stuck into her bosom and making a frame for her face: those that were handsome of course looked so much the more piquantes from the bizarrerie of this mask, but the plain ones looked frightful; wearing this machine to throw out their chest and keep their head back they were regularly drilled like soldiers'. Ordinary dancing was not permitted, but the callisthenics teacher was in fact a former dancing mistress who had joined the Plymouth Brethren, and who now looked on dancing as a great sin; 'she does not think Callisth^cs so near akin to dancing as I do.'

A History of Secondary Education, 1800-1870

Very similar to this institution, Romilly noted, 'is the Boys School for sons of the clergy at Marlboro wčh is just come into operation: it is for 200 and the charge if £30' (see p. 165).

There, with the callisthenics exercises at St Mary's Hall, we must leave the girls' schools. Much of what they did remains in the shadows because there is much less information available about them than about the boys' schools. Their great weakness was that mistresses had no systematic education or training. They could not teach what they had not learned. The girls' schools came under severe criticism, most of it justified, but there were exceptions to the general rule of mediocrity where good work was being done. Certainly Frances Power Cobbe's judgment on 'heterogeneous studies pursued in this helter-skelter fashion' in her own school was all too often justified.[35] By mid-century, however, there were many able women and some men who were determined on radical changes to increase the opportunities open to their sisters.

NOTES AND REFERENCES

1. Leinster-Mackay D P 1984
2. Arnold, Matthew 1910 pp 122-4 (from Arnold's General Report of 1867). There is a similar example in Bucks RO (136/48 Arch. Soc). A boy at Chiltern House Academy, Wendover, is writing to his parent just before Christmas 1841. Part of the letter reads as follows: 'The imperceptible though rapid flight of Time is hastening on that season of the year 'when happy faces meet around the taper's light', and the visible decrease in the length of day, emblematic of the shortening of my stay at school, encourages me to hope that I shall shortly join the happy group that circles around the family hearth.'
3. Hopkinson, David 1981 p 82. The date of this report is not given
4. *SIC* IX, pp 253-77. The quotation is on p 267
5. The following is based on Collins, Philip 1963 esp. pp 11-13, 98-116
6. Quoted in *ibid.* p 12
7. 'Mr George Clarkson and Mr William Shaw Drt. Agreeᵗ relative to Bowes Hall Academy Jany. 1810.' Clarkson was to pay Shaw £42 per annum for 3 years, at the end of which time half the boys boarded in the school were to be considered the scholars of William Shaw who was to make Clarkson a payment of £5 for each scholar (Hanby Holmes (Solicitors) Papers, Co. Durham RO)
8. Quoted in Collins, Philip 1963 p 105 (from Morley, John 1920 *Life of Richard Cobden* 14th edn p 4)
9. *SIC* I, p 560; *SIC* IX, p 282, where J G Fitch wrote: 'One lady prides herself on taking pupils exclusively from "county families", another draws the line at wholesale trades, and refuses to receive the daughter of a shop-

keeper. Thus each school is obliged to content itself with pupils of a particular social grade. When once this is fixed it is next to impossible for the mistress to get a new pupil from a family which considers itself to belong to a higher *stratum*, while the mistress not infrequently promises the parents that she will not receive pupils from a lower.'

10. See West, Katharine 1949
11. Bolam, David W 1952 pp 99-100
12. Peck, Winifred 1952 pp 61-2
13. *SIC* IX, pp 278-301 (J G Fitch). The quotation is on p 290. Fitch is using the word 'governess', as was quite common at the time, in the sense of 'schoolteacher'
14. *SIC* I, p 570
15. Greenberg E L 1953
16. Scottish Institution for the education of young ladies *CSE 1st Publication* 1837: 360-4
17. Howson J S 1859: 308-16
18. Liverpool Mechanics' Institution. *Report on the Proceedings of a Public Meeting held on the 29th of January 1844, in aid of the establishment of a girls school* ... p 17; *Annual Report 1845*, p 18; *Annual Report 1846*, pp 16-17 (Liverpool Central Library). Tiffen, Herbert J 1935 pp 104-7. On the schools of the Liverpool Institute, see pp 200-1
19. Battersby W J Educational work of the religious orders of women 1850-1950, in Beck G A (ed) 1950 p 340
20. Sturge, H Winifred, Clark, Theodora 1931 pp 88-9
21. Watts R E 1980: 273-86
22. Carpenter R L (ed) 1842 pp 209-10; Manton, Jo 1976 pp 38, 79-80
23. McLachlan H 1935 pp 109-17. Sarah Dendy (née Beard), born 1831, died 1922. For William Field (1768-1851), see McLachlan H 1934 p 124
24. The following on Miss Pipe is drawn from Stoddart, Anna M 1908. See also Binfield, Clyde 1981. This lecture introduced me to Miss Pipe
25. Stoddart, Anna M 1908 p 113
26. *Ibid.* p 60
27. *Ibid.* pp 175ff
28. Binfield, Clyde 1981 p 22
29. Davies, Kathleen 1981. For the daily programme, see p 28
30. My own edition is dated 1882, and is described as 'new and improved'
31. Briggs W G 1957: 24-32
32. Gérin, Winifred 1976 p 29. Ch III deals with Elizabeth Stevenson's schooling. On the Byerley sisters and their school, see Hicks, Phyllis D 1949
33. Lowther Clarke W K 1944 pp 135-7. Gaskell, Elizabeth C pp 47-61
34. Romilly, Joseph Diary 5 September 1843 (Cambridge University Library Add MSS 6822)
35. Cobbe, Frances Power 1904 p 68

CHAPTER ELEVEN
The religious impulse and the boarding school

The 'private foundation schools' formed a kind of half-way house between the private school, which was the property of an individual master or mistress, and the endowed school which had revenues and legal personality ensuring its continuity from one generation to another. The movement to create schools of a more permanent nature than the traditional private academy was controlled by three major forces; class, religion and professional aspirations. There was a growing reluctance to tolerate the education of children of different social ranks within the same school. In a private school the problem solved itself through the interaction of the wishes of the principal and the pressures of the parents. The unit was small enough for such personal pressures to be effective. In a proprietary school, set up as a public establishment and anxious to attract pupils in large numbers, the problem was more difficult. One means of securing the social standing of the school was by giving the directors a veto on the transfer of shares or on the admission of the pupils. The Taunton Commission was well aware of this tendency[1]:

> At Cheltenham College and some other schools of this class it is understood that the sons of shopkeepers would not be admitted. 'At Clifton College and at Sydney College, Bath', says Mr Stanton, 'the governing body retain in their hands the power of rejecting any boy whom they do not consider qualified socially for the school; and as a fact would not admit the son of any resident tradesman.'

Since boys of different social levels had different educational needs it was common to think in terms of separate schools for boys who wished to leave at different ages. The Taunton Commission recommended schools of three grades – with leaving ages of 14, 16 and

160

18/19 respectively, and Nathaniel Woodard, among others, had planned his schools on similar lines a good deal earlier. An educational case could be made for these divisions, but they also had the practical advantage of separating the sons of professional men, of the bulk of business men, and of artisans and small shopkeepers. In broad terms each group slotted into a separate grade and the divisions had a class as well as a curricular purpose.

Religion and education had always been very closely linked, not least because so many heads of schools were themselves clergymen or ministers, or lay people, both men and women, of strong religious convictions. There were economic links too. Many a country clergyman depended on his private pupils to supplement an inadequate stipend, and it was perhaps to accommodate these pupils that many of the spacious Victorian rectories were built. The dependence of many Dissenting ministers on their schools was even greater, and in relation to education, there was little difference between them and their brethren of the Establishment. The Dissenting academies of the eighteenth century had educated both lay and ministerial students.[2] Though the distinctive tradition of the academies had weakened after the outbreak of the French Revolution, some of it lingered in the schools of Unitarians like Lant Carpenter of Bristol and John Relly Beard of Manchester. 'There was no such thing as a dead particle in your father's faith', wrote James Martineau of Lant Carpenter, 'it was instinct with life in every fibre. Religion in his house, was not that shadowy, dreamy, distant thing which it often becomes; and many who came thither were startled, I doubt not, to find it there on the spot, and awake, and positively busy with the duties of every day.'[3] Beard was a man who spread his energies over many fields – minister, schoolmaster, publicist, writer on theological and educational topics.[4] Both he and Carpenter contributed too to that characteristic genre of the time, the literature of self-improvement for those who had left school or who had never received any systematic instruction.[5]

Beard did not die until 1876, having retired from ministerial and academic work a few years earlier. By that time, though the religious impulse in secondary education remained very strong, it had become identified with institutions much more than with individuals. Beard and Carpenter and hundreds of other clergymen and ministers had conducted their schools as individual enterprises. When they became old or died, their schools had closed and had been passed on to someone else as a private speculation. After about 1840 the type of clergyman-educator who would in an earlier generation have run his own private establishment was sometimes establishing a school on a more permanent footing or was becoming head of a school on a foundation established by someone else. Secondary schooling, like much else in Victorian society, was becoming institutionalized. The individual teacher remained important, but the parent or old boy began to look much more to the continuing tradition of the institution than to the personality or abilities of the individual master or mistress. Schools still suffered greater fluctuations than they do in the twentieth century, but once a school had established itself, it was more likely to maintain itself for a long time at the level which it had reached. Once again the forces of differentiation were at work to build up different levels of status. Within the newer corporate framework, the influence of religion remained very great, especially in boarding schools where community life provided special opportunities for the creation of a religious atmosphere. Religious ideas were pre-eminent in the mind of Nathaniel Woodard, the most important of the Anglican school-founders, and they strongly influenced the policies of many others like J L Brereton of the County Schools. They played a large part in the work of headmasters like G E L Cotton who in 6 years (1852–58) set Marlborough, which had had a shaky start as a school intended to provide a semi-charitable education, on the path towards becoming part of the most important of the new public schools.

Professional aspirations are more difficult to track down than the influence of either class or religion. Some of the private schools, as we have seen, offered directly vocational studies, but this was not characteristic of the private foundation schools which modelled themselves on the traditional patterns with some concessions to a more modern curriculum. The new schools were founded to meet a demand for more and better education. The middle classes were expanding both in size and in wealth, and were demanding better opportunities for their sons, though hardly, until the last third of the century, for their daughters as well. The prime objective of the proprietary schools was to provide a better education than the local grammar school could usually offer.[6] In Bristol, Clifton College began its highly successful life in 1862 after two earlier proprietary schools had failed. Among the leading members of the original College Council were several clergymen, one of whom, Henry Moseley, had a more than local reputation as an educationalist,[7] several bankers, a local physician, and a barrister/conveyancing counsel. Their object was to provide 'for the sons of gentlemen a thoroughly good and liberal education at a moderate cost'.[8] They were in fact making an institution for their own and their friends'

children, and similar groups must have been the creators of many
similar schools. By the time Clifton was started England was moving
into the era of competitive examinations, and 'a thoroughly good and
liberal education' offered direct prospects of financial benefit, though
only to those who could meet the challenge. A group like the Clifton
Council could help itself but there was much concern about poorer
professional men, especially the clergy, who needed help to get a good
education for their sons and daughters. Marlborough College for
boys, opened in 1843, and St Mary's Hall for girls, founded in 1836,
aimed to meet the needs of the sons and daughters of the clergy at very
moderate cost. That poorest of poor clergyman, the Rev. Josiah
Crawley, had a son at 'Marlbro' School' whence he was to proceed to
Cambridge at the expense of his godfather.[9] Among the Dissenting
bodies, the Wesleyan Methodists maintained Kingswood and Woodhouse Grove for the sons of their ministers as the Congregationalists
maintained Silcoates and Lewisham for theirs.[10] In 1859 the
foundation of Wellington College aimed particularly at helping the
sons of deceased army officers. In schools like Marlborough and
Wellington the education provided was shared from the beginning by
many others than the original beneficiaries, whereas at Kingswood
and Woodhouse Grove that happened much later.[11] All the boys in
these schools shared an education which aimed at sound religion,
sound scholarship and a preparation for life appropriate to young
men who had their own way to make in the world.

There was no single reason for this shift away from the individual
to the corporate ownership and management of schools. As
education became more complex and more subjects were required, it
was easier to provide them in a school which did not depend on the
professional effectiveness or the financial resources of a single
individual. The proprietary schools used the device of joint-stock
financing which had constructed the canals and the railways.
Through the device of shareholding large sums could be raised to buy
land and erect buildings, while individual subscribers needed to
produce only modest sums, and might, if the venture was successful,
even make a profit. In fact few proprietary schools broke even
financially, quite apart from earning a dividend, but the issue of
shares to subscribers primed the pump at the crucial moment and
enabled the new ventures to get under way. In many less successful
schools the headmaster himself took over financial responsibility for
the school after a few years. In others, as at Clifton, the shareholders
surrendered their rights when a royal charter was obtained.[12]

Financial pressures were not the only reasons for change. The

National and British Societies had introduced the idea of corporate
direction into elementary education, and in the late 1830s/early 1840s
the National Society was active in promoting middle-class education
as a means of strengthening the hold of the Church over social groups
in which Dissent was strong.[13] The efforts of the National Society
were not successful, but their area of concern was similar to that
discussed by Woodard in his *Plea for the Middle Classes* of 1848.
Finally, personal influences were influential in promoting the new
schools, though it is difficult to be specific about them. Woodard
himself became the centre of one such circle. When, for example, P R
Egerton thought of opening a school at Bloxham in Oxfordshire, he
consulted Woodard about the school coming under the latter's
control. Egerton began the school himself in January 1860 when
Woodard was unable to help.[14] The most important figure at the
centre of these circles of influence was Thomas Arnold of Rugby. It
was he more than anyone who saw the schoolmaster as a creative
figure with a strongly spiritual purpose working within the
corporate framework of the school. For 20 years after his death in 1842
Arnold does not seem to have had a strong influence in the 'great
schools' – he was, after all, a very controversial figure. But many of the
heads of the new schools had been Rugbeians or Rugby masters like
Cotton and G G Bradley of Marlborough and E W Benson of
Wellington. In creating the traditions of these schools the Rugby
influence was very important.

Many of the new schools situated in the towns like the proprietary
schools were day schools, but boarding schools grew steadily in
numbers and in prestige. They offered the master much greater
opportunities for religious and moral control. Their pupils could be
drawn from a much wider area, and travel, as communications
improved with the coming of the railways, became much easier and
cheaper by 1850 than it had been in 1800. As more money was made by
manufacturers and business men and as local isolation broke down,
many parents were willing, even anxious, to remove their children
from the local environment. The provision made to meet the demand
was, as we have seen, largely controlled by religious and denominational initiative. The Church of England, the Dissenting bodies, the
Roman Catholics were all involved in founding schools or in
developing those which already existed. Pre-eminent, as was natural,
stood the Church of England. It was the Established Church with the
greatest financial resources and the support of many men of authority
in the state. Since it controlled the ancient universities, it had a
monopoly of those clergy and teachers who enjoyed the best formal

education of the day. Through its own groupings – Evangelical, Broad Church, Tractarian/Anglo-Catholic – it marshalled great reserves of energy and enthusiasm. Though by the 1830s its traditional authority in the state lay under serious threat, the very fact that this was so nerved Anglicans to new and greater efforts in education as in other spheres.

Most of the new foundations were Anglican in inspiration and character. The successful schools quickly aligned themselves with the older public schools, and strongly reinforced that small group which, in the early part of the century, was small in total numbers, and in the case of some schools, like Winchester and Westminster, not very flourishing (see pp. 228-9). The movement across the private school/public school line is clearly seen in the chequered early history of Marlborough College, founded in 1843,[15] which was to become one of the most prominent of later Victorian public schools. The main aim of the founders was to provide education at a low cost for clergymen's sons. They were to form two-thirds of the total number of pupils and to pay thirty guineas a year. The 'lay' boys paid more. Admission was to be gained through the nomination of life governors and governors who paid £100 and £50 respectively for the privilege. The governing council had in addition power to fill up a limited number of places. In terms of numbers the school was almost embarrassingly successful. Two hundred boys arrived on the first day and by 1848 this had risen to 500. It looks as though the numbers were simply too great for the first head, Matthew Wilkinson, and his staff to manage, the fees were very low, and the school was soon in serious financial difficulties. At the end of the 1840s authority in the school was weakening and in 1851 there was a rebellion in which the boys did no work for several days, broke out of the school, smashed windows and rifled masters' desks. This was followed by Wilkinson's resignation in 1852. He had come to Marlborough from the headship of Kensington Grammar School in London[16] and under him the place seems to have been run like a very large private school.

His successor, G E L Cotton, had been a Rugby master under Arnold, and he adopted what were becoming the standard public school methods. Able young masters were attracted, most of them Rugbeians. More authority was given to the sixth form. The houses were reorganized and organized games started. A speech made by Cotton in his early days to the school has survived, and it sums up very neatly the changes which he introduced. The council when he was appointed had told him that boys should only be allowed to go out in pairs with a master.

> I told them I could not accept office upon such terms, that the School
> I hoped to govern was a public school, not a private one, and I would
> try to make it govern itself by means of prefects. The School knows
> now how matters stand. They must either submit to the prefects, or be
> reduced to the level of a private school and have their freedom
> ignominiously curtailed. The prefects are and shall be, so long as I am
> head, the governors of this School. As soon as I see this impracticable
> I will resign.[17]

Under Cotton's rule (1852-58) the tide turned, though the financial
situation continued to be very serious until the mid-1850s. His
successor, G G Bradley (1858-70), was another Rugby master who
consolidated what Cotton had begun. In 1859 the school won both
Balliol scholarships and by the following decade its old boys had
attained a prominent place at Oxford, both in scholarship and in
sport. Marlborough had won its place as an established public school,
but its beginnings had been very modest and its early history very
chequered.

Rossall near Fleetwood in Lancashire was a northern school which
developed on similar, though more modest lines, to Marlborough. Sir
Peter Hesketh-Fleetwood of Rossall Hall had laid out large sums of
money in developing Fleetwood as a port and watering place. A hotel
was built and the manager, a Corsican named Vantini, suggested the
establishment of a large school for boys and another for girls. A
public meeting called to launch the scheme decided to go ahead with
a Northern Church of England School for boys and leased Rossall
Hall for a period of 21 years, Hesketh-Fleetwood himself heading the
subscription list. Rossall must be unique in deriving from the
initiative of a Corsican hotel-keeper, though its other sponsors
belonged to the more usual type of benevolent Victorian. Indeed one
of them, G H Bowers, Dean of Manchester 1847-71, had already been
active in the foundation of Marlborough. A council was got together
and a limited company formed. As at Marlborough the original fees
were £30 a year for the sons of clergymen nominated by governors,
with higher fees for others. The school opened in 1844 and at the end
of the first year 150 boys had been nominated for admission, with
£6,539 10s. received in subscriptions. The first headmaster ran into
difficulties and resigned in 1849. Under his successor, W A Osborne
(1849-70), the school went steadily ahead. A surviving Annual Report
of 1857 records the winning of three open scholarships at Oxford, and
a profit on the year's working of £619. There was still, however, a
need for a more rapid reduction of the debt on the capital account and
for more life governors who could provide nominations for
impecunious parents. When Osborne resigned in 1870 there were 297

boys. He had been to Rossall, wrote A F Leach, 'what Bradley was to Marlborough and Thring to Uppingham'.[18]

Marlborough and Rossall are both examples of schools which, in one generation, crossed the line from the private foundation to the public school. The same course was taken, though more slowly, by the schools founded by Nathaniel Woodard (1811-91).[19] Woodard's aims were not limited to a single school. Eventually he planned his St Nicolas College as a national organization with centres in five geographical divisions, which were to be 'the right hand of the Church's system all about the country'.[20] His starting-point was the estrangement of the middle classes from the Church and the need to win them back to Anglican loyalty and practice. He saw his schools as a means of training in sound religion the sons – and to a much lesser extent the daughters – of middle-class families from gentlemen and professional men of small means at one end of the scale to tradesmen and hucksters at the other. The teaching of his schools was strongly Catholic, based on the tradition of the Oxford Tractarians. He came under heavy criticism, for example, because the practice of confession was used in his schools, though it was voluntary and parents had to consent to it. In one sense the credal associations of his schools weakened the national standing which he had hoped to acquire. On the other they gave him a permanent basis of support on which, since he was an excellent business man and organizer, he was able to capitalize. In 1890 eleven of his schools were in operation, a remarkable achievement for a man who had begun with no social and academic advantages, and had in 1847 launched his first day school in the dining room of his parsonage house at New Shoreham in Sussex.

Woodard first expounded his ideas in a pamphlet of 1848 which talked of schools of two classes[21]:

> the first would be suitable for the sons of the higher kind of tradesmen, professional men, and gentlemen of limited means; the second for the children of quite small tradesmen or even hucksters. These latter are a very important class, perhaps the most important; and with a little diligence and management might be *picked up by thousands.*

Very soon the original two classes had become three with the bifurcation of the higher group into a school for the sons of gentlemen of limited means and another for the sons of tradesmen and farmers. The original core of schools was in Sussex. In the early 1850s the first-class school had been established at Lancing, the second-class school at Hurstpierpoint. The third-class school at Ardingly followed a few years later for the class of people who,

Woodard wrote, were trying to maintain their families in a respectable way on £150 to £200 a year. They were the families, he argued, which would produce the missionaries and the schoolmasters, men who were not likely to be produced by richer families. 'Is it not fair to expect that Public Boarding Schools for the Lower Middle Classes would furnish a good quota of such men as could do good services in each of these capacities, both at home and abroad.'[22]

'Public Boarding Schools ... ' – though in his original pamphlet of 1848 Woodard had written about both boarding and day schools, the day schools quickly disappeared from the discussion. The boarding school was to conform 'as far as may be to the rule of Winchester',[23] and the public school model remained very much in his mind, though his second- and third-grade schools were institutions very different in kind from Winchester or Eton. In 1878 the annual payments at the three Sussex schools were as follows: Lancing from £60 to £100 a year, Hurstpierpoint £30 to £35, Ardingly only fifteen guineas.[24] Lancing remained the only first-grade school. The later schools in the Midlands and the west were all second or third grade. Woodard, since he had cast his net right across the great range of the middle classes, had to use the mechanism of differentiation which, as we have seen, had become universal in his day. Much the same threefold pattern had been worked out in the schools of the Liverpool Collegiate Institution and the Liverpool Institute in the 1840s (see pp. 191, 200–1) and it was to be put forward in the 1860s in the Report of the Taunton Commission.

To Woodard differentiation was not incompatible with underlying unity. All the schools of whatever grade shared the same religious teaching, based on Anglo-Catholic principles, and all were directed by clergymen. All the schools and their chief supporters, clerical and lay, were incorporated into the society of St Nicolas College which offered to all a bulwark of union and security. There were opportunities for able boys to move up the ladder from school to school. At Hurst there was a training college for commercial schoolmasters which helped to provide the necessary teachers. Woodard's achievement was remarkable but in his own terms limited. His ideal of providing middle-class education on national lines through a private corporation was hardly practicable, particularly since the schools were exclusively Anglican in character. The teaching was conservative, and little attempt was made to broaden the curriculum. Yet Woodard and his collaborators like E C Lowe[25] made a remarkable attempt to provide a boarding school education to boys (and some girls) for whom such opportunities had not been available before, and in their planning they made much use of ideas deriving from the ancient public schools. Eventually the Woodard schools were to become public schools themselves.

Another pioneer who thought in terms of a structure of interrelated schools was Joseph Lloyd Brereton (1822–1901). His work is much less widely known than Woodard's and was ultimately much less successful.[26] Brereton and Woodard sometimes came close together in their ideas and sometimes diverged. Woodard himself had been educated privately. Brereton was a public-school man himself, a boy at Rugby under Dr Arnold, whose ideas, particularly on the relationships between Church and state, affected him profoundly. Unlike Woodard he put little emphasis on strict Churchmanship. He wanted Anglicans and Nonconformists to co-operate and was anxious to create an atmosphere in his schools which would make this possible. His own direct concern with middle-class schools came through his interest in the education of farmers' sons, a very important group in a still agricultural England and one whose needs attracted a great deal of attention. For example, B F Duppa, secretary of the Central Society of Education (1836–40), had put forward in one of the society's publications a plan for 'County Colleges of Agriculture' which was remarkably similar to Brereton's later County Schools.[27]

Brereton and Duppa both suggested that the necessary money should be raised through the purchase of shares which would pay a dividend – the proprietary principle in fact. Some of the costs should be met by the labour of boys on the farm which would be part of the school and which would produce food for its use. Brereton, after several London curacies, became rector of West Buckland in Devon in 1852. There he gained the support and interest of the great local family, the Fortescues, busied himself with rural matters, put forward a plan for 'county examinations', and in 1858 opened a 'Farm and County School'. The fees, he explained, were to be graded from £45 to £10, according to the amount of farm-work done, and he hoped for a school of 50 boarders with 100 acres of land.[28] Brereton and his friend, the third Earl Fortescue, both wrote extensively on educational topics. His own plans were most completely set out in a book published in 1874.[29]

Like Woodard and the Taunton Commission Report, he talked of schools of three grades. The farmer who worked 200/300 acres was, he argued 'the midmost man in England', and on an average income of £200 he could not afford to pay a boarding fee of more than about thirty guineas, the approximate charge at the Devon County School,

West Buckland. Below that in the hierarchy a school for the sons of small farmers and bailiffs could be provided at £15–20 per annum for a school of fifty boys if the boys also did some agricultural work. In Brereton's structure such a school represented the third grade, West Buckland the second grade, and a first-grade school could be provided at fees of about fifty guineas per annum. The proposed fees for second- and third-grade schools were similar to what Woodard charged at Hurstpierpoint and Ardingly, though Lancing was considerably more expensive than Brereton's projected first-grade school. Brereton also thought in terms of a national organization, but his local unit was to be the county. He wished to conciliate Nonconformists who would find a secular unit acceptable. He wished also to appeal to local loyalty and local initiative, since he was hostile either to interference by, or financial support from, central government. He proposed that, in each poor-law union, there should be a third-grade school, in each county a second-grade school, and in a division of several counties a first-grade school. At the summit the country should be divided into four provinces, each based on a university, with a council to conduct examinations and certificate masters, and a County College. This would enable students to obtain a degree at a moderate cost and at a lower age than the normal and would also help to train secondary teachers. Some of the finance would be raised through the sale of shares with limited liability, some through the use of existing endowments as capital to provide buildings.

> A moderated desire for commercial profit, combined with an
> honourable concern for public interest would, I believe, in any district
> bring together out of the gentry, farmers and tradesmen, a body who
> would do their best (and perhaps, on the whole, *the* best) for the
> schools entrusted to their care.[30]

While Brereton was working out his ideas, other men were establishing moderately priced boarding schools on similar but independent lines. Some of these established themselves successfully, the best known being Framlingham in Suffolk and Cranleigh in Surrey. Both opened in 1865.[31] Brereton's own schemes had a much more chequered career than Woodard's. The school at West Buckland survived, though it had its ups and downs. The scheme of combining education with farm-work never became established because parents disliked it. In 1867 Brereton had succeeded his father as rector of Little Massingham in Norfolk, and in 1872 another County School was established in that county. With fees of about £50 for boarders it represented a first-class school in standard. In 1873 a County College

– later Cavendish College – was opened at Cambridge to offer an inexpensive degree course to entrants below the normal age. The later history of Brereton's ventures lies outside the scope of this volume. His ideas of commercial financing and local effort proved incompatible with the growth of centralized state power in the latter decades of the century. Schools which appealed particularly to farmers inevitably suffered in the great agricultural depression. The Norfolk County School closed in 1891 and Cavendish College closed the following year. Brereton's plans for the education of girls had to be abandoned. He lived on until 1901, struggling with a heavy burden of debt.

The comparisons with Woodard are striking. The contrast between their religious policies has already been examined. Both of them aspired towards a national organization of schools, based on a division into four or five provinces. Both of them used the graded structure so widely accepted at the time. Some of the biggest contrasts lay in financial management. Woodard had been highly successful in appealing for money, but he had never used the commercial principle of share and dividend. Brereton was a reckless and over-ambitious financier who never established, as Woodard did, a firm financial basis for his schemes. Both of them attempted tasks of national organization which could be accomplished successfully only by the resources of the state. Both of them saw the need to provide better opportunities for middle-class families for whom little was being done by existing institutions. Woodard created a pattern of schools which continues to flourish in the later twentieth century. Measured by that standard, Brereton was a failure, but he remains of interest because his Broad Church religious ideas, his belief in commercial financing, his rejection of state control embody many of the most characteristic themes in the life of mid-Victorian England.

There is space here to refer to only two more Anglican clergymen who were involved with similar new foundations. Both Bloxham and Bradfield proved to be successful ventures, though their origins were very different. Bloxham in Oxfordshire was founded in 1860 by P R Egerton, who had purchased in 1859 an empty building opened only a few years before as a school but closed within a short time. Egerton saw it when walking through the village of Bloxham with a companion who suggested that he should restart the school. Egerton said later that he had at the time no such intention, but, after thinking the matter over, he decided to purchase, was successful, and devoted the rest of his working life to building the place up. The original prospectus announced 'a Grammar School, for the education of the

Sons of Tradesmen, Farmers, Clerks, and others of the Middle Classes'. The instruction given was to include English, French and Latin, vocal music, writing and arithmetic and 'the other details of a sound commercial education'. The boarding fee was low – £25 4s. per annum, less than in Woodard's and Brereton's second-grade schools. The religious atmosphere was strongly Anglo-Catholic; confession was practised on the same basis as in the Woodard schools. Egerton's links with Woodard were always close. In 1884 he handed the school over to trustees and in 1896 it was transferred to the Woodard Corporation.[32]

Bradfield in Berkshire was founded in 1850 by Thomas Stevens, squire and rector of the parish, on the model of Winchester, and it seems from the beginning to have set a higher social and educational level than the schools which have just been described. It was considerably more expensive – the fees which began at £50 had been raised to £100 by 1854. From the beginning the school had good connections with the universities and won a number of successes there. The school constitution did not lead to harmony. Stevens was warden of the college. He appointed a headmaster but kept the real control in his own hands, and the relationships between the two officers were not always easy. In the 1870s the financial situation became very serious. At the end of 1879 the headmaster and some of his staff resigned, and 2 years later Stevens himself went bankrupt. H B Gray, who became headmaster in 1880 and warden the following year, pulled the situation round and by the end of the 1880s the school was flourishing. Gray remained at Bradfield until 1910.[33]

NOTES AND REFERENCES

1. *SIC* I, p 317
2. There is a considerable literature on the academies; see, for example, McLachlan H 1931
3. Carpenter R L (ed) 1842 p 351
4. McLachlan H 1935 esp. pp 33–4
5. Shepherd W, Joyce J, Carpenter, Lant 1822 Carpenter wrote on philosophy and logic. Beard J R 1859
6. At Sheffield the two proprietary schools, the Collegiate School and Wesley College, were set up because it was 'felt that the Grammar School and other educational establishments in the town were insufficient to meet the demands for a superior, classical and scientific training for the sons of the more wealthy inhabitants . . . '. Hunter J 1869 p 225

7. See Layton, David 1973 pp 75-94
8. Christie O F 1935 pp 17-29
9. Trollope, Anthony *The Last Chronicle of Barset* (Nelson edn) p 16
10. Lewisham School removed to Caterham in 1884
11. Ives A G 1970; Pritchard F C 1978 p 205 gives 1883 as the date when laymen's sons were admitted to Woodhouse Grove
12. Christie O F 1935 pp 91-2. The charter was granted in 1877
13. Roach J 1971 pp 44-8
14. *History of All Saints' School, Bloxham 1860-1910* (Bloxham 1910). published at the school, pp 7-8
15. The following is drawn from Bradley A G *et al.* 1923. The original proposals are set out in Bowers G H 1842, which includes the prospectus drawn up by the provisional committee. See also *DNB*: Bowers, George Hull 1794-1872
16. Wilkinson had been headmaster at Kensington 1840-43 and previously principal of Huddersfield Collegiate School 1838-40 (Venn J A 1940-54) vol. VI
17. Bradley A G *et al.* 1923 p 168
18. This is based on Leach A F 1908 Rossall School *VCH Lancashire* vol II pp 614-15. and on some of the early reports of the Northern Church of England School (Crawford Papers (Wigan and District Affairs Correspondence), John Rylands Library, Manchester). The account of the early years of the school in Furness W (ed) 1945 is very brief
19. On Woodard, see Heeney, Brian 1969; Kirk K E 1937; Otter, Sir John 1925
20. Woodard N 1883 p 19
21. Woodard N 1848 p 13
22. Woodard N 1858 pp 9-10
23. Quoted in Heeney, Brian 1969 p 99
24. Woodard N 1878 p 6
25. First headmaster of Hurstpierpoint and later first provost of the Society of St Mary and St John of Lichfield. Lowe was a more liberal man than Woodard with a much stronger interest in educational ideas
26. There is a good discussion of Brereton in Honey J R de S 1977 pp 58-101. See also Searby P 1974: 4-14
27. Duppa B F County Colleges of Agriculture *CSE 3rd Publication* 1839 (reprinted 1968): 59-86
28. Roach J 1971 p 52
29. Brereton J L 1874
30. *Ibid.* pp 89-90
31. Honey J R de S 1977 pp 65-7. The head of Framlingham, the Rev. A Daymond, gave evidence to the Taunton Commission, *SIC* V, pp 588-605
32. *History of All Saints' School, Bloxham 1860*-1910 (Bloxham, 1910) pp 4-5 (Egerton's account of his decision to buy the school), p 12 (the first prospectus). See also Kirk K E 1937 pp 135-8
33. See Blackie, John 1976 esp. pp 2-9 (on the founder), 70-4 (on the financial crisis of 1880-81). See, also Leach A F (ed) 1900

CHAPTER TWELVE

Nonconformist and Roman Catholic schools

The part played by Anglicans in founding new schools looms very large in the story because the Church of England was the biggest and richest of religious bodies, but Anglican efforts did not stand alone. The religious impulse also operated strongly among both Dissenters and Roman Catholics, with the same object of serving and propagating their own faith. They ran many private schools, sometimes limited to their own adherents, sometimes not. In the vicinity of London, Tottenham was a centre for Quaker schools.[1] Benjamin Disraeli, the future prime minister, attended for 4 years a school at Walthamstow, kept by a Unitarian minister, Eliezer Cogan (1762–1855). Cogan was, Disraeli wrote later, a good teacher and a first-rate scholar. When he left the school, he 'was quite fit to have gone to a university – I mean, I did not require any preliminary cramming at a private tutor's'.[2] The prospectus of Henry Frederick Smith's school, in the Quaker centre of Darlington, announced that he aimed to give a 'liberal and guarded education' to Friends' children.[3] For boys over the age of 12 he charged fifty guineas per annum. Smith's prospectus is unusual because he announced a course of higher study for young Friends who, at a time when the universities were closed to them, had no other access to higher education. The full course lasted for 5 years, though it was also possible to attend only certain classes. There is no record of how many students were attracted to this higher programme. Probably the school was not successful. Smith took it over in 1817 and left in 1827 – he is said to have gone to America. In 1831 the building was sold, 'the contiguity of the boys and girls schools recently established at York' making it unlikely that anyone would carry the school on.[4] The schools at York were Bootham and The Mount,[5] for boys and girls respectively. Both of them were owned and managed by the York Quarterly Meeting of the Society, which clearly felt the need for more permanent establishments than could be provided by private masters and mistresses. Bootham had in fact begun as a private school. William Tuke, a prominent York Friend, had long been closely involved with the Retreat, the Quaker home for the insane. In 1818 he proposed the foundation of a boys' school. Money was collected, but the scheme was not carried through. In 1821 Tuke and his grandson, Samuel, invited a master named William Simpson to start a school in part of the Retreat building. After some years, Simpson began negotiations to sell the school to John Ford, but the Quarterly Meeting took the school over itself and Ford became superintendent of their school instead of an independent master.[6] The girls' school, The Mount, was launched by the Quarterly Meeting in 1831 – once again with a pre-history. A group of women Friends, under the leadership of William Tuke and of Esther, his wife, had opened a girls' school in 1785 which had closed in 1814. The new girls' school was a success. Twenty-five years later an appeal for money to acquire a new site argued that the Quarterly Meeting had succeeded in their aim of providing a liberal education for the daughters of Friends 'more completely and with less fluctuation than attaches to private schools'.[7]

For such a small body the Society of Friends, usually through its local meetings, undertook a substantial responsibility for schools. The pioneer foundation at Ackworth 'for members of the Society not in affluence' had been founded in 1779; 2 years later there were 310 boys and girls.[8] Similar schools were founded at Sidcot in Somerset in 1808 and at Wigton in Cumberland in 1815.[9] An earlier workhouse school (which gradually developed on the same lines as these three), moved from Islington to Croydon in 1825 and to Saffron Walden in 1879.[10] At Ackworth, which was probably representative of the group, the education seems to have been solid and thorough, but necessarily limited in scope since the pupils left at 14–15.[11] Bootham and The Mount aimed at a higher social clientele and provided a more liberal curriculum, though the girls' school is likely to have been the more limited of the two. When Fitch visited Bootham for the Schools Inquiry Commission he thought that in the classics the boys were 'on a par with pupils of the best grammar schools', while their education in history, English literature, mathematics and natural sciences was far superior.[12]

As was so often the case, the Quaker schools had differentiated themselves according to respective needs, though, so far as I know, they did not theorize about it. Bootham and The Mount represented a first grade, Ackworth and Wigton a second grade. The third grade consisted of a group of schools for the 'disowned', those who had left the society but remained in sympathy with it and who needed assistance with their children's education. For them an education in the basic subjects was provided with manual work to reduce the expense.[13] Schools of this kind were founded at Rawdon (1832), Penketh (1834) and Great Ayton (1841), all in the north of England, and at Sibford in Oxfordshire (1842). A circular sent out when Sibford was being planned explained[14]:

> Friends have therefore contemplated the establishment of a School to combine labour with a guarded and religious education in accordance with their principles ... , into which children of the classes in question should be received upon the payment of Terms suited to the circumstances of their Parents, and from which, children who are members of the Society, should not be excluded.

As usual school fees provide a useful guide to status. At Rawdon the average cost of education in the 1840s was about £12. At Ackworth in 1840 it was £20 19s. 6d.[15] Bootham had in 1829 proposed £30 with additional charges for Latin, Greek, French and German.[16]

The Sibford circular already quoted comes from the papers on educational matters of John Pease of Darlington, dating from the 1840s and 1850s. There is other material in the papers about Sibford – a paper about the cost of the children's clothing and a long description of the annual examination. There is an advertisement for a new housekeeper at Great Ayton and a list of the occupations of former scholars. There is an appeal for funds and other correspondence about a new building for the girls' school at York and about the training of women teachers. There is a paper about the Flounders Institute which trained male teachers. There is the prospectus of Henry Frederick Smith's school at Darlington which has already been mentioned. There are a few letters about projects in other places in the North.[17] Taken together this material throws some interesting light on the range of the educational work for which Friends were responsible.

Their work was naturally centred on their own community. A school which set out to serve the general Dissenting interest was the Protestant Dissenters' Grammar School at Mill Hill in Middlesex, founded by a group of London merchants and opened in 1808. The annual fee for boarders was £45 with reductions for ministers' sons and those in especial need. Under Thomas Priestley who became head in 1834, the school flourished. In his early years, out of a week's school time of 42 hours, 15 were given to the classics, 8 to mathematics, 3 to geography, 3 to writing, 5 to English language and history, 5 to French, 2 to German and 1 to a biblical lecture – a full and varied curriculum for the time. After Priestley's day the school declined, was closed for a time, and then reopened in 1869 on a new foundation sanctioned by a Chancery scheme. In this, it was stated, 'the classical languages and literature hold the principal place in the course of study'.[18] This had clearly not been so in Priestley's time. By the late 1860s the reports of the Clarendon and Taunton Commissions had concentrated attention on the status of schools. First-grade schools were primarily classical schools and it may be that the stress on the classics was a means of claiming for Mill Hill first-grade status and public school rank.

Both the Congregationalists and the Wesleyan Methodists maintained schools for the sons of their ministers. The Congregationalists had two: one at Lewisham, Surrey, founded by John Townsend of Jamaica-row Chapel, Bermondsey, in 1811, and a northern school at Silcoates near Wakefield, opened in 1831 after an earlier Dissenters' Grammar School had collapsed. The numbers were small. Lewisham varied from fifty in 1840 to thirty-five in 1851, Silcoates in 1843 had thirty-seven boys, fifteen of them from Lancashire and Yorkshire. The ages at Lewisham stretched from 11 to 15.[19] Of the two Wesleyan schools Kingswood had been established by John Wesley himself in 1748; Woodhouse Grove at Apperley Bridge in the West Riding was opened in 1812.[20] The Wesleyan Methodist Conference laid down that no boy might stay at the two schools for more than 6 years – originally from 8 to 14. This age-range varied a little because the Schools Inquiry Commission report on Woodhouse Grove says that the boys came at 9 and remained for 6 years. The schools did not suffer from the common problem of very short school life, but the early leaving age obviously limited the boys' attainments. At Woodhouse Grove much of the teaching was classical, but in the 1850s both Conference and the headmaster were anxious that attention should be given to subjects like writing, arithmetic, English composition and the elements of natural science since most ministers' sons were likely to earn their livings in commerce and trade.[21] An account of the books in the library given by Benjamin Gregory, who was a boy in the 1830s, suggests that an intelligent boy could find plenty to read. He mentions the *Spectator*, Locke on *Education*, the histories of Hume and William Robertson, books on travel like Cook's *Voyages*, Mungo Park's *Interior of Africa* and Bruce's *Abyssinia*, and many of the standard works of the day on history and mythology.[22] Many better-known institutions would not have provided such good opportunities for a boy of intellectual tastes.

Neither Kingswood nor Woodhouse Grove did anything for the sons of lay members of the Connection, many of whom wanted, and could afford, a good education for them. If the boys were sent to non-Methodist schools, they might be lost to their church or to religion altogether, and at the least might suffer persecution for their opinions. Among those anxious to remedy these deficiencies was the Rev. S D Waddy, who was stationed in Sheffield in 1834 and who played a large part in the opening of a Wesleyan proprietary school there which opened in 1838.[23] The school, later known as Wesley College, was planned on an ambitious scale. The handsome building contained

> one large and six smaller school-rooms, nine dormitories, in which each pupil has a bed to himself, a spacious dining-hall, amphitheatre for lectures, laboratory, museum and library, reading-room and music-room, warm and shower baths, and, lastly, a beautiful and commodious chapel. There is also a spacious swimming bath on the premises, detached from the main building.

In the first year 161 pupils entered, most of them from the north of England and the Midlands, though there was a group from London and the south-east and a few from other parts of the kingdom. The boarders predominated; there were only thirty-five boys from Sheffield itself.[24] Initially £13,000 was subscribed, and the total cost of the land, buildings and furniture was almost £28,000.[25] After a promising beginning the school soon ran into financial difficulties. Waddy left Sheffield in 1840, but in 1844 he returned as governor and chaplain, a post which he retained until 1862.[26] Soon after his appointment the school became a College of the University of London which meant that students were able to work for a university degree while they still resided in Sheffield. Under Waddy's rule numbers recovered; in 1856 there were 185 boarders and 11 day boys.[27] A prospectus of that period[28] records a headmaster and 15 assistants, with a course covering the basic English subjects, 'all the requisites of a good Commercial Education', mathematics (elementary and advanced), Greek, Latin, Hebrew, French, Spanish and German. The terms for boarders varied from £35 to £55 according to age. Religion was taught 'as held and taught by the Wesleyan Methodist Church', though, according to Alfred Gatty, the college was not restricted to the sons of Wesleyans.[29] Shortly after the beginnings at Sheffield a West of England Wesleyan Proprietary School was opened at

Taunton (1843). It also became a collegiate institution of the University of London, and its development ran on lines so similar to those of Wesley College that there is no need to review the story in detail. The most distinctive feature of this school, which took the title Queen's College, Taunton in 1888, was that its first headmaster, Thomas Sibly, was one of the pioneers of school science teaching (see p. 132).

The last major group to be discussed are the Roman Catholics, and the story of their schools during this period is one of great interest. The religious communities established in France and the Low Countries during the penal times came back to England during the French Revolution, and their refounded schools, like Stonyhurst, Downside and Ampleforth, were to become the major Catholic public schools of the twentieth century. Roman Catholics attained full political equality after Emancipation in 1829, and their numbers steadily grew, partly as the result of Irish immigration and partly from the conversions set off by the submission to the Church of Tractarian leaders like J H Newman and H E Manning. For a long time, however, the Catholic social and educational picture was a distorted one because the middle class formed a very small part of the community. At one end of the scale stood the old Catholic families, at the other the large group of the Irish poor, living under wretched conditions in the towns and cities. Institutions existed to cater for the gentry. For many years the first priority was to provide elementary schools for poor children, and it was not until about 1870 that schools for the middle classes began to assume a higher priority.

In the middle of the century there were only a few Catholic schools for boys.[30] Some of them, following the example of the English College at Douai, closed in 1793, educated both those who were candidates for the priesthood and those who were receiving an ordinary lay education. Both St Edmund's, Old Hall, Ware (1793) and Ushaw near Durham (1808) filled this dual role. During this period the leading schools for Catholic boys of the upper classes were the Jesuit foundation, Stonyhurst (1794) and Oscott, also opened in 1794, though the latter became exclusively a seminary after 1889. The Benedictines maintained Ampleforth and Downside, established on their present sites in 1802 and 1814 respectively, though both of these suffered severely when Bishop Baines tried to establish a new school for sons of the gentry together with a seminary at Prior Park, Bath. Prior Park ran into serious financial problems and closed in 1856.[31] Soon after that, Newman founded the Oratory School in Birmingham (1859) to meet the demand of many parents, particularly converts, for a Catholic education on English public school lines. Newman maintained a very close connection with it, and it educated many men who became prominent in public life.

Most of these schools eventually achieved public school status in the twentieth century but they did nothing to meet the needs of the Catholic middle class which was beginning to develop as the community became more established. As early as 1763 Bishop Challoner had opened a boarding school at Sedgley Park near Wolverhampton which catered largely for the commercial middle class and for farmers. Boys generally entered at about 10, and, in the early part of the century, stayed for 3 or 4 years. In 1863 there were 155 boys. Ten years later, since the original site had been held only on a short lease, the school was transferred to Cotton Hall in Staffordshire.[32] Town day schools began with the establishment by the Jesuits of St Francis Xavier's Day School in Liverpool (1840). Ten years later a Catholic middle school was opened in the same city to give 'a commercial education combined with religious instruction at a low fee of four or five guineas a year'.[33] The Jesuits opened the Preston Catholic College in 1860, and in Manchester the Belgian Xaverians, who had begun work in English elementary schools in 1848, opened a college in 1862. All these schools were in Lancashire, the English county with the strongest Catholic presence. The De la Salle brothers came to London in 1855. Their day and boarding school at Clapham offered a non-classical curriculum at fees of £9 for day boys, £21 for boarders.[34] They opened a second school at Southwark in 1860. Middle-class education was an important priority in the mind of H E Manning who became Archbishop of Westminster in 1865. His own venture was St Charles's College in Kensington, opened in 1874. By the time of his death in 1892 there were over a dozen middle-class schools in London.[35]

Both Manning and his predecessor, the first Archbishop of Westminster, Nicholas Wiseman (1850–65), actively encouraged congregations of nuns to come to England and open girls' schools. The most active and efficient of them were the new teaching orders, many of them founded in France and Belgium in the early part of the century. They gave up the idea of strict enclosure; they were centrally organized and so found it easy to set up new houses; they were active in maintaining both parish schools and middle-class schools.[36] Only a few of the many orders can be mentioned here. The Faithful Companions of Jesus came to this country in 1830 and the sisters of Notre Dame de Namur in 1845. In 1842 the Society of the Sacred Heart opened a house in Ireland and another near London, which was moved to Roehampton in 1850.[37] The foundress, St Madeleine Sophie Barat, had started teaching at Amiens in 1801. The society's plan of studies, first drawn up in 1805, had been several times revised. The basic subjects had been Bible history and Church history, French grammar and language, literature and arithmetic, which included the new metric system and bookkeeping. The 1850 programme added foreign languages and natural history. The older girls were to study translations of classical and foreign literature. When Mother Barat died in 1865 the society had eighty-four houses in Europe, North and South America. In the early days the teaching in many of them, including Roehampton, was almost entirely in French.

It was the unreadiness of some English Catholics to accept what they saw as a foreign-type of education which led Wiseman to favour a distinctively English teaching order of women. In 1846 he summoned the American convert Cornelia Connelly to start a teaching community in England and to take over a school for the Catholic poor. The new Society of the Holy Child Jesus began at Derby and moved in 1848 to St Leonard's in Sussex.[38] The society ran a boarding school at St Leonard's, houses were set up in other towns, and its work spread to America, where a school was established in Philadelphia. In 1863 Mother Connelly produced the *Book of Studies*, which both embodied her general ideas about education and provided detailed instructions about teaching methods. The curriculum of the boarding school was that of the superior girls' schools of the day, but Mother Connelly was very anxious to meet new needs as they arose. She was interested in drawing and in the arts and in drama. She wanted her girls to have independence and self-government. Later, and ahead of most girls' schools, her nuns introduced games and gymnastics. One of her early pupils wrote[39]:

> the general atmosphere of St Leonards was one of joy and contentment. There was no spying on the part of the nuns, but we were greatly trusted, and trained to a high sense of honour – a method that completely achieved its end. There was a sense of freedom and broadmindedness about the school that was delightful.

During Manning's long archiepiscopate the secondary schools of the religious orders for women grew steadily in number. The powers of thought and organization deployed by the best of the nuns were considerable. Because they stood rather aside from the main stream of development, they have never had their proper recognition in the story of women's education in England.

NOTES AND REFERENCES

1. Bryant M 1969 in *VCH Middlesex* vol I p 261; Stewart W A C 1953 p 76
2. Monypenny W F 1910 p.24. For Cogan, see McLachlan H 1934 pp 106–7
3. Hodgkin Papers (Durham RO)
4. Durham County Friends' School 1929: 29–31. See also Darlington schoolboy's diary 1927: 21–30
5. The girls' school moved to The Mount in 1857
6. Pollard F E (ed) 1926 pp 21–8, 36–7
7. 'York Quarterly Meeting's School for Girls and the Training of Female Teachers', Hodgkin Papers (Durham RO). A covering note is dated 3mo 7th (7 March) 1856
8. Stewart W A C 1953 p 49
9. *Ibid.* pp 61, 63. There are some papers about the foundation of Wigton in a file of papers about Quaker education in Cumbria RO. See also *A History of Wigston School 1815 to 1915* (Wigston, 1916)
10. Bolam, David W 1952
11. Thompson, Henry 1879 p 312. For a picture of the school at mid-century, see Wallis, Isaac Henry 1924 pp 17–31. Andrews, who was later headmaster, was a boy in the school, 1859–64. He was head of the school at 14 years of age
12. Pollard F E (ed) 1926 pp 49–50
13. Stewart W A C 1953 pp 66–75
14. 'Proposed "Friends' Agricultural School" for Berks, Oxon, Bucks, Northampton, and such others of the Midland and Southern Counties as may incline to unite therein', 28 Dec. (?1840), Hodgkin Papers (Durham RO)
15. Stewart W A C 1953 p 83
16. Pollard F E (ed) 1926 p 30
17. 'Society of Friends Schools and Education' Hodgkin Papers (Durham RO)
18. Brett-James N G n.d. p 212. See also his *Mill Hill* (1938) p 34 for the curriculum under Priestley
19. Stafford, Hugh 1945. The school moved in 1884. Oakley H Hislop 1920
20. For the Methodist schools in general, see Pritchard F C 1949
21. Pritchard F C 1978 esp. pp 30, 169–70, 132, 143. For the careers of old boys see Table 9 (p 145)
22. Gregory, Benjamin 1903 pp 119–21. Gregory became a Wesleyan Methodist minister himself
23. Waddy, Adeline 1878 pp 110–13; Pritchard F C 1949 pp 136–44
24. *The Establishment, Principles, Discipline and Educational Course of the Wesleyan Proprietary Grammar School, Sheffield. With a list of the officers, proprietors, trustees and pupils; and a copy of the deed of settlement* (1839), esp. pp 16, 39–43 (Sheffield Local Studies Library)
25. Hunter J 1869 pp 226–7
26. The governor in a Methodist school was a minister who took charge of the whole establishment and was the headmaster's superior
27. For S D Waddy's governorship see Waddy, Adeline 1878 pp 175–278; Pritchard F C 1949 pp 162–3

28. *Wesley College, Sheffield* (leaflet, not dated) (Sheffield Local Studies Library)
29. Hunter J 1869 p 227
30. For the following, see Barnes A S 1926; Evennett H O 1944; Battersby W J Secondary education for boys, in Beck G A (ed) 1950 pp 322-36
31. See Roche J S 1931
32. For the history of the school, see Buscot W 1940
33. Battersby W J Secondary education for boys, in Beck G A (ed) 1950 p 327
34. See also Battersby W J 1953
35. McClelland V A 1962 pp 51-3, 67
36. Battersby W J Educational work of the religious orders of women 1850-1950 in Beck G A (ed) 1950 pp 337-64
37. O'Leary M 1936 pp 233-4. The material about that society is taken from this book
38. For the following, see Marie Thérèse, Mother, SHCJ 1963; *Cornelia Connelly 1809*-1879 by a religious of the Society 1950
39. *Ibid.* p 151

CHAPTER THIRTEEN
Urban proprietary schools

The emphasis in Chapter 12 was on boarding schools. In this chapter the focus will switch to the urban scene and to the new day schools provided for different sectors of the urban middle class. Once again it is very difficult to draw firm lines. Both boarding and day schools were set up on the proprietary principle. Many urban proprietary schools were day schools, though sometimes like Cheltenham College and Wesley College, Sheffield they attracted boarders in large numbers. The religious impulse has already been fully discussed. It also had a strong influence on the town proprietary schools – often to their detriment since religious rivalries led to the over-provision of schools. However the education of the urban middle classes does provide a distinct theme in the story. The proprietary schools served chiefly the sons of business and professional men. Efforts were also made to educate the sons of the shopkeeper and the artisan – the people for whom Woodard had planned his third-grade schools. Sometimes schools were provided in alliance with the new teachers' training colleges. In a few cases they were linked with Mechanics' Institutes. With the institutes formal education shades over into informal methods of self-improvement, and the centre of interest switches away from the adolescent to the adult.

Proprietary schools as corporate enterprises needed formal regulations and a number of these have survived. Of those which I have seen there are differences in detail, but the general structure is much the same. Among the many London schools the Pimlico regulations were published in the *Quarterly Journal of Education* (1831).[1] The following are the rules of St Paul's School at Southsea near Portsmouth, established in 1825.[2] In order to purchase a site and erect buildings £2,300 was to be raised, the total sum to be divided into 100 shares of £23 each. The buildings and premises were to be conveyed to seven trustees to hold in trust for themselves and the other shareholders 'for the purposes of the Institution'. Each shareholder might send one pupil to the school in the right of each share but no pupil who was not the son of a shareholder might be admitted without the consent of the superintending committee, who also had to approve the transfer of shares. Each shareholder was required to pay eight guineas annually 'for the support and maintenance of the School' on each share whether the boys nominated on that share were their own sons or not, and shareholders were responsible for this subscription if the places were unfilled. There was to be an annual general meeting of shareholders which, among other duties, was to elect a superintending committee of fifteen (in other examples called the directors) which was to meet monthly, to appoint visitors to visit and examine the school and to draw up an annual report. Three masters were to be appointed by the shareholders at fixed salaries. The head and first assistant were to be 'well skilled both in Classical and Mathematical learning'. The head was to be a graduate of an English university and a member of the Established Church. The second assistant was to teach classics and mathematics to the junior classes in addition to writing. There were to be French and drawing masters paid on a per capita basis. All the masters were permitted to take boarders from among the scholars. Rules were laid down about attendance and holidays, about discipline, and about the timetable. There was to be a half-yearly examination, and medals were to be awarded to those who distinguished themselves in English, Latin and Greek, to the best mathematical scholar, and to the boy whose general industry and proficiency were outstanding. Every scholar on admission was to be able 'to read and spell English, and to write legibly from dictation'.

Proprietary schools suffered many divergent fates. At St Paul's, Southsea some ninety pupils were examined in 1841, but by 1848 the proprietors had decided to close the school.[3] In many cases it proved much easier to start a school than to maintain it in prosperity when established. The schools were always under-capitalized, and since they generally had ambitious, and therefore expensive aims, finance was a constant problem. Sometimes the proprietors handed the school over to the headmaster who assumed full financial responsibility for it. There was a fairly small demand for a high-quality education, and even in large towns with little or no comparable grammar school provision, the support of middle-class parents was limited. Where party feelings and prejudices were aroused, they were normally linked with religion and with the increasingly embittered relationships between Churchmen and Dissenters. The former were determined to maintain their traditional position as educators of the nation. The latter were very conscious of their growing numbers and their increasing wealth, and they were not prepared to accept a position of subordination to the Establishment. In the larger towns where Dissent was usually strong, the two forces met on a level of equality and Churchmen enjoyed little of the protection so long secured to them by the traditional institutions of the state.

The power of the religious impulse is undoubted. As we saw in Chapter 12, many schools would never have existed without it. In London many of the new proprietary schools came into union with the Anglican King's College, their pupils being able to enter the college as second year students, and this union scheme may have given an impetus to new foundations.[4] In the urban context, however, the general power of religion seems to have been destructive as much as constructive in its effect on the fortunes of the new schools. Examples can be given from three towns, Leicester, Hull and Huddersfield. In Leicester the grammar school was in decline, and in 1835 a company was set up to found a new school on the lines already described. The 'Leicester and Leicestershire Collegiate School' opened in 1836 and attracted a fairly steady number of about 100 boys. The early decision that the headmaster and second master should be clergymen of the Church of England and graduates of Oxford or Cambridge alarmed the strong Dissenting element in the town, which then organized a second company and in 1837 opened a second school, the 'Proprietary School for Leicester and Leicestershire' which provided no religious instruction. The new school opened with 128 boys, but the fees were too low, it never managed to pay its way, and it lasted only for 10 years. The Collegiate School, which was burdened by a heavy mortgage, lasted until 1866 when the shareholders decided to close the school and to allow the mortgagee to sell the property.[5]

In Hull events moved on very similar lines. The Anglican Kingston College and the non-sectarian Hull College both opened in 1837. Both schools ran preparatory departments and both made provision for boarders. Both had a very short life, Hull College closing in 1845 and Kingston College in 1847. In both cases the headmaster continued the school for some years as a private venture.[6] In Huddersfield the Huddersfield College Company launched by a Dissenting minister opened a school in 1839. It was established, according to a brochure of 1843, 'by a propriety [*sic*] of gentlemen entertaining various religious opinions, with the design of providing for the youth of the middle and upper classes a sound Classical, Mathematical and Commercial Education, upon a scriptural foundation'.[7] A parallel school with an Anglican bias, the Huddersfield Collegiate School, had been built in 1838, and the two schools coexisted for many years. Numbers at the College fell in the late 1850s,[8] recovered in the 1860s and early 1870s when they rose to 226 in 1874 and then declined again. In the mid-1880s the headmaster of the Collegiate School suggested an amalgamation of the two schools, the Collegiate School premises were sold, the pupils and staff moved to the College and a new company was formed. However competition from other schools was too strong and the company was wound up in 1893.

These three examples are all different. The schools proved to be least successful in Hull, rather more successful in Huddersfield. It would be an over-simplification to argue that religious dissensions were the only reason for failure in any of these cases. Financial pressures were always severe. The depressed economic conditions of the 1840s did not provide the best of opportunities for new ventures to establish themselves. In two cases financial problems led to the purchase of a proprietary school by a grammar school foundation. At York the Collegiate School was established in 1838. A few years later the new school had buildings and pupils but little money. St Peter's, the school of the Dean and Chapter, had endowments, but few boys and an unsatisfactory headmaster. In 1844 the Dean and Chapter bought the Proprietary School, the head of which, the Rev. William Hey, became head of the combined school. At Midsummer 1844, the combined school had 101 boys, 18 from St Peter's and 55 from the Collegiate School.[9] At Wakefield the West Riding Proprietary School had been opened in 1834. In 1835 there were 175 boys, but ominously, since there was a debt of £1,800, the directors decided to increase the number of shares. Ten years later it had become clear that the school would not be able to continue. In 1854 the grammar school governors purchased the buildings for £4,050 and the Grammar School was transferred to the proprietary school site.[10]

Proprietary schools may have suffered too as many middle-class parents, particularly the more affluent, came to prefer a boarding school education for their sons. The development of boarding schools which was reviewed in Chapter 12 was bound to make the going harder for all town day schools, grammar and proprietary alike. But it is probable that, in a middle-sized or even a large town, two schools were very likely to fail where one might have succeeded. It has been earlier argued that in the grammar schools, sectarian divisions were not important (see p. 82), but the situation as between the two groups of schools was not strictly comparable. Grammar schools were Anglican foundations where Dissenters were often allowed on sufferance. In the proprietary schools the two great religious forces met as equals and as rivals. The harmful competition between them was a price which education had to pay for the clash between Churchman and Dissenter.

Despite all these difficulties some proprietary schools did establish themselves and survive for a number of years, though in the latter part of the century they proved vulnerable to the competition provided by the reformed grammar schools and by public bodies like the School Boards and the Technical Instruction Committees. Of those which aimed to secure public school status the most successful was Cheltenham College. Established in 1840 the regulations provided that no one might become a shareholder 'who should not be moving in the circle of gentlemen'.[11] The town with its population of retired Indian civilians and military men offered a favourable recruiting ground for a school of high quality. Its organization into two departments – classical and military – reflected the career aspirations of the parents for their sons. It began with 120 pupils; 49 day boys, 21 half-boarders and 50 boarders. By 1845 there were 303, by the late 1850s about 600, and Cheltenham must be one of the very few schools where the shares had appreciated in value. Until new regulations were made in 1862 the organization was very different from that of the Arnoldian public school. The directors were in charge of the discipline (except in the classroom) and of the boarding houses, and the head's powers were consequently limited. After 1862 the principal had full responsibility as in other public schools.

Many proprietary schools were established in the London area because there were many Londoners who wanted to give their sons the kind of education which these schools provided. One of the most successful, which eventually acquired a status as a major day school comparable with St Paul's or City of London, was University College School, founded by a group of proprietors in connection with the new London University (University College) and opened in 1830. The curriculum was original for its day. There was little Greek and no Latin verse-making. Nearly all the boys learned French and many German. Much attention was given to mathematics and chemistry with some work in other sciences. There was no religious teaching and no corporal punishment. 'The quality of the education which was provided, and the character of the place', wrote H Hale Bellot, 'attracted those who were not content to stand upon the ancient ways.'[12]

University College School represented the Liberal/Utilitarian side of the new University of London. On its Anglican side some of the schools 'in union' with King's College were also noteworthy. One of the most successful of them was Blackheath which began in January 1831 with twenty-five boys and which survived until December 1907. The 1845 prospectus claimed a number of successes at Cambridge and at the East India Company's colleges at Haileybury and Addiscombe. In 1856 a special department was set up for boys who wanted to become civil engineers or who were intended for direct commissions or military cadetships. Four years later a master was appointed to teach mechanical drawing and physical science. In the mid-1840s numbers fell, but the school prospered under E J Selwyn (1847–64). In 1862 there were 248 boys.[13] Another successful south London head was Charles Pritchard, head of Clapham from 1834 to 1862, about whom a good deal has already been said, particularly about his work as a pioneer in science teaching. He had been for a year (1833–34) head of a school at Stockwell, but he could not work with the proprietors, and his supporters started up a new school for him at Clapham. This was very successful and after 7/8 years the committee handed over complete control to him. He was clearly a brilliant teacher with a very wide range. He taught mathematics and science, he helped boys to understand the beauties of Latin literature, he read English poetry and Bible stories with them. He took a keen interest in the school chapel and its music. He taught the boys geography and made them draw maps. Sir George Grove the musicologist who was an early pupil wrote[14]:

> I had been at two other schools which were considered good of their class; but with Pritchard the atmosphere was very different. The master was younger and more sympathetic; also, he had a great power of explanation and illustration, and took constant interest in his boys.

Such teaching power, Grove thought, perhaps existed in the public schools, 'yet in schools of our class it was a great novelty'.

Blackheath and Clapham were clearly good schools. Yet resolute effort and high standards of work did not always bring the success which Selwyn and Pritchard enjoyed in south London. Sheffield was another large provincial town in which two proprietary schools were established. The foundation and early history of Wesley College has already been reviewed (see p. 178). It had opened in 1838, 2 years after the Anglican Collegiate School which had opened in July 1836. In one sense the Sheffield story is happier than some others because both schools survived into the twentieth century.[15] Yet the Collegiate School, about which a good deal of information has survived, had a history of disappointment and unfulfilled hope. G A Jacob, who was head from 1842 to 1853, went on to the headmastership of Christ's Hospital in London. When a public dinner was given to mark the award of his DD degree in 1852, the sense comes over very clearly in the speeches that the school was not well supported in the town.[16] Thirty years later a local pamphleteer wrote that under Dr Jacob 'the school is said to have prospered, but it is doubtful whether it ever made such an income as to afford the headmaster any profit'.[17]

After Jacob's resignation a local business man became lessee of the property until the Rev. G B Atkinson became headmaster in 1860. He was a man of ability who tried to run the school on the public school model, and J G Fitch, after a visit in 1865, wrote favourably about the standard of the work. However the financial situation remained grave. Alfred Gatty, writing in the late 1860s, pointed out that no dividend had ever been paid to the shareholders and that there was a heavy burden of debt. Atkinson had leased the school at a rent sufficient to pay for repairs and debt interest. When in 1871 the chief mortgagee had not received his interest, he put the school up for auction. In the same year Atkinson resigned.[18] In his resignation letter he spoke of his disappointment and his plans to open another school in Shrewsbury 'under brighter skies and in a more genial educational atmosphere'.[19] The Sheffield Collegiate School was a good school and Jacob and Atkinson were able men. Their comparative failure shows how difficult it was, in one large provincial town, to get the necessary support, particularly when there was a comparable institution in Wesley College not half a mile away from the Collegiate School.

All the schools which have so far been described in this chapter aimed to serve an upper-middle-class clientele of professional and business men. Efforts were also made in many places to meet the needs of less affluent parents who wanted a briefer and less ambitious education for their sons, but who were not satisfied with what was offered by the National and British schools. In the terms used both by Woodard and by the Taunton Commission such parents wanted an education of the third grade for boys who would leave school at about 14 or, in some cases, of the second grade for boys who would leave at 16. It was widely argued at the time that this social group was very poorly served, particularly since many of the private schools which catered for it were very bad. Liverpool, a town with no endowed school,[20] provides some interesting examples of the principle of differentiation, so often discussed in these pages, applied to an urban setting. Two private institutions each organized a group of schools for different levels of age and curriculum. The schools of the Mechanics' Institution will be discussed later (see pp. 200-1). The Collegiate Institution 'for the general instruction of all classes combining scientific and commercial with sound religious knowledge' was founded in 1839-40. Its chief object, as defined in a speech made at the laying of the foundation stone of its building, was 'to furnish to the middle classes of society an education which shall be commensurate with their wants, and which hitherto they have not had the opportunity or the means of obtaining in such a way as it is desirable that they should obtain it'.[21]

The plan envisaged an upper school with a classical curriculum and both middle and lower schools, and when they opened in 1843, the numbers in the different schools were 40, 175 and 130 respectively.[22] Under J S Howson, principal from 1849 to 1865, the schools prospered; his account of them given in 1858 to the Social Science Association, is of considerable interest.[23] It is noteworthy that the first problem to which he addresses himself was that of religion. In the school religion according to Church of England doctrines was taught, but the sons of Dissenters were not required to learn the catechism. This arrangement had been successful, and in Howson's view 'the religious difficulty will normally give way under the action of good temper and good sense'.[24] He also analysed the social background of the boys by parental occupation; the figures specifically refer to the first quarter of 1858, but they were, he says, typical of the whole period since the opening of the schools in 1843. The statistics of both religious affiliation and parental occupations are given in Table 11.

The allocation of social groups to schools is very much what might have been expected, though it is strange that some boys from business and professional families were attending the lower school. Tradesmen, hotel-keepers and publicans, bookkeepers and cashiers were strongly represented in both the middle and lower schools as they would have been in similar schools in any town. The master mariners' and pilots' sons reflect the concerns of a great port. The large number of widows' sons in the middle and lower schools is likely to reflect the fact that these schools were inexpensive. Widows came from many social groups, but were alike in their straitened means. The lower school had also attracted a number of the sons of mechanics and domestics.

Table 11 Statistics of the Liverpool Collegiate Institution, 1858

	Upper	Middle	Lower
(a) Religious affiliation (March 1855)			
Church of England	104	175	211
Dissenters (all bodies)	11	57	89
	115	232	300
(b) Social backgrounds of boys by parental occupation (1858)			
Bankers, merchants, shipowners, etc.	47	38	9
Clergymen	22	5	2
Dissenting ministers	0	1	0
Physicians and surgeons	12	11	4
Manufacturers	10	15	5
Lawyers	7	2	1
Brokers, Agents, etc.	7	9	21
Gentlemen and professional men	14	20	6
Widows	5	25	22
Architects, builders, surveyors, etc.	2	7	1
Officers in excise and customs, registrars, etc.	7	8	9
Bookkeepers and cashiers	3	21	34
Farmers	0	4	8
Estate agents and accountants	0	8	4
Millers, corn and flour dealers	0	2	9
Contractors and stevedores	0	6	2
Hotel keepers and licensed victuallers	1	9	13
Tradesmen	0	51	111
Master mariners and pilots	0	9	18
Car and cart-owners	0	3	3
Miscellaneous	0	3	22
Mechanics and domestics	0	1	26
Promoted boys	6	2	0
	143	260	330

Source: Howson J S 1858: pp 241–9.

NOTES AND REFERENCES

1. Proprietary Schools: an abstract of the rules adopted by the proprietors of the Pimlico Grammar School 1831: 199–202
2. *Laws and Regulations of St Paul's School, at Southsea, near Portsmouth* 1831 Portsea. (Atkinson Collection, Hants RO). Other examples are: *Rules and Regulations of the West Riding Proprietary School, as*

prepared by the Committee, and approved of and adopted by a General Meeting of the Subscribers held on the 30th May, 1832 (Wakefield, 1832); *Rules and Regulations of the Huddersfield College, established 1838, incorporated with London University, 1844* (Huddersfield, 1850) (Starkey of Norwood papers, Notts RO)

3. *A List of the Pupils at St Paul's School, Southsea, as determined by the General Examination, Christmas 1841* (Portsea, 1842); Leinster-Mackay D P 1972

4. *VCH Middlesex* vol I p 258; *QJE* I (1831): 202-3 lists four proprietary schools in connection with King's College: Hackney (107 pupils); St Peter's Pimlico (78 pupils); Islington (67 pupils); Blackheath (which was to be opened in Jan 1832)

5. Martin, Janet D 1958 in *VCH Leicestershire* vol IV pp 334-5; Crook Z, Simon B 1958 Private schools in Leicester and the county, in Simon B (ed) 1968 pp 121-9

6. Lawson J 1969 in *VCH Yorkshire East Riding* vol I p 353; Lawson J 1952: 15-26

7. Quoted in Brook, Roy 1968 p 199

8. There is some correspondence in the Starkey of Norwood papers, Notts RO, about the problems which arose in launching a new Huddersfield College Company, 1859-60

9. Raine, Angelo 1926 pp 120-3

10. West Riding Proprietary School Wakefield 1835: 197-8; Leach A F 1907 in *VCH Yorkshire* vol I p 444; Peacock M H 1892 pp 28-31

11. Morgan M C 1968. The following material comes from Morgan's book, pp 1-53

12. Bellot, H Hale 1929 pp 169-71. Felkin F W 1909 is very brief

13. Kirby J W 1933 pp 1-76

14. Quoted in Pritchard, Ada 1897 pp 72-3

15. The Collegiate School united with the old endowed Grammar School in 1885. The so-founded Royal Grammar School united with Wesley College to form King Edward VII School, opened in 1905 (Armytage W H G Education in Sheffield, in Linton D L (ed) 1956 p 206)

16. (Jacob G A) 1852 pp 32, 38. This and material quoted in ensuing references are in the Sheffield Local Studies Library

17. 'An Oxonian' (Addy S O) 1883 p 9

18. Hunter J 1869 p 226; W(allis) P J 1950 237-9

19. Atkinson Collection (Hants RO). The letter is dated 3 Oct 1871

20. The grammar school had been discontinued when the master died in 1803, *CCR* 20, p 91

21. Wainwright, David 1960 pp 28, 33

22. *Ibid.* p 53

23. Howson J S 1858: 241-9

24. *Ibid.* p 245. The proposal not to make learning the catechism compulsory seems to have deterred the 24th Earl of Crawford and Balcarres from subscribing to the institution (Crawford Papers, Lancashire and Cheshire affairs, Correspondence, John Rylands Library, Manchester)

CHAPTER FOURTEEN
Schools for the lower middle class

Many attempts were made to provide better schools for the lower middle class, though most of these efforts were not very successful until public money was injected through the School Boards and the Science and Art Department in the latter part of the century. In a few cases – notably at Liverpool – Mechanics' Institutes set up day schools. There were pioneers in London, notably the layman William Ellis and the clergyman William Rogers. Most important of all were the plans made by the Church of England, particularly through the National Society's campaign of 1838–39 to create both 'middle schools' and training colleges for schoolmasters.[1] The two institutions, it was thought, would complement one another. They could be supervised by the same principal. Since the middle schools would charge fees, they might make profits which would help to meet the costs of the teacher training establishment. The training students would be able to teach in the middle school, and thus increase their practical experience. The schools, providing a good non-classical or commercial education, would meet a real need among farmers and tradesmen, and would extend the influence of the Church among classes where Dissent was very strong. The Winchester Diocesan Board of Education discovered that in the diocese the education of 'yeomen, tradesmen and superior mechanics' was conducted to a large extent by Dissenters.

> ... But for the effort now making on the part of the Church, through her incorporated National Society, and the Diocesan Boards in connection with it, the youth of the Church, among the middle classes, would have been suffered to remain almost entirely consigned to teaching foreign to her polity. The Board have endeavoured to call attention to this great want on the part of the middle classes, in the hope of being enabled to relieve it.[2]

The history of this 'middle school movement' has never been properly studied and the information about these schools is distinctly patchy. Many schools were certainly set up, though in some cases they did not long survive, and in others their ultimate fate is not recorded. In some cases, as already explained, middle schools were linked with training colleges, in others they were independent foundations, and examples will be provided from either group. Yet the information provided here offers only a brief vignette of a movement which deserves much fuller attention.[3] Linked training and middle/ commercial schools were set up in a number of cathedral cities. At Canterbury the commercial school curriculum included religious instruction, English grammar and spelling, writing, arithmetic, bookkeeping, history, geography, natural history, mensuration and mapping, practical mechanics, vocal music, linear drawing, and – at an additional charge – French. In 1842 there were forty-three pupils and when in 1845 the diocese was enlarged by taking in some parishes from the see of Rochester, another middle school was set up at Maidstone. However diocesan activity in teacher training did not continue for very long. The Diocesan Board closed their training institution in 1849 because they lacked the money to carry it on, and it is not clear what happened to the middle schools thereafter.[4]

At Bristol the cathedral school had been united with a training and middle school. In 1845 the Diocesan and Cathedral Training and Middle Schools had seventy-six pupils – five of them training pupils, eight cathedral choristers, and sixty-three pupils in the middle school. The fees for pupils over the age of 10 had been increased to £8 8s. per annum.[5] The training school was closed in the early 1850s when the diocese of Bristol combined with Oxford for educational purposes. There were differences of opinion between the Diocesan Board and the Dean and Chapter about the middle school, and both bodies withdrew their support from it, while the headmaster of the cathedral school tried 'to establish a school of somewhat higher pretensions'.[6] In 1846 the York and Ripon Diocesan Boards founded a 'Yeoman School' in connection with the Training College at York. By 1848 the school had moved to buildings adjacent to the college; there were eighty-six boarding pupils and the fees were £22 a year. A witness to the Taunton Commission explained that since the fees had been kept very low in order to attract farmers' sons, the school had got into debt. Many parents had been frightened by what was regarded as 'very high church teaching'. In 1858 the Yeoman School was amalgamated with Archbishop Holgate's School.[7]

At Lincoln the middle school founded by the Diocesan Board was for a decade much more successful than its efforts to provide teacher training.[8] From the beginning a middle-class school providing a general education was as prominent among the board's objectives as a training school for masters, and they decided to establish 'one General School' to meet both objectives.[9] There is no suggestion in the board's records – in the early years at least – that they appreciated the problems of managing within a single institution both young boys who would leave school at 14 or 15 and older youths who needed to acquire professional skills and to be mature enough at the end of their course to take up posts in schools. Initially the training students were admitted at 15, then the age was raised to 19, then it was reduced to 15 again with arrangements to send the students to the training school at Westminster for further professional experience. In fact, during the first decade, the Lincoln Board succeeded in training very few teachers indeed. The Annual Report for 1852 gives the total number since the beginning as eighteen, six of whom were in the school at that time.[10]

The school, on the other hand, seemed set for success. The curriculum included religious instruction, English, French, writing, arithmetic, elements of mathematics and of natural history and philosophy, history and geography and vocal music, with Latin, Greek and linear drawing 'if required'. A site of six acres was purchased, and a school and master's house built. A master, the Rev. F R Crowther, was appointed in June 1841 and in August of the same year teaching began. By 1843 there were fifty-four boarders and twenty-eight day boys, and the master had agreed, in return for the fees, to undertake the financial responsibility, thus relieving the burden on the board.[11] The boarders' numbers kept up until the end of the decade. In 1850 there were still forty-five of them,[12] but the numbers of day boys declined into single figures. The board and the committee of management were very concerned about the problem. Some friction seems to have arisen as a result of the master's custom of keeping boys back after school hours, a practice which Mr Crowther promised to change. The board looked into the general question whether an adequate 'commercial education' had been provided and decided that, since there had been deficiencies in teaching French and linear drawing, an additional master should be appointed for that purpose. No blame, they thought, attached to Mr Crowther. The small number of day boys 'arises from no neglect or partiality on the part of the Master, and is to be attributed to the distance of the school from the town, the number of other schools in more central situations, and other local causes which need not be enumerated'.[13] It is possible, though there is no evidence of this, that the townspeople disliked the strongly Anglican atmosphere of the school. For whatever reasons, it had not proved popular with Lincoln parents.

After 1850 the boarding side declined too. In 1851 there were thirty-seven boarders and two day boys, the decline, the board argued, being due to 'the extended usefulness of the Grammar Schools at Lincoln, Grantham and Boston'.[14] As we have already seen, competition among schools was very keen in the 1850s, and at Lincoln the decline was rapid. In 1853 there were sixteen boarders and one day boy. Mr Crowther, finding it financially impossible to continue, resigned at Christmas 1853. The board expressed their sympathy with his financial plight, but pointed out that they possessed no means 'to render him any efficient aid'.[15] If the school could not pay its way, it could not continue.

The board was still determined to continue its teacher-training work and was confronted with the problem how best to achieve this objective. With little delay the decision was taken not to continue the school in its existing form, and the reasons were set out in an interesting report adopted by the board in March 1854.[16] The report began by arguing that the system adopted for the training of masters had not been a success. Of those trained less than half had become National schoolmasters, the remainder having become ushers in private schools and similar establishments. The system of the Diocesan School had little in common with that of the National Schools. Consequently it was not likely to train students 'efficiently as Masters for schools for the poor'. Once that argument had been put forward, it was natural to argue that the middle school in its existing form should not be reopened. Its objectives had not proved to be compatible with those of a training school for masters. There was no reason to suppose that another master of the middle school would have any greater success since there was no fault to be found with Mr Crowther or his system of management. There were external factors too which argued against continuance. It was likely that a middle school would be set up at Lincoln, and possibly another at Market Rasen, endowed from the revenues of the Spital and Mere charities. Middle schools 'without a foundation to rest on' had usually proved failures in other places, and the education of the sons of small farmers was likely to be best supplied by providing efficient masters for national schools.

The middle school was not revived after Mr Crowther's resignation, and the building was eventually adapted for a women's training college opened in 1862.[17] The arguments accepted by the

Lincoln Board in the 1854 report were well considered, and the decisions to discontinue other middle schools linked with training institutions must have been affected by similar reasoning. It had appeared in 1840 that a training institution and a middle school might reinforce one another and economize by using the same teaching staff. In fact the experience of a decade had shown that it was very difficult to combine a school for young boys or girls with a training institution for older adolescents or young adults. By the 1850s the growing likelihood of the redistribution of educational endowments imperilled the position of non-endowed institutions, which were very vulnerable to short-term fluctuations in numbers. By that time too the introduction of state aid for teacher training presented serious problems to institutions with both training students for whom government grants might be claimed and middle-school pupils for whom no such aid was available. For a whole series of reasons an idea which had seemed very attractive in the late 1830s/early 1840s had proved difficult to work in practice, and the Lincoln story provides a model of what is likely to have happened in other places as well.

The most remarkable of these middle or commercial schools was certainly the Science School at Chester, directed by Arthur Rigg, the first principal of the Training College, though his pioneering plans were eventually abandoned.[18] The Chester training institution was planned to consist of a training school for fifty to sixty students and a commercial and agricultural school for sixty to seventy boys. The school opened in January 1843. Rigg was an unusual man with an enthusiasm for technical subjects and for making both boys and students proficient in practical skills. The Science School – to give it its later name – had sixty-eight pupils in 1855, the average number between 1855 and 1867 being forty-six. During the 1860s the number of training students declined sharply, while the number of boys in the school had risen after a decline in the late 1850s, and Rigg's interest seems to have been largely concentrated on it.[19] Clearly the school aimed at a higher level than those which have been described in other cathedral cities. A prospectus of about 1850 gives the fees for boarders over the age of 12 as £17 per term, there being three terms in the year.[20] In 1860 it was 'certified as satisfying all the requirements of the Engineering Department of Public Works in India for the preparation of candidates for the Indian Service'.[21] In 1862 the school gained three out of the ten places offered in the competitive examination for the Indian Engineering Department,[22] and a number of old boys, including one of Rigg's sons, joined that service.[23] The school attracted the sons of men like Henry Cole and Richard Redgrave of the Science and Art Department, and some of its old pupils rose high in the engineering and chemical industries.

A description of the college by an Irish visitor who went there in 1850 mentions a blacksmith's forge in which Rigg himself was working and a large basement room in which both young men and boys were busy with a variety of tasks.[24] Rigg resigned the principalship in 1869 and his distinctive ideas did not long survive him. The ruling opinion of the day did not favour his emphasis on industrial skills for the student teacher. In secondary education majority opinion favoured the literary tradition rather than practical or technological skills. The Science School had made a contribution to the expenses of running the college and it continued until 1883. By that time other voices were urging the claims of technical studies in secondary and higher education. Rigg's work, had it survived, would have contributed additional force to the pressures for a more practical and vocational curriculum.

Middle or commercial schools were set up on an independent basis by groups of Churchmen in several parts of the country. The first in London was a school in Rose Street, Soho Square, founded in 1839. Another was the East Islington Commercial School for the sons of 'respectable tradesmen' opened in 1841.[25] In Manchester Dean Herbert and a group of prominent Churchmen established the Commercial Schools in Stretford Road (1846), which are said to have been, in the 1850s and 1860s, 'the leading public High School in Manchester'.[26] In Bristol Canon Henry Moseley, former HMI and active advocate of teaching science in elementary schools, played a leading part in the foundation (1857) of the Bristol Trade School which took boys at the age of 12 and gave them a scientific training for 2 or 3 years to prepare them to work in local trades and industries.[27] In the small town of Dursley in Gloucestershire the initial meeting to discuss setting up a middle-class school in connection with the Diocesan Board attracted a gathering of ten clergymen and nine laymen (16 March 1840). The school began in hired premises,[28] but within a short time a building had been provided by a member of the committee, Mr Henry Vizard, in return for which it was agreed that a certain number of boys from Dursley, Cam and Stinchcombe should be accepted as free scholars. By December 1844 there were thirty boys – twelve on the foundation and eighteen paying scholars, ten of whom were boarders. By autumn 1849 the number of boarders had risen to thirty-one. Initially things seem to have gone well; examiners' reports were favourable and in 1847 the schoolroom was extended. The following year fortune changed. The master, Mr Huthersall, resigned at Christmas 1848. There appear to have been personal difficulties between the master and his wife, and it seems that he went bankrupt. His successor, appointed in November 1848, resigned after only a month, before he took up office. In 1851–52 there were negotiations with the then master, Mr Want, about his assuming the financial responsibility for the school, which he finally agreed to do. The minute book ends with a shareholders' meeting in March 1852, though the school went on certainly into the early 1880s, because the foundation boys continued to be regularly appointed until that time. The first twelve free scholars appointed in 1844 were the sons of a baker, a law-clerk, a millwright, a pawnbroker, an excise officer, a farmer(2), a pork-butcher and beerseller, a veterinary surgeon, a tailor, a writer, and the master of a blue-coat school. The youngest came at 7, the oldest at 15. Most stayed only a year or two. The 7-year-old stayed for 7 years, as did another boy who came at 8. Another boy came at 10 and stayed for 5 years.[29] Unfortunately no comparable information has survived about the fee-payers.

The Church of England held no monopoly in providing urban secondary schools of this type. In three major cities – Liverpool, Leeds and London – other agencies were at work, usually on a non-sectarian or secular basis. In both Liverpool and Leeds initiatives were taken by the Mechanics' Institution as an extension of the original objective of providing education for adult workers. At Liverpool the Institution had been founded in 1825. Eight years later two of its directors, James Mulleneux, a wine merchant and distiller, and R W Yates, an iron merchant, offered money for the foundation of a day school on condition that the balance of the cost was raised by public subscription. The effort was a success and the school opened in 1835.[30] This was an elementary school. In January 1838 another school – a high school – was opened, 'designed for the sons of the more opulent members of the community'.[31] The 'system of education' for the two schools, dated 1837, shows the lower school teaching French and navigation and nautical astronomy in the top class. The high school was to teach Latin and Greek and some natural science as well as mathematics and French. Members of the institution paid £1 15s. per annum in the lower school, eight to ten guineas in the high school, non-members paying slightly more in each case. In 1844 a girls' school was opened in addition, a building having been provided for it through the generosity of the shipowner George Holt.[32] This school was designed to meet 'the educational wants of the daughters of tradesmen, clerks, shop-keepers, mechanics'.[33] The curriculum covered the English subjects (including geography and history), arithmetic, writing, drawing and needlework. A small number of girls also learned French.[34]

The girls' school grew to about 300 pupils, and remained stable at that level. The lower school, by the late 1850s, had about 600 boys.[35] Clearly the level of work had quickly risen above the elementary. A programme dated 1852 shows that the top boys were studying simple and quadratic equations, plane trigonometry and chemistry, though they did not study Latin, and French and German were extras at an additional fee.[36] In 1856 the school was renamed the Commercial School,[37] and in the following year it received a very favourable report from Mr Morell, HMI, who commented that it provided the only systematic chemistry course which he had seen.[38] In the High School numbers fluctuated greatly. After a strong start they had fallen as low as 70 by the mid-1850s.[39] By December 1863 they had risen to 165 when there were 665 boys in the Commercial School.[40] By that time the schools were building up a credit balance. Up to 1854 there was a considerable deficit which was cleared up through the efforts of George Holt and other benefactors. However they always depended considerably on gifts from wealthy men in the city of Liverpool.[41]

Two features of the Liverpool Institute schools deserve special comment. Firstly their supporters were very proud of their position about religious teaching. They had, claimed George Holt in 1857, 'given a perfect example upon a large scale of the successful education of 1,000 to 1,500 young people of both sexes upon non-sectarian principles'.[42] Secondly, they were very early to take advantage of the new University Local Examinations which began in 1857–58 (see pp. 293–4). In 1859 there were four senior and nine junior candidates in the Oxford Locals.[43] In 1862 the schools had, in the Oxford and Cambridge examinations taken together,[44]

> passed the largest number of Senior candidates in the country, viz. nine; the second largest number of Senior and Junior candidates combined, viz. twenty-eight; and it also carried off the second largest number of first-class honours in the country, viz. six.

By the 1860s the Institute Schools had established themselves on a solid basis. It is remarkable that in this period Liverpool had developed two similar groups of schools because the Collegiate Institution, already described, served much the same clientele as the Institute Schools. Both adopted a liberal religious policy. The Institute Schools were non-sectarian. The Collegiate Institution gave Anglican religious teaching, but did not require Dissenters to learn the catechism.

The story of the Leeds Mechanics' Institution schools is similar and can be dealt with quite briefly.[45] The boys' school opened in 1845. It consisted of three departments – Junior, English and Commercial – and the original fees were 12s. a quarter. By 1847 there were 150 pupils. It seems that the second headmaster, Mr Bedford, appointed at the end of 1847, aimed at a more ambitious curriculum than had hitherto been offered. By 1849 the classics were being taught and the school was described as a 'Commercial, Classical and Mathematical Day School'. In 1853 the fees were considerably increased to meet the costs of these changes, and it looks from the Reports as if the new programme was too ambitious for the clientele which the school could attract. Consequently the school ran into a period of serious financial difficulty. In 1854 Mr Bedford left for a post in Scotland, and the committee had difficulty in retaining a competent head because of the difficulties of providing a sufficient salary. While the boys' school had been experiencing these difficulties, a girls' school had been started in 1854. By Christmas 1857 it had 80 pupils which had risen to 140 by Christmas 1863. By that time the boys' school was also prospering with 188 boys, and both schools were making an income slightly in excess of their expenditure. At Leeds as at Liverpool the annual reports in the early 1860s make much of successes in the Local Examinations. Leeds indeed mentions not only Oxford and Cambridge but also the examinations of the University of Durham, of the Royal College of Surgeons, of the Science and Art Department and of the Society of Arts, for the last of which the girls' school also entered candidates. It is possible that these new examinations did provide a stimulus to the teaching in this kind of school and attract more pupils to them.

The day schools of these Mechanics' Institutions formed only a part of their total effort in education, much of which was concentrated on their lecture courses and their classes for adult workers. The early nineteenth century linked formal with informal education in a fashion to which the late twentieth century, with its talk of 'continuing education', is only just beginning to return. The point has already been made that many schoolmasters were closely involved with the self-improvement of adults. The Hill brothers, for example, were interested in the Society for the Diffusion of Useful Knowledge, in the *Penny Magazine* and the *Penny Cyclopaedia*,[46] and many provincial schoolmasters were active in societies in their own areas. These men were very concerned that the educational processes which had begun in the school should provide both stimulus and discipline for adult life. Schooling was ineffective unless it produced the power of self-help as well as abstract knowledge. Voluntary societies of all kinds proliferated in British urban life.[47] Not all of these were educational, but a surprising number of them, like the retail co-operative societies, saw the better education of their members as a major means of attaining their objectives. There was throughout the century a secular dynamic of change which ran alongside the religious dynamic which is better documented and more widely known. The Utilitarians were by no means the only thinkers who preached a gospel of secular improvement based on a better understanding of the economic and political structure of society.

One very interesting thinker and practical educationalist who stood in this tradition was the London business man, William Ellis, founder of the Birkbeck Schools, which took their name from Dr George Birkbeck, creator of the London Mechanics' Institution.[48] The Birkbeck Schools stand on the extreme fringe of secondary education as defined here. Indeed they might be better described as offering a sound elementary course to upper-working-class/lower-middle-class parents who could afford to pay fairly well for it. Ellis told the Schools Inquiry Commission that the pupils – they taught both boys and girls – had in most cases left by the age of 13 and the school fees were generally 6d. to 1s. per week.[49] However Ellis' work was so closely linked with the urban tradition of education and self-improvement that it would be difficult to exclude him from this discussion. He began to try out his social ideas by undertaking some teaching in a British school in 1846, and he opened his first school 2 years later. His basic plan was to structure the curriculum round an understanding of the laws of political economy – what he called 'elementary social science'. This meant the interpretation of these laws in terms of the *laissez-faire* economic doctrine of the period. It was essential, he believed, that children should understand how strikes happen and why the prices of commodities rise and fall. He did not believe that these things could be explained by lectures. They had to be approached through the Socratic method of question and answer, so that the child would himself find the answers to the teacher's questions. To do this effectively was to lay the true basis for morality which depended on the understanding of social laws. Ellis explained his method as follows[50]:

> I began by asking the children why people dig and plough, why they build, and why they spin and weave, smelt, and perform all the various industrial works, why all this is done, and from that I go up to the highest questions in morals, my object being to tell the children nothing but to make them tell me . . . .

In this fashion the child would learn to understand his duty to his neighbour, and since in Ellis's view this was the primary moral duty, he did not provide any religious teaching in his schools. He was also anxious that children should learn the basic laws of physical science, and he emphasized the effect upon them of the general school environment. There were no blows struck, no harsh words. 'The whole school is conducted on a principle of order and appeal to intelligence.'[51]

Ellis opened several schools in various parts of London after the first began in 1848. He provided the buildings – usually old chapels or halls adapted for their new purpose – and the schools were then expected to be self-supporting. Infants of both sexes were educated together, but boys and girls were taught separately. A description in a book of 1871 of the Peckham School, opened in 1852, mentions 600 children under 14 teachers. There were separate junior and upper schools and in the latter the payments were higher and the children belonged to a higher class. The ordinary elementary subjects were taught together with geography, history, French, drawing, elementary and practical science. An example cited in this account about the nature of the skin and its uses illustrates the way that science was taught to the children. The physiological properties of the skin would be explained and then its commercial uses 'as in the manufacture of leather and glue, and experiments made showing the processes used in these arts'. No religious instruction was given, but the moral tone of the teaching was favourably commented upon.[52] However this was not a unanimous view; a local clergyman criticized the same school as Socinian and godless, fitting children neither for this world nor for the next![53] Most of the Birkbeck schools closed when the School Board provided acceptable alternatives after 1870. The Gospel Oak School in North London, founded in 1862, survived and was reopened in 1889 as a secondary school for 200 boys under the name, William Ellis School.

Ellis did not limit his concerns to his own schools. Among other pioneers whom he supported was the Rev. William Rogers, perpetual curate of St Thomas Charterhouse and later rector of St Botolph's, Bishopsgate in the City of London.[54] Rogers was incumbent of St Thomas's, a very poor district inhabited by costermongers, from 1845 to 1863. He started schools, he explained in his autobiography, so that he might reach the children in his parish since he had little hope of influencing their parents. A whole group of schools and of evening classes, a clothing club and a provident club, a reading room and a lending library were set up. In the usual way differing needs led to differentiation in the schools provided. In 1859 a middle-class school was opened which Rogers described as 'one of the pioneers of middle-class education'.[55] In 1872 this school was charging four guineas a year for 'training boys for "commercial pursuits, the competitive examinations in the Civil Service and the University Local Examinations"'.[56]

After he moved to St Botolph's in 1863 Rogers concentrated his efforts on middle-class education, since there was very poor provision in London for the children of tradesmen and commercial men who had to rely on unsatisfactory private schools. The argument is a familiar one, which we have met many times before. He hoped to meet the need through a schools corporation financed by the revenues of the City parochial charities. The large funds which would have been required for this never became available, but he did succeed in raising enough money from City companies and commercial houses to found a middle-class school in Cowper Street, City Road, Finsbury. which educated 1,000 boys. The school was non-sectarian and children were admitted irrespective of religious opinions. The Bible was taught, and there had, Rogers explained, never been any difficulties about religious practice. There was no corporal punishment and there had never been any difficulties about discipline.

The Cowper Street school was a success, but it was much less than Rogers had hoped to achieve. 'I wish', he wrote in his autobiography, 'I could see some early prospect of an organized system of secondary education for London.'[57] The provision of second-grade, and even more of third-grade, schools had presented major problems throughout the period. Many of the efforts made to meet these needs have been reviewed here – the Yeoman Schools and Commercial Schools of the Diocesan Boards and the National Society, the ventures at Liverpool and Leeds, the efforts of William Ellis and William Rogers in London. Much had been attempted but, in relation to the size of the problem, very little had been achieved. The report of the Taunton Commission commented that good schools of the third grade were the most pressing need. ' ... the artizans, the small shopkeepers, the smaller farmers are in many places without any convenient means of educating their children at all, and still more often have no security that what education they do get is good'.[58] There was a constant lack of money since schools at this level found it difficult to finance themselves and it was not easy to tap endowment funds. There was the constant nagging problem of religious teaching. Parents were ignorant, suspicious, and not always clear about what they wanted. Eventually the central government and the local authorities were to offer solutions to the problem, but that was a long process and one which involved its own difficulties in determining what kind of curriculum should be provided.

NOTES AND REFERENCES

1. Roach, John 1971 pp 45–8
2. Quoted in Rose, Martial 1981 p 10
3. A first step would be to analyse the reports and other papers of the various Diocesan Boards of Education
4. Berry M H A The Canterbury Diocesan Training School 1840–9, in Berry M H A, Higginson J H (eds) 1976 pp 123–31
5. *English Journal of Education* IV (1846): 57–8
6. *CathC* 1st Report, pp 743–4
7. Craig M 1961 in *VCH Yorkshire, City of York* p 458. For Archbishop Holgate's Free School, see *CCR* 12, p 689
8. For the following, see Lincolnshire Committee of the Diocesan Board of Education, Minutes (1838–66) (Lincs Archives Office). I have not distinguished between the meetings of the board and of the committee of management which are both contained in the book. There is also a printed set of *Reports of the Diocesan Board of Education on the principles of the Established Church for the County of Lincoln* 1840–55
9. Minutes, 31 Jan 1839
10. Minutes, 28 Oct 1852
11. Minutes, 12 May, 26 Oct 1843
12. Minutes, 24 Oct 1850
13. Minutes, 28 Oct 1847
14. Minutes, 28 Oct 1851
15. Minutes, 27 Oct, 9 Nov, 23 Nov 1853
16. Minutes, 14 Dec 1853, 7 March 1854
17. Zebedee D H J 1962
18. For the Chester Science School, see Foden F E 1959: 105–18; Bradbury, John L 1975 esp. pp 133–8
19. These figures are taken from Rigg's reports in Chester Training College, Minute Book 1854–67 (Chester City RO). In June 1867 there were 5 training students plus another preparing for the admission examination, and 51 boys in the school
20. Chester City RO, CR 86/12/17
21. *Vocational Aspect* XI: 111
22. Chester Training College, Minute Book, 12 June 1862
23. Obituary of Rigg, *Chester Courant* 15 Sept 1880, in Letters and Papers relating to the Rev. Arthur Rigg (Chester City RO)
24. *Vocational Aspect* XI: 110
25. *VCH Middlesex* vol I p 259
26. Mumford A A 1919 pp 293–8
27. See Moseley's evidence to the Taunton Commission, *SIC* IV, pp 198:1923–206:2025. On p 214 the trades entered by 57 boys who had left

the upper part of the school in the two previous years are given: 10 became engineers, 8 miners, 13 clerks, 3 sailors, 2 watchmakers, 11 other mechanical trades, 5 warehousemen, 1 still unsettled, 4 left for other schools. On Moseley's ideas see Layton, David 1973 pp 75–94

28. The following is based on the records of the Dursley Agriculture and Commercial School (Glos RO)
29. Foundation Register, Dursley School (Glos RO)
30. For the following, see *Reports of the Liverpool Mechanics' Institution (Liverpool Institute)* vols I–IV (1825–79) (Liverpool Central Libraries). The name was changed to Liverpool Institute in 1856. See also Tiffen, Herbert J 1935
31. 'Plan for the establishment of a High School', 7 Nov 1836, *Reports* vol I
32. *Annual Report* 13 March 1844 pp 47–8
33. *Report of the proceedings of a Public Meeting held on the 29th January 1844, in aid of the establishment of a girls' school . . .* p 17, *Reports* vol III
34. *Annual Report,* 11 March 1846 pp 16–17
35. *Annual Report,* 18 January 1860 pp 6, 8
36. Drawn up by the headmaster, Alexander MacIlveen, who was clearly an enthusiastic and competent teacher (in *Reports,* vol III)
37. Tiffen, Herbert J 1935 p 68
38. *Annual Report,* 20 Jan 1858 pp 8–11
39. *Annual Report,* 21 Jan 1857 pp 6–7
40. *Annual Report,* 8 Feb 1864 pp 3, 5
41. Tiffen, Herbert J 1935 pp 128–9
42. *Annual Report,* 21 Jan 1857 p 9
43. *Annual Report,* 18 Jan 1860 pp 7–8
44. *Annual Report,* 4 Feb 1863, Appendix p 24
45. For the following, see Leeds Mechanics' Institution and Literary Society, *Annual Reports* 1842–51, 1852–61, 1862–75 (West Yorkshire Archive Service, Leeds District Archives)
46. Dobson J L 1959–61 III(12): 80–3
47. Morris R J 1983: 95–118 is interesting on the background of co-operation and voluntary activity behind groups like Mechanics' Institutes
48. For Ellis, see Stewart W A C, McCann W P 1967 pp 326–41; Wickenden T D 1962. For contemporary accounts, Blyth E K 1889; Ellis, Ethel E 1888
49. *SIC* V, pp 502:13856; 503:13866
50. *Ibid.* p 505:13880. Ellis is describing his book, *Progressive Lessons in Social Science*
51. *Ibid.* p 513:13918
52. Bartley, George C T 1871 pp 419–26. The quotation is on p 425
53. Stewart W A C, McCann W P 1967 p 335
54. The following is based on Rogers, William 1888; see also Rogers W 1851
55. *Reminiscences* p 88
56. *VCH Middlesex* vol I p 260
57. *Reminiscences* p 210
58. *SIC* I, p 79

PART THREE

The great schools

CHAPTER FIFTEEN

The schools embattled

The last group of schools to be examined is the major public schools – the seven or nine of the Clarendon Commission of 1861–64. The commissioners examined Eton, Winchester, Westminster, Charterhouse, Harrow, Rugby, Shrewsbury, together with the two London day schools, St Paul's and Merchant Taylors', which were not included in the Public Schools Act of 1868. The seven great schools, largely boarding schools attracting boys from many parts of the country, formed the nucleus of the much larger group of 'public schools' in the modern sense of the term which developed in the 1870s and 1880s. The appellation has never been a precise one. The first *Public Schools Year Book*, published in 1889, limited the coverage to thirty schools, though that number was quickly enlarged.[1] Classification has always been imprecise around the edges since there are clear differences between the large nationally known boarding schools, the smaller boarding schools and the large urban day schools, all of which have claimed the title. Many schools with good reason claim it, but it has always meant different things under different circumstances to different people.

The boarding non-local element has always been important, though the public schools have always included a non-boarding element and, as we shall see, there were during the nineteenth century many battles about the respective rights of boarders and of local boys. Sir William Grant, Master of the Rolls, handed down an important judgment in 1810 in a case brought by some of the parishioners of Harrow about the purposes for which the foundation was being used. In the course of his remarks Sir William compared circumstances at Harrow with a recent case decided by the Lord Chancellor about Rugby School. Both (Harrow and Rugby) had, Grant said, in the course of time become 'a great Public School ... and the scholars who paid for their education, greatly outnumbered those on the Foundation; sometimes in the proportion of *ten* to *one*'.[2] Sydney Smith, writing in the *Edinburgh Review* in the same year, followed the same line of thought and produced a similar definition[3]:

> By public school we mean an endowed place of education, of old standing, to which the sons of gentlemen resort in considerable numbers, and where they continue to reside, from eight or nine, to eighteen years of age.

The historian A F Leach, writing at the end of the century after a major increase in the number of these schools, does not alter the definition. He speaks of 'an endowed grammar school which was wholly or almost wholly a boarding school for the wealthier classes'.[4]

The point has already been made that in the eighteenth and early nineteenth centuries the fortunes of the endowed grammar schools fluctuated with the ability and success of individual masters. A school as prominent as Shrewsbury, which in the sixteenth and early seventeenth centuries had been one of the foremost in the country, went into a long period of decline in the eighteenth century, and when Samuel Butler became headmaster in 1798 he found about twenty boys of whom all but two were the sons of burgesses of the town.[5] Yet throughout the eighteenth century there were always a few schools which enjoyed without a break a position of national importance. The most important of them were the three schools linked with ecclesiastical foundations – Eton, Winchester and Westminster. The first two were grammar schools linked with colleges of priests which had survived the Reformation. The third was the school belonging to the Dean and Chapter of Westminster Abbey. By 1800 a few more schools were gaining a national reputation similar to that which the collegiate trio had long enjoyed. Harrow and Rugby emerged from the ranks of local grammar schools, in both cases under the influence of Etonian masters. Charterhouse, the school attached to Sutton's Hospital, had become prominent in London. Shrewsbury produced a long list of classical scholars under the long headmastership of Samuel Butler (1798–1836).

This group of major schools was first formally defined when the Charity Commission was set up in 1818, since six schools – Eton, Winchester, Westminster, Harrow, Rugby, Charterhouse – were excluded from the inquiry. On that occasion Shrewsbury, which had very good historical claims to inclusion, was left out. Butler protested against the decision and the reasons he gave are worth noting because they emphasize the points by which he thought that the status of a public school could be judged. Shrewsbury attracted boys from all parts of the kingdom. It had a substantial endowment and numerous exhibitions. It had a distinguished record of university success, and a large number of pupils.[6] Butler's criteria of public school status were well chosen, and the points he made will recur in our later analysis. When the Public Schools Commission was set up in 1861, Shrewsbury was added to the six schools of 1818, all of whom kept their places. Its record of distinction under Butler and his pupil and successor, B H Kennedy (1836–66), would have made exclusion impossible.

By the time the Clarendon Commission reported the title 'public school' could be extended more widely than the seven so far discussed. The commission itself examined two of the great London day schools – St Paul's and Merchant Taylors'. Howard Staunton in his book *The Great Schools of England* considered the nine plus Christ's Hospital, which has always stood in a category of its own, and he also gave brief accounts of the four 'Chief Modern Proprietary Schools' – Cheltenham, Marlborough, Rossall, Wellington – and of Dulwich College, which in its reorganized form under the Act of 1857 resembled St Paul's and Merchant Taylors' (see pp. 12–13 on the London schools).

The 'public schools', in the modern sense of the term, which emerged as a coherent body in the 1870s and 1880s, were formed from three groups. First in prestige and historic pre-eminence were the seven schools of the Clarendon Commission and the Public Schools Act. Second came the old endowed grammar schools which, because they maintained their positions over a long period of time, made good their claim to high status. Among them were Repton and Tonbridge, which have already been mentioned (see pp. 13–14). Uppingham joined the group in the 1860s as a result of the work of a very able, though highly idiosyncratic headmaster Edward Thring (1853–87), of whom more will be said in Ch. 17. Finally there were the most successful of the new schools, like Cheltenham, Rossall, Marlborough and Lancing (see Ch. 11). An expanding demand for education and a growing middle class produced many new schools in early Victorian England, and only a few of them achieved secure status as public schools. Other new schools which became very prominent were Wellington, opened in 1859 as a memorial to the great Duke,[7] Haileybury and Clifton, both opened in 1862, and Malvern, opened in 1865. Schools like these led by men of great ability like E W Benson and John Percival, established themselves very quickly, and were soon ranked as equals with their older contemporaries. After the late

A History of Secondary Education, 1800–1870

1860s there were few new foundations. The list of public schools continued to grow through the upgrading of schools which already existed in the categories which have been described.

The public schools have attracted much attention from both popular and semi-popular writers and from modern scholars; indeed, apart from histories of individual schools, this is the one part of the story of Victorian secondary education which has been treated very much at all.[8] The story of the public schools is interesting. It brings in many remarkable individuals, it deals with an important period in the lives of many of those who were to become the nation's leaders, it relates to themes like the growth of organized games, of patriotism and of Empire which are of concern to many people. Yet the total number of boys who have received a public school education has always been small. Before 1860 it was very small, and between about 1820 and 1850 the total number of boys in the great schools did not grow, though within the group some went up and some down.[9] When the public schools are related to the grammar schools and private schools as part of the total national provision of secondary education, they do not loom so large as when they are discussed, as they usually have been discussed, in isolation.

One of the main arguments of this book has been to stress the connections and interrelationships between the different sectors of secondary schooling. In a situation of free competition, schools of all kinds operated within a constantly fluctuating market where success and failure could lie perilously close together. During the first half of the century the public schools – which I define here as the seven great schools – were not in general very prosperous, while many of the grammar schools declined. At the same time the private schools seem to have been expanding and to have achievements to their credit which have often been neglected by historians. After about 1850 the balance changed again. The 1850s was a difficult decade for the grammar schools, though many of them were being reformed. The public schools began to move forward, partly through the revival of older schools and partly through the foundation of new ones. The deeper reasons for these changes remain to be considered, but the coming of the railways must have had an effect in helping to concentrate boys into a comparatively small number of large boarding schools. As the public schools expanded and the grammar schools slowly put their house in order, the private schools relatively declined. By the 1860s the tides of popularity, which had been flowing their way in the 1820s and 1830s, had turned against them.

The discussion in these chapters will be largely limited to the seven

214

great schools, though to illustrate the point that by the 1860s they had
ceased to stand alone, something will also be said about two other
headmasters who were themselves old boys of those schools, Edward
Thring of Uppingham, who was an Etonian, and William Sewell of
St Columba's and Radley, who was a Wykehamist. The seven schools
collectively enjoyed considerable endowments, though there were
wide disparities between them, and the gross incomes given by the
Clarendon Commission were spent on many purposes other than
running the schools. For example the large incomes of Eton and
Winchester supported the provost and fellows/warden and fellows of
these colleges, and most of the wealth of Charterhouse went to
Sutton's Hospital. The Clarendon figures – approached with these
reservations – were as given in Table 12. Both Eton and Winchester
used the old system of fine and renewal of leases which has already
been described (see p. 34). The Clarendon Report pointed out that in
both cases the provost and fellows/warden and fellows had divided
the renewal fines among themselves, and had not brought them into
the general income, though at Eton they had contributed from the
fines money to extraordinary expenses.[10] At Charterhouse, on the
other hand, the receiver had told the Select Committee of 1816 that all
the estates were let at rack rent and none upon fines, 'and generally
upon twelve year leases; the estates have increased more than double
within the last twenty-seven years'.[11]

Table 12 Endowments of major public schools, 1864

	Annual income	
Eton	*c.* £20,000	
Winchester	£15,494	
Westminster	(£1,400)	
Charterhouse	£22,747	(of which about £8,000 was spent on the school)
Harrow	Less than £1,100	
Rugby	£5,623	
Shrewsbury	*c.* £3,000	

Source: PSC I. pp 58 (Eton); 134 (Winchester); 177 (Charterhouse); 208 (Harrow); 230 (Rugby); 303 (Shrewsbury). John
Sergeaunt 1898 p 230 says that in the 1820s and 1830s the
Chapter gave Westminster school 'scarcely £1,400 a year out
of revenues which were perpetually increasing'.

The management of the seven schools, as in the case of all the endowed schools, came under much criticism as the century went on. At Eton and Winchester the headmaster was closely controlled by the provost or the warden. At most of the other schools he was subject only to the rather intermittent control of a governing body of local gentlemen which met once or twice a year. At Rugby Arnold was very much his own master, though he was once almost dismissed over his article on 'The Oxford malignants'.[12] At Winchester, his own old school, he would not have had the freedom to achieve what he did at Rugby. In the great schools, as in every grammar school in the land, the governing body and the headmaster were managing an enterprise which was partly public and partly private. The point has already been made that those grammar schools which were successful had become so because their masters had succeeded in attracting boarders and paying day boys in addition to those boys who were entitled under the foundation to claim either a free education or an education at very low charges (see pp. 7–8). Exactly the same is true of Eton or Winchester, Harrow or Rugby. All the great schools consisted both of foundation boys and of other boys – usually boarders – who paid full fees and whose presence made it possible for the head and his assistants in a successful school to enjoy large incomes.

The Clarendon Report gives the numbers of foundation and non-foundation boys in all the schools at the close of 1861 (Table 13). There was a wide difference between the position in the three ecclesiastical colleges and in the four other schools. At Eton, Winchester and Westminster the scholars – seventy in each of the first two and forty in the last – were both educated and housed by the

Table 13 Major public schools: foundation and non-foundation boys, 1861

	Foundationers	Non-Foundationers
Eton	61	722
Winchester	69	128
Westminster	40	96
Harrow	33	431
Rugby	68	397
Shrewsbury	26	106
Charterhouse	45	71

Source: PSC I, p 8. The Shrewsbury figure covers sons of burgesses.

foundation. They formed the original core of the school round which everything else had grown and they maintained a separate identity as the schools increased in size. At Eton, by the nineteenth century, they formed only a small part of a very large school. At Winchester and Westminster their proportionate importance was much greater.

The conditions under which scholars lived were often bad, and this was particularly the case at Eton. They were poorly housed and fed, locked up every night without supervision. Since the college provided so little, their parents had to incur considerable expense and the total costs were not much less than those of the oppidans, the fee-paying boys.[13] Edward Thring, who went from college at Eton to King's in 1841, wrote 20 years later[14]:

> A mob of boys cannot be educated. Not five and twenty years ago, with open gates up to eight o'clock at night, and sentinels set the winter through, as regularly as in the trenches before Sebastopol, to warn us of the coming master, the boys of the finest foundation in the world starved their way up to the university.

Thring like many Etonians had gone up as an oppidan and had transferred into College because only collegers were eligible for the scholarships and fellowships at King's College, Cambridge. Even with that substantial bait on offer, College at Eton in the early nineteenth century was never full. The entrance examination was a farce and the vice-provost and fellows told the Clarendon Commission that in about 1830 'the number did not amount to 50, and at previous times the deficiency has been great'.[15] Thring himself was the son of a landed gentleman in Somerset, but since the conditions in college were so bad, many of the places were filled by boys of a much humbler origin – the sons of Windsor tradesmen or the occasional boy from a country grammar school.[16] The situation was drastically changed by Francis Hodgson, who became provost in 1840, and under a headmaster, E C Hawtrey, who was sympathetic to reform.[17] The living conditions were improved, better food provided and a serious entrance examination for scholarships introduced. As a result of the changes, the places were all filled and there was keen competition for entry. But open competition, as often happened in Victorian England, brought greater social exclusiveness because it favoured those candidates whose parents were in a position to buy the best preliminary education for them. The tradesmen's sons disappeared, as places in College became more attractive to boys of good family.[18] Arthur Coleridge, who was at Eton in the 1840s and who like Thring had been both an oppidan and a colleger, wrote in later life[19]:

> The Eton Collegers of to-day are certainly not the poor lads whose
> education was the object of our founder. A year or two since I heard
> the Head Master calling 'absence', and the names of 'Peel, K S'
> 'Talbot, K S' 'Fremantle, K S' etc., made me rub my eyes like Rip van
> Winkle. We never affected such purple blood in our time.

The Clarendon Report observed that the condition of poverty had
been given up and no inquiries were made about the financial
circumstances of candidates for College or their parents.[20]

Westminster was a school in which conditions seem to have been
poor and life harsh for everyone.[21] The account of Dacres Adams, who
was a junior King's scholar in 1820, paints a picture of constant and
oppressive fagging with little time even to eat his meals.[22] Moreover
the value of scholarships had declined, and parents had to pay nearly
£100 a year.[23] Yet the scholars' places were prestigious because the
awards were purely competitive. The scholarships were given to boys
who were already in the school after a series of verbal challenges
stretching over many weeks. As a result, they were much sought after.
Mr Cambell, one of the ushers, told the Select Committee of 1816 that
they 'were obtained by an examination, and creditable; boys of
distinction and all ranks are anxious for it'.[24] The Clarendon Report
recommended that the competition should be opened to boys
educated elsewhere and a wider range of subjects offered. As at Eton,
the scholars' conditions had been much improved in the previous 20
years.[25] At Westminster a traditional form of competitive test had
survived. At Winchester the scholars had been nominated by the
electors until in 1854 competition had been introduced on the Eton
model. The headmaster, George Moberly, had originally opposed the
change, but he told the Clarendon Commission a few years later that
the results had been outstandingly successful.

> We were comparatively poor in boys. The open competition brings
> boys of all abilities, of all families, from all parts of the country, and
> so spreads our connexion very widely.

In 1862 there were 137 competitors for 7 vacancies at Winchester. The
commission commented on the improvement in the treatment of
scholars there. They were well lodged and educated with very little
expense to their parents. The opening of scholarships to competition
had also, the commissioners thought, increased the number of
commoners.[26]

Competition was one of the great bywords of the mid-Victorian
reformers. They argued that the use of endowment money could be
justified only if it was spent on the most able scholars whose
subsequent achievements would reflect credit on the foundation. In

practice much of that money had always been spent on boys whose claim to receive it had nothing to do with their ability but arose solely from their birth or residence in certain places. Three of the great schools – Harrow, Rugby and Shrewsbury – had to deal with conflicts of interest between the boarders, on whom both the prestige and the financial stability of the school really depended, and the local boys. From this point of view they were in the same position as many grammar schools all over the country. In these three schools the foundation boys were in a quite different position from the collegers of Eton, Winchester and Westminster. The collegers, like the oppidans, were boarded as well as taught, and both were receiving the same kind of education. The Harrow, Rugby and Shrewsbury foundationers were day boys living locally whose requirements about lesson times, curricula and games were not necessarily the same as those of the boarders. They could, and often did, form a very indigestible element in the general composition of the school.[27]

The foundationers themselves were not a homogeneous group. At Harrow and Rugby a few of them were boys of a fairly humble background claiming their traditional right to a classical education (see p. 37) though, as we have already seen, that type of education became less and less attractive to many boys and their parents as the century went on. Increasingly at both schools the foundation rights were claimed by 'incomers' or 'squatters' as they were sometimes called who came to reside in the town in order to enjoy for their sons a good education at a very low price. In one sense the 'incomers' provided a more difficult problem for the school authorities and in another sense an easier one. Socially the people who took a good house in order that they might send their sons to a major public school were likely to be of much the same standing as the parents of the boarders. They were likely to want the same kind of education and they did not bring down the social level. On the other hand they were likely to be more numerous than the genuine local parents, and if they became too numerous, they would threaten the profits which were largely made from the boarding side.

It will probably be clearest to say something separately about each of the three schools before looking at the recommendations of the Clarendon Commission which gave a good deal of attention to the problem. At Harrow a group of parishioners went to Chancery about several matters related to the school trust, the most important of which was the general constitution of the school and the rights of local boys. In his judgment (1810) the Master of the Rolls, Sir William Grant, denied that the school had been conducted in such a way as to damage the interests of the parishioners. They had no complaint if they did not choose to take advantage of the classical curriculum established by the founder. 'I can by no means admit', Grant argued, 'that the propriety of any expenditure is to be measured by the number of Parish boys, who are to be immediately benefited by it; provided it is an expenditure, fairly referable to the purposes of the School'.[28]

Grant's judgment did nothing to promote the interests of local boys at the expense of the boarders, though it probably made the governors more cautious in keeping to the letter of their rules and statutes.[29] Both Christopher Wordsworth (1836-44), under whom numbers plummeted, and C J Vaughan (1844-59) under whom they increased rapidly, had problems about the admission of the sons of 'incomers'. Vaughan also came under local pressure to provide a commercial education for the sons of tradesmen and, since the governors refused to take any action, he set up in 1853 on his own responsibility the so-called 'English Form', a separate school in which Latin was taught free and £5 a year was charged for other subjects. The boys in the new school were kept entirely separate from those in the public school, and the accommodation was poor – it was said to have been a converted stable. The English Form was a poor satisfaction to local claims. H M Butler, Vaughan's successor, told the commissioners that the tradespeople and farmers were glad to have it, though there were only twenty-two boys in it. The numbers had been much the same since he had been at Harrow, that is from 1859. None of this social group sent their sons to the public school. There were about thirty foundationers in that school, 'the children of parents belonging to the higher classes' and many of them the sons of widows who had come to Harrow to enjoy the inexpensive schooling for their sons.[30]

The Rugby foundationers fell into the same two groups as at Harrow. The return to the commissioners showed 61 foundationers, together with 6 other boys residing with their parents who presumably paid fees. There were 396 boarders.[31] The clerk to the trustees' solicitor explained that a 2-year residence requirement, imposed in 1830, had checked the numbers. Incomers often came to the town before their boys were old enough so that they could go on to the foundation as soon as possible. These people moved away again after their boys had left the school, and they were quite a different type of person from the local people for whom the founder had made provision. However no distinction was made between them and bona fide local residents, and any Rugby tradesman could send his son to the school.[32] However, the incomers were important as well. It has been shown that between 1844 and 1863, 130 families came to reside in the town for the purpose of educating their sons. Such a comparatively large group in a small town was of some importance to its economy.[33]

Disputes over the rights of local boys led to a Chancery case during Arnold's headmastership. It seems that Arnold deliberately set out to exclude the youngest boys, so that by 1838, the two lowest forms, through which local boys would be likely to enter, had disappeared.[34] The matter was taken to court by a local solicitor, W F Wratislaw, who had sons in the school, and by another local parent, W S Gibb. Their complaints against the trustees covered the award of exhibitions, the imposition of a 2-year residence qualification, and – most importantly – the discouragement of the admission of younger boys. From the point of view of Wratislaw and Gibb this meant that their sons, if they hoped later to become foundationers, had first to receive a preparatory education, for which they had to pay, before they could claim their privilege at a higher level in the school. The Master of the Rolls, Lord Langdale, did not find for the petitioners in all points, but he did see substance in the complaint about the younger boys, finding that the entrance of those under 12 had been discouraged and that this was not in accordance with the objects of the charity.

> The school is by the founder designated as a grammar school; but the boys are to be taught writing and arithmetic in all its branches, i.e. more than grammar and classical learning is to be taught; and taking the test mentioned in the affidavit of Dr Arnold, it appears to me that those who are qualified in other respects ought to be admitted if they can read English and are capable of being taught the first elements of grammar.[35]

No order was made by the court because the trustees expressed their desire to give effect to the judgment, but nothing seems to have been done at the time. The evidence from the Clarendon inquiry is rather conflicting. The trustees in their evidence said that there was no minimum age of entry to the school. In general boarders would not be admitted younger than 12. Town boys would be admitted earlier 'if competent to commence learning Latin'.[36] A boy might have been expected to have started Latin at a considerably earlier age than 12. The report on the school again says that there was no minimum age, but that there were only nine boys below the age of 12, which suggests that the younger foundation boys had disappeared.[37] The whole issue of the younger boys is a puzzling one. It is possible to interpret Arnold's policy towards the younger boys as ruthless and unscrupulous, a deliberate act to take away from local boys rights which they had previously enjoyed. In his day many boys went to boarding schools at a very young age and he seems to have been against the admission of all boys under the age of 12, so that he might have argued that he was not treating foundationers in any way differently from boarders. Wratislaw, the prime mover in the 1839 Chancery case, was a professional man himself and in social rank probably not very different from the parents of many of the boarders. Though Wratislaw was a Rugby resident, socially he was much more on a par with the 'incomers' than with the local tradespeople, and Arnold may have argued that, if it was desirable to limit the age-range of boys in the school to those over 12, this was a greater good than the loss which might be suffered by some local boys and a loss which Wratislaw and Gibb were in a good position to sustain. Yet it is difficult to avoid the impression that headmasters like Arnold were behaving in an increasingly arbitrary fashion towards local rights, because most of the boys who enjoyed those rights did not, as they saw it, contribute a great deal to the success of the school. Certainly the Clarendon Report itself, as we shall see, adopted a high-handed and dogmatic attitude towards the rights of local boys.

The position at Shrewsbury was rather different from that at the other two schools. It was the only school in which foundation rights were enshrined in a recent Act of Parliament (1798) but they were limited to the sons of burgesses, not of residents, and new burgesses had not been created since the Municipal Reform Act of 1835. Consequently the boys entitled to free education were a declining group. Finally it was the only one of the three places which was a corporate town, and the corporation of Shrewsbury took an active interest in the education provided and pressed for money to be spent on a commercial school. In 1843 the corporation proposed to the trustees that they should establish 'a branch school of a commercial character', and the trustees decided to apply to Chancery for permission to use surplus funds for this purpose. B H Kennedy, the headmaster, opposed the plan, arguing that the sons of burgesses had no preferential claim on the funds and that the intention of the founders had been to provide a classical education. Finally a new scheme was agreed in 1853. The trustees were given a somewhat freer hand to dispose of surplus income, and Kennedy won his main point that the way in which school revenues were spent should not be changed.[38]

Kennedy did set up a 'non-collegiate' class, but this does not appear to have been very successful. The commissioners found only twenty boys in it.[39] The townspeople thought it insufficient and the trustees feared the development of a commercial school. The corporation and some of the townspeople made it very clear to the commissioners what they wanted. In a formal memorial the town council claimed that it would serve the general interests of the townspeople if the school were to give not only a classical education suited for scholars bound for the university or the professions but also 'an education of a liberal character adapted for and suitable to the requirements of the middle classes'. Several individuals also gave evidence, in particular Mr Southam who was a large ratepayer but not a burgess (and therefore not entitled to any foundation privileges). The existence of the school as it stood prevented, he claimed, the foundation of other schools which would have provided education for the middle classes. He needed an education at four/five guineas per year for his large family. He appreciated that this payment would not cover the cost, but he thought that the school ought to make some provision for helping him, as a large ratepayer, and the charge on the endowment would not be very great because there would be a considerably greater number of boys if these changes were made. Other schools available to him were very expensive, costing sixty/eighty guineas per annum, 'but when you have five or six sons to send it is a heavy charge upon a tradesman'.[40]

The commissioners, in their report on Shrewsbury, quoted Mr Southam's arguments, but their recommendations were directly opposed to what he wanted. All local privileges should, they argued, be abolished.[41] Their viewpoint was worked out in detail in the reports on the individual schools, but their general view was something like this. All the schools from the beginning had contained a non-local boarding element which had everywhere come to predominate until the schools formed part of a national grouping of public schools, attracting boys of high social status and teaching a classical curriculum. The local boys had very largely dropped out, or they had been replaced by 'incomers' who could lay no real claim to participate in the bounty of the founder. To make the schools once again schools for the sons of farmers and local tradesmen would mean 'the restoration of a small local benefit at the expense of a great public loss'.[42] The commissioners also made use of the argument about free competition which has already been stressed. All the major schools operated in a national market in which competition was keen and now that scholarships were awarded on a competitive basis at Eton and Winchester, that competition was bound to become keener. This argument, so typical of its day, was worked out most fully in the case of Rugby. At Rugby, as at all schools, 'free and charitable education' could be given to only a small number of boys. If that money were spent on the results of a competitive examination, it would be given to those who were most likely to profit from it and whose success would contribute the most to the future well-being of the school. The foundation boys under these circumstances would act as a leaven to the whole lump and would help to advance the status of the whole school. In a market which had become national, no school could afford to lag behind. Those schools would achieve the most which were able to attract the highest talent.

> If the best talents and proficiency of the kingdom are drawn to Winchester and Eton, they are so far to a certain degree drawn away from Rugby and Harrow. The former will tend to exhaust the best raw materials, so to say, of all Public Schools. Those greater powers, whether in the form of natural ability, or acquired mental habit, which under one universal system of indiscriminate gratuitous education, would be distributed casually amongst all the schools, will now rush to those whose system selects and rewards them .... If any school, therefore, possessing funds for gratuitous education, perseveres in bestowing them upon objects arbitrarily or indiscriminately taken for that purpose, it undertakes to contend against heavy odds in its struggles not only for honour but also for efficiency ... [43]

The argument of the commissioners does not only stress the element of competition. It also tends very strongly to take the schools out of their local context and to see them as national institutions meeting the social and educational needs of a limited and privileged group. The growth of the public school community, as sketched at the beginning of this chapter, was already well on the way. This division or differentiation was inevitably on class lines because it was only the comparatively wealthy who could afford boarding fees or the expensive preparatory education necessary to win competitive awards. Yet on this theme the commissioners did not speak with one voice. At Harrow, the most meanly endowed of the seven schools, it was accepted that the interests of the classical school should not be sacrificed to the interest of those parishioners who did not want a classical education, but money should be spent on providing a building and proper staff for the existing English Form.[44] The attitude towards the comparable 'non-collegiate class' at Shrewsbury was much more suspicious, possibly because its existence was regarded as much more of a threat to the classical school. The commissioners would have liked to abandon it, but since this was not possible, they urged the governors to watch carefully and see that it did not harm the primary objectives of the foundation, and to ensure that the fees were the same as in the classical school. If the fees were kept up, this would prevent the admission of boys of a lower social standing.[45]

The age of reform and competition was not to be an egalitarian age. The opening to competition of the Eton scholarships had raised the social rank of collegers. The new proprietary schools like Cheltenham had taken careful measures to exclude the sons of retail tradesmen (see p. 160). In an older England wide disparities of rank had not prevented boys of very different backgrounds sitting on the same benches, though no one supposed that they were 'equal' with one another. In the new age there was much more equality of condition within the institutions, but this had been achieved by ruthlessly excluding all those who did not meet the conditions by which equality was defined. The Clarendon Commission swept aside in what seems to us a very arbitrary fashion rights and privileges which had centuries of prescription behind them, and they did this in the name of a concept of 'the public school' which was a comparatively new creation when they reported. Just as Arnold had done with the first two forms at Rugby, they were prepared to sweep away with very little ceremony rights which did not fit into their preferred pattern of what a public school should be. Moreover they were successful, and their model imposed itself as the standard for the new schools which were developing so rapidly. The post-Clarendon public school was to be emphatically non-local and socially exclusive.

The story in these schools does have an epilogue after the passing of the Public Schools Act in 1868. At Shrewsbury the new statutes simply provided for the gradual phasing out of the burgesses' rights to free education.[46] At Harrow there was continued agitation over the rights claimed by incomers, but eventually these difficulties were overcome and a new building was opened for the Lower School in 1876.[47] At Rugby Temple had favoured the creation of a Lower School giving a semi-classical and commercial education and, although here too there was much controversy about what was to be done, the buildings of the school, later known as the Lawrence Sheriff School, were completed in 1878.[48] At Rugby and Harrow these new schools did provide in a significant way for the local boys who no longer found a place in the public school itself. In an age when stratification and differentiation were the keynotes, this had proved to be the only possible answer to the problem. The old local rights ran directly counter to the ideals and objectives of the new age.

NOTES AND REFERENCES

1.   Honey J R de S 1977 p 250
2.   For Grant's judgment, see Carlisle, Nicholas 1818 vol II pp 138–45. The quotation comes from p 144
3.   Remarks on the system of Education in Public Schools *ER* XVI (1810)) 327
4.   Leach A F (ed) 1900 p 2. See also his *History of Winchester College* (1899) pp 5–8
5.   Fisher G W 1899 p 264
6.   Butler, Samuel 1896 vol I pp 197–8 (in a letter to the Hon H G Bennett, MP, 20 Sept 1820)
7.   On the interesting history of Wellington and its first master, E W Benson, see Newsome, David 1959
8.   Modern scholarly books include Newsome, David 1961; Wilkinson, Rupert 1964; Bamford T W 1967; Simon B, Bradley, Ian (eds) 1975; Honey J R de S 1977; Mangan J A 1981; Chandos, John 1984
9.   Bamford T W 1961 The prosperity of public schools 1801–1850: 85–96
10. *PSC* I, pp 59, 135–6
11. *Report from SC, House of Commons* 1816 p 242
12. Bamford T W 1960 pp 99–103
13. *PSC* I, p 65
14. Parkin G R 1898 vol I p 23
15. *PSC* II, p 110
16. Hollis, Christopher 1960 pp 174–5
17. Maxwell-Lyte H C 1875 pp 415–24
18. Hollis, Christopher 1960 pp 248–9, 289–90
19. Coleridge, Arthur 1921 p 79
20. *PSC* I, pp 67–8
21. *PSC* I, pp 162–3
22. Carleton J D 1965 p 51
23. Sargeaunt, John 1898 p 231
24. *Report from SC, House of Commons* 1816 p 251. The system of examination is described on p 250
25. *PSC* I, pp 160–1
26. *PSC* I, pp 137–9
27. At Charterhouse the Gownboys do not seem to have formed such a distinct group. The Select Committee of 1816 was told that they were boys of the same general description as the town boys, generally 'the sons of gentlemen of very confined income and of large families' (*Report from SC, House of Commons* 1816 pp 273, 311)
28. Quoted in Carlisle, Nicholas 1818 vol II p 143
29. The following account of events at Harrow is based on May, Trevor The other Harrovians: local boys at Harrow School in the nineteenth century, in Searby P (ed) 1981 pp 86–112
30. *PSC* I, p 211; *PSC* IV, pp 158–61
31. *PSC* II, p 303
32. *PSC* IV, p 252
33. Bamford T W 1957–58: 25–36
34. Bamford T W 1960 ch XII. M H Bloxam, a former foundationer and a

Rugby solicitor, specifically accused Arnold of this, and of appointing to teach the younger boys two men who were quite incompetent for the work (*Report from SC, House of Lords* 1865, pp 45:21-3; 46:32-5

35. Beavan, Charles 1840 vol I (1838, 1839, 1 & 2 Vict.) p 466
36. *PSC* II, p 304
37. *PSC* I, p 235. M H Bloxam claimed that the younger boys had been 'virtually driven away from the school' (*Report from SC, House of Lords* 1865 p 45: 21)
38. Oldham, J Basil 1952 pp 111-13
39. *PSC* I, pp 307, 311
40. *PSC* IV, pp 325-9. There is also some interesting evidence by Mr J H Edwards who was Shrewsbury-born but not a burgess
41. *PSC* I, p 11
42. *PSC* I, p 10
43. *PSC* I, pp 269-71
44. *PSC* I, p 227
45. *PSC* I, p 322
46. Oldham, J Basil 1952 p 127
47. May, Trevor The other Harrovians: local boys at Harrow School in the nineteenth century, in Searby P (ed) 1981 pp 103-4
48. On developments at Rugby, see Hope-Simpson J B 1967 pp 56-7, 94, 108-11. The *Report from SC, House of Lords* 1865 says a good deal about this: p 37 (views of local opponents of Temple's scheme); pp 139-66 (Temple's evidence, including his proposal for a 'first-rate middle school' and his views about the 'sojourners' in the town)

CHAPTER SIXTEEN
The coming of reforms

Overall numbers in the great schools did not grow during the first half of the nineteenth century. At the beginning of the century there was rapid growth (1805-11), followed by a period of fluctuating prosperity (1811-31). Between 1831 and 1843 there was a sharp fall, and by 1850 numbers had returned again to about the 1811-31 level.[1] The general advance began in the 1850s and 1860s with the growth of the new schools. The Clarendon Report gave a total, at Christmas 1861, of 2,696 boys for the nine schools (that is including St Paul's and Merchant Taylors'). Since the two London schools had 415 boys the boys in the seven schools numbered 2,281.[2] The advance may also have been accelerated by the generally favourable judgments of the commission and even more by the more stable economic conditions of the mid-century. But the causes for both stagnation and growth need more careful examination than they have hitherto received.

Before that is attempted, something more needs to be said about the individual schools and about the social background of the boys who attended them. John Keate at Eton (1809-34) had to struggle with major problems. He confronted a disorderly school with only a small staff of assistant masters, who were not all very trustworthy. He himself attempted to teach a class of boys so numerous as to be unmanageable. One Etonian of his period remembered being one of 198 boys in the headmaster's division. 'Songs and even choruses used to be sung in school, but Dr Keate was seldom able to ascertain whence the sounds proceeded.'[3] He distrusted the boys' honour, accused them of lying, and flogged incessantly, but he still waged a rather unsuccessful battle with schoolboy lawlessness. Any chance of reform was made impossible by the rigid conservatism of the provost, Joseph Goodall (1809-40). Nevertheless the school remained much the largest of the public schools and preserved its strong aristocratic connection. Under Hodgson (provost 1840-53) and Hawtrey (head-master 1834-53) Eton moved slowly but definitely into the age of reform.

Harrow, the other school strongly connected with the aristocracy, was prosperous at the beginning of the century, but suffered a period of major decline between 1825 and 1844. Under Christopher Wordsworth (1836-44) numbers fell as low as seventy-eight,[4] though they rapidly recovered under his successor C J Vaughan. Winchester had a rather stagnant period under the long reign of George Moberly (1835-66), though numbers did begin to grow towards the end of his time. The school was deserted by many families which had sent boys there for generations, and it may have suffered too from the High Church views of Moberly and his second master, Charles Words-worth. Moberly's daughter commented that for 30 years he was never asked to preach in any but one of the Winchester parish churches while his wife and daughters were for many years never invited to join in any parish work. Such isolation is not likely to have been good for the school.[5]

Four of the nine schools included in the Clarendon inquiry were in London. Two of these, St Paul's and Merchant Taylors', were day schools. The commissioners found them both well conducted, though they thought that at St Paul's the school's objectives were set at too low a level and the numbers ought to be increased.[6] Westminster and Charterhouse had not flourished in the preceding half-century. Charterhouse grew in numbers for a time under John Russell (1811-32) who introduced the monitorial system of teaching, but numbers fell again before the end of his time.[7] At Westminster, which in the eighteenth century had attracted many boys of the best families, they fell even further. In 1841 the Queen's scholars actually outnumbered the town boys. The school received only meagre financial support from the Dean and Chapter and conditions in the boarding houses were crowded and poor. In 1846 a visitation was held after a parent had complained to Sir Robert Peel about the state of the school. The captain of the school was expelled and the headmaster, Richard Williamson, though he was not entirely to blame for what had happened, resigned.[8] Under his successor, H G Liddell, things began to improve but, as the Clarendon Report explained, the situation was not favourable to boarding schools in central London. The growing emphasis on health and on organized games had led parents to prefer rural schools which had also become more accessible than formerly. In the case of Westminster the view was clearly expressed by the commissioners that it was extremely difficult to combine boarders and day boys in the same school. The governing body ought to make a choice – either to make the school a day school or, if they wished it to remain a boarding school, they should remove it into the country. There was, the commissioners thought, a large demand in London for good day schools and, in order to meet this, St Paul's and Merchant Taylors' ought to be expanded, either on their existing sites or on new sites in the suburbs.[9] Most of what they recommended came to pass. Charterhouse moved to Godalming in 1872, and Merchant Taylors' moved on to its old site. St Paul's moved to West Kensington in 1884. Only Westminster stayed in its original home and continued in its old shape as part day, part boarding school.

The two schools which, in rather different ways, were successful throughout the period were Shrewsbury and Rugby. Butler, a Rugbeian of Thomas James's day, built up the school from nothing to be the leading classical school in England, and the high level of scholarship which he achieved was continued under his successor, B H Kennedy. Yet successes at the universities had not brought large numbers. Kennedy thought that the school had suffered from the competition of proprietary schools and from the defects of its buildings.[10] Moreover the town lacked good communications. Rugby, though things did not always go well, was the great success story of the seven. Thomas Arnold, when he was appointed in 1827, went to the headship of a well-known and successful school. It had risen in repute under the Etonian Thomas James (1778–94), and Arnold's predecessor, John Wooll (1806–28) had trained some distinguished men, though numbers fell during his last few years, and he had also seen the school rebuilt.[11] Of Arnold as of Samuel Butler of Shrewsbury more will be said later (see pp. 244–8). It is not easy to estimate Arnold's influence on English education, which has probably been exaggerated. Yet the position which the school had built up by mid-century was remarkable. The Clarendon Commission dealt with it at great length and with almost exaggerated respect. Its headmaster in the 1860s, Frederick Temple – 'Granite on Fire' as he was described – was a very remarkable man, and the school had more influence than any other of the seven on the new schools which were developing. The French observers, Demogeot and Montucci, visited it during Temple's period and, reviewing the report of the commissioners, spoke of the 'public confidence which Rugby School has enjoyed for many years and never more completely, since Arnold's time, than at the present day'.[12]

Some light has been cast on the social background and career destinations of the boys who went to the great schools, though there are major topics – particularly the important question when manufacturers and commercial men started sending their sons to public schools in large numbers – about which very little is known. The status of the parents of boys entering Eton, Harrow and Rugby has been classified, and the figures for the period 1831–40 are given in Table 14. The occupations of fathers of Wykehamists, born between 1820 and 1829, and therefore covering much the same period as the above, have also been worked out (Table 15). The form of the list is somewhat different, but not so much so as to make comparison impossible. The usefulness of the lists is much reduced by the large number of 'others' – people about whom nothing is known – though one would not expect their social status to have been very different from that of the other groups on the list.

There were wide variations from school to school and in the proportion of the different groups which sent their sons to public schools. The Winchester analysis shows a strong representation of clergy and professional men with fewer gentry than in other schools – that is, if 'gentlemen of leisure' in one case can be equated with 'gentry' in the others. The same social groups were strongly represented at Rugby. A Rugby master, Charles Evans, told the commissioners that the pupils were 'members for the most part of the working upper middle class'.[13] Figures based on eight schools (the seven plus St Paul's) show very different proportions of attendance at public schools among different groups. Over the first half-century to 1850, boys entering the schools numbered less than one in ten of sons of serving officers and less than one in five of clergymen, with few from medicine, law and teaching. Among the gentry the proportion was less than one in two and among the titled aristocracy more than one in two.[14] Another calculation shows that among Cambridge

Table 14 Status of parents of boys entering Eton, Harrow and Rugby, 1831–40

	Lower	Middle	Profes- sional	Clergy	Services	Gentry	Titled	Others	Total
Harrow	0	0	39	62	28	210	117	119	575
Rugby	0	11	12	154	29	494	59	129	888
Eton	0	7	61	44	27	389	232	536	1,296

Source: Bamford T W 1961 Public schools and social class, 1801–50: 225.

Table 15 Occupations of fathers of Wykehamists, born 1820–29

Church	117	(43.2%)	Law	23	(8.5%)
Medicine	14	(5.2%)	University teaching and research	4	(1.5%)
Schoolteaching	5	(1.8%)	Other professions	0	
Engineering	0		Business	8	(2.9%)
HM forces	40	(14.8%)	Government service	10	(3.7%)
The arts	0		Farming	0	
Other occupations	1	(0.4%)	Gentlemen of leisure	49	(18.1%)

Total occupations Known 271 (64.8%)
Not known 147 (35.2%)
Total 418

Source: Bishop T J H, Wilkinson Rupert 1967 p 104; see also Bishop T J H 1962.

alumni – a very restricted group – 80 per cent of the sons of the landowning class had been educated in first-grade public schools and 10 per cent in other public schools during the nineteenth century.[15]

Figures of careers followed by boys who were at public schools during the 1830s – and which can therefore be compared with parental occupations already given for the same period – show a similar pattern to that already cited (Tables 16 and 17).

By the 1860s, according to the sources already used, fewer boys were going into the Church and more were taking up careers in business. It has been argued that, from quite early in the century, wealthy men in

Table 16 Careers of boys entering Harrow and Rugby in 1835

	Armed forces	Church	Law	Administration and politics	Scholastics	Business
Rugby	11	19	9	8	0	0
Harrow	7	6	3	10	0	2

	Overseas	Medicine	Science and engineering	Other occupation	Died young	No information
Rugby	0	1	0	0	4	21
Harrow	1	0	0	0	0	8

Source: Bamford T W 1967 p 210.

Table 17 Careers of Wykehamists, born 1820–29

Church	121	(34%)	Law	48	(13.5%)
Medicine	7	(2%)	University teaching and research	23	(6.5%)
Schoolteaching	8	(2%)	Engineering	3	(0.8%)
Other professions	2	(0.6%)	Business	23	(6.4%)
HM forces	69	(19.4%)	Government service	17	(5.2%)
The arts	0		Other occupations	0	
Farming	2	(0.6%)	Gentlemen of leisure	31	(8.8%)
			Total 354		

Source: Bishop T J H, Wilkinson, Rupert 1967 p 64.

industry and business were beginning to send their sons to the public schools and that, as a result, the older ruling and professional classes fused with the new wealth to create a new ruling group for late-nineteenth/early-twentieth-century England.[16] There is probably much truth in this argument, but it would, I think, be impossible to establish it by evidence which could be quantified, since the detailed investigations have not been carried out. The process certainly happened very early with some families of great wealth. Peel was sent to Harrow and Gladstone to Eton before Christ Church and a political career, financed by Lancashire cotton in the one case and Liverpool shipping in the other. But for families of more modest wealth, who formed the majority of the social group in question, only hints can be given, and they come from the end of the period. J G Fitch, reporting for the Taunton Commission on the grammar schools of the West Riding, commented that the gentry and the manufacturers normally sent their sons out of the county for their education.[17] At much the same time both Kennedy and Thring made reference to boys from Lancashire. On June 24th 1864 Thring recorded in his diary his deep appreciation of the gift of £100, with promise of further aid, to a fund for carrying out their plans. The donor was a Manchester merchant whose boy had been for three years at Uppingham and who wished to do what he could to help the school's work. At Shrewsbury some of these boys stayed only a year or two 'before they go into some active profession or business'.[18] The rather later comic novel *Vice Versa. A Lesson to Fathers* by 'F Anstey' (T A Guthrie) (1882) depicts a situation which must have occurred in many real middle-class families. The city merchant, Paul Bultitude, and his son, Richard, exchange roles through the agency of the magic Garuda stone. Paul has received a commercial education. Richard, when the story begins, is at a private school with a classical curriculum. He wants to be taken away and sent to a public school, and, at the end of the story, he is sent to Harrow. This upward social movement – commercial school, classical private school, public school – reflects real changes in middle-class aspirations during the century.

The success and popularity of the late-nineteenth-century public schools were slowly won. Before they were likely to attract the real-life Paul Bultitudes in any number, they had to overcome two major lines of criticism. The first and more serious was the growing attack on their discipline and moral atmosphere. The second was the attack on the dominance of the classics and the very limited nature of the curriculum. The two complaints were often combined, though they were in essence separate, and they were not resolved in the same way. Nineteenth-century boarding schools remained by modern standards rather rough places. The exploits of the bully Flashman took place in the Rugby of the reforming Dr Arnold, but in Part II of *Tom Brown's Schooldays*, Thomas Hughes entitled the first chapter 'How the tide turned'. At the end of the eighteenth and the beginning of the nineteenth centuries all the major schools confronted serious problems of order. Sometimes, as in College at Eton, the boys lived under very poor conditions. Punishment was harsh, but headmasters and their staffs, often too few in number for the work they had to do, were still unable to maintain effective control.

Christopher Hollis, in his book on Eton, made the point that there are arguments for systems of wide freedom and of rigid discipline ' ... but the schools of the eighteenth century seemed to have the worst of both systems without any redeeming features. Barbaric anarchy reigned and at the same time a system of discipline which was both utterly savage and at the same time utterly ineffective.'[19] Serious rebellions were not uncommon. At Winchester trouble broke out in 1793 and 1818, when the Riot Act was read and soldiers sent for.[20] At Rugby there was a serious outbreak in 1797 – another occasion on which the Riot Act was read.[21] In 1818 Eton was in a state of uproar for several days over changes in locking-up times.[22] In the same year there were disturbances at Shrewsbury. The boys got up fights in the town, a placard was put up threatening Dr Butler with personal violence, and the painted glass in the school library was broken by stones.[23] In 1818, in fact, three schools – Eton, Winchester, Shrewsbury –

experienced major breakdowns in discipline. There were occasional problems afterwards, but that seems to have been the high point of disaffection.[24]

Relationships between masters and boys got better in the 1820s and 1830s, but many problems remained over the rights of the prefects and the fagging duties of the younger boys. Though these relationships were regularized and to some extent humanized as the century went on, they long continued to cause difficulty and produced the occasional scandal, with a flurry of pamphlets and press articles. This happened, for example, at Winchester when there was a rebellion against the authority of the commoner prefects in 1828,[25] and in 1872–73 when there was a sharp controversy over the punishment of a boy who had received thirty strokes across the shoulders, five ground-ashes being broken during the punishment.[26]

It was a Wykehamist, Sydney Smith, who had begun the public criticism of the whole system as early as 1810.[27] Every boy, Smith argued, was 'alternately tyrant and slave', and the older boys were given 'an absurd and pernicious opinion of their own importance'. The schools were too big, there was too little supervision, and those of middling talent had no incentive to improve themselves. 'Boys, therefore, are left to their own crude conceptions, and ill-formed propensities; and this neglect is called a spirited and manly education.'

Criticism became much keener in the 1830s, that great decade of reform. It continued the line of attack which Sydney Smith had initiated into the bullying and tyranny inherent in the system, and opened a new assault against the teaching. A purely classical education did not meet the demands of the age and moreover the classics were not taught well, so that boys after devoting years to studying them, left school with only a desultory knowledge of the subjects to which they had devoted all their time.[28] Lytton Bulwer, writing in 1833, complained: 'Religion is not taught – Morals are not taught – Philosophy is not taught – the light of the purer and less material sciences never breaks upon the gaze. The intellect of the men so formed is to guide our world, and that intellect is uncultured!'[29] The *Quarterly Journal of Education* contains a very interesting series of articles on the public schools in the early 1830s – interesting not least because they gave Thomas Arnold an opportunity to reply to their criticisms, though it was not convinced by what he said. An Etonian, the *Journal* argued, might well acquire the tastes of a glutton or a drunkard, a skill in brutal sports and a relish for degraded female society.[30] Fagging led to brutality on the one side and to subservience on the other. Punishments ought not to be awarded capriciously or passionately. They should lie in the hands of the master and not of other boys. Moral and religious education had often become a mere matter of form.[31]

Arnold made two contributions to the discussion. One of these was a defence of classical education. The second confronted the critics of moral tone and discipline head on, and is of considerable importance in the rehabilitation of the public school idea which was beginning when Arnold wrote.[32] A boy was, he argued, naturally inferior to his parents and teachers and since this was so, he could not be degraded by physical chastisement. As he grew older and developed more fully as a moral being, his change in status would be marked by his emancipation from punishments of this kind. When boys lived together in a school, some services were bound to be demanded from the younger by the older. The objective of the school should be to organize these services under the control of older boys who represented a constituted authority sanctioned by the headmaster and in close contact with him. If this were done with strictness but without cruelty it formed no mean part of education. 'Many a man who went from Winchester to serve in the Peninsula in the course of the last war must have found his school experience and habits no bad preparation for the activity and hardship of a campaign; not only in the mere power of endurance, but in the helpfulness and independence which his training as a junior had given him.' It was very difficult, Arnold urged, to make a large school a place of Christian education because a boys' society was dominated by low standards. The best way of changing the situation was through 'the peculiar relation of the highest form to the rest of the boys'.

Arnold's arguments about the gentling and Christianizing of boy society were of great importance for the future of the public schools but they had not become generally accepted at the time when this article was published. The 1830s were a decade of declining numbers in the great schools, which suggests that they were not holding their own among the social groups which had traditionally used them, nor were they recruiting new adherents among the men of new wealth in industry and commerce. Society, under the influence first of the Evangelicals then of the Tractarians, laid an increasing emphasis on high moral standards and devout religious observance. Children were valued more highly and great interest was taken in giving them good moral and religious training. The new men of wealth came from backgrounds which laid great stress on these values. What they could learn about heavy punishments, the oppressive treatment of younger boys and hidebound and traditionalist teaching was likely, I think, to deter, rather than encourage them, from sending their sons to public schools. Sydney Smith, in the *Edinburgh Review* article of 1810 which has already been quoted, complained that in large public schools boys were neglected. If it was not possible to combine domestic with school life, boys were best taught in groups of twenty to thirty. The private schools, with their smaller numbers and closer supervision, provided what Smith wanted. It has already been argued that the first half of the century was the period in which the private schools reached their greatest importance. What they could offer in close contact between master and pupil and in innovative teaching seemed to many people in the 1820s and 1830s to make good the defects of the major public schools. The stagnation of one group was counter-weighed by the expansion of the other.

It seems likely that these arguments may have weighed strongly with the new men, who wanted and could afford a good education for their sons, but who had no hereditary predisposition, like the gentry and the more affluent professional men, for the public schools. In the 1830s there was a strong tide of liberalism running in the country, and the great schools were associated with the *ancien régime* and its abuses which liberals wished to destroy. Brougham's committees of 1816 and 1818 had taken evidence about some of the schools, and the committee of 1818 had complained that the authorities of Eton and Winchester had deviated from the intentions of the founders and had paid more attention to the interests of the fellows than of the scholars.[33] The investigation into Winchester, in particular, turned into a tussle between the witnesses, who were unwilling to reveal information which they had sworn not to disclose, and the committee, whose questions harped on the theme that the statutes of the college were not being observed and that the warden and fellows were profiting substantially from the endowments.[34] By the 1830s more and more people had come to share the committee's views. Now that the rotten boroughs have gone, wrote Lytton Bulwer, political advancement will no longer lie through the public schools.[35] The Eton system of education, wrote the *Quarterly Journal*, does not belong to the present age. 'It is the offset of a system of jobbing and corruption in all departments of church and state, when patronage was the all-in-all of our aristocratic institutions ....'[36] If the public schools were to go forward, they had to free themselves from the incubus of what many people regarded as a reactionary past.

One aspect of that reactionary past which was very evident to the critics of the 1830s was the fact that the great schools were emphatically classical schools. One of the critics' major demands was a broader curriculum, including mathematics and the sciences, modern languages, geography and history. The abler boys at the head of the school did gain a good education – and one which was in fact a good deal broader than the critics often appreciated – but certainly many boys, especially those who left fairly young, gained very little from their years of linguistic grind, particularly since the classical programme allowed very little room for anything else.[37]

The case for the classics – to put the matter in that way – was made in rather a similar way by two headmasters of Rugby, Thomas Arnold and Frederick Temple. Arnold argued that knowledge of the ancient world in and for itself is not sufficient. The classical teacher must be well acquainted with modern history and modern literature. Yet the truths expressed by the great writers of antiquity are of permanent value to modern man, and they come to him freed from the trappings of immediate circumstance. What matters is the process rather than the detail. As an educational objective the acquisition of 'useful information' can be overvalued. It is the teacher's prime task to help his pupils to gain information 'hereafter for themselves, and to enable them to turn it to account when gained'. The great value of the classics lies in training the judgment and the memory and in teaching the pupil to learn for himself.[38] Temple told the Clarendon Commission that the classics are the best instruments for the highest kind of education because they give us the knowledge of men and of their thoughts and deeds at the highest level. 'The studies pursued at a public school and the method of study do not always give a boy the precise thing that he wants for immediate use in life; but they give a training which enables him to study almost anything afterwards with ease.'[39]

Despite the clamour of the 'modernist' critics the social groups who sent their sons to the public schools must have been broadly satisfied with this defence of the classical curriculum because, although the supremacy of the ancient languages was modified by the 1860s, it was not destroyed. Mathematics and modern languages were introduced, but only in subordinate roles. The people who sent their sons to public schools in early Victorian England were Liberal but not Radical in these as in many other matters. The classics had occupied the field for many centuries, the best teachers were classical scholars, and there was no other organized body of knowledge to take their place in the schools. The attack on the classical curriculum was perhaps the least important of the attacks levied on the public schools in the 1830s. Yet it is likely to have had some effect in deterring parents from entering their sons, and possibly the expansion of the 1860s and 1870s would not have come about on such a scale if the schools had not, by that time, considerably widened the programme of study which they offered. By the time of the Clarendon Report the great schools were offering mathematics and some modern languages. At Harrow, for example, all boys had to learn mathematics and either French or German, though German was not taught below the fifth form.[40] The door had not always been opened very wide. At Eton the mathematical masters complained of the inferior position which they held and the small amount of time devoted to their study.[41] On science the door had hardly been opened at all. Rugby was the only one of the seven schools in which it was taught on a regular basis,[42] and Moberly of Winchester, where a course of lectures was given every year, told the commissioners that for the great majority of boys science was 'worthless as education'.[43]

The neglect of mathematics and science in the public schools was commented upon by three foreign observers, the German Ludwig Wiese, writing about 1850, and the Frenchmen Demogeot and Montucci, writing in the 1860s. They both noted an emphasis on facts and on memory work and a neglect of controversy and critical ideas. The instruction, they thought, was mechanical. Everything learned, wrote Wiese, 'should be able to bear the test of examination'.[44] Demogeot and Montucci spoke of 'this regular continuous, positive work, which can be measured and counted'.[45] What these French and German observers noticed can be related to the growing emphasis of the day on competition and emulation. That which was most appropriate to be learned was that which could be most readily tested. By the 1860s the competitive principle had gained more influence in some public schools than in others. Shrewsbury under Butler and Kennedy had been a pioneer in emphasizing promotion by merit. 'The principal stimulant to work at Shrewsbury appears to be the desire to obtain a high place in the school. Boys mix freely by proficiency . . . ', observed the Clarendon Report which made similar comments about Rugby.[46] On the other hand, Eton made very little use of competition, and in the last two years there were hardly any examinations at all.[47]

The stimulus of competition probably raised the standard of the abler boys, but to judge from the commissioners' remarks, it can have had little effect on the work of the majority. They spoke of the ignorance of many boys at the end of their school course, since they knew little of the classics or of anything else.[48] Even those who went on to university spent their first two years on what was essentially school work.[49] The commissioners considered the school curricula to be lacking in breadth and flexibility, but, despite all these criticisms of a system which devoted most of its time and energy to classical studies, they strongly recommended that the great schools should remain pre-eminently classical schools. It was an extraordinary vote of confidence in a system which had clearly been unsuccessful in providing an effective intellectual training for many – perhaps the majority – of those who had experienced it. The doubt remains whether the commissioners and most of their contemporaries were very interested in the academic studies of the majority of the boys. What really concerned them was that the public schools provided an excellent moral education and a sound character training for boys who had practical work to do in the world. The high academic achievements of the few certainly brought a school prestige. For the majority the classics occupied satisfactorily enough the time not devoted to the many activities which went on outside the classroom.

The commissioners' ideas about the curriculum were clearly expressed in their discussion of 'modern' departments such as those which existed at schools like Cheltenham. They were against such departments in the great schools for many reasons, and in particular because 'they are, and we think they ought to be, essentially classical schools, and we do not think it advisable that they should propose to their scholars two alternative courses of study … '.[50] One of the great services of the schools, the report commented, had been 'the maintenance of classical literature as the staple of English education'.[51] I have already argued that the attack on the classical curriculum was the least important of the attacks made on the public schools since the 1830s, but it had been made and it must have had some effect on parents who were likely patrons. Now an official inquiry, with all the prestige which such a body could bring, gave an endorsement to the traditional system. Yet, characteristically for a liberal age, it was a qualified endorsement. The classics were to remain the core of instruction, but more attention should also be given to the other subjects which had previously been neglected. The report produced a suggested distribution of time for both school work and preparation. A school week of 20 hours should, it was suggested, be divided as follows: classics with history and divinity, 11 hours; arithmetic and mathematics, 3 hours; French or German, 2 hours; natural science, 2 hours; music or drawing, 2 hours. Of 19 hours' preparation time, classics was to have 10.[52]

By the time the report was published in 1864 the tide was flowing strongly in favour of the public schools old and new. The schools had, in the first half of the century, been confronted with three major problems: the issue of morals and discipline; the identification with an outmoded political order and its abuses; the debate over the nature of the curriculum. The future progress of the schools depended on the solution of all three problems, and particularly of the first. By the 1860s success was on the way, and the next chapters will show how it was achieved.

NOTES AND REFERENCES

1. See Bamford T W 1961 The prosperity of public schools 1801–1850: 85–96. Bamford gives charts of the entrants to the seven schools plus St Paul's, 1801–50
2. *PSC* I, pp 11, 190, 202
3. Maxwell-Lyte H C 1875 p 369
4. May, Trevor The other Harrovians: local boys at Harrow School in the nineteenth century, in Searby P (ed) 1981 p 78
5. Moberly C A E 1911 p 83; Leach A F 1899 pp 430–5. For Charles Wordsworth, see his *Annals of my early life 1806–46* (1891)
6. For the report on St Paul's, *PSC* I, pp 187–201; for the report on Merchant Taylors', *ibid.* pp 202–7
7. Jameson E M 1937 p 20
8. Sargeaunt, John 1898 pp 229–42; Carleton J D 1965 p 54
9. *PSC* I, pp 51–2; pp 170–1 (Westminster); p 184 (Charterhouse); p 199 (St Paul's)
10. *PSC* IV, p 324
11. Rouse W H D 1898 pp 192–219 covers the Wooll period
12. Demogeot J, Montucci H 1868 p 238 (my translation)
13. *PSC* II, p 314
14. Bamford T W 1961 Public schools and social class: 233
15. Jenkins H, Caradog Jones D 1950: 113
16. Kitson Clark G 1962 pp 273–4
17. *SIC* IX, p 148
18. *PSC* II, p 324; see also Parkin G R 1898 vol I p 141
19. Hollis, Christopher 1960 p 172
20. Leach A F 1899 pp 403–6, 419–22
21. Rouse W H D 1898 pp 182–6
22. Maxwell-Lyte H C 1875 pp 361–2
23. Butler, Samuel 1896 vol I pp 156–7
24. For the school rebellions in general, see Lamb G F 1959 pp 69–94. Lamb considers that the first of them took place at Eton in 1768
25. Mack E C 1938 pp 158–60; Ward, Wilfrid 1889 pp 15–17
26. For the case of 'Tunded Macpherson' see Dilke, Christopher 1965 pp 82–90
27. Remarks on the system of Education in Public Schools *ER* XVI (1810) 326–34

28. *ER* LI (1830): 65–81; LIII (1831): 64–82
29. Bulwer, E Lytton 1833 (repr 1970) p 161
30. Eton School 1834: 286
31. Flogging and Fagging at Winchester 1835: 84–90; On the discipline of large boarding schools 1835: 82–119
32. The Discipline of Public Schools, reprinted in Arnold, Thomas 1845 pp 361–79
33. *Third Report, SC* 1818 p 60; see also Mack E C 1938 p 135
34. *Third Report, SC* 1818 pp 132–45. Those examined from Winchester were David Williams, second master; Liscombe Clarke, fellow and bursar; James Ralfe, auditor and steward; Philip Williams, barrister-at-law and fellow of New College, Oxford
35. Bulwer, E Lytton 1833 (repr 1970) p 156
36. *QJE* VIII (1834): 292–3
37. There are several contemporary accounts in some detail of the classical curricula in the schools. See *QJE* III (1832): 1–17 (Harrow); V (1833): 30–52 (Westminster); VII (1834): 234–49 (Rugby – by Thomas Arnold, and reprinted in his *Miscellaneous Works* (1845) pp 339–60). Bache, Alexander Dallas 1839 gives an account of both Rugby and Harrow, and considers the Rugby course the better of the two. The interesting and comprehensive classical notebook of Richard Williamson, headmaster of Westminster (*c*. 1840) is in Cambridge University Library (Add. MSS 5979). See also Demogeot J, Montucci H 1868 pp 122–38 which covers work at Eton, Winchester, Westminster, Charterhouse, Harrow and Rugby. For Thomas James's account of Rugby studies, see Butler, Samuel 1896 vol I pp 25–38
38. Arnold, Thomas 1845 pp 348–57. The quotation is on p 356
39. *PSC* II, pp 311–12
40. *PSC* II, p 276
41. *PSC* II, pp 167–8
42. *PSC* II, pp 252–3; Meadows A J, Brock W H Topics fit for gentlemen: the problem of science in the public school curriculum, in Simon B, Bradley, Ian (eds) 1975 pp 95–114
43. *PSC* I, pp 146–7
44. Wiese L 1854 p 93
45. Demogeot J, Montucci H 1868 p 138
46. *PSC* I, p 312 (Shrewsbury); p 244 (Rugby)
47. *PSC* I, p 90
48. *PSC* I, p 26. Demogeot J, Montucci H 1868 p 149 draw a contrast between the results achieved with able and with less able boys: 'powerful action exercised on the intelligence of the able, extreme connivance with the idleness and incapacity of ordinary abilities'
49. *PSC* I, pp 24–5
50. *PSC* I, p 39
51. *PSC* I, p 56
52. *PSC* I, p 34

CHAPTER SEVENTEEN

Some great headmasters

Though the Clarendon Report was in some ways critical – for example, of the low standards of attainment reached by many boys – the final verdict was almost fulsome.

> It remains to us to discharge the pleasantest part of our task, by recapitulating in a few words the advances which these schools have made during the last quarter of a century, and in the second place by noticing briefly the obligations which England owes to them – obligations which, were their defects far greater than they are, would entitle them to be treated with the utmost tenderness and respect.[1]

With such an endorsement it was not surprising that the public schools rose in popularity and esteem. The difficulties which had held them back have already been outlined. It is time now to explain the tide of success which flowed so fully between 1860 and the First World War.

One reason was the high ability and strong powers of leadership of many of the headmasters, men who had clear views of what they wanted to achieve and the power of persuading parents of the value of what they had to offer. If some of them like Arnold were controversial figures as well, at least that quality got the school talked about.[2] Sometimes the advance of the schools has been attributed largely to Arnold and his successors at Rugby, though that is a rather uncritical view. For example, both Eton and Winchester were unaffected by 'Arnoldism'. Yet Arnold and his influence were important. He should be seen as one of a whole group of men who established a new concept of the role of the headmaster and of the moral and intellectual objectives of the school. It is impossible within a brief treatment to discuss all the leading personalities of the time. Four vignettes will be offered – two from the great schools and two from the old grammar schools and the new foundations which were to coalesce with them to form the public school community of the 1870s and 1880s.

From the great schools I have chosen Arnold himself and Samuel Butler. From the other groups choice is much more difficult, but I have chosen two men who were themselves products of the major schools, Edward Thring and William Sewell. Samuel Butler has not enjoyed his due measure of attention among the great nineteenth-century headmasters.[33] He was the first of them, and he reigned at Shrewsbury for 38 years (1798–1836). Unlike Arnold, who took over a school with a distinguished recent history, he built up a great school from almost nothing. Butler was a brilliant teacher, and his pupils had a remarkable record of university successes. B H Kennedy, for example, won the Porson Prize at Cambridge in 1823 while he was still at school, and T Brancker did the same in 1831 with the Ireland Scholarship at Oxford. Butler, more than any other headmaster, created the link between the public schools and university achievement which was one of the main reasons for their growing success as the century went on. Indeed so successful was he as a teacher that he had to face accusations, which he indignantly denied, that he directly crammed boys for success in examination. Certainly he put great emphasis on competition, though he would have insisted that this was not incompatible with a broad education. Kennedy wrote about him long afterwards: 'his crowning merit was the establishment of an emulative system, in which talent and industry always gained their just recognition and reward in good examinations'.[4] Butler can be called one of the creators of the competitive spirit so characteristic of mid-Victorian England.

He was a good deal more than a fine scholar and a good teacher. He was a good administrator; he was for many years the conscientious archdeacon of Derby and he brought to a successful ending a lawsuit about the school property which had dragged on for over 200 years.[5] He was consulted both by C T Longley of Harrow and by E C Hawtrey of Eton when they were appointed to their headships. His letters give the impression of a man who understood boy nature very well. This is the headmaster writing in 1827 to an assistant whom he felt that he had to support but who was clearly much too severe[6]:

I know you mean well, but you expect more than human nature is capable of . . . I have always flogged them that I might support your authority, but without always feeling that it was likely to prove a serviceable correction. I have more than once thought that it was only hardening them, and that the despair of doing anything that would be accepted by you if it was not quite correct drove them to do nothing at

all. The strong and serious case which I have had to-day induces me
to beg that you will remit something of this extreme vigour without
giving way to too much laxity. All great severity destroys its own
effect.

Clearly Butler had serious problems in running the school. Like
Keate at Eton he had frequent difficulties about discipline; his
grandson's *Life* contains many letters to parents, the constant theme
of which is that, if they are not ready to support his authority, they
must remove their boy from the school.[7] He had to work for 37 years
with an ineffective second master with whom he communicated only
in writing. His most serious weakness seems to have been that he gave
the boys little moral or religious leadership, and that, it has been
argued, is what the public schools of his day really needed. This is a
strange judgment on a man who became a bishop. Sincerely religious
himself, he had an almost morbid fear of religious 'enthusiasm',
which was more characteristic of the eighteenth century than of the
nineteenth. The school's priorities are suggested by the story of Butler
and C J Blomfield in chapel together at Shrewsbury. Butler and
Blomfield as young men had clashed about Butler's edition of
Aeschylus. Long afterwards Blomfield, who was then Bishop of
Chester, paid the school a visit, went to morning chapel with the
boys, 'and was much scandalised at seeing Dr Butler, towards the
close of the service, begin to cut his pencil so as to be ready for
marking and correcting exercises'.[8]

It is difficult to conceive of Thomas Arnold sharpening his pencil
in Rugby chapel. Arnold did a great work in a comparatively short
time; he was at Rugby for 14 years (1828–42), as against Butler's 38
years at Shrewsbury. He died just before his forty-seventh birthday
when he might have been expected still to accomplish much more. He
was a greater figure than Butler and a much more complex one.
Though there are many books about him, it is not easy to get a clear
picture of his personality or to assess his influence on the
development of the public schools.[9] Much of the legend was built up
by two remarkable books written by his own pupils, the *Life* by A P
Stanley, published in 1844, only two years after his death, and *Tom
Brown's Schooldays*, the greatest of all school stories, written by
Thomas Hughes and published in 1857. In the twentieth century
Arnold's posthumous fortunes were to change. He was a good
candidate for the 'debunking' to which so many of the leading figures
of his era were exposed. Lytton Strachey, in *Eminent Victorians*
(1918), noted that he had rather short legs and a somewhat puzzled
look on his face.[10]

One major point about Arnold is that he saw his work at Rugby as only part of his total experience. He was accused, both of neglecting the school and of trying to influence the boys towards his own view on controversial subjects, both of which charges he strongly denied.[11] Yet his heart lay at least as much in his writings on religion and politics as in the school, and he is in that respect unique among the great headmasters. He was absorbed by the problems of political and religious reform, by the nature of the Christian community, by the relationships between the Church and state. In public matters he was a reformer – indeed a Radical. 'My love for any place or person, or institution', he told Stanley, 'is exactly the measure of my desire to reform them.'[12]

In fact he was much more of a reformer in political theory than in the practical affairs of school. Essentially what he did at Rugby was to take the traditional system, to broaden it and to refine it. He did not in essence change it. The point can be illustrated by two examples. He is remembered as the headmaster who gave wide authority over the school to his praepostors or prefects. Yet he did not create the system. What he did was to regularize and moralize, to put a weight of responsibility upon his prefects which they had not carried before. He addressed them in a sermon like this[13]:

> I cannot deny that the oldest and most advanced among you have an anxious duty, a duty which some might suppose was too heavy for your years. But it seems to me the nobler as well as the truer way of stating the case to say, that it is the great privilege of this and other such institutions, to anticipate the common term of manhood . . . .

Similarly in his classical teaching, he modified but he did not transform. Increased emphasis was given to the history of the ancient world. Time was found for mathematics and other modern subjects, but the curriculum was not fundamentally changed.

Where Arnold was an innovator was in his emphasis on moral and religious training. Quite early in his time at Rugby he got the trustees to appoint him chaplain and he preached regular sermons of urgent moral exhortation, inflamed by a personal sense of the truths of religion and his own love and adoration for the person of Christ. This was all something new. Butler, it has been suggested, made little or no attempt to give direct and personal religious teaching. Arnold, and others of his contemporaries among the younger generation of headmasters, began the moral transformation of the public schools. In 1815 the moral argument had worked against them. By 1850 it was beginning to work in their favour. Men began to believe not that boys were corrupted by their public schools, but that those schools were raising them to a higher spiritual and moral level than they had enjoyed before.

If there is one image above all of Arnold which it is essential to convey, it is Arnold pleading and exhorting in the pulpit. Yet it was no comfortable message which he preached. He had a deep sense of the evil in boy nature, of its tendency to frivolity, of its propensity, unless carefully watched, to establish low values and bad conduct. For a man who was happily married and an affectionate father, this sense of the deep-rooted evil of boyhood is difficult to understand. Before he took up his Rugby duties, he wrote to a friend, ' . . . my object will be, if possible, to form Christian men, for Christian boys I can scarcely hope to make'.[14] The impression thus expressed grew no weaker as the years went on. Boyhood to him was a transition period between childhood and manhood. It was expedient to shorten it as much as possible so that boys might quickly pass from a state of carelessness and ignorance to one of maturity and responsibility. Since the moral stakes were so high, it was an important duty for the headmaster to weed out unsatisfactory boys on the way. One of the major duties of the prefects was to help the head and his assistants to bring the change about, a task of high seriousness which, some critics argued, made them priggish and old before their natural time. The resultant confusions between the serious and the trivial were neatly satirized by Fitzjames Stephen[15]:

> . . . how can football be puerile; how can it be a vulgar incident to kick your fag for not toasting your sausages when every motion of the hand, tongue or foot involves the idea of the πολις and asserts the identity of the Christian Church with the Christian State.

Arnold and his sixth form are easy enough to satirize, but there was more to them than that. George Moberly of Winchester, looking back on his memories as a Balliol tutor, wrote of the impact of Arnold's pupils at Oxford, where they brought with them a new and different personal stamp (see p. 259). Twenty years later a Rugby master told the Clarendon Commission that the school had produced 'a large number of Christian-minded, conscientious, hard-working men'.[16] It is, of course, very difficult to calculate how great was the personal influence of Arnold, and particularly of his preaching, on the ordinary boy. Many must have been untouched, but it has been recently argued that the pious moralistic tone of the second part of *Tom Brown* does represent the tone of the school as Hughes would have experienced it himself.[17] Certainly, for those who were affected, the message was strongly practical. One of Arnold's Laleham pupils said that 'every boy was made to feel that there was a work for him to do'.[18] That was the message which Arnold, throughout his career and with considerable success, tried to inculcate.

Rugby under Arnold was a successful school. Numbers remained high, and he weathered the storm of controversy aroused in the mid-1830s by his controversial views. In the final 2 or 3 years before his death he had reached a secure position of acceptance and success. Rugbeians did well at the universities. Not only were they respected for their moral character, but they were successful as scholars, one of the leading figures being A P Stanley himself, who had a distinguished career at Oxford. What is sometimes overlooked about Arnold is that he was a pioneer in his treatment of the assistant masters.[19] He insisted that they should not take local curacies and that they should devote all their time to the school, but he put all the boarding houses into their hands and ensured them good salaries. He held regular masters' meetings and was anxious to improve the status and position of his staff. He is so often thought of as the very authoritarian headmaster that it is worth emphasizing the reference in the Clarendon Report on the school to 'that general love of equality which marked his character'.[20] One of his ablest assistants, James Prince Lee, when appointed to a headship, wrote to Arnold to thank him for 'your invariable kindness, courtesy and liberality, for the information and advice I have gained from you, and the advancement and support you extended to me in the school'.[21] That kind of gratitude from an assistant to a headmaster is not a common thing.

Arnold's reputation as a schoolmaster had certainly grown before his early death. The American A D Bache, writing in 1839, considered Rugby to be one of the first of English schools 'from the character of its headmaster and his associates'.[22] Very soon after Arnold's death T W Jex-Blake, who was himself to be headmaster of the school (1874–87), was sent to Rugby at very short notice after his father had read Stanley's *Life*; [he] 'told me that he had no idea that any public school attempted to act on the Xan ideal'.[23] Arnold's work became known abroad; the German Ludwig Wiese explained that Arnold's career had begun his interest in English education.[24] The commemorative *Book of Rugby School*, published in 1856, spoke in terms of veneration of the great headmaster, who had died only 14 years before. It is entirely appropriate that Arnold is described in the book reading the Bible at evening prayers in the school-house hall.[25]

By the 1860s, as we have seen, the term 'public school' was being extended to include not only the seven great schools but also some of the old grammar schools and the new schools of private foundation. The successful schools in both groups naturally owed a great deal to their headmasters, though there is space here only to offer a brief sketch of one man from each group. Edward Thring reigned at Uppingham for 34 years (1853–87), almost as long a period as Butler's term at Shrewsbury. Much of his important work falls therefore outside the limits of this book, and this study concentrates on the years up to about 1865, though by that time he had clearly worked out the kind of school he wished Uppingham to be. There was a mystical intuitive quality about him which set him aside from other men. He ploughed his own furrow, and by the end of his life – for he died in office like Arnold – he had probably failed to achieve his real aspirations. Uppingham had become, and was to remain, a successful school but it was hardly the school of Thring's vision.[26]

He was an Etonian and a colleger who had been captain of the splendid and extravagant Montem of 1841.[27] However he had little sympathy with the great schools, referring in his diary (19 November 1869) to their 'inefficiency and lying efforts and lying glory'.[28] His own interest in teaching had been aroused when he taught in the National School in the Gloucester parish in which he had served as curate, and – perhaps because he had begun with that very difficult work — he was much more concerned than the other heads of his day with the theory and practice of the art of teaching. He wrote a good deal on this and his ideas are still of value.[29] When he was appointed to Uppingham in 1853 he found a school which had a good reputation under his predecessor, but which numbered only 25 boarders and 6/7 day boys.[30] When he was examined 12 years later by the Schools Inquiry Commission, the day boy numbers had remained the same and there were 296 boarders.[31] In terms of numbers he had achieved a resounding success; moreover he had created a new kind of school. He valued the old foundation as a link with the past and because of the university exhibitions which it provided and which attracted boarders. His relationships with the trustees – local gentry and clergy – were not always easy; one senses that they were alarmed by what must have seemed wildly ambitious schemes. What Thring achieved was won through his own financial investment and that of the masters whom he persuaded to work with him and to build boarding houses at their own expense. For years he bore a heavy burden of debt and he often became discouraged, but by the mid-1860s the school, which he did not wish to grow in size beyond 300, was full.[32] Thring planned Uppingham on two clear principles. The first was that every boy, however clever or stupid, must receive individual attention. The second was that for this attention to be provided effectively there must be proper buildings and facilities to support a wide range of activities – the doctrine in his own words of the 'almighty wall'.[33] He provided a gymnasium and a swimming bath. Carpentry and metalwork were taught, and much attention was given to music. Games were encouraged, and Thring himself played football with the boys – at least until he was about 40.[34] He was very concerned to achieve small and manageable units. Not only were total numbers to be limited to 300, but each boarding house was to contain no more than 30 boys and each class no more than 20/25. He was very anxious that boys should have privacy; each boy had his own cubicle in the dormitory and a small study to himself. No headmaster of his day tried so hard to make education a valuable experience for each individual.[35] 'That is a great part of our system', he told the Schools Inquiry Commission, 'that every boy shall have something to do which interests him. We take each boy, clever or stupid; we consider we are bound to train him, irrespective of his abilities, to the best of our power . . . .'[36] Indeed the school tended to get more than its fair share of dull boys because of its reputation for managing them well, but by the mid-1860s university distinctions were also being won. In 1864 R L Nettleship won the first Balliol scholarship, to be followed by a string of university prizes and scholarships at Oxford.[37] When in 1865 Thring was summoned to give evidence to the Schools Inquiry Commission he could look back on a decade of remarkable success. The school was full. In the early years he had had his troubles with some members of staff, but he had gradually collected congenial colleagues around him. He wrote in his diary that he had been pleased by his examination before the commissioners, which had enabled him to bring out the principles he cared about.[38] His reactions to the commissioners' report and its aftermath were less favourable, but those reactions, and the realignment of forces which led to the creation of the Headmasters' Conference in the 1870s, form part of a later story.[39]

Thring took little from his experience at Eton; William Sewell was a devoted Wykehamist. 'To Winchester College', he wrote, 'I owe everything', though he felt that he had been given no religious guidance there.[40] He had been elected to a fellowship at Exeter College, Oxford in 1827 and he was a prominent tutor and lecturer in the Oxford of the 1830s, sympathetic with the Tractarians yet the author of a somewhat critical *Letter to Pusey*, written after the publication of *Tract 90* in 1841. By that time he had been drawn by a group of Irish gentry and clergy into the project of founding a school in Ireland. Roman Catholic influence was to be countered by training boys, who would become Ireland's natural leaders, in the Irish language in a school controlled by a collegiate body where the warden and fellows were to live together as in an Oxford college. The collegiate idea was Sewell's, and he was deeply involved in the beginnings of the College of St Columba, opened in 1843. However he withdrew in 1846 under circumstances which are not entirely clear.

Though circumstances had led him to be the co-founder of a school in Ireland, he wrote much later that he had been thinking ever since 1832 of a school in England for the sons of the upper classes[41]:

> Thousands were labouring for the education of the poor, I thought of the education of the rich; not as if the soul of Dives was more precious than the soul of Lazarus, but because a single Dives, once filled with the spirit of a Christian, will shower blessings on a multitude of Lazaruses.

Soon after his withdrawal from the Irish venture he and his friends opened St Peter's College at Radley near Oxford under the same warden, R C Singleton, who had started St Columba's.

The principles of the two schools were much the same. Strong emphasis was laid on Church principles and on collegiate management. The warden and fellows were to regard their work as a task of Christian duty and love. Radley opened in 1847 with a warden, four fellows and three boys. The early years were difficult, and in January 1853 Sewell himself took over the wardenship. It was a brave decision for a man of some 50 years of age who had no previous experience as a schoolmaster but it seemed the only way of saving the school. For some years his rule was a success. Numbers rose to a peak of 156. He was himself an affectionate, warm-hearted man who saw the school as a large family where the warden was the father and the assistant masters the elder brothers of the boys. 'I resolved', Sewell wrote, 'to try the experiment of education by a family of Christian gentlemen.'[42] Masters and boys were to share a common life in handsome and dignified surroundings. Pictures and fine furniture were bought, and lavish hospitality given. For a new foundation with only modest resources Sewell's schemes were too ambitious. He was an original thinker with some forward-looking ideas, but he was not a practical manager. In 1861 the school had to be rescued from financial disaster by a parent who was a London business man. Sewell had resigned in December 1860; he died in 1874, having played no part in educational work after he left Radley.

Sewell's concept of education, with its emphasis on the close ties between masters and boys and on the family life of the school enjoyed in a dignified environment, was very different from that of most of his contemporaries. Thring was tougher and much more experienced, for he had the advantage of becoming a headmaster as a much younger man. Yet there are marked similarities between them – their strong religious principles, their concern for close personal relationships, their interest in the setting in which school life was to be lived. Sewell never talked about the 'almighty wall', but he would have understood what Thring meant.

. These four men selected for more detailed study – Samuel Butler, Thomas Arnold, Edward Thring, William Sewell – were only some of the leading figures. They are not unique, but rather characteristic of the new impulses affecting all the schools. Eton and Winchester had moved slowly, but definite progress had been made under E C Hawtrey and George Moberly. Three of the seven schools were in or near to London. The problems confronted by Westminster and Charterhouse have already been outlined (see pp. 229–30). Though progress was slow, Westminster started to move forward under H G Liddell (1846–55) and C B Scott (1855–83). At Charterhouse W Haig Brown, appointed in 1863, planned the move out to Surrey which was carried out in 1872. Harrow, after a very bad period in the 1830s, was built up again by C J Vaughan (1844–59) and his achievement was confirmed by his successor, H M Butler (1859–86). Vaughan was a Rugbeian and the only one of Arnold's pupils to become head of one of the seven schools.[43] The opening in recent years of the manuscript memoirs of J A Symonds has produced an explanation of Vaughan's resignation in the full tide of success: that he had been detected in a love affair with a boy. The story, if true, did not become generally known, and no harm was felt by the school.[44]

Vaughan left Harrow in 1859. By that time the growing success of both the Clarendon schools and of their newer competitors could be attributed in large part to the abilities of a very able group of headmasters whose talent and personality helped to attract a bigger clientele to their schools. A few of the new men like Arnold had Radical leanings; most of them can best be described as liberal conservatives. All of them in their different ways helped to remove from the schools the stigma of obscurantism, the taint of the *ancien régime* which had hung over them in 1830. They brought the public schools forward into the new age of liberalism and progress.

This new age, as has often been suggested, was an age of competition, and the competitive principle in public life gained its first success in the honours examinations at Oxford and Cambridge.[45] Both universities moved steadily forward after the stagnant years of the eighteenth century. By 1815–20 the prestige of the Oxford Schools and the Cambridge Tripos was high. Standards of scholarship, though narrowly based, were rising. Numbers of students were increasing. The Oxford Commission of 1850 put the number of matriculations in recent years at about 400; between 1800 and 1813 the average had been 267.[46] At Cambridge the average between 1767 and 1799 had been 153. It rose to 342 between 1800 and 1833. In 1850 there were 441, and in the following year about 40 per cent of men graduating took honours degrees.[47] The increase in numbers and the rise in standards were not spectacular but they were steady. Arnold, who was keenly aware of what was going on around him, picked up the point in a sermon[48]:

> What was accounted great learning some years ago, is no longer
> reckoned such; what was in the days of our fathers only an ordinary
> and excusable ignorance, is esteemed as something disgraceful now. In
> these things, as in all others, never was competition so active, – never
> were such great exertions needed to obtain success.

There was a two-way traffic in this success between the universities and the public schools. Many fellows of colleges had always moved on to become headmasters of schools, but in that generation there was a particularly close link between the leading heads, some of whom have already been discussed, and those colleges which stood foremost at Oxford and Cambridge. Arnold had been a fellow of Oriel when it was the leading Oxford college. Moberly of Winchester was a fellow of Balliol as were both Tait and Temple of Rugby, both of whom became Archbishops of Canterbury. Arnold's pupil, C J Vaughan, was a fellow of Trinity College, Cambridge, as, among the Rugby masters, were James Prince Lee of Birmingham, E W Benson of Wellington, later Archbishop of Canterbury, and G E L Cotton of Marlborough. So too were H M Butler of Harrow and C B Scott of Westminster. The remarkable Shrewsbury trio – Samuel Butler, B H Kennedy, H W Moss – whose reigns spanned more than a century – were all fellows of Trinity's great Cambridge rival, St John's. The fact that the leading schools could appoint heads of this calibre – many of them men who later moved on to high office in the Church – must have increased the drawing power of the schools and made them more attractive to parents. The one exception to the argument about university influence is the greatest school of all – Eton, which remained throughout the period a very closed world. It simply was not worth while moving on from there, and the connection with King's College, Cambridge, was not fruitful until that college was opened up about 1870.

A History of Secondary Education, 1800–1870

The able men – both heads and assistants – who came from Oxford and Cambridge trained able boys who themselves in their turn became candidates for academic honours. One very important measure of a school's standing came to be its record of university success. Samuel Butler of Shrewsbury was the pioneer in creating this link between the public schools and academic honours. It has already been noted that, when he was trying to establish Shrewsbury's claim to rank as a public school, he counted its record of university success as one of the justifying criteria (see p. 213). As numbers at the universities grew and success in their examinations became more important, so those schools which had a strong representation at Oxford and Cambridge were likely to gain in popularity. The public schools, comparatively large and well staffed, were in the best position to profit from the changing situation. A D Bache wrote that success at the universities was 'the standard by which all the public schools in England are tried'.[49] It was a standard which they measured up to better than other kinds of school.

Both Royal Commissions of the 1860s gave detailed information about boys leaving school and entering universities. The Clarendon Report calculated that about one-third of Oxford undergraduates and about one-fifth of Cambridge undergraduates came from the nine schools, and of these totals about three-quarters came from Eton, Harrow and Rugby. Their figures for the individual schools, averaged over a 4-year period, were as given in Table 18. This gives an average entry to the universities from all nine schools of about one-

Table 18 Major public schools: numbers leaving school and those entering universities, *c.* 1860

	Total no. leaving	Total no. going to universities
Eton	160	62
Winchester	24	13
Westminster	27	12
Charterhouse	25	8
St Paul's	17	7
Merchant Taylors'	52	9
Harrow	139	52
Rugby	130	38
Shrewsbury	43	12
Totals	617	213

Source: PSC I, pp 26, 27.

third of the grand total of leavers, though the proportion varied
greatly from school to school. At Winchester, calculated over 10-year
periods, it remained steadily over 50 per cent, though that was a high
percentage of a small total.[50]

The Taunton Commission provided figures which make it
possible to compare numbers from different types of school, though
their sample, taken from returns made in May 1867, is not complete
(Table 19). Though the arithmetical figures give only a very crude
result, the differences between the three main groups of schools are
significant. The average numbers per type of school are 63.09 (the
nine plus Marlborough and Cheltenham); 5.37 (43 proprietary
schools); 4.65 (139 grammar schools). Of the total numbers returned
(1949), the nine schools plus Marlborough and Cheltenham make up
35.6 per cent. The number of undergraduates from private schools.
was, as might have been expected, negligible. Of the considerable
number from private tutors many had probably spent some years in
one of the nine schools or at Marlborough or Cheltenham, and had
been sent to a tutor to achieve the final polish for university entry. So
the total proportion of undergraduates who were ex-public-school
boys is likely to have been even greater than the figures of the
Taunton Commission show.

Table 19 Undergraduates at Oxford and Cambridge from different types
of school, 1867

	Total no.	*Oxford*	*Cambridge*
The nine schools plus			
Marlborough and Cheltenham	694	487	207
139 Grammar schools	647	352	295
43 Proprietary schools	231	123	108
31 Private schools	45	16	29
Private tutors	239	123	116
Scotland and Ireland	48	30	18
Channel Islands,			
colonial, foreign	45	23	22
Totals	1,949	1,154	795

Source: SIC I, *Report,* Appendix VII, p 161 (Table II). The returns are of
undergraduates 'who having been two years at one school or other place of
education, had gone to either University within one year after leaving school
or other place of education'. There are also figures for undergraduates who
had gone up within 2 years of leaving school but these are few in number. The
returns were made by about three-quarters of Oxford undergraduates and
more than one-half of Cambridge undergraduates.

It is important not to exaggerate. The Taunton figures are not complete; at Cambridge rather more than half the men sent in a return, and even at Oxford, where they were much stronger than they were at Cambridge, the public-school boys were not in a majority. But they had become the largest and the most clearly defined and recognizable group. Success in the academic world grows by what it feeds on. Higher standards in the universities had helped to promote higher standards in the public schools. In turn more schools were providing a large proportion of the undergraduates for the expanding universities. Many of the men, as we shall see, were ill-prepared for academic study, but the best of them were very able. Schools became known by their record of academic success, and many parents were likely to send their sons to schools with a reputation for winning scholarships and future first classes. As university success became more important, so did those schools advance which could help the most to achieve it. That very achievement became a major reason for the popularity and success of the major public schools.

NOTES AND REFERENCES

1. *PSC* I, p 56
2. Bamford T W 1967 p 159
3. The following is based on Butler, Samuel 1896. There is a useful modern treatment in Percival, Alicia 1973 pp 65–91
4. Butler, Samuel 1896 vol I p 252
5. For the case of the Albrighton tithes, see Oldham, J Basil 1952 pp 84–5
6. Butler, Samuel 1896 vol I p 334
7. Chandos, John 1984 pp 184–95 takes a much less favourable view of Butler than I have expressed. He particularly stresses Butler's bad relations with many boys, and particularly senior boys
8. Butler, Samuel 1896 vol I p 161
9. Of the many books on Arnold, see Stanley A P 1875; Findlay J J (ed) 1914; Whitridge A 1928; Wymer N 1953; Bamford T W 1960 and 1970. For Arnold's own works, see his *Sermons* (1878) and *Miscellaneous Works* (1845). On family and pupils, Woodward, Frances J 1954; Trevor, Meriol 1973
10. Strachey, Lytton 1948 p 194
11. William Sewell, who had examined at Rugby, wrote of Arnold: 'he had too much confidence in himself, too much desire to impress his own ideas upon others'. (Sewell W) 1938 p 65
12. Stanley A P 1875 vol I p 340
13. Bamford T W (ed) 1970 pp 83–4
14. Stanley A P 1875 vol I p 71
15. (Stephen J F) 1858: 186

16. *PSC* II, p 314 (Charles Evans)
17. Scott, Patrick The school and the novel: *Tom Brown's Schooldays*, in Simon B, Bradley, Ian (eds) 1975 pp 48, 52
18. Stanley A P 1875 vol I p 33 (Bonamy Price)
19. Rouse W H D 1898 pp 235-7; Wymer N 1953 p 176
20. *PSC* I, p 233
21. Quoted in Wymer N 1953 p 176
22. Bache, Alexander Dallas 1839 p 390
23. Quoted in Hope-Simpson J B 1967 p 102
24. Wiese L 1854 pp 6-7
25. Goulburn E M (ed) 1856 pp 52-3 (by E W Benson, later master of Wellington and Archbishop of Canterbury)
26. On Thring, see Skrine J H 1890; Parkin G R 1898; Rigby, Cormac 1968. Hoyland, Geoffrey 1946 is very brief, but it does convey a lively impression of the man
27. For the Montem festival, held for the last time in 1844, see Maxwell-Lyte H C 1875 pp 451-73
28. Parkin G R 1898 vol I p 165
29. He had a strong influence on the distinguished Education Officer of the West Riding of Yorkshire, Sir Alec Clegg
30. From Thring's evidence to the Schools Inquiry Commission (*SIC* V, p 104:9997)
31. *Ibid.* p 93:9865. Thring explained that there was little local demand for education in a first-class classical school
32. Parkin quoted many extracts from Thring's diary which reveal strain and discouragement. Cormac Rigby argues that these passages, confided to a private journal, were not typical, and that Thring was basically a buoyant and confident man
33. Parkin G R 1898 vol I p 68 quotes a statement made to the trustees in 1875; see also p 76
34. *Ibid.* vol I pp 118-19. The diary entry of 14 Feb 1862 records playing football, though he had not for a long time done this regularly. He was born on 29 Nov 1821
35. For an early statement of his views see *English Journal of Education* XII (1858): 143-7. 268-70. This was only five years after his appointment to Uppingham
36. *SIC* V, pp 96-7:9913
37. Parkin G R 1898 vol I pp 143, 156; *DNB*: Nettleship R L
38. Parkin G R 1898 vol I pp 150-1
39. Which I hope to tell in a later volume
40. This account of Sewell is based on James L 1945; (Sewell William) 1938
41. *Ibid.* p 74
42. *Ibid.* p 76
43. The Rugby influence was, I think more marked in the new schools, though not all embracing even there. Demogeot J, Montucci H 1868 p 317 described Marlborough as a Rugby on less expensive and still more innovating lines
44. Symonds J A 1984 and Grosskurth P 1964 pp 32-40
45. For a fuller treatment of this point, see Roach J 1971 pp 12-22
46. Mallet C E 1927 p 304 and n 2

A History of Secondary Education, 1800–1870

47. *VCH Cambridgeshire* vol III pp 235, 242
48. Quoted in Bamford T W (ed) 1970 p 117
49. Bache, Alexander Dallas 1839 p 400
50. Bishop T J H, Wilkinson, Rupert 1967 p 123 gives a table of university entrants, calculated over 10-year periods and beginning with those born between 1820 and 1829

CHAPTER EIGHTEEN

An ideology triumphant

Two major reasons for the increasing success of the public schools in the 1850s and 1860s were the great ability of many headmasters and the close interconnections between the schools and Oxford and Cambridge. These are both factors which can to some degree be measured. Equally significant were moral and emotional factors which are impossible to quantify, but which were as important, if not more so, in popularizing both the old and the new schools. One of the most serious problems faced by the schools in the early part of the century was the attack on their discipline and moral atmosphere, an attack far more serious than the criticism, which often accompanied it, of the classical curriculum. By the time of the Clarendon Report the earlier attacks had been replaced by praise which was almost fulsome. This change must now be examined in more detail if we are to understand the great wave of success which was to buoy them up during the last third of the century.

Moberly of Winchester, who had been a Balliol tutor, wrote a letter to A P Stanley in which he reflected on the religious atmosphere at Oxford. When Moberly himself was an undergraduate, the tone of college society, and of public-school men, had been very irreligious. A great change had come about which was not entirely due to Arnold but of which he had been a pioneer.

> It soon began to be a matter of observation to us in the University that his pupils brought quite a different character with them to Oxford than that which we knew elsewhere. I do not speak of opinions; but his pupils were thoughtful, manly-minded, conscious of duty and obligation, when they first came to college.[1]

Moberly's comments are the more valuable because he was himself a High Churchman and, as he makes clear, out of sympathy with many of Arnold's most deeply held opinions.

Moberly's judgment, which dates from the early 1840s, can be compared with that of the Oxford and Cambridge dons who gave evidence to the Clarendon Commission 20 years later.[2] Many undergraduates, they thought, were idle and ill-prepared by their schools, especially in mathematics. On the whole those who did best were men from schools like Rugby, Marlborough and some of the old grammar schools who needed to achieve university success if they were to carve out good careers for themselves. Many Etonians and Harrovians, on the other hand, had no incentive to do well. But there was general testimony to the general improvement of moral character, not least among public-school boys. G Rawlinson, Camden Professor of Ancient History at Oxford, gave a similar explanation to Moberly's: 'The change dates from the time when Arnold's pupils began to come up to Oxford .... '[3] Henry Latham of Trinity Hall, Cambridge, thought that public-school boys 'have decidedly improved in point of moral training and character within the last 20 years'.[4] D P Chase of St Mary Hall and Oriel College, Oxford, commented on the high character of public-school religious training, on the greater interest in games, largely promoted by public-school men, which had removed temptations to immorality and extravagance, and on the beneficial effects of competitive examinations.[5] Finally – an important point to which we shall return – the Vice-Chancellor of Cambridge, Edward Atkinson of Clare, argued that public-school boys possessed in a pre-eminent degree 'that quality of readiness and self-possession in the face of unforeseen difficulties, intellectual and physical, which forms one of the most useful preparations for the duties of active life'.[6]

The Clarendon Report, looking at all the products of the schools and not merely at the minority which went to Oxford and Cambridge, re-echoed the same sentiments. In fact the report made two very different judgments. They were very critical of the low intellectual attainments of many of the boys, which resulted 'either from ineffective teaching, from the continued teaching of subjects in which they cannot advance, or from idleness ... '.[7] On the other hand they spoke in the highest terms of the moral and religious training provided by the schools. In these the most enduring friendships and the most lasting habits have been forged. 'They have had perhaps the largest share in moulding the character of an English gentleman.'[8] If, the commission seemed to think, the scholastic record was open to many criticisms, these were more than counterbalanced by the value of the character training provided. The judgment is interesting and perhaps rather strange; if there was to be a choice between thought and action, the latter was the more important of the two. The function of England's leading schools was to be, not so much to provide intellectual leadership, but to train the practical men who would direct the course of English social and political life. A great deal of the evolution of British state and society in the half-century up to 1914 was implicit in that judgment of the purposes of a public school education.

Praise of the moral training which boys received was remembered from the Clarendon Report, not its criticism of the teaching and of the attainments of many of them. As a result of the changes of the preceding 20 or 30 years the moral argument had, so as to speak, been stood on its head. Whereas at the beginning of the century the schools had been attacked for their low moral and religious standards, by the 1870s they were praised as the training grounds for a more moral and more serious generation of future leaders of the nation and Empire. The schools had incorporated a creed of personal and religious discipleship which was new. Some of this change was the work of Thomas Arnold (see pp. 246–8. We have already looked at his concept of the school as a place of moral struggle in which boys might overcome the evil inherent in their natures and develop into Christian gentlemen. Arnold was not unique; he was one deeply religious man in a religious age, but he did forge a link between religion, education and character training which had not existed before. B H Kennedy of Shrewsbury told the commission that Arnold[9]

> had shown (what previous educators, conscientiously fearing to profane holy things or to promote hypocrisy had doubted or denied) – that it was possible to bring religious influence to bear on boys in public schools.

The point has already been made that Kennedy's predecessor, Butler, though a sincerely religious man himself, had a horror of enthusiasm in religious matters (see p. 245), and that characteristic was true of other headmasters. Arnold was less inhibited. Though he and his Rugby successors were criticized for producing a morbid and self-conscious religiosity in some boys, they did provide what mid-Victorian England wanted – men who regulated their lives by a clearly proclaimed moral standard. The same attitudes characterized those who stood in the Arnoldian tradition like Cotton, Vaughan and Benson. In the latter part of the century the religious atmosphere sometimes became a thin veneer to cover what was essentially the worship of good form. In Arnold and his immediate successors the religious impulse went much deeper than that and contemporaries recognized and valued it as a major contribution to the training of leaders in all walks of life.

The Arnoldian tradition was not, however, the only teaching which proclaimed higher standards of moral excellence. There was another, more High Church tradition stemming from Winchester which was important and which has been less often stressed. Moberly's praise of Arnold's work has already been noted. His own approach was more reserved, more traditionally High Church; he was himself a neighbour and a friend of John Keble at Hursley vicarage. His second master, Charles Wordsworth, wrote later that in what he had written about Arnold's influence, Moberly had done less than justice to his own efforts and to those of other heads[10]:

> The truth is, there was a general awakening, which in many instances, as with us at Winchester, *partook decidedly of a church character*, such as Arnold's teaching and example, however excellent in their way, had little or no tendency to create.

The Winchester influence was strong in some of the new schools, among founders and heads who were themselves High Churchmen. William Sewell of St Columba's and Radley has already been studied, as – much more briefly – has Thomas Stevens of Bradfield (see p. 172). Charles Wordsworth himself was the first warden (1847-54) of Trinity College, Glenalmond, of which W E Gladstone was a principal begetter and which was established to promote the revival of the Episcopal Church in Scotland.[11] And, most influential of all, Nathaniel Woodard desired his first boarding school to be 'conforming as far as may be to the rule of Winchester'.[12]

The Clarendon Commission believed that, as a result of the moral revolution which had taken place, the 'old roughness of manners' had largely disappeared, along with 'the petty tyranny and thoughtless cruelty' which had accompanied it.[13] The core of the issue lay in the institutions of boy self-government – the prefect system and the fagging of the younger boys by the older which accompanied it. These institutions had been regulated by Arnold and the other reforming heads, but they had neither wished, nor would they have been able, to sweep them away. The authority of the prefects, particularly their power to inflict corporal punishment, was a problem which rumbled on, producing a crisis from time to time (see p. 235), but, as the century went on, the view steadily gained ground that, if operated under proper safeguards, the authority exercised by the older boys as prefects and the service rendered by the younger boys as fags helped to produce a manly and independent character by creating a blend of liberty with discipline which was highly favourable to personal self-development.

Though the Clarendon Commission commented unfavourably on abuses of fagging at Westminster, its general judgment on the monitorial system, both in the main report and in the reports on the individual schools, was highly favourable.[14] What the commission said echoed what it had been told by the schoolmaster witnesses like Richard Elwyn, headmaster of Charterhouse: 'I do consider such powers to be essential and useful to the effectual maintenance of school discipline . . . . I believe that the system is the very best which can be devised for suppressing tyranny of the stronger boys over the weaker . . . .'[15] The headmasters' position is very clearly set out in a pamphlet written in 1854 by C J Vaughan after a case, in which a boy who had answered back to a monitor and had received thirty-one strokes, had been taken up by *The Times*.[16] The matter is a choice of alternatives, Vaughan argued. Either you must have constant supervision of the boys on the model of foreign schools, or a monitorial system under due safeguards. He had no doubt of his own choice. 'I see many difficulties, some evils in the present system; some advantages, many plausibilities in its opposite; and yet I believe the one to be practically ennobling and elevating – the other essentially narrowing, enfeebling, and enervating.'[17] The doubt always remains how much headmasters knew about their own schools. The charges made about Harrow by J A Symonds are now well known.[18] A J C Hare's account of a year in the school in 1847–48 is one of ceaseless fagging and constant bullying and cruelty.[19]

If such evils occurred along the way, they were probably considered to be exceptional, and in the eyes of contemporaries they were far less important than the manly independence which the system was believed to inculcate. Here the evidence of the French observers, Demogeot and Montucci, is interesting. They were not convinced by the arguments for corporal punishment, and fagging they considered a 'vicious institution'. Yet they were very impressed by the freedom which the boys enjoyed and by their ability to rely on themselves. 'The masters', they observed, 'work . . . to make themselves useless.'[20] Over and over again the schoolmaster witnesses to the commission stressed the qualities of self-reliance and adaptability as the point of a public school education. Moberly thought that 'the characteristic stamp of a Winchester man' was 'a self-reliance, a modesty and a freeness of behaviour towards other people which fit men, eminently well, for the actual work of life'.[21] S T Hawtrey, mathematical master at Eton, praised the achievement of a young man, who 6 weeks after he had left Eton, had taken charge of 600 men trooping from Malta to the Crimea. 'But he had been "captain of the boats" at Eton, and the "service" then had the benefit of the experience and power of exercising a moral influence over others which he had gained in his previous training.'[22] By the 1860s and 1870s the public was convinced that this case was valid. The public schools combined stability and tradition with adaptability and change. The self-reliance which they prized so highly was an amalgam of high moral character, of training for leadership, of personal preparedness, of team-work on the games field, of manliness in general. Here, in these qualities, lies the final key to the success of the public schools in mid-Victorian England.

That period was not only a great age of innovation; it was also an age which laid much emphasis on history and tradition. It was the age of the Gothic Revival, of the rediscovery of the Catholic heritage of the Church, of a revived creed of chivalry. Perhaps the most characteristic building of an age which faced both ways is St Pancras Station in London – a modern train shed of glass and iron at the back, a turreted Gothic palace in front. The public schools had needed to reform themselves, but since they were already old and prestigious institutions, they also benefited from the historical romanticism of the age and from the growing attachment of old boys to their schools. This filial feeling, wrote Ludwig Wiese, did not blind men to the schools' deficiencies, but it made them confident of the powers of development inherent in the old roots.[23]

As this old-school romanticism developed, it was yet another force attracting boys to their father's old school and winning a new clientele of boys who would in turn themselves be old-boy parents. Historical sentiment attached itself most naturally to those schools which possessed ancient and beautiful buildings, the most obvious sign of the links connecting the present with the past. Schools like Eton and Winchester enjoyed these advantages to the full. Other schools which were less fortunate were conscious of the deficiency and anxious to do what they could to repair it. Thomas Arnold was a Radical and a Broad Churchman, but he was also a Wykehamist and a devoted son of Oxford. When that other Wykehamist, William Sewell, was visiting Rugby, Arnold said to him: 'Sir, in this place we want antiquity. You cannot educate well except under the shade of antiquity.'[24] There was, Arnold said in a sermon, 'something very ennobling in being connected with any establishment at once ancient and magnificent: where all about us, and all the associations belonging to the objects around us, should be great, splendid, and elevating'.[25] Very soon Arnold was deemed by his successors to have created traditions worthy to rank with the old. *The Book of Rugby School* (1856) commented on his interest in historical associations. Alongside the royal memories of Eton and the antiquity of Winchester could now be placed 'the possession of these lively memorials of Thomas Arnold'.[26]

All the public schools, by mid-century, were in the myth-making business because the myths of antiquity, religion and leadership contributed to the type of education which the upper and middle classes wanted for their sons. As the historical myths developed, they increased the drawing power of the public schools as against that of their rivals. The older schools did possess a genuine history and tradition; the newer schools did not find it difficult to acquire these things. This was an ideology which the private school or the tutorial establishment could not rival. They might be successful for a time, but their success was too ephemeral to compete with a corporate tradition which strengthened with the passage of each boy generation.

There is another feature of this romantic historicism which is important: that it tended to exalt institutions as against individuals. There had never been any lack of able heads who had built up successful schools and much has been said in earlier chapters about some of them, in both grammar and private schools. But their success, because it was very personal to themselves, was also ephemeral. It did not, in most cases, survive their own individual health and vigour or the particular circumstances which favoured their work. In one sense the emphasis which has been laid here on the contribution made by individual heads to the success of the public schools is misleading because it does not bring out the difference between their achievements and those of most of their predecessors. Arnold was successful not only as an individual but as headmaster of Rugby. Because his personal contribution was made to an institution which had already gathered strong loyalties to itself, what he did was carried forward and multiplied in a historical sequence of the work of many other men. As was often the case in Victorian life, the contributions of individuals were subsumed into a corporate whole and made much more enduring as a result. *The Book of Rugby School* brings out the point very clearly. Boys must learn to be attached to the school as a whole, 'to the ideas of Law, Order, System, Organization, as distinct from any individual through whom, as the executive power, these things are carried out .... At a Private School the Master may legitimately be everything .... Public Schools should claim a reverence and love as Institutions, independently of the men to whom their interests have been entrusted for a time.'²⁷ That the public schools succeeded in combining loyalty both to individuals and to the institution was another reason for their growing success.

Loyalty to the institution took many forms. The tensions in the mid-Victorian age between tradition and change have already been pointed out. In pre-industrial English society and among the social groups who had traditionally used the public schools, the first loyalty was owed to the family. As new wealth was made from an ever-expanding industry and commerce, there were more and more men, who could afford to give their children a good education, who had moved out of the social milieu in which they or their parents had been born. For these new men the family could not provide the focus of identity and socialization which it gave to people of more established social rank. It has already been argued that the public schools may have played an important part in creating a new ruling class for late-nineteenth-century England (see p. 233). An important part of that process lay in the civilizing, socializing role played by the public schools for many boys who had no other such centre of loyalty. Once again the public schools were much better placed to provide this kind of training than any of their rivals. They provided it partly through the experience of school life itself, though much more came through the games field than the classroom. Secondly, they created the ideal of careers in the public service. The army and the Empire overseas ranked ahead of commerce and industry as proper arenas for the development of the public school spirit.

The ideology of the public schools is very clearly expressed in that commemorative volume of 1856, *The Book of Rugby School*, which has already been quoted. There is a deep veneration for the memory of Thomas Arnold who created the tradition. There is a strong emphasis on the moral value of the school games which elicited the qualities of courage and tenacity later displayed on the battlefields of India and the furthest corners of Empire. The spell of the cricket match on the Close at Rugby is broken, as the match ends, by the whistle of an approaching train.

> Into that great world the waves of this little world must flow; those ardent cricketers, who so lately filled this great field with life, must be born by that Railway to other scenes than the Close, to other struggles than a Pie Match, to every corner of England, and to many corners far away from England, but the moral of the close is this, that they will be Rugbeians still.²⁸

The author of those words was one of the doctor's sons, William

Delafield Arnold, of the Bengal Native Infantry and later Director of Public Instruction in the Punjab, who expressed in his own life the links between public school training and service in the greater world.[29]

The stress on character training through games is very important to the development of the public school ethos. Boys had always played games, though they were not highly organized, and were often opposed, or at least restricted, by the school authorities. The early-nineteenth-century public-school boy was left very free in his out-of-school hours, and he spent much of his time roaming the countryside and engaging in occasional forays with keepers and farmers. The idea of organizing boys' games and giving them a formal status within the general curriculum appears to date from the 1850s. It has recently been argued that the two headmasters who, at much the same time, were the major pioneers in this were Cotton of Marlborough and Vaughan of Harrow. Cotton, as we have seen, succeeded to the headship of a school which was very new, very large and very disorderly. A general subscription for games would, he wrote to parents in 1853, prevent the boys from wandering round the countryside damaging their neighbours' property and would keep them 'as much as possible together in one body in the College itself and in the playground'. In the same year as Cotton's letter, the Philathletic Club was founded at Harrow to promote 'a stronger feeling of interest in manly exercises and amusements' and to foster 'a spirit of sociability and concord throughout the members of the school'. Games, it was claimed, would keep boys out of mischief and would get rid of 'the general apathy and want of spirit'. Boys who played well could generally be expected to work well.[30]

The school games of early years, like the Big-Side Match at Rugby between 40 boys of the sixth and 200 from the rest of the school which began on 26 September 1845 and went on for 3 days,[31] were very unlike the formalized and structured rituals of later Victorian times. After about 1850 the organization improved and by about 1880 compulsion was general and the games cult had become fully established. The Clarendon Commission, in general, approved. Games, they thought, were likely to prevent some boys from overworking and others from idling away their time.[32] Some influential witnesses were highly supportive. Edmond Warre, then an assistant master and later headmaster and provost of Eton, who had a major influence in promoting games in the school, argued that active participation in them produced both moral and physical benefits. It cut down the class of idlers and was 'quite compatible with very steady reading'.[33] H M

Butler of Harrow testified to the very strong interest of the boys throughout the school[34]:

> There is no subject on which even the oldest and most intellectual boys are so eager to talk. A boy who was believed to take no interest in the favourite games, especially cricket, would, however distinguished, be somewhat looked down upon by his schoolfellows.

It is not surprising that boys in the enclosed world of the boarding school should have taken their games so seriously. What is surprising is that their masters should have become such enthusiastic proponents of the cult. One aspect of this was the belief that games promoted the desirable moral qualities – co-operation and team spirit, the ability to win gracefully and to lose without complaint, the power to endure fatigue and physical pain. The hard-fought contests of the playing field were seen as rehearsals for the battles of the world outside. Secondly, these battles were seen through a haze of historical romanticism. The mid-Victorian age was deeply affected by the ideal of chivalry. It was the era of the Eglinton Tournament,[35] of the Round Table and of the *Idylls of the King*. The athlete, like the soldier, seemed a modern version of the knight in shining armour. Very often the boy who excelled in the first role later won fame as a man in the second.

One individual who drew these threads together was the Eton master, William Johnson (later Cory), who taught at the school from 1845 to 1872. He wrote beautiful and rather melancholy verse commemorating his affection for his pupils. He actively encouraged school games, and in 1863 he wrote the 'Eton Boating Song'. He told the commission that every Etonian wished to be distinguished in bodily exercises and many wanted to do well in both work and games. 'Games come first. Books second.'[36] He was a strong patriot and a great admirer of soldiers. If he heard a detachment march by his pupil-room, he would shout 'Brats, the British Army', and he and his pupils would hurry into the street and stand till the men had marched by.[37]

The army, the Empire and public service were the great fields of action for the moral values proclaimed by the public schools and tested on their playing-fields. The Clarendon Report said that the number of public-school boys who entered the army, either through direct commissions or through entry to Sandhurst, was small,[38] but some of their detailed evidence does modify that judgment to some degree. Harrow in 3 years sent up sixty-two candidates for commissions of whom forty-two passed, most of them after further

private tuition. In the one year 1861–62, thirty-eight Harrovians went
to Oxford and Cambridge.[39] William Johnson gave evidence that 'the
only profession which it is worthwhile to consider with reference to
Eton boys is the army',[40] by which he presumably meant that while
many Etonians did not need to follow a profession, the army attracted
many of those who did. Other schools had strong army and Empire
links. Several Wykehamists had been prominent in the Napoleonic
Wars,[41] and a strong contingent from Rugby had been attracted to the
army and to service in India at least as far back as the days of John
Wooll, Arnold's predecessor.[42] Arnold himself was keenly aware of
the English overseas. He preached a sermon just before he died in
which he referred to the scattering of boys from an English school
'over the whole habitable world'.[43] The career of his own son William
has already been mentioned, and one of his old boys was the Indian
Mutiny hero, Hodson of Hodson's Horse, who captured the King of
Delhi. A favourite Victorian hero-figure was the Christian soldier,
and a famous example of the class was another Mutiny paladin, Sir
Henry Havelock, who had been at Charterhouse.[44] Of the memorial
windows presented to Rugby chapel in the 1850s one was a gift from
Rugbeians serving in India, and another commemorated the twenty-
five old boys who fell in the Crimea.[45]

This legacy of imperial service was further reinforced by the new
schools like Cheltenham, Marlborough and Wellington with their
army sides. It relied very much on the traditions of self-reliance and
personal independence which the public schools claimed to foster.
The point has been noted by several modern writers. Honey speaks of
'manliness',[46] Newsome of 'godliness and manliness'.[47] All these
phrases express the same creed of patriotism, duty, personal
hardihood and self-denial which was deemed to be characteristic of
public-school men. It proved a potent and popular doctrine. In an age
when British interests were expanding all over the world and young
men – sometimes little more than boys – had to undertake major
responsibilities, the creed – self-reliance, manliness, call it what you
will – answered a real demand. To meet that demand was a major
objective of the schools which educated the sons of the ruling class.
The public schools, with their historic traditions, their chapels and
playing-fields, their memories of loyalty and communal life for both
master and boy, were uniquely well placed to offer what upper-class
Englishmen wanted for their sons. Their growing popularity reflects
the success with which they met those needs.

The years 1850–70 were years of growing prosperity for the middle
and upper classes. There was more money for them to spend on a wide

variety of goods and services, one of which was education.[48] Much of that money was spent on sending boys to public schools, though it is an over-simplification to argue that, if the education market was expanding, the public schools had inevitably to be the major beneficiaries of the growth. Around 1830 these schools seemed to be falling behind, and in the 1850s competition between schools was still keen. The swing towards the public schools was a long and complex process. What I have tried to do is explain why they overtook their rivals, particularly the private schools, and gained a victory so complete that the fact that there was ever a struggle has been almost forgotten. Perhaps the generally favourable verdict of the Clarendon Commission promoted their interests and helped to make victory certain.

NOTES AND REFERENCES

1. Stanley A P 1875 vol I p 153
2. *PSC* II, pp 9-30 (correspondence with professors and tutors at universities)
3. *Ibid.* p 14
4. *Ibid.* p 28
5. *Ibid.* p 18
6. *Ibid.* p 24
7. *PSC* I, p 26
8. *Ibid.* p 56
9. *PSC* II, p 327
10. Wordsworth, Charles 1891 p 278
11. See St Quintin G 1956 chs I, II
12. Quoted in Heeney, Brian 1969 p 99
13. *PSC* I, p 56
14. *Ibid.* pp 43-4; p 152 (Winchester); pp 221-2 (Harrow); p 258 (Rugby). On Westminster see pp 162-3
15. *PSC* II, p 225
16. Vaughan C J 1854; see also Mack E C 1938 pp 379-80; Chandos, John 1984 p 239
17. Vaughan C J 1854 p 23
18. Grosskurth, Phyllis 1964 pp 32-40
19. Hare A J C 1896 pp 214-28, 236-7, 241-6
20. Demogeot J, Montucci H 1868 pp 18, 41, 58, 164
21. *PSC* II, p 188
22. *Ibid.* p 161
23. Wiese L 1854 p 117; see also Mack E C 1938 p 108
24. (Sewell William) 1938 p 2
25. Bamford T W (ed) 1870 p 45
26. Goulburn E M (ed) 1856 p 59 (written by E W Benson)
27. *Ibid.* p 219

28. *Ibid.* p 193
29. On W D Arnold, see Woodward, Frances J 1954 pp 180–228 and also his own novel about India, *Oakfield: A Fellowship in the East* (1853, reprinted Leicester 1973)
30. See Mangan J A 1981. The Harrow and Marlborough documents are on pp 223–30
31. As described by W D Arnold in Goulburn E M (ed) 1856 pp 155–69. See also the account given in *Tom Brown's Schooldays*
32. *PSC* I, p 41
33. *Ibid.* p 97
34. *PSC* II, p 282
35. On the Eglinton Tournament of 1839, see Anstruther, Ian 1963. On the idea of chivalry generally, see Girouard, Mark 1981
36. *PSC* II, p 128
37. For an account of William Johnson, see Hollis, Christopher 1960 pp 276–81. For the story of the detachment of troops see also Girouard, Mark 1981 p 175
38. *PSC* I, p 27
39. *Ibid.* p 223
40. *PSC* II, p 127
41. Leach A F 1899 pp 413–14
42. Rouse W H D 1898 pp 208–10
43. Bamford T W (ed) 1970 p 146
44. For a study of Victorian interest in the army and navy, see Best, Geoffrey Militarism and the Victorian public school, in Simon B, Bradley, Ian (eds) 1975 pp 129–46
45. Goulburn E M (ed) 1856 pp 78, 85
46. Honey J R de S 1977 p 209
47. Newsome, David 1961 p 216
48. See the general argument of Banks J A 1954 esp pp 189–90

PART FOUR

The 1860s

CHAPTER NINETEEN
Reform and its limitations (i)

The Clarendon Commission on the major public schools was appointed in 1861, in the same year as the Newcastle Commission on popular education published its report. In 1864, when Clarendon reported, the Schools Inquiry or Taunton Commission was set up to investigate the schools – both endowed and private – which had not been examined by the other two. Already, during the 1850s, the universities of Oxford and Cambridge had come under scrutiny. During the decade ending in 1868 when the Schools Inquiry Commission reported, the whole range of English schools had come under review. Major political changes were also taking place. The year 1868 was also that of the first and greatest victory of W E Gladstone, when the Liberals profited from the political changes introduced by the Conservatives in the Reform Act of 1867. Among the achievements of the new liberalism were the Education Act of 1870 and important measures to deal with the endless problems of Ireland.

The 1860s were also a decade of active educational debate, much of it centred on the demand for the fuller recognition of science in the curriculum. Herbert Spencer, in his *Essays on Education* published in 1861, made a plea for scientific education on the ground that only science is really useful and that it is scientific knowledge which enables man to live and flourish in the world. 'Thus to the question we set out with', Spencer wrote, 'What knowledge is of most worth? – the uniform reply is science. This is the verdict on all the counts.'[1] A more moderate, but more influential voice on the same side was that of T H Huxley, himself a scientist of distinction. Huxley appreciated the value of the traditional disciplines, but he claimed that, unless it provided a thorough grounding in experimental science, no education could be considered complete.[2]

In 1868 *Essays on a Liberal Education*, a collection of essays by a group of teachers writing from within the traditional education structures, expressed a similar view. Though they appreciated the virtues of the classics as one subject among others, they wanted to end the classical dominance of the curriculum. They were critical of the neglect of the sciences and of English. The traditional methods of learning classics, they argued, imprisoned boys within a pedantic routine, so that they never learned to grasp the ancient languages properly and they had no time for anything else. The philosopher, Henry Sidgwick, for example, denied that there was any necessary antagonism between science and literature so that a choice had to be made between one and other. In the mid-Victorian age an education in physical science was the natural form for education to take because 'the external world forces itself in every way, directly and indirectly, upon our observation'.[3] By the end of the decade the same pressures were reinforced by the fear of competition in international trade and of British backwardness in comparison with her foreign rivals. In 1868 the Select Committee on Scientific Instruction, chaired by the great industrialist Bernhard Samuelson, recommended better facilities for scientific education, and these pressures were to grow steadily during the 1870s.[4]

The debate over science and technology is important. It attracted much attention in the press and in Parliament, and many people of distinction contributed to it, but it seems to have had fewer results on the mainstream of school activities than might have been expected from those facts. One of the remarkable features of the general debate about secondary education in the 1860s and 1870s is the absence of any clearly defined core curriculum to meet the requirements of a rapidly changing world. Important changes took place, but there was no overall strategy. Perhaps, in the English system of divided control and individual responsibility, it was too much to expect that such a strategy should emerge. Most upper- and middle-class Englishmen were reasonably content with what they had – and where they accepted changes, these were to be as few as possible. The Schools Inquiry Commission, in its report, emphasized language as the primary subject of instruction and quoted the weight laid by their expert witnesses on Latin.[5] The ramparts of a liberal education still stood firm against attack.

If curriculum was one major issue of contemporary debate, organization was another. The best-known critic of the disorder of English education and of the harmful results for the middle classes which resulted from it was Matthew Arnold. England lacked a concept of the national interest rising above the conflicts of classes and based on rational principles. In France, Germany and Switzerland, he argued, education was a matter of state organization. It was planned centrally, though wide latitude was left to local administrators, and in consequence educational opportunities were available which did not exist on a comparable scale in England. Arnold thought that the middle classes suffered greatly from England's lack of system, so that they could be judged the worst educated in the world. England possessed a few public schools which were excellent, but below that level there was nothing to compare with the state secondary schools of France and Germany. As the result of its educational deficiencies England was not ready to meet the demands of the modern epoch.[6]

Because Matthew Arnold is a major literary figure and a very persuasive writer, it is easy to exaggerate his influence. It would be difficult, I think, to show that his ideas had a direct effect on the practical men who were wrestling with the problems of secondary education. Though the Taunton Commission made inquiries in foreign countries, there is not much sign that foreign influence had any great effect. Indeed it may have been less powerful in that generation than in the days of Pestalozzi and Fellenberg. Yet Arnold had put his finger on a problem which was critical to the concerns of mid-Victorian reformers – the question of organization at both national and at local level. In the mid-Victorian period narrow limits were set to the intervention of the state in education, particularly in the case of schools for the middle and upper classes. Yet the state was forced to take a hand to regulate the large endowments enjoyed by those schools. We have already considered the inquiries of the 'Brougham' commissioners of 1818–37 and the establishment, after long delays and with insufficient powers, of the Charity Commissioners in 1853 (see p. 93). The information made available by the 'Brougham' inquiries had made it clear that reform was essential, while it was equally clear that the rigid processes of the Court of Chancery – which were the only means generally available of revising existing schemes of management – were an expensive and ineffective method of achieving this.

The original objective of reformers had been to improve the management of individual charities, but it soon became obvious that it would be difficult to do this effectively without creating a central department with overall control and with some means of linking charities in the same area with one another, possibly through county or borough boards of education. The problem was taken up in the

Newcastle Commission Report of 1861, which has a section on charitable endowments. The powers of the Charity Commissioners, the report suggested, should be transferred to the Privy Council; 'that the action of a central authority is necessary in this case seems to us past dispute'.[7] The Privy Council's duties should include any necessary modifications in the instruction given in endowed schools and in the distribution of funds between the various objects of the foundation. The Privy Council should also give attention to the improvement of school premises, the relaxation of restrictions and the extension of endowments to cover new districts, the combination of small endowments, the acquisition of new sites, and the reorganization of boards of trustees.[8]

A few years before the Newcastle Report a similar argument was advanced from the provinces in an article by the Manchester educationalist Canon Richson. Richson was largely concerned with elementary education, though he also discussed 'intermediate education', up to the age of about 16. There should, he thought, be a minister of public instruction with power to appoint inspectors for both primary and middle-class schools and to provide for 'the Visitation of Schools publicly endowed'. All schools should submit to 'Periodical Public Examinations'. Most important of all was 'the proper application of Charitable Endowments; because I consider that no effort ought to be spared to develope [sic] fully and for the most advantageous and consistent purposes, the immense educational resources, which in such Funds, this country possesses'.[9]

The same demand for public control and more effective management runs through much of the evidence presented to the Taunton Commission, as well as being a major theme in their final report, though that report does not go so far as to propose a Ministry of Education. The comment of D R Fearon, assistant commissioner for the metropolitan district, is typical of the argument repeated many times in the commission's papers[10]:

> I only wish to point out, what is apparent to all who have studied the history of English education what very inadequate results from magnificent means, what abortive creations, what mischievous or undesigned effects, in short, what a lamentable *waste of power* has been occasioned, by the want of any superintending and directing intelligence, by that prevailing mistrust of authority and love of independent ill-directed action which is so peculiar to Englishmen.

The opportunity was to be missed. After 1870, little was done to create the central mechanism which the Schools Inquiry Commission had recommended, though much was achieved to improve the management of individual schools. The central authority for secondary education, towards which Taunton had looked, was not be created until the Education Act of 1902 – and then in a very different form.

In 1860 all that lay in the future, though it was already clear that the state intended to take a much more active interest than it had done previously in the conduct of universities and of schools of all kinds. The increasing commitment of public funds to elementary education had led to the appointment in 1858 of the Newcastle Commission whose report of 1861 was followed by Robert Lowe's Revised Code, imposing much more rigid controls over elementary school curricula and over the spending of public money on the system as a whole. While Newcastle was deliberating, public attention was directed towards the major public schools when a new burst of criticism broke out, much of it directed at Eton.

The movement of opinion which resulted in the appointment of the Clarendon Commission was initiated by two Etonians, a journalist M J Higgins ('Paterfamilias') and a high court judge, Sir John Coleridge. Coleridge – naturally enough – was the more measured critic of the two, but what they both said was in essence very similar. Their comments brought together the complaints which had been repeated for a generation: the excessive powers of the provost and fellows and the concentration of a large part of the endowment in their hands; the fact that there were too few masters, that they were chosen among a very narrow circle of Kingsmen and that they were considerably overworked; the neglect of subjects like modern languages and mathematics; the idleness and extravagance of the boys.[11]

The debate extended into other journals, and the scope widened beyond the affairs of Eton. Even the *Quarterly*, anxious to defend the schools, admitted that the boys were idle and that teaching methods needed improvement.[12] It was Henry Reeve in the *Edinburgh* who widened the whole debate. He repeated the criticisms made about the management of Eton and argued that much might be learned there from the arrangements made at the new foundation of Wellington College. But, he argued, the matter extended beyond Eton. The public schools should be dealt with in the same way as the universities of Oxford and Cambridge[13]:

> The only remedy adequate to the case is a Royal Commission, armed –
> by Parliament if necessary – with full visitatorial powers, which ought
> to comprehend within its range the other great public schools of
> Westminster, Winchester, Harrow and Rugby. These are no longer
> monastic establishments or private corporations, they are the great

seminaries of learning in this land and their welfare and progress concerns in the highest degree the Empire itself.

Henry Reeve's assertion of the claims of the public interest against the private interests of individual foundations is very significant of the mood of the day, but it was an assertion which the men of that time were prepared to push only up to a certain point. Their mood was, as has already been argued, reforming rather than Radical, and the Clarendon Commission treated the great schools with considerable – sometimes almost exaggerated – respect, though they were critical of the teaching and of the standards achieved by the boys. From the constitutional point of view there was a major difference between the tasks of the Clarendon and Taunton commissions. Clarendon was dealing with a small number of institutions – nine initially, seven as covered by the Public Schools Act of 1868. They made general suggestions for the management of the schools, but they saw each of them as an entity demanding separate treatment. Reeve's comparison with Oxford and Cambridge is worth bearing in mind here. The Taunton Commission, whose report covered 782 schools, faced an entirely different problem. Their schools varied widely in numbers, in wealth, in prestige, in curriculum. Instead of dealing with a small number of major institutions, they were attempting to create a national pattern out of the most disparate elements. In managerial terms their problems were infinitely more complex than those of the Public Schools Commissioners, and indeed those problems proved too complex to be solved at that time in the ways which they recommended.

The Report of the Clarendon Commission (1864) recommended the reform of the governing bodies and the revision of the statutes. The new governing bodies should, it was argued, contain 'men conversant with the world, with the requirements of active life, and with the progress of literature and science'.[14] The assistant masters should form a formal council to advise the headmaster and with the right to address the governing body. All payments for instruction should be paid into a tuition fund out of which the head and assistants were to be paid their salaries.[15] It was 4 years before legislation was passed. One problem which caused delay was that of foundationers' rights at Rugby, Harrow and Shrewsbury (see pp. 219-25). In the House of Lords the Conservatives worked hard to alter the original form of the bill. They prevented the appointment of the new governing bodies by Parliament itself, as originally proposed, but they were unsuccessful in reducing the authority of the proposed executive commission which as in the case of Oxford and Cambridge 10 years earlier, was to watch over the work of the new governing bodies.[16] The Public Schools Act 1868 (31 & 32 Vic., c. 118) gave the existing governing bodies powers, to endure until 1 May 1869, to make statutes to decide the constitution of the new governing bodies. After that the statute-making power passed to the special commissioners. The new governing bodies were given power to make statutes to remove local restrictions on foundation boys and to make admission to the foundation dependent on competitive examination. They might also abridge or extend foundation privileges, alter regulations for scholarships and exhibitions, establish subordinate schools, and in the case of Winchester and Eton, regulate the numbers and the income of the warden/provost and fellows. All new statutes were to be submitted to the special commissioners and then to the Privy Council. The new governing bodies were also given power to make regulations about numbers of boys, fees, attendance at divine service, holidays, new branches of study, and the number, position and rank of assistant masters. Other clauses protected the rights of those residents at Harrow, Rugby and Shrewsbury who enjoyed them when the Act was passed, and provided that the Eton and Winchester estates should be let at rack-rent instead of by leases and fines.

The establishment of the Schools Inquiry Commission in 1864 had been preceded a year earlier by a petition from that sounding board of progressive opinion, the Social Science Association, for the appointment of a Royal Commission to examine the present state of the education of the middle classes.[17] In the year when the commission began work the association's education section heard a number of papers on that topic from speakers, some of whom were to play a part in the commission's work. The subjects discussed illustrate some of the major concerns of such a group. They include the problem of gratuitous education and the advantages of modern departments in which Greek was not taught;[18] the possibility of selecting within an area a small number of grammar schools for advanced work with a structure of 'middle schools' beneath them;[19] the utility of examinations and the best way of organizing them.[20] Emily Davies read a paper on the need to provide adequate secondary education for girls,[21] and there was discussion about the need to reform ancient trusts, accompanied by concern about the impact that such reforms might have on the interest of poor but able boys if traditional rights were abolished. George Griffith, the West Midland advocate of local rights, read a paper on the misuse of endowments and on the desirability of electing school trustees in the same way as guardians of the poor.[22]

The papers published by the Schools Inquiry Commission (1868) are so massive in scale that to do them justice would demand a book in itself. They consist of a lengthy general report and recommendations, the examination of numerous witnesses, surveys of schools in other countries, eight substantial reports by assistant commissioners on different areas of the country, and reports on the individual schools. Seven hundred and eighty-two endowed schools were reported on; 36,874 boys were educated in them (9,279 boarders, 27,595 day boys). The net endowment income was £195,184. Eight school had incomes of more than £2,000, 13 of more than £1,000, 55 of at least £500.[23] For the numbers in private schools they were able to provide no reliable estimate, but they had no doubt that these were very large. They thought that 52,000 boys were in both endowed and proprietary schools, and they estimated that 255,000 boys in total required secondary education; therefore 'nearly eighty per cent of the whole are educated in private schools, or at home, or not at all'.[24]

Much of the Taunton survey repeats the observations of the 'Brougham' Commission which have already been examined in the earlier chapters in this book. The endowed schools as a whole were not full. In many of them the teaching was ineffective, and sometimes many of their resources were committed to teaching a few boys Latin. Many of them had ceased to be classical schools and had sunk to the level of poorly run elementary schools, which, since they already existed, prevented the creation of effective National Schools. Many endowments were tied to small villages or devoted to objects of limited utility, and it was very difficult and expensive to reform them. Masters, particularly those with freehold offices, were inefficient, and trustees were not effective managers. In many areas it was impossible for parents, who were prepared to pay for good teaching, to find it since grammar schools had ceased to prepare boys for the universities or for professional careers. Only 166 endowed schools (including the 9 Clarendon schools and Marlborough) sent boys to the universities, and only about 80 or 90 schools were sending one student a year. Three hundred and forty or 43 per cent of the total number of schools did not teach Latin and Greek.[25] J G Fitch thought that in the West Riding, though a few schools had been reformed, the majority were degenerating rather than improving[26]:

> It not infrequently happened that on visiting foundation schools which are now sunk to a far lower level than an ordinary national school, I have been met by trustees who are now magistrates and country gentlemen, and informed me that in their youth they received a good drilling in Latin and Greek within the same walls.

The commission did not limit itself to endowed schools; it also reported on private and proprietary schools. In the private sector they found much to criticize and some things to praise – on lines similar to those outlined in earlier chapters of this book. In all these schools they laid much stress on the power of class distinctions so that these schools were not always open to parents who were ready to pay the fees.[27]

The Schools Inquiry Commission did much more than repeat and further reinforce complaints about endowed and private schools which had been well known for a generation. They showed both that the endowed schools were not providing sufficient places in the areas where they existed and that there were many important centres with no grammar school provision at all. There were major deficiencies in London; there were 73 towns in the West Midlands, the north-west and Yorkshire with a population of 1,164,098 with no grammar school endowments at all.[28]

In order to meet these deficiencies as far as possible they suggested a policy of grading schools, similar to that already adopted under differing circumstances by both Nathaniel Woodard and by the Liverpool Collegiate Institution (see pp. 167, 191). They recommended schools of three grades. The first grade would be basically classical, would be based on the requirements of a university course, and would take boys up to the age of 18. The second grade, taking boys up to about 16, would prepare boys for business and for many professions. Parents of such boys had no desire for Greek and little for Latin, while there was a strong interest in English, mathematics, natural science and modern languages. The third grade would take boys up to about 14. These schools would be designed for the sons of small farmers, shopkeepers and superior artisans. There was hardly any public provision of such schools, and it was of great importance to make this deficiency good. In some cases it might be possible to link these schools with existing elementary schools.[29]

The commission further envisaged that within particular areas there might be co-ordination between schools of different grade, with exhibitions to enable boys to pass from one grade of school to another. Such exhibitions might be financed from school endowments, and would be an appropriate use of such funds.[30] Several of the assistant commissioners made specific proposals for their own areas which illustrate what was intended. T H Green in the West Midlands thought that both Warwickshire and Staffordshire might maintain one 'high school'. This would contain both classical and modern departments, would have provision for boarders, and would be centrally situated and easily reached by rail. Board and teaching might be offered for £40 a year and there should be exhibitions 'of 25l. a year tenable at the school, most of which, if not all, should be appropriated to boys either resident or trained at schools, public and private, in the county'. Other grammar schools, if they had an endowment income of much less than 1,000l. a year should act as preparatory to the proposed high schools and should not attempt to keep their boys much beyond the age of 15.[31] For the West Riding with its many endowments J G Fitch suggested six high schools and a larger group of twenty-five secondary schools. The remainder might be managed in the same way as National Schools and should include higher departments for the sons of farmers and small tradesmen which might be financed from the endowments.[32]

Such plans for reorganization, if they were to be realized, would demand a new administrative structure for secondary education. The demand for such a structure is the major theme of the final report of the Taunton Commission and an important strand in the reports of the assistant commissioners. J G Fitch pointed out that opinion in the West Riding favoured both a central administrative authority for 'middle and higher instruction', and county or local boards to inspect schools, to award exhibitions, and to keep a register of teachers.[33] James Bryce, in his report on Lancashire, argued that a central authority would be able to help boards of trustees and to provide a wider view of contentious local issues. The jurisdiction of the Court of Chancery was too rigid and legalistic and the influence of the Charity Commission, though useful, was not adequately felt.[34] There was a great need, Bryce wrote, for an outside stimulus 'whether by the State, or by local public bodies, or by combined voluntary effort, to offer to parents a better education for their children'.[35]

The final report reiterated these points. It pointed out that the French, Prussian and Swiss systems owed their success to the completeness of their public organization.[36] In England, on the other hand, the state exercised no control over the training of teachers, the examination of scholars, or the management of schools.[37] What was needed was a comprehensive plan giving control to an administrative board with powers to initiate reform.[38] During the 1850s Parliament had taken a first tentative step on the road towards the better regulation of endowments by creating the Charity Commission (see p. 93). Its powers had been extended by another Act of 1860, but it is clear, both from its annual reports and from the evidence of the legal and official witnesses to the Taunton inquiry, that its powers were still quite insufficient. In the case of charities with an income of over

£50 a year – in other words in the case of all charities of any importance – they could take action only with the consent of the majority of the trustees, and there was a practically unlimited right of appeal to the Court of Chancery against their decisions.[39]

The official witnesses considered that the Charity Commission had, even under these difficulties, done useful work and they recommended the extension of its powers.[40] The commission complained in its own reports of the very tight legal constraints within which it was forced to operate and of the way in which the 'vehement opposition of interested parties' had sometimes foiled its proposals.[41] What this meant in practice is outlined in D R Fearon's report on London schools[42]:

> ... in very many instances in which their interference is most wanted they have no power to move, and of course cannot for a moment aspire to forming out of our present chaos a thorough system of grammar school education for the metropolis. Even where they can move they are checked at every step by the Court of Chancery, and it is not uncommon to find the whole power of the Board paralysed by a small but active knot of partisans in a parish who have perhaps nothing whatever to do with the management or control of the school. The master and all the governors and trustees of a school may be strongly in favour of a scheme sanctioned by the Board, but if there is the least appearance of opposition in the locality the Board cannot act ....

What were needed, it was argued, were flexible rules of administration. What existed was a rigid system of law, which attempted to interpret the intentions of founders, formulated under quite different circumstances, yet embodied in perpetual trusts which it was very difficult to change. The Court of Chancery, and therefore the Charity Commission, applied in these matters the *cy près* rule, which insisted that charitable bequests be regulated as nearly as possible by the founder's original intentions. In a complex legal matter it is best to quote the evidence of lawyers. Lord Romilly, Master of the Rolls, explained the rule like this[43]:

> The founder of many of these charities has endowed schools and charitable institutions with a view to his notion of the state of society at that time, and fettered by such rules as he thought desirable. The Courts of Chancery have followed that as far as they possibly could, but where the objects have utterly failed they applied them *cy près*, that is, as nearly as may be, but when they have not failed, generally speaking the Courts have held themselves to be bound by the rules, however foolish, and however absurd, imposed by the founder.

Not surprisingly, under these rules, the court had had considerable trouble over charitable bequests for the relief of slaves captured by the Barbary pirates!

Not only was the system rigid: it was also uncertain. One of the Charity Commissioners pointed out the difficulties caused to them from the fact that different judges had taken different decisions on similar subjects.[44] One of these judges, Sir William Page Wood, cited the admission of boarders to grammar schools as one subject on which decisions had varied a good deal. The opinion of the court was, he thought, moving towards generally accepting boarders,[45] though this can have been little consolation to schools which had gone to the court when a more rigid view prevailed. Page Wood also suggested that there ought to be a general power to revise charitable bequests after 60 years.[46] To end legal perpetuities would break the grip exercised by the past over the present.

There was a strong feeling that endowments should be managed according to equity and common sense rather than through 'the technical forms of contentious jurisdiction'.[47] Such a change would mean the transfer of control to some kind of administrative body. Many of the witnesses wanted to extend the powers of the Charity Commission. Sir James Kay-Shuttleworth, who had unique experience of educational administration, suggested a more ambitious scheme. He proposed a department of public charities, working under the Privy Council on lines parallel to the existing Education Department for elementary education – or even identical with it. The new charities department would be represented in Parliament through the same ministers who spoke for elementary schools. It would be divided into two branches, scholastic and legal, each with its own inspectorate. Unlike many other witnesses, Kay did not favour the creation of local boards. His clear purpose was to bring together elementary and secondary education so as to provide a progression from the lowest levels of the system to the highest. Though he does not say this, the achievement of his proposals would have created a Ministry of Education long before such a department was set up.[48]

Any reorganization of endowments was likely to lead to many problems. One issue, which caused so much bitterness in the elementary schools throughout the century, was that of religious education and the conscience clause. In the grammar schools there were few difficulties on this score. The Attorney-General, Sir Roundell Palmer, explained that a conscience clause had been included in recent schemes.[49] C H Stanton in Devon and Cornwall found few complaints of exclusion on religious grounds.[50] James

Bryce in Lancashire said that parents were not sensitive about religious teaching, and that schoolmasters, if they were tactful, 'find it perfectly easy ... to give such teaching dogmatic or undogmatic, as they think it their duty to give, without either violating the conscientious feelings of any parent or interfering with the organization of their school'.[51]

Just as the religious issue was the major point of conflict in the elementary schools, the primary problem in the grammar schools was what to do about the traditional rights to free education. The concept of a 'free grammar school' has already been discussed. In the 1860s the general tone of opinion was against free schooling unless it were linked with the award of exhibitions to boys of academic merit. This grammar school debate runs parallel with the controversies about foundationers' rights at Harrow, Rugby and Shrewsbury which have already been examined (see pp. 219–25), and is related to the mid-Victorian emphasis on competition and on examination.

The Schools Inquiry Commission papers show a general dislike of what the men of the time regarded as indiscriminate charity. Page Wood said that for 30 years the Court of Chancery had, as much as possible, discouraged 'purely gratuitous education'.[52] T H Green judged that the result of free admission to schools was 'so to lower the general character of the school as to deprive promising boys of the humbler classes of any real benefit they might gain by entering it. It leads to the invasion of the school by a 'mixed multitude' of boys too numerous to be absorbed in a higher element than their own, who get no good from it themselves which they might not get elsewhere and prevent its doing good to others.'[53] Green laid much emphasis on the advantages of a system of exhibitions as a means of bringing forward promising boys.[54] Bryce thought that the endowment of a school might be divided between a number of exhibitions, each of which would equal in value the normal fee paid by a paying pupil.[55] J G Fitch was the most outspoken of all. The poor, he claimed, do not value free education. They have got used to fee-paying in schools under the Committee of Council and they disdain free provision. The endowments should supplement what middle-class people were prepared to pay for their children's education. It was perfectly fair to do this now if government paid grants towards maintaining schools for the poor.[56]

The difficulty with the Fitch argument is that it implied a clear division between the education of the middle classes and of the poor which the traditional grammar school system, for all its faults, had avoided. The person who saw most clearly the importance of preserving educational opportunities for humble boys was Kay-Shuttleworth. If free education were to be abolished, it should be replaced by scholarships covering both education and something for clothing and maintenance. The first charge for endowments, he thought, should be to enable boys of humble birth to enjoy a good education. Grammar schools should have preparatory departments in which a boy might gain a good English education and enjoy the opportunity by means of scholarships, of a full grammar school course.[57]

It is not difficult to find out from the sources the views on these subjects of lawyers and professional men such as those who have been quoted. It is much more difficult to discover the views of the tradesmen and artisans whose sons might benefit from the opportunities which Kay was anxious to keep open. One voice expressing what may be called a 'provincial view' is that of the West Midland corn merchant, George Griffith, whose ideas have already been discussed (see pp. 95–8). After a period of quiescence he returned to the problems of the grammar schools in the late 1850s. He published a survey of Staffordshire schools in 1859 and of the educational and charitable institutions of Birmingham, his home town, in 1861.[58] He tried unsuccessfully to get himself appointed an assistant commissioner under the Taunton Commission.[59] He continued to write and to speak on much the same lines as in the 1850s,[60] defending the rights of local boys, criticizing the admission of boarders, demanding that the classics be replaced by commercial and scientific studies. He opposed the introduction of school fees, arguing that the Charity Commissioners had imposed them even when the school funds were large enough to make them unnecessary. The value of the endowed school properties was so great, he argued, that it would provide £6 per annum for every poor boy and girl between the ages of 8 and 14, and if properly utilized, would 'do away with our immense public grants for education'.[61]

On free education the final report of the commission took the same line as T H Green – that the indiscriminate admission of free boys flooded a school with those who demanded the rudiments of knowledge only. It would be best, they thought, to award free places by competition.[62] On the general questions of management and administration their recommendations were radical.[63] A strengthened Charity Commission would become a central authority with power to accept or reject schemes for the settlement of trusts and to submit them to Parliament. They should appoint inspectors of endowed schools, audit accounts and inquire into useless or obsolete charities.

Beneath the central authority there should be provincial authorities, one for each of the Registrar-General's eleven divisions. These provincial authorities would settle the various grades of school and would draw up schemes to be submitted to the central body. There should be a general conscience clause and trustees should not be required to be members of the Church of England or masters to be Anglican clergymen. The prime charge on endowments should be for buildings. Indiscriminate free instruction should be abolished and free education given only as a reward for ability and attainment. Restrictions on beneficiaries based either on poverty or on residence in particular areas should disappear. The qualifications for exhibitions should be widened as much as possible. They should be awarded for forms of advanced education other than the university and they should be awarded from a lower to a higher grade of school.

The new central body would enjoy the powers of the Court of Chancery except in cases involving claims to property or the misconduct of trustees. The central body would appoint an official district commissioner for each division who would be a salaried officer responsible for the inspection of educational schools and charities in his district. In addition to him there would be six or eight unpaid local commissioners, and county boards might be set up as well if there was sufficient demand for them. No compulsory rate for secondary education was proposed, but it was suggested that towns and parishes might if they wished be able to levy a rate for furnishing a site and buildings and for paying the fees of able boys selected from the elementary schools. Nor were examinations overlooked. These should be placed in the hands of a Council of Examinations, half of it appointed by the universities of Oxford, Cambridge and London and half of it by the Crown. The council would not only examine schools. It would also examine those who wished to qualify as schoolmasters. Private and proprietary schools should also be registered and submitted to the same conditions of inspection and examination.

The report thus recommended a bureaucratic structure for secondary education with tight controls at both central and local levels. If these plans had been fully implemented, they would have produced a revolution in the endowed schools, and the private schools could not have remained unaffected. The Endowed Schools Act of 1869 implemented only part of these proposals; the rest of the original bill never passed into law.[64] The commission's plans form one of the most fascinating 'might have beens' of English educational history. They might have created a national system of secondary education before the public schools had established the massive prestige and authority which they gained in the next 20 years. They might have combined the action of private endowments with that of the state so that each side supplemented the other. They might, if the grades of schools could have been organized, have produced an open system favourable to the poor but able boy or girl. As it was, free education often disappeared, but no exhibitions were set up to replace it. The report did not seriously discuss how much its scheme would cost. It certainly recognized that in some cases endowment provision would have to be supplemented from the rates, but this seems to have been regarded only as a subsidiary resource. It is impossible to say how far the endowments and the fees paid by parents could have covered the necessary costs. Perhaps an awareness of this financial uncertainty was one reason for caution at a time in the late 1860s when it was clear that the state was likely to increase its financial commitment to the elementary schools. It was not a good time to take measures making possible claims on the public purse in the interests of people who, in theory at least, could pay for the education of their own children.

NOTES AND REFERENCES

1. Spencer H 1949 p 42
2. For Huxley's ideas, see his *Science and Education: essays* (1910). See also Bibby, Cyril (ed) 1971
3. Sidgwick, Henry The theory of classical education, in Farrar F W (ed) 1868 p 139
4. Argles M 1964 pp 26–7
5. *SIC* I, pp 22–7
6. Arnold wrote extensively on these themes; for a good example of his arguments see A French Eton or middle-class education and the state (1864), in Smith P, Summerfield G (eds) 1969 pp 76–156
7. *NC* I, p 491
8. *Ibid.* p 548
9. Richson C 1855–56: 1–20 and Appendix. For the quotation about endowments, see Appendix p iii. For Canon Richson, see Roach, John 1971 pp 59, 97–8
10. *SIC* VII, p 271
11. The three letters of 'Paterfamilias' are in *Cornhill Magazine* I (Jan–June 1860): 608–15; II (July–Dec 1860): 641–9; III (Jan–June 1861): 257–69. Coleridge, Sir John T 1860
12. Public School Education 1860: 418, 420–1
13. Eton College 1861 *ER* CXIII: 387–426. The quotation is on p 426
14. *PSC* I, p 5

15. *Ibid.* pp 52-6
16. Mack E C 1941 pp 42-9
17. *TSSA* 1863: 361
18. Hey (Canon) 1864: 360-6
19. Robinson (Canon) 1864: 367-79
20. Fitch J G 1864: 380-93
21. Davies, Emily 1864: 394-404
22. Summary of Proceedings: Middle-Class Education, *TSSA* 1864: 454-64. For George Griffith, see pp 95-8
23. *SIC* I, pp 109-10, 434
24. *Ibid.* p 434
25. *Ibid.* pp 127-32
26. *SIC* IX, p 109
27. *SIC* I, pp 309-17
28. *Ibid.* pp 340, 411. For the calculations about school places in particular areas, see ch III of the report (*SIC* I): on the revenues and local distribution of the endowments for secondary education
29. *SIC* I, pp 20-1, 78-83
30. *Ibid.* p 96
31. *SIC* VIII, pp 225-6, 229
32. *SIC* IX, pp 214-17
33. *Ibid.* pp 330-1
34. *Ibid.* pp 444, 460
35. *Ibid.* p 790
36. *SIC* I, p 77
37. *Ibid.* pp 107-8
38. *Ibid.* pp 469-70
39. *Ibid.* pp 466-9; Owen, David 1965 pp 207-8
40. See, for example, the evidence of James Hill, Charity Commissioner, *SIC* V, pp 363-79; Sir William Page Wood, Vice-Chancellor, pp 382-3; Thomas Hall, Inspector of Charities, pp 399-418
41. For example, Charity Commissioners for England and Wales *15th Report* 1867-68 pp 18-21
42. *SIC* VII, p 325
43. *SIC* V, pp 465-6: 13433
44. *Ibid.* p 371: 12701-2 (James Hill)
45. *Ibid.* pp 386-7: 12828 (Sir William Page Wood)
46. *Ibid.* pp 391-2: 12855
47. *Ibid.* p 404: 12932 (Thomas Hare)
48. *Ibid.* pp 897-923 (Sir James Kay-Shuttleworth). His proposals are summarized on pp 922-3: 17568. See also his article, 1866: 330-48
49. *SIC* V, p 547: 14137. Palmer as Lord Selborne was Lord Chancellor 1872-74, 1880-85
50. *SIC* VII, p 54
51. *SIC* IX, p 517
52. *SIC* V, pp 389-90: 12844
53. *SIC* VIII, p 170
54. *Ibid.* pp 109-10, 207-8, 232-3
55. *SIC* IX, p 479
56. *Ibid.* pp 146-7, 153-4

57. *SIC* V, pp 909–10: 17490–7; 913:17510; 915:17519
58. Griffith G 1860 and 1861
59. Griffith G 1870 vol II pp 638–9, 651–3, 668–79
60. See Griffith G 1864
61. Griffith G 1870 vol II p 682
62. *SIC* I, pp 148–9, 151–2, 158
63. For the recommendations, see *ibid.* ch VII
64. Roach, John 1971 pp 231–2

CHAPTER TWENTY
Reform and its limitations (ii)

Two other topics to which the commission devoted much attention were school examinations and the education of girls. The proposal in the general recommendations for a national Council of Examinations, although it came to nothing, represented an important strand in the social thinking of the time. Achievement in academic competition brought forward the meritorious, and ensured success to those who had both the intellectual and the moral qualities to deserve it. Such was the basic case for opening the Civil Service appointments to competition. This was achieved for the Indian service by the Act of 1853. For the home service limited competition was achieved in 1855 and a fully competitive entry in 1870. Arguments of the same kind were used in the case of the schools. However there was a major difference between the schools and the Civil Service. The latter was concerned solely to get the best candidates – however 'best' might be defined. It had no obligations to the unsuccessful. The schools also had a responsibility to bring forward talent; hence all the plans about exhibitions for promising boys and transfers to schools of a higher grade. Yet they had a second and equally important responsibility to secure that all their pupils – dullards as well as high-flyers – received a sound education. If examinations were to be used on a wide scale they would need to promote both objectives – and that was to prove very difficult to achieve.

The inspection and examination of schools was one of the subjects set out in the assistant commissioners' instructions. In the decade preceding their inquiry there had been major developments. The College of Preceptors had introduced a system of school examinations between 1850 and 1854. Much more important was the intervention of the universities. The Oxford Local Examinations had been established in 1857, and the Cambridge Locals followed in 1858. In 1862 Cambridge introduced a scheme for the examination of schools as a whole, and in 1865 the Cambridge Locals were opened to girls after a successful experimental examination in December 1863.

Neither the assistant commissioners nor the final report limited their comments to the Locals. The examinations of the College of Preceptors were thought to be well planned, but the college lacked the prestige to provide the basis for a general system.[1] A few able boys took the matriculation examination of the University of London as a final test of school work. It was considered suitable for this purpose, but it was not widely used. J G Fitch considered it to be rather more difficult than the Oxford and Cambridge senior examinations.[2] Most of the comments made related to the Locals, and the judgments of their success were mixed. It was generally agreed that they had provided a valuable stimulus to school work. On the other hand only a few candidates took them since pupils were entered as individuals and were examined at local centres. Consequently they did not benefit the work of schools as a whole. The minority who entered were often over-taught to achieve success and, since candidates had to pay an entrance fee and to be examined outside their own schools, they were expensive for parents.

Though there was a general consensus among the assistant commissioners in these judgments, there were variations. At Brighton there was a large and successful centre, but the statistics for the years 1858–61 showed that 'with one or two notable exceptions, the schools can only manage to send in from one or two qualified candidates apiece for each examination'.[3] In London no grammar school at the time of the inquiry had adopted the examinations at all.[4] At the other end of the country, in Northumberland, there was no centre and only one private school appeared ever to have sent in candidates. In Norfolk, Norwich Grammar School had refused to send in candidates in the first year and most of those who entered from the smaller grammar schools and private schools had failed. After that there had been a steady improvement, though not many distinguished candidates had come forward.[5]

In the great manufacturing centres T H Green reported on Warwickshire and Staffordshire, J G Fitch on the West Riding of Yorkshire and James Bryce on Lancashire. Green found that King Edward's, Birmingham, had held aloof. The school felt that it could supply competition enough within itself and it was unwilling to make its own course of instruction conform to that which the Oxford examination demanded. Other West Midland schools had, however, sent in candidates. The most successful of them was Brewood in Staffordshire which had sent up candidates for both senior and junior Cambridge examinations and which had also sent up several boys over the last few years to Cambridge who had done well there. Though Green's remarks about the Locals were somewhat patronizing, he claimed that their effect had been to extend the length of school education by at least a year.[6] In the West Riding the Locals had not been used very much. In 1864-65 sixty-four endowed schools produced only six successful candidates and only thirteen private schools had made use of them.[7] Bryce in Lancashire put forward the usual arguments for and against the system. He thought it might be made much more useful if the pass standard were lowered, if whole classes instead of selected individuals were sent in, and if more weight were laid on language and mathematics rather than on 'crammable subjects like history and geography'.[8] The final report summed up what the assistant commissioners had said[9]:

> On the whole it is clear, that the local examinations, as now used, fail to reach a large majority of the schools; fail to test the whole school work of all, except a very small number of the schools which they do reach; fail to distinguish with certainty between good schools and bad. Yet they have done much good; with some important modifications and with a power to examine, not scholars, but whole classes, they might supply what the schools appear to need.

One major initiative taken by the Schools Inquiry Commission had been to investigate the education of girls. By the time the commission was set up the women's movement had made considerable progress.[10] People like Madame Bodichon (Barbara Leigh Smith), Jessie Boucherett, Emily Davies, Frances Buss, Dorothea Beale and Elizabeth Garrett were already active in promoting better education and wider professional opportunities for women. When the commission was appointed, Emily Davies, the future foundress of Girton, and a number of her associates promoted a memorial urging that girls should be included in the inquiry. They were told that this would be done though with certain inevitable limitations, since neither domestic education nor private tuition were covered, and since few endowments were devoted to the education of girls. However the assistant commissioners were asked to report on girls' schools and the commission itself would be prepared to hear witnesses.[11] The promise was fully kept, and the commission's papers give a very valuable account of the position of girls' education at that time.

The fact that the commissioners agreed to investigate at all perhaps recognized the fact that much had been achieved to improve girls' education in the preceding two decades and that pressure was building up for further change through bodies like the Social Science Association in which women had from the first played an active role. The movement for change began in the 1840s. The distress and poverty suffered by many governesses led to the foundation of the Governesses' Benevolent Institution, of which in 1843 David Laing, vicar of Holy Trinity, Kentish Town, became honorary secretary. It soon became clear that one reason for the poverty of many governesses was their ignorance and incapacity to teach. Consequently Laing and Miss Murray, maid of honour to the Queen, decided to establish a college and called on the aid of some of the professors of King's College, the most prominent among them being F D Maurice. As a result of these efforts Queen's College in Harley Street opened in the spring of 1848.[12] Queen's was Anglican and 'Establishment' in general tone. A year later another college opened in Bedford Square with a very different background. Bedford College (to give it its later name) was founded by a Unitarian, Mrs Reid, and among its supporters were other Unitarians and men of unorthodox views like F W Newman, younger brother of the future cardinal. It was closely linked with the unorthodox University College, and in the early days the taint of heresy caused some trouble; for example the principal of King's College refused to allow two members of his staff to teach there.[13]

Both institutions aspired to be colleges rather more than mere schools. Bedford, in its first prospectus, announced that ladies over 12 years of age would be admitted, and that instruction would be given in biblical teaching, English grammar and literature, moral philosophy, ancient and modern history, mathematics, natural science, astronomy and scientific geography, Latin, German, French and Italian, elocution, vocal music, harmony and drawing, all of them to be taught by men professors.[14] The original Queen's curriculum was similar, though it offered less in mathematics and science and included principles and method of teaching.[15] There must, of course, have been many discrepancies between what was offered and what could actually be taught because of the very poor initial education of the girls. Both colleges set up schools for younger pupils, but the difficulties about preliminary training took a long time to overcome.

Despite these general similarities there was one major difference between the two institutions. Queen's was governed by men and the only administrative function of women was to act as lady visitors or chaperones. At Bedford women formed part of the body of management from the first. Indeed Mrs Reid, who lived until 1866, seems to have distrusted the men professors who, she thought, favoured the interests of the school as against those of the college. When in 1860 she set up the Reid Trust to help finance the higher education of women, she gave the control over it to women trustees. In the late 1860s the women on the college council were anxious to ensure that Bedford concentrated on the higher education of women and they excluded the men teachers from any real control of its affairs.[16]

The foundation of Queen's and of Bedford opened a new and wider opportunity, though the scale was small at first. Among the early Queen's students were people of the first importance in the history of the women's movement like the two headmistresses, Frances Buss and Dorothea Beale, and the pioneer physician, Sophia Jex-Blake, foundress of the London Medical School for Women, who, after unhappy experiences in other schools, found Queen's 'an elysium on earth'.[17]

Dorothea Beale, daughter of a physician, was a day student who for several years acted as a tutor. In 1857 she became for a short and unhappy period headteacher at the Clergy Daughters' School at Casterton in Westmorland, and in 1858 was appointed principal of the Ladies' College at Cheltenham, a proprietary school for girls which had been established in 1853.[18] Though public memory has always linked Miss Buss and Miss Beale together, their backgrounds were very different. Dorothea Beale came from a family in comfortable circumstances. Frances Buss was the daughter of an artist and drawing master, who began to teach in her mother's private school when she was 14. She was greatly influenced by David Laing, and through that connection she became one of the first pupils at Queen's, though she was only able to attend the evening classes after she had done a day's teaching. The college, she said, 'opened new life to me', though she was not a student for very long. In 1850, at the age of 23, she became headmistress of the reconstituted family school, christened the North London Collegiate School for Ladies.[19] In the early years the school was very much a Buss family affair.

During the 1850s, while Miss Buss and Miss Beale were learning their professional skills, the women's movement was broadening out. Here the crucial figure, because she had links with so many activities, was Madame Bodichon, born Barbara Leigh Smith, and like Mrs Reid the product of a Unitarian family. She organized a petition to Parliament against the laws which put the property of married women entirely into the possession of their husbands. She helped for some years to finance the Portman Hall School, off the Edgware Road, which was taught by her friend Elizabeth Whitehead and which was both mixed and undenominational. She was one of the founders of the *Englishwoman's Journal*, established in 1858.[20] This brought into her circle Jessie Boucherett, who in 1859 started the Society for Promoting the Employment of Women, the first women's employment agency. The problem of employment was one of particular difficulty since there were so few careers open to women. And it was particularly serious because the 1851 census had shown that there were 870,000 more women than men, so marriage was not an option available to all.[21] Mme Bodichon and Miss Boucherett explained their ideas about the education of middle-class girls to the Social Science Association in 1860. There was a need for an investigation of the existing position. Schools at fees of 6d. or 1s. per week should be set up, though these would need charitable support; schools at fees of 15s. or £1 a quarter might make a profit. Schools should be open to inspection and should be in correspondence with 'the Queen's College, and similar London Societies'. Finally endowments should be used to support girls' schools.[22]

By that time a circle of like-minded women was gathering in London, particularly linked to the *Englishwoman's Journal* and the Employment Society. Emily Davies, daughter of a Co. Durham clergyman and sister of one of F D Maurice's friends, got in touch with the group in 1859–60, and in 1862 she and her mother came to live in London after her father's death.[23] She was a friend and supporter of Miss Garrett in her attempts to obtain a medical qualification. She was the prime mover in the successful attempt in 1862–63 to open the Cambridge Local examinations to girls.[24] By the middle of the decade she had concentrated on the higher education of women after school,[25] an interest which led her to found Girton and which provided the major purpose of her later life. Another pioneer of higher education who came to London at much the same time was Miss A J Clough. Born in Liverpool, she had started a school at Ambleside in the 1850s. After the death of her brother Arthur in 1861 she came to live partly near Kingston upon Thames and partly in London, getting to know Mme Bodichon, Miss Davies, Miss Buss and Miss Bostock, who was a close associate of Mrs Reid's and one of her trustees. At the end of the decade she returned to work in Liverpool and became a leading member of the North of England Council for the Higher Education of Women. The council did not last for very many years, but out of her involvement with it grew Miss Clough's life-work at Newnham College, Cambridge.[26]

The exploration of these connections has taken us somewhat outside the limits of secondary education, but it has established the point that, by the time the Taunton Commission decided to consider girls' education, there was in existence a group of like-minded women who had seriously considered the problems and done something practical about solving them. There is a broad distinction in tone between the evidence given to the commission in London and the reports of the assistant commissioners. The witnesses were, on the whole, the leaders of innovation. The assistant commissioners reported on the ordinary girls' private schools which had been much less touched by pressures for change. The evidence sheds light on a number of topics, many of them re-echoed in papers given to the Social Science Association in 1864 and 1865. There was a desire to make endowments available for girls' education, particularly for scholarships and exhibitions, though Miss Wolstenholme, head of a private school at Manchester, did not want them used to pay stipends.[27] Comment was also made about the provision of schools. Miss E E Smith, a member of the Bedford College Council, wanted to see 'in every large town in England a thoroughly good day school giving instruction to pupils from ten years of age and upwards'. These schools, she thought, would also raise the standards of teaching in private schools.[28] Miss Davies thought that in large towns it would be best to have day schools with boarding houses attached to them. There were great advantages in large schools; 'a clever girl is not likely to be made much of among a larger number as when she is the only one of 10 or 12'.[29]

There was general agreement, both that teachers needed to be trained and that pupils came to school very badly prepared. Both Miss Buss and Miss Beale, whose schools had been very successful, emphasized the second point. Miss Buss had begun in 1850 with 35 pupils.[30] She told the commission that there were 201 day scholars and the highest number of boarders had been 18.[31] Miss Beale had begun with many difficulties, not least over what subjects might be taught. She had not dared to teach Euclid, but she had managed to teach some science camouflaged as physical geography. However after 1860 the tide had turned, and by 1864 there were 130 girls.[32] Yet entry standards were poor. Miss Beale, for example, gave the commission a long list of errors in simple arithmetic, French and spelling, made by girls who had entered the school over 15 years of age.[33] The position in the case of many older women was no better; Miss King, secretary to the Society for the Employment of Women, said a good deal in her evidence about the poor education of the women who came to the office to seek employment.[34] Miss Buss complained of the difficulty of getting good teachers and urged that all of them should possess certificates of attainment and go through a course of training.[35] Miss Beale, on the other hand, had not experienced such problems since she had been able to appoint her own pupils, though she argued in favour of a national board to examine both teachers and schools.[36]

Since the opening of the Cambridge Local examinations to girls was a major issue of the time, these examinations were much discussed. Miss Buss had sent up candidates for the trial examination of 1863, and she supported the development.[37] Miss Wolstenholme thought that the Locals had had a good effect in Manchester and that they had helped teachers by bringing defects to light.[38] Opinion was not unanimously favourable. Miss Martin, head of the Bedford College school, thought that the Locals system was likely to foster vanity and that independent examinations were unnecessary in a well-conducted school.[39] Miss Beale, though she was not hostile to examinations as such, had doubts about the Locals on two grounds. Firstly, she thought the subjects in some respects unsuited for girls and the system likely to stimulate undesirable rivalries between them.[40] Secondly, for her school there was a social problem[41]:

> The brothers of our pupils go to the universities. Now, generally speaking, those who go in for the local examinations occupy a much lower position in the social scale, and our pupils would not like to be classed with them, but regarded as equal in rank to those who pass at the university. These feelings are stronger in a small place.

The Locals raised the familiar issue of class – that bugbear so ready to present itself in Victorian discussions about education. Miss Beale explained the entrance policies of her school, which were the same as those of nearby Cheltenham College (see p. 160). 'None are admitted', she explained, 'but the daughters of independent gentlemen or professional men', and she answered 'yes' to a question whether 'the object of the whole institution is that girls only of a certain class of life should be admissible to the school'.[42] Miss Buss's policy was much more open; her pupils were admitted on a footing of equality whatever their fathers did. A list of parents' occupations made about 10 years after her school opened included, alongside gentlemen and professional men, 'a zinc worker, a fish salesman, a cricket warehouseman, a licensed victualler, a linen draper, a cheese factor, a horse dealer, a pianoforte tuner and a Berlin wool worker'.[43]

Behind all the questions lay the fundamental issue: did girls possess the same abilities as boys and should they follow the same course of study? Miss Buss was explicit. When she was asked whether there was any distinction between the mental powers of boys and girls, she replied: 'I am sure that the girls can learn anything they are taught in an interesting manner, and for which they have some motive to work.'[44] The introduction of public examinations raised the issue in a very direct form. Miss Eleanor Smith did not wish to see 'a special standard created for women'.[45] The basis of every test, said Miss Wolstenholme, 'should be the admission of the principle of a common education for men and women. Anything short of that I should regard as but a partial good.'[46] Miss Beale was rather less definite. She argued that the male and female minds are similar but not necessarily that they should move in the same channel.[47]

The most outspoken advocate of an education of a common type and standard for both boys and girls was Emily Davies. In her writings during the 1860s she returned to the same points over and over again. A better education for women would bring men and women together and enlarge their community of interest. For a woman to be told that she belonged to an inferior class for whom sustained intellectual effort was impossible was infinitely depressing and frustrating. Whatever a girl's abilities might be, let her succeed or fail as an individual, according to standards applied to other individuals, regardless of sex[48]:

> To make the discovery of individual incompetence may be
> wholesomely humbling or stimulating as the case may be, but no one
> is the better for being told, on mere arbitrary authority, that he
> belongs to a weak and incapable class and this, whatever may be the
> intention, is said in effect by the offer of any test of an exclusively
> female character.

Miss Davies, after she had been examined, wrote to Mme Bodichon, that she had found the commissioners well disposed. 'The Assistant Commissioners, with scarcely an exception go in for the girls, and it is most useful to have them going about stirring up and encouraging the school-mistresses.'[49] In a few, though not in all cases, there was opposition to the inquiry on the ground that it was an interference with the rights of parents and an intrusion into the mistresses' privacy.[50] The district reports exposed the deficiencies which have already been described (see pp. 151-2), and the remedies which they suggested were very similar to those suggested by the woman witnesses. As in the case of boys' schools, the schools of the third grade were particularly bad. In Lancashire, according to James Bryce, the girls who were sent to cheap day or boarding schools 'learn to read, to write badly, to execute elaborate uglinesses in thread or Berlin wool.

That is all that school teaches them, and except for the sake of getting that, they might as well stay at home and mind the baby.'[51]

The assistant commissioners expressed general support for reorganizing endowments so as to give girls a share in them. In the West Riding, according to J G Fitch, there was only one endowed school – at Rishworth near Huddersfield – which gave girls any instruction above the elementary, but even there, both in numbers and in terms of the course of study available, the balance had been tilted far too much towards the boys.[52] D R Fearon reported that opinion in London favoured an educational board to reform endowments and to set up schools for different age groups.[53] London opinion may have been influenced by Miss Davies and her friends, who were likely to be in advance of general thinking. However both Green in the West Midlands and Bryce in Lancashire mentioned the desirability of setting up public high schools for girls in each considerable town. The fees should be kept as low as possible and Green argued that, to complete the scheme, a certain number of free places should be offered.[54]

The final report of the Taunton Commission found for the critics and the innovators. The defects in the curriculum of girls' schools were once again emphasized; too much time was often given to instrumental music and too little to any form of exercise. The schools were not solely to blame, for one major obstacle to improvement was the apathy of parents and their unwillingness to pay for sound teaching. So far as natural ability was concerned, American experience had shown that girls had similar capacity for intellectual attainment to boys, though a complete assimilation should not be attempted. The extension of the Cambridge Locals to girls had been a success, and it was not true that women were likely to suffer in health from greater intellectual effort. The question of the mixing of classes had caused more trouble in girls' schools than in boys'. Many who favoured such admixture in boys' schools were very against it in girls' schools. An especially important issue was that of improving the standards of teaching. There was a need for efficient systems of school examination and inspection and for further education for women, both for those who wished to teach and for those who did not. Better education for women in general was more likely to improve the standard of teachers in girls' schools than the creation of special training institutions for them. The same certification arrangements should be created for women teachers as those suggested for men. The almost total exclusion of girls from educational endowments was unjust and inexpedient and should be changed, though girls were not likely to get the same share in them as boys. The report was strongly in favour of a higher college or colleges for women, though it was difficult to see how much demand there would be for education at that level.[55]

Such higher institutions for women were soon to emerge. Emily Davies's college at Hitchin, which was to move to Cambridge 3 years later, was opened only 1 year after the publication of the report. The support given by the Taunton Commission to the cause of better education for women was very important. It was attuned to a major need of the time, and many of the objectives of the women's campaign had been realized by the end of the century.[56] The commissioners' main recommendation – their plan for a complete structure of secondary school administration – was never achieved. Much useful work was done after 1869 to reform endowments, but it was done in a piecemeal fashion. The country had to wait until the twentieth century for an overall design. The passing of the Public Schools Act of 1868 and of the Endowed Schools Act of 1869 marks an important stage in the story of nineteenth-century secondary education, and an appropriate place to bring this part of the story to a conclusion, though other important developments were going on independently of this legislation.

While the royal commissions had been hard at work, the foundation of new schools on the public school model had continued. Wellington, founded in 1859, had been planned primarily to educate the sons of deceased officers. Under E W Benson, who had been a Rugby master, it developed into a successful public school, giving considerable attention to modern studies.[57] Among major foundations of the 1860s were Haileybury and Clifton, both opened in 1862, and Malvern (1865). The Taunton Report commented that parents who sent their sons to first-grade schools appeared on the whole to prefer boarding schools. 'This is proved by the fact that all the great schools are now full, and that within the last twelve years several others have been established and all readily filled.'[58] By the time the report was published the foundation of new schools had come to an end. In the 1870s the public schools were consolidating as a group, two major landmarks being the foundation of the Headmasters' Conference and of the Oxford and Cambridge Schools Examination Board.

The second development, at the other end of the educational spectrum, was the Forster Act of 1870, which set up the School Boards to fill the gaps in provision left by the existing voluntary schools.

This expansion of elementary schooling had two major effects on secondary education. First of all, the growth of the elementary schools in numbers and the rising standard of their work made it much easier to argue for the reorganization of the endowed schools on lines which largely confined them to members of the middle class. After 1870 the claim could more cogently be made that the needs of the poor were being met in institutions specially designed to cater for them and which were being paid for by the taxpayer at considerable expense. Secondly, by 1880 some of the large urban boards were opening higher-grade schools which were very similar to the third-grade schools suggested by the Taunton Commissioners. These higher-grade schools became important providers of lower secondary education in industrial towns like Bradford and Sheffield. They also exposed the old grammar schools to new competition. The School Boards represented public educational provision at local level. At national level such provision was represented by the Science and Art Department set up in 1853 to encourage the teaching of the applied sciences. The department paid grants to schools and to other bodies on the basis of annual examinations. By 1873 it was responsible for 1,182 classes and 24,674 candidates, and its work was steadily expanding.[59]

It has already been argued that the secondary schools responded rather slowly to pressures for change. There was a demand for more science and technology, but this had less effect than might have been expected. There was a more ready reaction to other demands of the society around them. The schools were strongly influenced by the stress on emulation and competition which was so powerful in the mid-Victorian world. One example of this was the growth of public examinations. However, competition hardly led on to meritocracy in the full sense because society did not for a generation create a way of advancement for poor but able boys, the need for which had been so strongly emphasized by Kay-Shuttleworth in his Taunton Commission evidence (see p. 288). Competition was to operate within the ranks of those who could pay for education of a certain kind. Another way of making the point is to say that Victorian society was strongly influenced by concepts of class, which made it more difficult than had been the case in earlier periods for people of different social groups to be educated together. The concentration of so many boys of ability and of good family into a small number of public schools must have accentuated this social differentiation. The schools had also to respond to business and professional demands. Here they were probably more successful in training for the service of Empire and for certain of the older professions than for business and industry, and this deficiency was linked with the limited penetration of the system by science and technology. The influence of the ideal of Empire on English secondary education between 1870 and 1914 would be a major research topic in itself.

The Clarendon and Taunton Commissions were the most extensive exercise in state intervention in secondary education since the days of the Tudors and Stuarts. Before 1860 each school had wrestled with its problems as best it could. The masters and trustees of the endowed schools struggled to manage their properties, to maintain their numbers of pupils, to enlarge their curricula. The private-school masters and mistresses set out to provide what middle-class parents wanted, some selling shoddy merchandise, some doing an honest but unimaginative job, some introducing new ideas. The private foundation schools of various types met the needs of religious groups or offered high-grade teaching when it could not be obtained anywhere else in the area. The public schools had begun the century badly. Their prestige and authority had steadily grown, though these depended more on moral and emotional values than on educational efficiency.

After 1870 state authority loomed larger, because only the state had been able to break the dead hand of custom and tradition which lay so heavily on the schools. Much less had been done, however, than the reformers of the 1860s had planned because so many influential groups had a deep-rooted fear and suspicion of state power and of what was seen as outside interference with educational work (see p. 110). Over the next generation the balance between the schools of various types changed considerably. The public schools were in the lead and the more successful of the private foundation schools were assimilated to them. The grammar schools followed a similar path with more or less success. The private schools, though they retained some importance, especially for the education of girls, fell behind. Society now expected to educate its young people in corporate institutions which had built up a reputation over a long period of time. More ephemeral institutions dependent on private individuals could not compete. On the whole these changes were probably an advantage. Yet the decline of the private schools represented loss as well as gain, for it had been through them that many innovations had been introduced. Something of the innovatory tradition of the private schools was perpetuated in new foundations like Abbotsholme and Bedales at the end of the century, but there were not very many of them in comparison with the many private schools of an earlier period. It was probably inevitable that later Victorian secondary schools should become larger, more public, more formalized, but the change brought with it its own rigidities and made adaptation to change more difficult. The private schools had many faults, but they made a contribution to secondary education in the first half of the nineteenth century which has never been fully recognized.

NOTES AND REFERENCES

1. *SIC* I (Report), pp 329-30; *SIC* VII, p 379 (D R Fearon)
2. *SIC* I, pp 327-8; *SIC* IX, p 311 (J G Fitch). See also Fitch J G 1864: 392
3. *SIC* VII, p 168 (H A Giffard)
4. *Ibid.* pp 316-19 (D R Fearon)
5. *SIC* VIII, pp 267, 342-3 (J L Hammond)
6. *Ibid.* pp 144, 175-80. For Brewood School, see pp 21-3
7. *SIC* IX, pp 210, 307 (J G Fitch)
8. *Ibid.* p 776
9. *SIC* I, p 336
10. There is a very large literature on the women's movement. See Strachey, Ray 1928; Rowbotham, Sheila 1973; Delamont, Sara, Duffin, Lorna (eds) 1978; Vicinus, Martha (ed) 1972 and 1977. On education, Kamm, Josephine 1965; Burstyn, Joan N 1980
11. Stephen, Barbara 1927 pp 131-2
12. See Grylls, Rosalie Glynn 1948
13. Tuke, Margaret J 1937 pp 24-5, 64-5
14. *Ibid.* Appendix II
15. Grylls, Rosalie Glynn 1948 Appendix I
16. Tuke, Margaret J 1937 pp 99, 115
17. Grylls, Rosalie Glynn 1948 p 35
18. Most of the material on Miss Beale is taken from Raikes, Elizabeth 1908. Casterton School was the descendant of the clergy daughters' school at Cowan Bridge, Charlotte Brontë's 'Lowood'
19. Most of the material on Miss Buss comes from Ridley, Annie E 1895; Burstall, Sara A 1938. The quotation comes from *ibid.* p 25
20. See Burton, Hester 1949
21. Delamont, Sara, Duffin, Lorna (eds) 1978 p 139
22. *TSSA* 1860: 432-3
23. Stephen, Barbara 1927 pp 52, 67-8
24. Roach, John 1971 pp 108-12
25. Davies, Emily 1866
26. See Clough B A 1903 esp. pp 107-8
27. *SIC* V, pp 235:11236 (Miss Davies); 255:11490 (Miss Buss); 744:16228 (Miss Wolstenholme)
28. *Ibid.* p 701:15773
29. *Ibid.* p 245:11356
30. Kamm, Josephine 1958 p 41

31. *SIC* V, p 252:11442-3
32. Raikes, Elizabeth 1908 pp 113-14, 121
33. *SIC* V, p 724:16082. See also Beale D 1865: 275. Miss Buss's comments about entry standards were similar (*SIC* V, p 257:11522)
34. *SIC* V, pp 718-22 (Miss Gertrude King)
35. *Ibid.* pp 255:11484; 259:11549
36. *Ibid.* pp 729-30:16126-8
37. *Ibid.* pp 253-4:11467-8; 258-9:11543; 262-3:11597-9
38. *Ibid.* pp 741:16192-9; 745:16234
39. *Ibid.* pp 683:15493-5; 685:15553
40. *TSSA* 1865: 285-6
41. *SIC* V, p 730:16129
42. *Ibid.* p 722:16073-6
43. Kamm, Josephine 1958 p 47
44. *SIC* V, p 254:11471
45. *Ibid.* p 705:15821
46. *Ibid.* p 747:16264
47. *Ibid.* p 734:16164-5
48. Davies, Emily 1910 Special systems of education for women (1868) p 132. See also Davies, Emily 1864: 394-404, and 1866 pp 122-8
49. Stephen, Barbara 1927 p 138
50. *SIC* VII, pp 68-9 (C H Stanton, referring to Clifton and Bath); *SIC* VIII, p 485 (J L Hammond on Norfolk)
51. *SIC* IX, p 834
52. *Ibid.* p 197
53. *SIC* VII, pp 412-13
54. *SIC* VIII, p 242 (T H Green); *SIC* IX, pp 836-7 (James Bryce)
55. *SIC* I, pp 546-70 ('Girls Schools')
56. On endowments, see Fletcher, Sheila 1980; on the general background Dyhouse, Carol 1981
57. Staunton H 1869 p 405
58. *SIC* I, p 47
59. Argles M 1964 p 21

Bibliography

(All books are published in London, unless another place of publication is cited.)

1. Manuscript sources in Record Offices and Libraries

Record Offices are generally designated only by the name of the county or town. Libraries are cited separately. Some printed sources are included where they are contained in special collections. All this material has been used by kind permission of the principal archivists and librarians concerned. Special acknowledgements are included where necessary. Reference numbers are generally given for documents cited.

Buckinghamshire RO

Accounts of insolvent debtors 1807–46. Accounts of Joseph Randell (Q/DA/31 1 & 3)
High Wycombe, Royal Grammar School:
  Minute book of the trustees of the Wycombe charities 1838–65 (CH1 AM1)
  Miscellaneous papers relating to the school (CH1 AP14/1–22; CH1 AP 13/15; CH1 AP14/96; AP10/36)
Letter from James Griffin, Chiltern House Academy, Wendover, 3 Dec 1841 (136/48 Arch. Soc.)
Uthwatt MSS, Papers relating to the education of G B Mansell, son of M D Mansell, at Chiswick and Westminster Schools 1815–20 (D/U/9/ 1 & 2)

Cambridge University Library

Diary of Joseph Romilly 1843 (Add MSS 6822)
Richard Williamson, headmaster of Westminster School, Classical
notebook *c.* 1840 (Add MSS 5979)

Chester, City RO

Chester Training College:
  Minute book 1854-67 (CR 86/1/1)
  Letters and papers relating to the Rev Arthur Rigg, principal of the
  college 1839-69 (CR 86/13/4)

Chester, King's School (by permission of the headmaster)

Hughes Thomas, List and index of King's School scholars, revised
  by G D Squibb
Letters and papers found in the register of foundation scholars,
  c. 1812-1969

Cheshire RO

Finney, Peter Davenport III (1824-40), Papers relating to the
  education of, (DFF/54/1-42)
Latham family of Sandbach, Letters from and to John Henry
  Latham at Rugby School 1835-39 (DDX 232/1-9)
Macclesfield, King's School, Minute books 1773-1859, 1860-88
  (SP/3/1/2 & 3)
Warrington, Grammar School:
  Trustees' minute books 1820-40, 1840-89 (SL 382/1/1 & 2)
  List of scholars presented or admitted ... commencing 21 Jan 1822
  (SL 382/4)
Witton (Northwich), Sir John Deane's Grammar School, Subject file:
Witton. Legal papers (*Report of the Master in Chancery* 1851; *Order
  of Vice-Chancellor Stuart* 1855)

Cumbria RO (Carlisle)

Bootle, Hycemoor Grammar School, Vestry minutes 1807-1931 and
  minutes of meetings of ratepayers and trustees of Bootle School
  1811-1910 (SPC/27/2)

Brampton, Croft House Academy:
  School magazines 1843, 1859 (DX/610/1; DX/182/4)
  Examination list June 1859 (DX/182/4)
Penrith:
  Register book of the free school of Penrith (from 1699) (DEC 2/2)
  Commonplace book, kept by James Gordon, headmaster (from 1865) (DEC 2/3)
Silloth, Green Row Academy:
  Books of mathematical problems, including a series of five books written by Daniel Jennings 1835–38 (DX/300)
  Letters from Joseph Harris to his brother 1825–26 (D/WM/7/26)
  Miscellaneous papers including list of pupils June 1841 (PR/122/98)
Uldale, Trustees' minute book 1726–1886 (DS/15/1)
Wigton Friends' School, File of papers about Quaker education, including some material about Ackworth School (FCF/2/75)

Co. Durham RO

Hanby Holmes (Solicitors) Papers, Agreement between George Clarkson and William Shaw relating to Bowes Hall Academy Jan 1810 (D/HH/3/8/3/2)
Headlam A W, Letters about the unpaid fees of a private tutor 1861–62 (D/HH/2/11/62/1-17)
Hodgkin Papers, 'Society of Friends Schools and Education' (papers about Quaker schools 1819–56) (D/10/X7)
Houghton-le-Spring parish records, Papers relating to the Kepier Grammar School, especially for the period 1845–60 (EP/HO 274-9)

Essex RO

Brentwood School:
  List of former pupils 1819–23 (microfilm) and other papers (TB 223/ 3,5,6).
  Newspaper cuttings about the proper use of the endowment 1828– (TB 223/4)
Colchester Free Grammar School:
  Register of scholars 1637–1892 (microfilm) (TB 217)
  Correspondence of Charles Gray Round as trustee of the school about its rebuilding 1851–52 (D/DR 018)
Dedham, Free Grammar School, Record of the boys at the school 1767–1820 (transcript of original)

Round (Birch Hall) Papers, Felsted School, Papers relating to the reorganization of, 1851-55 (D/D Rb 07,08,09)

Sperling family of Great Maplestead, Correspondence about the education of C R, F V H, Rochfort, Rowland and Rosalie Sperling *c*. 1840-55 (D/D Se 29; D/D Se 33)

Gloucestershire RO

Blathwayt of Dyrham, Letters about the sons of Col G W Blathwayt *c*. 1840 (D 1799/ C 27)

Dursley, Records of the Dursley Agricultural and Commercial School (Dursley Middle School):

Committee minutes 1840-52 (D 981/1)

Board book 1846-49 (D 981/10)

Foundation register 1844-84 (D 981/11)

Marling family of Stroud, Letters from W H Marling to his parents from Dr Heldenmaier's school, Worksop, 1847-49 (D 873/ C 17)

Tetbury Grammar School, Correspondence about refoundation as a National School 1828-29 (D 566 R 5/1)

Wotton-under-Edge Grammar School:

Minutes of meetings of the trustees 1726-1858 (D 733/5/1)

Admission register of foundation scholars (at the other end of the same volume)

Hampshire RO

Alton, Eggar's Free Grammar School, Minute book vol II 1806-79 (39M 67/2)

Atkinson Collection (9M 49):

Papers relating to St Paul's School, Southsea *c*. 1840

Laws and Regulations of St Paul's School at Southsea, near Portsmouth, established 1825 (W Woodward Portsea 1831)

Atkinson G B, Letter on his resignation from the headship of the Collegiate School, Sheffield 3 Oct 1871

Basingstoke:

Holy Ghost Grammar School, Papers in Chancery proceedings 1850-53 (H 12 M 49/15)

Queen's Free School, Minutes of trustees (from 1854) (H 28 M 68)

Odiham Grammar School, Trustees' minute books and accounts 1789-1874 (21 M 51/19)

Queenwood College Stockbridge, Collection of papers about the school under George Edmondson (1798-1863) (47 M 72)

A History of Secondary Education, 1800-1870

Lancashire RO

Bispham Grammar School, Trustees' minute and account book
1830-78 (DDX/285/2)

Blackburn Grammar School:
Governors' minutes and accounts 1808-67 (DD Bk/2/3)
Volume of registration slips relating to scholars 1820-42
(DD Bk/3/15)

Bury Grammar School:
Trustees' minutes and accounts 1840-67 (DD By/2/1)
Examination questions (2 books)

Cartmel Grammar School, File of miscellaneous letters about school
property and schoolmasters 1844-82 (PR 2703)

Rivington Grammar School, Correspondence with the Charity
Commissioners 1858-61 (DDX 94/89)

Lincolnshire RO

Lincolnshire committee of the Diocesan Board of Education,
Minutes 1838-66 (DBE/1/1)

*Reports of the Diocesan Board of Education on the principles of the
Established Church for the County of Lincoln* 1840-55 (DBE
7/1/1-16)

Liverpool City Libraries

Liverpool Mechanics' Institution (Liverpool Institute) *Reports* vols I
(1825-38); II (1839); III (1840-54, 1856-58); IV (1859-79) (373 INS)

Manchester

Central Library Archives Dept (by permission of the City of
Manchester Leisure Services Committee)

Journal of Alice Southern at a boarding school at Lymm 1842
(M367/6/4/1)

John Rylands University Library (by permission of the Earl of
Crawford and Balcarres)

Crawford Papers (24th Earl of Crawford and Balcarres), Letters about
Lancashire schools, including early *Reports of the Northern
Church of England School, Rossall*). These are taken from 'Wigan
and District Affairs Correspondence' 25/13/1-217; 'Lancashire
and Cheshire Affairs Correspondence' 25/14/1-90

312

Norfolk RO

East Dereham, William Buck's private school, Ledgers 1799–1829 (MC 25)
Great Yarmouth, Proprietary Grammar School, Minute Book 1833–35 (Y/L16/24)
North Walsham, Paston Grammar School:
  Governors' order book 1769–1839, 1840–73 (MC 20/ 1 & 3)
  Correspondence from and about the Rev W T Spurdens 1817–25 (MC 20/17)
  Charity Commission papers 1853–1901 (WD 34 384 X 7)

Nottinghamshire RO

Starkey of Norwood Papers, Huddersfield College (DDSN IX/3):
  Rules and Regulations of the Huddersfield College, established 1838, incorporated with London University, 1844 (Waters Hardy, Huddersfield 1850)
  Papers about launching a new College Company 1859–60

Sheffield Local Studies Library

Correspondence between Rev Francis Hall and his son, John Hall 1838–43 (MD 2694/67–102)
Norton School:
  Register book of scholars at the school under the various charities ... 1759–64 (Sheffield OD 1554)
  Accounts 1822–47 (OD 1558)
Sheffield Collegiate School 1836–85, A biographical register compiled by P J Wallis (typescript) (by permission of Dr Wallis)

Staffordshire RO

Brewood Grammar School, Minute book 1801–77 (CEG 2)
Kinver Grammar School:
  Papers relating to additions to the school building 1845–47 and other correspondence (D 1197/7/1/3)
  Statutes and Orders to be observed by the Master and Scholars ... Dec 1848 (D 1197/7/1/4)

Suffolk RO (Bury St Edmunds)

Bury St Edmunds Grammar School, Governors' minutes 1776–1830, 1831–58, 1858–91 (E 5/9 202.2; 939/1; 939/2)

Wigan RO

Grammar School, Papers relating to the headmasters, in particular to Samuel Doria 1852-55 (RM 1634/A2 1-9)

Wiltshire RO

Ramsbury, Accounts of C E Meyrick's private school 1802-41 (31/1, 31/2)

Yorkshire, West RO (Leeds)

Leeds Mechanics' Institution and Literary Society, *Annual Reports* 1842-51, 1851-61, 1862-75

2. Official publications (arranged chronologically)

Abstract of the Returns of Charitable Donations for the Benefit of Poor Persons ... 1786-88, 2 parts 1816

Report from Select Committee of the House of Commons appointed to inquire into the education of the lower orders in the metropolis, 1816

Third Report of the Select Committee on the education of the lower orders, 1818

Reports of Commissioners to inquire concerning Charities. 1st, 1819; 2nd, 1819; 3rd, 1820; 4th, 1820; 5th, 1821; 6th, 1822; 7th, 1822; 8th, 1823; 9th, 1823; 10th, 1824; 11th, 1824; 12th, 1825; 13th, 1826; 14th, 1826; 15th, 1826; 16th, 1826-27; 17th, 1826-27; 18th, 1828; 19th, 1828; 20th, 1829; 21st, 1829; 22nd, 1830; 23rd, 1830; 24th, 1831; 25th, 1833; 26th, 1833; 27th, 1834; 28th, 1834; 29th, 1835; 30th, 1837; 31st, 1837-38; 32nd: Pt I, 1837-38; Pt II, 1837-38; Pt III, 1837-38; Pt IV, 1839; Pt V, 1839; Pt VI, 1840

Public Charities II *Digest of Schools and Charities for Education* as reported on by the Commissioners of Inquiry into Charities. Grammar Schools, 1842

Census of Great Britain 1851, Education, England and Wales *Report and Tables*, 1854

Report of Her Majesty's Commissioners appointed to inquire into the state and condition of the Cathedral and Collegiate Churches in England and Wales, 3 vols 1854-55

Annual Reports (nos 1-16) of the Charity Commissioners for England and Wales, 1854/1868-69

Report of the Commissioners appointed to inquire into the state of popular education in England ... (Newcastle Commission), 6 vols 1861

Report of Her Majesty's Commissioners appointed to inquire into the revenues and management of certain colleges and schools ... (Clarendon Commission), 4 vols 1864

Report from the Select Committee of the House of Lords on the Public Schools Bill, 1865

Report of the Commissioners appointed by Her Majesty to inquire into the education given in schools in England, not comprised within Her Majesty's two recent commissions on popular education and on public schools (Taunton Commission), 21 vols 1867-68

3. Theses

Benson Edwin 1932 A history of education in York 1780-1902, PhD London

Bishop T J H 1962 Origins and achievements of Winchester College pupils 1836 to 1934, PhD London

Board M J 1959 A history of the private adventure schools in Sheffield MA Sheffield

Greenberg E L 1953 The contribution made by private academies in the first half of the nineteenth century to modern curriculum and methods, MA London

Hey Colin G 1954 The history of Hazelwood School, Birmingham, and its influence on educational developments in the nineteenth century, MA Wales

Leinster-Mackay D P 1972 The English private school 1830-1914, with special reference to the private preparatory school, PhD Durham

Musgrove Frank 1958 The family as an educational institution, PhD Nottingham

Rigby Cormac 1968 The life and influence of Edward Thring, DPhil Oxford

Wilson G E 1952 A history of the Macclesfield Grammar School ... from 1503-*c*. 1890, MEd Leeds

4. Books, Pamphlets, Articles (published before 1901)

Abraham J H 1805 *Juvenile Essays: comprising in the order merit, the first and second half-yearly prize Compositions of the pupils belonging to the Milk Street Academy, Sheffield. To which is prefixed a brief history of Education and a table of the system pursued in the above academy* Printed for the proprietor, Sheffield

Adams J E 1853 *Remarks on the theory and practice of education: being an outline of the plan pursued at the Sheffield Commercial Classical and Mathematical School* Harrison, Sheffield

Ainsworth W H 1858 *Mervyn Clitheroe* G Routledge

'An Oxonian' (Addy S O) 1853 *Middle-Class Education in Sheffield* W C Leng, Sheffield

'Anstey F' (Guthrie T A) 1882 *Vice Versa. A lesson to fathers* Smith, Elder

Arnold Thomas 1845 *Miscellaneous Works* B Fellowes

Arnold Thomas 1878 *Sermons* 6 vols Longmans, Green

Arnold W D 1853 (reprinted 1973) *Oakfield. A fellowship in the East* University Press, Leicester

Bache Alexander Dallas 1839 *Report on education in Europe to the trustees of Girard College for orphans* Lydia R Bailey, Philadelphia

Bamford Samuel *Early Days* in Dunckley Henry (ed) (n.d.) *Bamford's Passages in the life of a Radical and Early Days* T Fisher Unwin

Bartley George C T 1871 *The Schools for the people* Bell and Daldy

Beard J R 1859 *Self-culture: A practical answer to the questions 'What to learn?' 'How to learn?' 'When to learn?' With Illustrative Anecdotes and Biographical Sketches, Courses of Reading and Lists of Manuals, comprising such as are necessary for the Civil Service Examinations; the whole forming a complete guide to self-instruction* John Heywood, Manchester

Beavan Charles 1840 *Reports of cases in Chancery, argued and determined in the Rolls Court during the time of Lord Langdale, Master of the Rolls* vol I (1838–39) Saunders and Benning

Blyth E K 1889 *Life of William Ellis (founder of the Birkbeck Schools) with some account of his writings, and of his labours for the improvement and extension of education* Kegan Paul

Bowers G H 1842 *A Letter addressed (by permission) to his Grace the Lord Archbishop of Canterbury, on the subject of the plan of a proposed school for Sons of Clergymen &* C B Fellowes

Brereton J L 1874 *County Education. A contribution of experiments, estimates and suggestions* Bickers and Son

Bulwer E Lytton 1833 (reprinted 1970) *England and the English* University of Chicago Press, Chicago and London

(Bury St Edmunds) 1850 *Record of the tercentenary of the foundation of King Edward VIth's Free Grammar School, Bury St Edmunds: containing the lord bishop of London's sermon; the head master's retrospective address; the proceedings of the day* G Thompson, Bury St Edmunds

Butler Samuel 1896 *The Life and Letters of Dr Samuel Butler, headmaster of Shrewsbury School 1798–1836* 2 vols John Murray

Carlisle Nicholas 1818 (reprinted 1972) *A Concise description of the endowed grammar schools in England and Wales* 2 vols Richmond Publishing Co

Carpenter R L (ed) 1842 *Memoirs of the life of the Rev Lant Carpenter LL.D., with selections from his correspondence* Philp and Evans, Bristol; Green, London

Coleridge Sir John T 1860 *Public School Education: a lecture delivered at the Athenaeum, Tiverton* John Murray

Collingwood C S 1897 *Dr Cowan and the Grange School, Sunderland With recollections by old scholars etc.* Simpkin, Marshall, Hamilton, Kent

Conybeare W J 1847 *The Liverpool petition to the House of Commons in favour of a measure for improving the character of the instruction received by the middle classes* J W Parker, London; Wareing Webb, Liverpool

Davies Emily 1866 *The Higher Education of women* Alexander Strahan

Demogeot J, Montucci H 1868 *De l'Enseignement secondaire en Angleterre et en Écosse. Rapport adressé à son Exc. M. le Ministre de l'Instruction Publique* Imprimerie Impériale, Paris

Edwards E 1823 *An Inquiry into the revenues and abuses of the free grammar school at Brentwood* C Roworth

Ellis Ethel E 1888 *Memoir of William Ellis and an account of his conduct-teaching* Longmans

Farrar F W (ed) 1868 *Essays on a liberal education* Macmillan

Fisher G W 1899 *Annals of Shrewsbury School* Methuen

Goulburn E M (ed) 1856 *The Book of Rugby School. Its history and its daily life* privately printed, Rugby

Griffith G 1852 *The Free Schools of Worcestershire and their fulfilment* Charles Gilpin

Griffith G 1860 *The Free Schools and endowments of Staffordshire and their fulfilment* Whittaker

Griffith G 1861 *History of the Free-schools, colleges, hospitals and asylums of Birmingham and their fulfilment* W Tweedie

Griffith G 1864 *The Endowed Schools of England and Ireland, their past, present and future* Whittaker

Griffith G 1870 *Going to Markets and Grammar Schools, being a series of autobiographical records and sketches of forty years spent in the Midland Counties from 1830 to 1870* 2 vols William Freeman

Hare A J C 1896 *The Story of my life* vol I George Allen

Hill Arthur 1855 *Hints on the discipline appropriate to schools* Longman

Hill Frederic 1836 *National Education; its present state and prospects* 2 vols Charles Knight

Hill M D 1825 *Public education of boys, or plans for the government and liberal instruction of boys, in large numbers; as practised at Hazelwood School* (2nd edn) C Knight

Holland G C 1843 *The vital statistics of Sheffield* Robert Tyas

Hunter J 1869 *Hallamshire. The history and topography of the parish of Sheffield* (new edn by A Gatty) Bell and Daldy, London; Pawson and Brailsford, Sheffield

(Jacob G A) 1852 *The Sheffield Collegiate School* ... Simpkin, Marshall

Leach A F 1899 *History of Winchester College* Duckworth

Leach A F 1900 (ed) *A History of Bradfield College By Old Bradfield Boys* Henry Frowde

Leader R Eadon (ed) 1897 *Life and Letters of John Arthur Roebuck ... with chapters of autobiography* E Arnold

(Leeds) 1819 *Rules and Orders for the management of the Free Grammar School in Leeds; as appointed by the Committee entrusted with its Guidance and Government, at their Court, holden January 20th A.D. 1819* B Dewhirst, Leeds

Manchester Statistical Society:

Report of a Committee on ... education in ... Liverpool ... 1835–36 (1836)

Report of a Committee on ... education in ... Manchester ... 1834 (2nd edn 1837)

Report of a Committee on ... education in ... Salford ... 1835 (1836)

Report of a Committee on education ... in Bury, Lancashire ... 1835 (1835)

Report of a Committee on ... education ... in York ... 1836–7 (1836–37)

Mangnall Richmal 1882 *Historical and Miscellaneous Questions for the use of young people with a selection of British and general biography &c* (new edn) Longman, Green

Maxwell-Lyte H C 1875 *A History of Eton College 1440-1875* Macmillan

Meiklejohn J M D 1883 *Life and Letters of William Ballantyne Hodgson LL.D.* David Douglas, Edinburgh

Parkin G R 1898 *Edward Thring. Headmaster of Uppingham Life Diary and Letters* 2 vols Macmillan

Payne Joseph 1883 *Lectures on the science and art of education* (2nd edn) Longmans

Peacock M H 1892 *History of the free grammar school of Queen Elizabeth at Wakefield founded A.D. 1591* W H Milnes, Wakefield

Pritchard Ada 1897 *Charles Pritchard ... Memoirs of his life* Seeley

Ridley Annie E 1895 *Frances Mary Buss and her work for education* Longmans

Rogers William 1851 *A Short Account of the St Thomas Charterhouse Schools: drawn up at the request of a patron* Longman Brown Green and Longmans

Rogers William 1888 *Reminiscences* (compiled by R H Hadden) Kegan Paul

Rouse W H D 1898 *A History of Rugby School* Duckworth

Sargant W L 1870 *Essays of a Birmingham Manufacturer* vol II Williams and Norgate

Sargeaunt John 1898 *Annals of Westminster School* Methuen

Shepherd W, Joyce J, Carpenter Lant 1822 *Systematic Education: or, Elementary Instruction in the various departments of Literature and Science; with practical rules for studying each branch of Useful Knowledge* (3rd edn) 2 vols Longman Hurst Rees Orme and Brown

Shoveller John 1824 *Scholastic Education: or, a synopsis of the studies recommended to employ the time, and engage the attention of youth; a suggestion of the most efficient methods of tuition; and a notice of the authors which may be advantageously used in a scholastic course* (2nd edn) G and W B Whitaker

Skrine J H 1890 *A Memory of Edward Thring* Macmillan

Slugg J T 1885 *Woodhouse Grove School: memorials and reminiscences* T Woolmer

Smith J F (ed) 1874 *The Admission Register of the Manchester School with some notices of the more distinguished scholars* vol III (May 1807-Sept 1837) Chetham Society: XCIII,XCIV

Speight Harry 1897 *Romantic Richmondshire. Being a complete account of the history, antiquities and scenery of the picturesque valleys of the Swale and Yore* Elliot Stock

Stanley A P 1875 *Life and correspondence of Thomas Arnold D.D.* (9th edn) 2 vols John Murray

Staunton H 1869 *The Great Schools of England* (new edn) Strahan

Thackeray F StJ 1896 *Memoir of Edward Craven Hawtrey D.D. Headmaster and afterwards Provost of Eton* G Bell

Thompson Henry 1879 *A History of Ackworth School during its first hundred years* Published by the Centenary Committee, Ackworth School

Vaughan C J 1854 *A Letter to the Viscount Palmerston, M.P. on the monitorial system of Harrow School* (2nd edn) John Murray

Vesey Francis jun 1806 *Reports of cases argued and determined in the High Court of Chancery during the time of Lord Chancellor Eldon* vol XI A Strahan

Waddy Adeline 1878 *The Life of the Rev Samuel D Waddy D.D.* Published at the Wesleyan Conference Office

(Wakefield) 1832 *Rules and Regulations of the West Riding Proprietary School, as prepared by the Committee and approved of and adopted by a general meeting of the Subscribers held on the 30th May 1832* John Stanfield, Wakefield

Ward Wilfrid 1889 *William George Ward and the Oxford Movement* Macmillan

(Wesley College Sheffield) 1839 *The Establishment, principles, discipline and educational course of the Wesleyan Proprietary Grammar School, Sheffield. With a list of the officers, proprietors, trustees and pupils; and a copy of the deed of settlement* John Mason

Wesley College, Sheffield (leaflet, not dated)

Wiese L 1854 *German Letters on English education* (trans W D Arnold) Longman Brown Green and Longmans

Woodard N 1848 *A Plea for the middle classes*

Woodard N 1858 *St Nicolas College: St Saviour's Lower Middle Class School*

Woodard N 1878 *The Society and Schools of St Mary and St Nicolas College*

Woodard N 1883 *The Scheme of education of St Nicolas College, with suggestions for the permanent constitution of that society, in a letter to the most noble the Marquess of Salisbury* (reprint of the original edn 1869) Parker, Oxford

Wordsworth Charles 1891 *Annals of my early life 1806–46* Longmans

Wyse Thomas 1836 *Education reform, or the necessity of a national system of education* vol I Longman Rees Orme Brown Green and Longman

Articles

(For an explanation of abbreviations of journal titles, see List of abbreviations, p xi

Acland T D 1859 On the Education of the Middle Classes *TSSA*

Beale D ('A Utopian') 1866 On the Education of Girls *Frasers Magazine* LXXIV

Beale D 1865 The Ladies College at Cheltenham *TSSA*

Bradley G G 1884 My Schooldays from 1830 to 1840 *Nineteenth Century* 15

Central Society of Education:
  1st Publication 1837 Scottish Institution for the education of young ladies
  2nd Publication 1838 (reprinted 1968): Resident Assistants in private boarding schools; (reprinted 1968): Ellis Mildred, The Education of young ladies of small pecuniary resources for other occupations than that of teaching
  3rd Publication 1839 (reprinted 1968) Duppa B F, County Colleges of agriculture

Davies Emily 1864 On Secondary Instruction, as relating to girls *TSSA*

Davies Emily 1868 Some account of a proposed new College for women *TSSA*

Eton School 1834 *QJE* VIII

Eton 1861 *Westminster Review* XIX (n.s.)

Fitch J G 1864 The proposed Royal Commission of inquiry into Middle-Class Education *TSSA*

Flogging and Fagging at Winchester 1835 *QJE* IX

Harrow School 1832 *QJE* III

Hey (Canon) 1864 Grammar Schools *TSSA*

Howson J S 1858 Statistics of the Liverpool Collegiate Institution *TSSA*

Howson J S 1859 On Schools for girls of the middle class *TSSA*

Humphreys E R 1857 The Plan and Objects of the Royal College of Preceptors, calculated to provide middle class education *TSSA*

Jacob G A 1862 The professional training and certification of middle class teachers *TSSA*

Kay-Shuttleworth Sir James 1866 What Central and Local bodies are best qualified to take charge of and administer Existing

Endowments for Education and what Powers and Facilities should be given to such Bodies *TSSA*

Maurice F D 1865 What better provision ought to be made for the Education of Girls of the Upper and Middle Classes *TSSA*

Melville David 1864 The Report of the Royal Commission on Public Schools *TSSA*

Moore Smith G C 1900 The Diary of a schoolgirl of eighty years ago *The Modern Language Quarterly* III

Norris J P 1864 On the proposed Examinations of girls of the professional and middle classes *TSSA*

On the discipline of large boarding schools 1835 *QJE* X

'Paterfamilias' (Higgins M J) 1860-61 Three letters *Cornhill Magazine* vols I, II, III

Proprietary Schools: an abstract of the rules adopted by the proprietors of the Pimlico Grammar School 1831 *QJE* I

Public Education – Hazelwood School 1825 *ER* XLI

Public School Education 1860 *Quarterly Review* **108**

Public Schools of England – Eton 1830 *ER* LI

Public Schools of England – Westminster and Eton 1831 *ER* LIII

Public Schools 1864 *Quarterly Review* **116**

(Reeve Henry) 1861 Eton College *ER* CXIII

Richson C 1855-56 On the Agencies and Organization required in a National System of Education *Transactions of the Manchester Statistical Society*

Robinson (Canon) 1864 Suggestions for the improvement of Middle Class Education *TSSA*

(Smith Sydney) 1810 Remarks on the system of Education in Public Schools *ER* XVI

(Stephen J F) 1858 Tom Brown's Schooldays *ER* **107**

Tod Isabella M S 1867 Advanced Education for girls of the Upper and Middle Classes *TSSA*

Westminster School 1833 *QJE* V

West Riding Proprietary School Wakefield 1835 *QJE* X

Wolstenholme Elizabeth 1865 What better provision might be made for the Education of Girls of the Upper and Middle Classes *TSSA*

5. Books, Pamphlets, Articles (published since 1901)

Adamson J W 1930 (reprinted 1964) *English Education 1760-1902* University Press, Cambridge

Allen Peter 1978 *The Cambridge Apostles: the early years* University Press, Cambridge

Anstruther Ian 1963 *The Knight and the Umbrella* Geoffrey Bles

Archer R L 1921 (reprinted 1966) *Secondary Education in the Nineteenth Century* Frank Cass

Argles M 1964 *South Kensington to Robbins: an account of English technical and scientific education since 1851* Longmans

Arnold Matthew 1910 *Reports on Elementary Schools 1852-1882* (new edn by F S Marvin) HMSO

Arnold Ralph 1961 *The Whiston Matter. The Reverend Robert Whiston versus the Dean and Chapter of Rochester* Rupert Hart-Davis

Ashford L J, Haworth C M 1962 *The History of the Royal Grammar School High Wycombe 1562 to 1962* Published by the governors of the school

Auchmuty J J 1939 *Sir Thomas Wyse 1791-1862: the life and career of an educator and diplomat* P S King

Bamford T W 1960 *Thomas Arnold* Cresset Press

Bamford T W 1967 *The Rise of the Public Schools: a study of boys' boarding schools in England and Wales from 1837 to the present day* Nelson

Bamford T W 1970 (ed) *Thomas Arnold on Education: a selection from his writings* University Press, Cambridge

Banks J A 1954 *Prosperity and Parenthood: a study of family planning among the Victorian middle classes* Routledge and Kegan Paul

Barnes A S 1926 *The Catholic Schools of England* Williams and Norgate

Battersby W J 1953 *Brother Potamian: educator and scientist* Burns Oates

Beck G A (ed) 1950 *The English Catholics 1850-1950: essays to commemorate the centenary of the restoration of the hierarchy of England and Wales* Burns Oates

Bellot H Hale 1929 *University College London 1826-1926* University of London Press

Berry M H A, Higginson J H (eds) 1976 *Canterbury Chapters: a Kentish heritage for tomorrow* Dejall and Meyorre International Publishers, Liverpool

Bibby Cyril (ed) 1971 *T H Huxley on Education* University Press, Cambridge

Binfield Clyde 1981 *Belmont's Portias: Victorian Nonconformists and middle-class education for girls* (Friends of Dr Williams's Library, 35th lecture)

Bishop T J H, Wilkinson Rupert 1967 *Winchester and the Public School Elite: a statistical analysis* Faber and Faber

Blackie John 1976 *Bradfield 1850–1975* Published for the Warden and Council of St Andrew's College, Bradfield

(Bloxham) 1910 *History of All Saints' School, Bloxham 1860–1910* Published at the school

Bolam David W 1952 *Unbroken Community: the story of the Friends' School Saffron Walden 1702–1952* Friends' School, Saffron Walden

Bradbury John L 1975 *Chester College and the Training of Teachers* Governors of Chester College

Bradley A G *et al.* 1923 *A History of Marlborough College* (revised edn) John Murray

Brett-James N G (n.d.) *The History of Mill Hill School 1807–1923* Thomas Malcomson, Reigate

Brett-James N G 1938 *Mill Hill* Blackie

Brook Roy 1968 *The Story of Huddersfield* Macgibbon and Kee

Bruce Sir Gainsford 1905 *The Life and Letters of John Collingwood Bruce* W Blackwood, Edinburgh and London

Burstall Sara A 1938 *Frances Mary Buss: an educational pioneer* SPCK

Burstyn Joan N 1980 *Victorian Education and the Ideal of Womanhood* Croom Helm

Burton Hester 1949 *Barbara Bodichon 1827–1891* John Murray

(Bury St Edmunds) 1908 *Biographical List of Boys Educated at King Edward VI Free Grammar School Bury St Edmunds. From 1550 to 1900* (Suffolk Green Books, no. XIII, Bury St Edmunds)

Buscot W 1940 *The History of Cotton College: at Sedgley Park 1763–1873; at Cotton 1873–* Burns Oates

Carleton J D 1965 *Westminster School: a history* Rupert Hart-Davis

Chandos John 1984 *Boys Together: English public schools 1800–64* Hutchinson

Christie O F 1935 *A History of Clifton College 1860–1934* J W Arrowsmith, Bristol

Clough B A 1903 *A Memoir of Anne Jemima Clough, First Principal of Newnham College Cambridge* Edward Arnold

Cobbe Frances Power 1904 *Life of ... as told by herself* Swan Sonnenschein

Coleridge Arthur 1921 *Reminiscences* (Fuller-Maitland J A ed) Constable

Collins Philip 1963 *Dickens and Education* Macmillan

Cornelia Connelly 1809–1879 Foundress of the Society of the Holy Child Jesus, by a religious of the Society (1950 4th edn) Longmans Green

Cox Marjorie 1975 *A History of Sir John Deane's Grammar School Northwich* University Press, Manchester

Craze Michael 1955 *A History of Felsted School 1564-1947* Cowell, Ipswich

Dare R A 1963 *A History of Owen's School* Carwal Wallington

Davies Emily 1910 *Thoughts on Some Questions Relating to Women* Bowes and Bowes, Cambridge

Davies Kathleen 1981 *Polam Hall: story of a school* G Prudhoe, Darlington

Delamont Sara, Duffin Lorna (eds) 1978 *The Nineteenth-Century Woman: her cultural and physical world* Croom Helm

Dictionary of National Biography

Dilke Christopher 1965 *Dr Moberly's Mint-Mark: a study of Winchester College* Heinemann

Dyhouse Carol 1981 *Girls Growing Up in Late Victorian and Edwardian England* Routledge and Kegan Paul

Elliott R W 1963 *The Story of King Edward VI School Bury St Edmunds* Published by the foundation governors of the school

Evennett H O 1944 *The Catholic Schools of England and Wales* University Press, Cambridge

Felkin F W 1909 *From Gower Street to Frognal: a short history of University College School from 1830 to 1907* Arnold Fairbairns

Findlay J J (ed) 1914 *Arnold of Rugby: his school life and contributions to education* University Press, Cambridge

Fletcher Sheila 1980 *Feminists and Bureaucrats: a study in the development of girls' education in the nineteenth century* University Press, Cambridge

Furness W (ed) 1945 *The Centenary History of Rossall School* Gale and Polden, Aldershot

Gardner Brian 1973 *The Public Schools: an historical survey* Hamilton

Gaskell Elizabeth C *The Life of Charlotte Brontë* (World's Classics edn)

Gérin Winifred 1976 *Elizabeth Gaskell: a biography* Clarendon Press, Oxford

Girouard Mark 1981 *The Return to Camelot: chivalry and the English gentleman* Yale University Press, New Haven and London

Godber Joyce 1973 *The Harpur Trust 1552-1973* The Harpur Trust, Bedford

Gregory Benjamin 1903 *Autobiographical Recollections Edited, with Memorials of his Later Life, by his Eldest Son* Hodder and Stoughton

Grosskurth Phyllis 1964 *John Addington Symonds: a biography* Longmans

Grylls Rosalie Glynn 1948 *Queen's College 1848–1948* George Routledge

Hans N 1951 *New Trends in Education in the Eighteenth Century* Routledge and Kegan Paul

Harrison J A 1958–69 *Private Schools in Doncaster in the Nineteenth Century* Pts I–VI Doncaster Museum Publications

Hearl T W 1966 *William Barnes 1801–1886 the Schoolmaster: a study of education in the life and work of the Dorset poet* Longmans (Dorchester)

Heeney Brian 1969 *Mission to the middle classes: the Woodard schools 1848–1891* SPCK

Hicks C R 1936 *Lady Barn House and the Work of W H Herford* University Press, Manchester

Hicks Phyllis D 1949 *A Quest of Ladies: the story of a Warwickshire school* Frank Juckes, Birmingham

Hodges Sheila 1918 *God's Gift: a living history of Dulwich College* Heinemann

Hollis Christopher 1960 *Eton: a history* Hollis and Carter

Holt R V 1938 *The Unitarian Contribution to Social Progress in England* G Allen and Unwin

Honey J R de S 1977 *Tom Brown's Universe: the development of the public school in the nineteenth century* Millington

Hope-Simpson J B 1967 *Rugby since Arnold: a history of Rugby School from 1842* Macmillan

Hopkinson David 1981 *Edward Penrose Arnold: A Victorian family portrait* Alison Hodge, Penzance

Hoyland Geoffrey 1946 *The Man who Made a School: Thring of Uppingham* SCM Press

Hutton T W 1952 *King Edward's School Birmingham 1552–1952* Blackwell, Oxford

Huxley T H 1910 *Science and Education: essays* Macmillan

Ives A G 1970 *Kingswood School in Wesley's Day and Since* Epworth Press

James L 1945 *A Forgotten Genius: Sewell of St Columba's and Radley* Faber and Faber

Jameson E M 1937 *Charterhouse* Blackie

Kamm Josephine 1958 *How Different from Us: a biography of Miss Buss and Miss Beale* Bodley Head

Kamm Josephine 1965 *Hope Deferred: girls' education in English history* Methuen

Kirby J W 1933 *The History of the Blackheath Proprietary School* Blackheath Press

Kirk K E 1937 *The Story of the Woodard Schools* Hodder and Stoughton

Kitson Clark G 1962 *The Making of Victorian England* Methuen

Lamb G F 1959 *The Happiest Days* Michael Joseph

Layton David 1973 *Science for the People: the origins of the school science curriculum in England* George Allen and Unwin

Leach A F 1903 *Early Yorkshire Schools* vol II (Yorkshire Archaeological Society Record Series XXIII)

Leech W H B 1932 *Queen Elizabeth's Grammar School Penrith* R Scott, Penrith

Leinster-Mackay D P 1984 *The Rise of the English Prep. school* Falmer Press

Lewis R R 1981 *The History of Brentwood School* Published by the governors

Lindley E S 1962 *Wotton-under-Edge: men and affairs of a Cotswold wool town* Museum Press

Linton D L (ed) 1956 *Sheffield and its Region: a scientific and historical survey* British Association for the Advancement of Science, Sheffield

Lowther Clarke W K 1944 *Eighteenth Century Piety* SPCK

McClelland V A 1962 *Cardinal Manning: his public life and influence 1865–1892* Oxford University Press, London

Mack E C 1938 *Public Schools and British Opinion 1780 to 1860* Methuen

Mack E C 1941 *Public Schools and British Opinion since 1860* Columbia University Press, New York

McLachlan H 1931 *English Education under the Test Acts* University Press, Manchester

McLachlan H 1934 *The Unitarian Movement in the Religious Life of England* vol I *Its Contribution to Thought and Learning* G Allen and Unwin

McLachlan H 1935 *Records of a Family 1800–1933: pioneers in education, social service and liberal religion* University Press, Manchester

Mallet C E 1927 *A History of the University of Oxford* vol III (Modern Oxford) Methuen

Mangan J A 1981 *Athleticism in the Victorian and Edwardian Public School: the emergence and consolidation of an educational ideology* University Press, Cambridge

Manton Jo 1976 *Mary Carpenter and the Children of the Streets* Heinemann

Marie Thérèse Mother, SHCJ 1963 *Cornelia Connelly: a study in fidelity* Burns Oates

Mitchell B R, Deane P 1962 *Abstract of British Historical Statistics* University Press, Cambridge

Moberly C A E 1911 *Dulce Domum: George Moberly ... his family and friends* John Murray

Monypenny W F 1910 *The Life of Benjamin Disraeli Earl of Beaconsfield* vol I (1804-37) John Murray

Morgan M C 1968 *Cheltenham College: the first hundred years* Richard Sadler, Chalfont St Giles for the Cheltonian Society

Mumford A A 1919 *The Manchester Grammar School 1515-1915; a regional study of the advancement of learning in Manchester since the Reformation* Longmans

Musson A E, Robinson Eric 1969 *Science and Technology in the Industrial Revolution* University Press, Manchester

Newsome David 1959 *A History of Wellington College 1859-1959* John Murray

Newsome David 1961 *Godliness and Good Learning: four studies in a Victorian ideal* John Murray

Oakley H Hislop 1920 *The First Century of Silcoates* Ed J Burrow, Cheltenham

Ogilvie Vivian 1957 *The English Public School* B T Batsford

Oldham J Basil 1952 *A History of Shrewsbury School 1552-1952* Blackwell, Oxford

O'Leary M 1936 *Education with a Tradition: an account of the educational work of the Society of the Sacred Heart* University of London Press

Otter Sir John 1925 *Nathaniel Woodard: a memoir of his life* Bodley Head

Owen David 1965 *English Philanthropy 1660-1960* Harvard University Press, Cambridge (Mass)

Owen Dorothy M, Thurley Dorothea 1982 *The King's School Ely: a collection of documents relating to the history of the school and its scholars* (Cambridge Antiquarian Records Society 5, Cambridge)

Parry R StJ 1926 *Henry Jackson O.M. ....: a memoir* University Press, Cambridge

Patterson A Temple 1971-75 *A History of Southampton 1700-1914*: 1971 vol II (1836-67); 1975 vol III (1868-1914) (Southampton Records Society 14, 18)

Peck Winifred 1952 *A Little Learning or a Victorian Childhood* Faber and Faber

Percival Alicia 1973 *Very Superior Men: some early public school headmasters and their achievements* C Knight

Pollard F E (ed) 1926 *Bootham School 1823-1923* Dent

Pritchard F C 1949 *Methodist Secondary Education: a history of the contribution of Methodism to secondary education in the United Kingdom* Epworth Press

Pritchard F C 1978 *The Story of Woodhouse Grove School* Woodhouse Grove School, Bradford

Raikes Elizabeth 1908 *Dorothea Beale of Cheltenham* Archibald Constable

Raine Angelo 1926 *History of St Peter's School, York, A.D. 627 to the present day* G Bell

Reeves Marjorie 1980 *Sheep Bell and Ploughshare: the story of two village families* Granada paperback edn

Roach John 1971 *Public Examinations in England 1850-1900* University Press, Cambridge

Roche J S 1931 *A History of Prior Park College and its Founder Bishop Baines* Burns Oates

Rose Martial 1981 *A History of King Alfred's College Winchester 1840-1980* Phillimore

Rowbotham Sheila 1973 *Hidden from History: 300 years of women's oppression and the fight against it* Pluto Press

St Quintin G 1956 *The History of Glenalmond: the story of a hundred years* Printed for Trinity College, Glenalmond, Edinburgh

Seaman C M E 1977 *Christ's Hospital - the Last Years in London: a fragment of Victorian history* Ian Allan

Searby P (ed) 1982 *Educating the Victorian Middle Class* (History of Education Society Conference Papers Dec. 1981)

(Sewell W) 1938 *Founder's Faith - Religio Fundatoris: a calendar of thoughts* (James L ed) Oxford University Press, London

Simon B 1960 *Studies in the History of Education 1780-1870* Lawrence and Wishart

Simon B 1968 (ed) *Education in Leicestershire 1540-1940* University Press, Leicester

Simon B, Bradley Ian (eds) 1975 *The Victorian Public School: studies in the development of an educational institution* Gill and Macmillan

Smith P, Summerfield G (eds) 1969 *Matthew Arnold and the Education of the New Order* University Press, Cambridge

Spencer Herbert 1904 *An Autobiography* vol I Williams and Norgate

Spencer Herbert 1949 *Essays on Education etc.* (Everyman edn)

Stafford Hugh 1945 *A History of Caterham School* Wilding, Shrewsbury

Stephen Barbara 1927 *Emily Davies and Girton College* Constable

Stewart W A C 1953 *Quakers and Education as Seen in their Schools in England* Epworth Press

Stewart W A C, McCann W P 1967 *The Educational Innovators 1750–1880* Macmillan

Stocks G A (ed) 1909 *The Records of Blackburn Grammar School* Chetham Society new ser: 66, 68

Stoddart Anna M 1908 *Life and Letters of Hannah E Pipe* William Blackwood, Edinburgh and London

Strachey Lytton 1948 *Eminent Victorians* Penguin edn

Strachey Ray 1928 reprinted 1969 *The Cause: a short history of the women's movement in Great Britain* Kennikat Press, Port Washington, NY

Sturge H Winifred, Clark Theodora 1931 *The Mount School York, 1785 to 1814, 1831 to 1931* J M Dent

Symonds J A 1984 *Memoirs* (Grosskurth Phyllis ed) Hutchinson

Tiffen Herbert J 1935 *A History of the Liverpool Institute Schools 1825 to 1935* The Liverpool Institute Old Boys' Association

Tompson Richard S 1971 *Classics or Charity? The dilemma of the 18th century grammar school* University Press, Manchester

Trevor Meriol 1973 *The Arnolds: Thomas Arnold and his family* Bodley Head

Tuke Margaret J 1937 *A History of Bedford College for Women* Oxford University Press, London

Venn J A 1940–54 *Alumni Cantabrigienses* Pt II (1752–1900) 6 vols University Press, Cambridge

Vicinus Martha 1972 (ed) *Suffer and Be Still: women in the Victorian age* Indiana University Press, Bloomington and London

Vicinus Martha 1977 (ed) *A Widening Sphere: changing roles of Victorian women* Indiana University Press, Bloomington and London

Victoria History of the Counties of England (see separate entry below)

Wainwright David 1960 *Liverpool Gentlemen: a history of Liverpool College, an independent day school, from 1840* Faber

Wallis Isaac Henry 1924 *Frederick Andrews of Ackworth* Longmans

Wenham L P (ed) 1965 *Letters of James Tate* (Yorkshire Archaeological Society Record Series CXXVIII)

West Katharine 1949 *Chapter of Governesses: a study of the governess in English fiction* Cohen and West

Whitridge A 1928 *Dr Arnold of Rugby* Constable

Wickenden T D 1962 *William Ellis School 1862–1962: the history of a school and those who made it* William Ellis School

(Wigton) 1916 *A History of Wigton School 1815 to 1915 with Lists of Scholars and Teachers* Published by the Wigton Old Scholars' Association

Wilkinson Rupert 1964 *The Prefects British leadership and the public school tradition: a comparative study in the making of rulers* Oxford University Press, London

Williamson J B 1903 *Memorials of John Bruce School-master in Newcastle-upon-Tyne and of Mary Bruce his Wife* Andrew Reid, Newcastle upon Tyne

Wilson Edmund (ed) 1906 *Leeds Grammar School Admission Books from 1820 to 1900* (Publications of the Thoresby Society 14, Leeds)

Woodward Frances J 1954 *The Doctor's Disciples* Oxford University Press, London

Wymer N 1953 *Dr Arnold of Rugby* Robert Hale

Zebedee D H J 1962 *Lincoln Diocesan Training College 1862–1962* Governors of the Lincoln Diocesan Training College

The Victoria History of the Counties of England

This History contains many useful articles on education and schools. Of particular importance is the article in

Middlesex vol I (1969) Bryant Margaret E, Private education from the sixteenth century

Articles in other volumes include:

Cheshire vol III (1980) Wardle David, Education before 1903

Essex vol II (1907) Fell-Smith C, Schools

Hampshire and the Isle of Wight vol II (1903) Leach A F, History of Schools

Lancashire vol II (1908) (various authors) Schools

Leicestershire vol IV (1958) City of Leicester. Martin Janet D, Primary and secondary education

Rutland vol I (1908) Fletcher F, Schools

Somerset vol II (1911) Holmes T Scott, Schools

Staffordshire vol VI (1979) (various authors) Schools

Surrey vol II (1905) Leach A F, History of schools

Sussex vol II (1907) Leach A F, Schools

Warwickshire vol VII (1964) City of Birmingham. Tyson J C, King
Edward VI Elementary Schools
Wiltshire vol V (1957) Butcher Emily E, Education
Worcestershire vol IV (1924) Leach A F, Schools
Yorkshire vol I (1907) Leach A F, Schools
Yorkshire City of York (1961) Craig Margaret, Schools and colleges
Yorkshire East Riding vol I (1969) City of Kingston-upon-Hull.
Lawson J, Education

Articles

Bamford T W 1957-58 Public school towns in the nineteenth century
British Journal of Educational Studies VI
Bamford T W 1961 The prosperity of public schools 1801-1850
Durham Research Review III(12)
Bamford T W 1961 Public schools and social class *British Journal of
Sociology* 12
Bartrip P W J 1980 A 'thoroughly good school': an examination of
the Hazelwood experiment in progressive education *British
Journal of Educational Studies* XXVIII(1)
Briggs W G 1957 Richmal Mangnall and her school at Crofton Old
Hall *Researches and Studies* (Univ. of Leeds Institute
of Education) no. 15
Darlington schoolboy's diary 1927 *Journal of the Friends' Historical
Society* XXIV
Dobson J L 1959-61 The Hill family and educational change in the
early nineteenth century *Durham Research Review* II(10): III(11);
III(12)
Durham County Friends' School 1929 *Journal of the Friends'
Historical Society* XXVI
Foden F E 1959 The Rev Arthur Rigg: pioneer of workshop practice
The Vocational Aspect of Secondary and Further Education XI
Hobbs J L (ed) 1960 The journal of John Wilson Soulby of Rampside
Academy, August-December 1847 *Transactions of the Cumberland
and Westmorland Antiquarian and Archaeological Society* LX
(n.s.)
Hunt Harold C 1942 William's schooldays at Ackworth in 1819
Friends' Quarterly Review 76
Jenkins H, Caradog Jones D 1950 Social class of Cambridge alumni
British Journal of Sociology 1

Lawson J 1952 Two forgotten Hull schools: the foundation of Hull College and Kingston College 1836 *Studies in Education* (Univ. of Hull) I(6)

Leinster-Mackay D P 1974–75 Private schools of nineteenth century Warwickshire *Warwickshire History* II (5, 6)

Leinster-Mackay D P 1980 Pioneers in progressive education: some little known proprietary and private school exemplars *History of Education* **9** (3)

Morris R J 1983 Voluntary societies and British urban élites, 1780–1850: an analysis *Historical Journal* **26** (1)

Musgrove F 1959 Middle class families and schools 1780–1880 *Sociological Review* n.s. V

Musgrove F 1959–60 Middle class education and employment in the nineteenth century *Economic History Review* 2nd ser. XII: 99–111 (and XIV: 122–30)

Perkin H J 1961–62 Middle class education and employment in the nineteenth century: a critical note *Economic History Review* 2nd ser. XIV

Roach John 1981 The idea of a liberal education *Education Research and Perspectives* (Univ. of W. Australia) **8** (1)

Sadler Michael 1923 A nineteenth-century experiment in education: the work of Matthew and Rowland Hill *The Forum of Education* I

Searby P 1974 Joseph Lloyd Brereton and the education of the Victorian middle class *Journal of Educational Administration and History* XI (1)

Shanks R 1956–57 The Flounders Institute: a Quaker experiment in teacher training *Educational Review* **9**

Simon Joan 1979 Private classical schools in eighteenth-century England: a critique of Hans *History of Education* **8** (3)

Spence B V 1972 The education of a north country family *Durham Research Review* VI (28)

Stones E 1960 The Rev Dr Jonathan Bayley of Accrington: a nineteenth-century educationalist *Transactions of the Lancashire and Cheshire Antiquarian Society* LXX

Stroud L John 1948 The Friends' School at Newton-in-Bowland *The Friends' Quarterly* n.s. **2** (1)

Thompson D 1955 Queenwood College Hampshire: a mid-19th century experiment in science teaching *Annals of Science* **11**

Tompson R S 1970 The Leeds Grammar School case of 1805 *Journal of Educational Administration and History* III (1)

Wadsworth F Arthur 1941 Two Nottingham schools *Transactions of the Thoroton Society of Nottinghamshire* XLV

W(allis) P J 1950 The Rev George Barnes Atkinson and the Collegiate School *King Edward VII (Sheffield) School Magazine* XII

Wallis P J 1964 The Educational Register 1851–5 *British Journal of Educational Studies* XIII (1)

Watts R E 1980 The Unitarian contribution to the development of female education 1790–1850 *History of Education* 9 (4)

Index

Index

Index

Index

Warwick, 83
Wellington College, 163, 213, 279, 303
Wesley College *see* Sheffield
West Buckland, Devon County School, 169–70
Westminster, 218, 229–30, 252
Widnes, 37–8
Wigton, 175
Winchester, 218, 229, 234, 235, 237, 250, 262, 281
Wirksworth, 42
Witton *see* Northwich
Wolverhampton
  GS, 72
  Sedgley Park *see* Cotton College

Woodhouse Grove, 132, 144–5, 163, 177–8
Wotton-under-Edge, 34, 47, 62–3, 89

Yarm, 38
York
  Bootham, 130, 174–5
  Collegiate School, 187
  private schools in, 120
  St. Peter's, 187
  The Mount, 139–40, 153, 174–5
  Yeoman School, 195
Yorkshire schools *see* Dotheboys hall